Critical Psychology

Critical Psychology

An Introduction

edited by

Dennis Fox and Isaac Prilleltensky

SAGE Publications
London • Thousand Oaks • New Delhi

ISBN 0-7619-5210-1 (hbk)
ISBN 0-7619-5211-X (pbk)
First published 1997
Reprinted 1999, 2001

SAGE Publications Ltd
1 Oliver's Yard
55 City Road
London EC1Y 1SP

SAGE Publications Inc
2455 Teller Road
Thousand Oaks
California 91320

SAGE Publications India Pvt. Ltd
B–42 Panchsheel Enclave
PO Box 4109
New Delhi 110 017

British Library Cataloguing in Publication data
A catalogue record for this book is available from the British Library

Library of Congress Control Number: 96072193

Printed digitally and bound in Great Britain by
Lightning Source UK Ltd., Milton Keynes, Bedfordshire

Contents

Contributors

Laura S. Brown is a feminist clinical and forensic psychologist in private practice and Clinical Professor of Psychology at the University of Washington, USA. She has written and taught extensively on questions of ethics in psychology. Her most recent books include *Subversive Dialogues: Theory in Feminist Therapy* (Basic Books, 1994), and with Ken Pope, *Recovered Memories of Abuse: Assessment, Therapy, Forensics* (American Psychological Association, 1996). In 1996 she was given an Award for Distinguished Professional Contributions to Public Services by the American Psychological Association.

Erica Burman teaches developmental psychology and women's studies at The Discourse Unit, The Manchester Metropolitan University, Manchester, UK. Her work revolves around representations of children, gender issues in development, the globalization of developmental psychology and critiques of dominant forms of subjectivity. In addition to *Deconstructing Developmental Psychology* (Routledge, 1994), her contributions to critical psychology include *Feminists and Psychological Practice* (edited, Sage, 1990), *Discourse Analytic Research* (co-edited, Routledge, 1993), *Qualitative Methods in Psychology* (co-authored, Open University Press, 1994), *Challenging Women: Psychology's Exclusions, Feminist Possibilities* (co-authored, Open University Press, 1995), and *Psychology, Discourse, Practice: From Regulation to Resistance* (co-authored, Taylor and Francis, 1996). She would very much like to network with other critical developmental psychologists with similar interests.

Zack Z. Cernovsky is Associate Professor in the Department of Psychiatry of the University of Western Ontario, Canada. He is the author of more than fifty articles on various aspects of personality assessment and research methodology and on other psychological issues. He has also written invited chapters in several medical textbooks, given numerous invited lectures at universities in other countries, and presented papers at various international scientific conventions on topics from psychology and psychiatry.

Michelle Fine is Professor of Psychology at the City University of New York, Graduate Center and the Senior Consultant at the Philadelphia Schools Collaborative, USA. Her recent publications include *Chartering Urban School Reform: Reflections on Public High Schools in the Midst of Change* (1994), *Beyond Silenced Voices: Class, Race and Gender in American Schools* (1992), *Disruptive Voices: The Transgressive Possibilities of Feminist Research* (1992), and *Framing Dropouts: Notes on the Politics of an Urban High School* (1992). She has provided courtroom expert testimony for a number of significant schools-related legal cases. In addition, she works nationally as a consultant to parents' groups, community groups and teacher unions on issues of school reform. She was awarded the Janet Helms Distinguished Scholar Award in 1994.

Blaine J. Fowers is an Associate Professor teaching in the Counseling Psychology Program in the Department of Educational and Psychological Studies at the University of Miami, Florida. His scholarly interests have involved inquiry into marital quality and positive illusions about marriage and now emphasize a hermeneutic approach to the philosophy of social science and its implications for psychological theory and practice.

Dennis Fox is Associate Professor of Legal Studies and Psychology at the University of Illinois at Springfield, USA. His work considers psychology's role in maintaining the legal, political, and socioeconomic status quo. Publications include essays in the *American Psychologist* ("Psychology, Ideology, Utopia, and the Commons," 1985; "Psychological Jurisprudence and Radical Social Change," 1993); in *Behavioral Sciences and the Law* ("The Autonomy–Community Balance and the Equity–Law Distinction: Anarchy's Task for Psychological Jurisprudence," 1993; "The Law Says Corporations Are Persons, but Psychology Knows Better," 1996); and in *New Ideas in Psychology* ("The Inescapable Nature of Politics in Psychology," with Isaac Prilleltensky, 1996). Fox founded and coordinates the international Radical Psychology Network with Isaac Prilleltensky. He serves on the Editorial Board of *Behavioral Sciences and the Law*, and can be reached on the Internet (fox@uis.edu or http://www.uis.edu/~fox).

Benjamin Harris is Professor of Psychology at the University of Wisconsin, Parkside (in Kenosha, Wisconsin). A Charter Fellow of the American Psychological Society, he is an advisory editor of *Contemporary Psychology* and is best known for his essays on the history of behaviorism (e.g., "Whatever Happened to Little Albert?" in the *American Psychologist* in 1979) and history of social psychology (e.g., "A History of Debriefing" in J. G. Morawski's *The Rise of Experimentation in American Psychology*). He is currently writing a political history of American psychology and psychiatry, portions of which have appeared in *The Journal of the History of the Behavioral Sciences, History of Psychiatry*, and *The Bulletin of the History of Medicine*.

Rachel T. Hare-Mustin is a feminist theorist and clinical psychologist. She and Jeanne Marecek published *Making a Difference: Psychology and the Construction of Gender* (Yale University Press, 1990). Her work includes critical essays on postmodern theory, family systems, and ethical issues in professional practice. Among recent publications is her article in *Family Process* ("Discourses in the Mirrored Room: A Postmodern Analysis of Therapy," 1994). She is a psychotherapist in independent practice.

Louise H. Kidder received her PhD in Social Psychology from North-western University. She has taught English in India and psychology in Japan. Currently she is Associate Dean and Professor of Psychology and Women's Studies at Temple University, USA. She co-authored the text *Research Methods in Social Relations* and co-edited *New Directions for Methodology of Social and Behavioral Science: Forms of Validity*. Her interests in Qualitative methods were formed more than twenty-five years ago during her graduate studies at Northwestern where she combined participant observation with quasi-experimental research.

Celia Kitzinger is Director of Women's Studies in the Department of Social Sciences at Loughborough University, UK. She has written widely on lesbian and feminist issues in psychology, including *The Social Construction of Lesbianism* (Sage, 1987), *Changing Our Minds* (New York University Press, 1993), and (with Sue Wilkinson) *Heterosexuality* (Sage, 1993). Her work has been honored with a Distinguished Publication Award from the Association for Women in Psychology, and with a Distinguished Scientific Contribution Award from Division 44 of the American Psychological Association.

Jeanne Marecek is Professor of Psychology and Women's Studies at Swarthmore College, USA. Her work includes essays on the study of gender in psychology; feminist theory and postmodern theory; and the uses of qualitative methods in psychology. She often works in Sri Lanka, where her focus has been on suicide, cultural constructs of distress and well-being, and culture-specific healing practices. She and Rachel T. Hare-Mustin published *Making a Difference: Psychology and the Construction of Gender* (Yale University Press, 1990).

Fathali M. Moghaddam, an Iranian born, British educated psychologist, joined the faculty of Georgetown University, Washington, DC in 1990. He previously taught at McGill University, Montreal, Canada. He is the author or co-author of numerous books and articles. His latest text, *Social Psychology: A Cultural Perspective*, will be published by Freeman.

Maritza Montero is Professor in the Department of Social Psychology of Universidad Central de Venezuela. She is author of *Ideología, alienación e identidad nacional* (*Ideology, Alienation and National Identity*, 1985), editor of two volumes on political psychology (1986, 1991) and co-editor of another two, one of them on Latin America (1995), the other on France, Spain, and Latin America (1993). Her primary work includes analyses of ideology and alternative modes of action, published in journals through the Americas and Europe.

Tor Neilands received his BA degrees in English Literature and Psychology from the University of California at Santa Cruz (1988) and his PhD in Social Psychology from the University of Texas at Austin (1993) with a minor in quantitative methods and psychometrics. Currently a Senior

Systems Analyst at the UT Austin Computation Center, he performs statistical software consulting and World Wide Web development. He also maintains the Radical Psychology Network World Wide Web pages (http:// uts.cc.utexas.edu/~neilands/radpsy). His research interests include self-esteem and the integration of self and society in Western cultures; social influence and conformity; and the impact of inequitable wealth distribution and materialism on individuals' well-being. He is currently working with others to develop an integrated theory of the self and society, blending mainstream and critical approaches to tie together disparate research areas in social psychology while simultaneously offering practical advice for individuals with low self-esteem. Neilands may one day return to academia to carry out critically driven research and teaching in psychology. He encourages readers to contact him at Com 1/G2700, UT Austin, Austin TX 78712 USA; via e-mail at t.neilands@cc.utexas.edu; or through his World Wide Web site, where samples of his past work are available (http:// uts.cc.utexas.edu/~neilands/psych/).

Geoffrey Nelson is Professor of Psychology at Wilfrid Laurier University in Waterloo, Ontario. He has served as Program Director for the MA program in Community Psychology at Laurier, as Senior Editor of the *Canadian Journal of Community Mental Health*, and as Chair of the Community Psychology Section of the Canadian Psychological Association. His research and action have focused on housing and community support for psychiatric consumer/survivors and community-based primary prevention programs for children and families.

David Nightingale is a Lecturer in Social Psychology at the Bolton Institute of Higher Education, UK. His particular research interests are the self, social constructionism, and the philosophy of the social sciences. He is the coordinator of the Radical Psychology Network e-mail discussion group (radical-psychology-network@mailbase.ac.uk). He is also a member of Psychology-Politics-Resistance, a UK-based group of critical psychologists. He encourages readers to contact him via e-mail at d.j.nightingale @bolton.ac.uk.

S. Mark Pancer is Professor of Psychology at Wilfrid Laurier University, Ontario, where he has been teaching social psychology and program evaluation since 1983. Prior to coming to Wilfrid Laurier, he was the Director of Research and Evaluation at a children's mental health center in Toronto, and previous to that he was an Assistant Professor in the Applied Social Psychology program at the University of Saskatchewan. Current research interests include the ways in which individuals negotiate major life transitions, the development of social consciousness in adolescence and early adulthood, and the evaluation of community-based primary prevention programs.

Ian Parker is Professor of Psychology at the Discourse Unit, Division of Psychology and Biology at the Bolton Institute of Higher Education, UK.

He is author of *The Crisis in Modern Social Psychology* (1989) and *Discourse Dynamics* (1992), and co-author of *Qualitative Methods in Psychology* (1994, with P. Banister, E. Burman, M. Taylor, and C. Tindall), *Carrying Out Investigations in Psychology* (1995, with J. Foster) and *Deconstructing Psychopathology* (1995, with E. Georgaca, D. Harper, T. McLaughlin, and M. Stowell-Smith). He is co-editor of *Deconstructing Social Psychology* (1990, with J. Shotter), *Discourse Analytic Research* (1993, with E. Burman) and *Psychology and Society: Radical Theory and Practice* (1996, with R. Spears).

Isaac Prilleltensky is Associate Professor of Psychology at Wilfrid Laurier University,Waterloo, Ontario. He is interested in the social, moral, and political consequences of psychological theory and practice. Through his work in critical psychology he is trying to show how psychology perpetuates an unjust societal status quo, and how it may serve emancipatory purposes. To advance these goals, he co-founded with Dennis Fox the Radical Psychology Network. Prilleltensky is a fellow of the Division of Community Psychology of the American Psychological Association, and the author of *The Morals and Politics of Psychology: Psychological Discourse and the Status Quo* (SUNY Press, 1994).

Julian Rappaport is Professor of Psychology at the University of Illinois at Urbana–Champaign, USA, where he is a member of both the Clinical/ Community Psychology and the Personality and Social Ecology programs. He is Past President of the Society for Community Research and Action (American Psychological Association, Division 27) and recipient of the Society's Distinguished Contributions Award. He is Editor Emeritus of the *American Journal of Community Psychology*. Rappaport's research and writing have been concerned with policies and programs in the mental health, legal and educational systems, particularly those that foster empowerment, mutual help and collaboration among human service professionals and citizens. His most recent interests are in understanding how community narratives influence personal identity stories.

Frank C. Richardson teaches in the Department of Educational Psychology at the University of Texas at Austin, USA. His interests are in counseling, personality, and philosophical psychology. During the first part of his career he published a book and research and theoretical articles in the areas of cognitive and behavior therapy. For the last twelve years his work has taken a strong critical turn. Over this time, he has published a number of articles dealing with the way in which modern psychotherapy theory and practice seem to reflect and even perpetuate some of the more shallow, narrowly individualistic, and even emotionally harmful aspects of modern culture. He is also contributing to current efforts to rethink the very nature of social theory and science in a post-positivist era. He feels that both critical psychology and contemporary hermeneutic (or interpretive) philosophy are vital resources for this undertaking. He is active in the

Theoretical and Philosophical Psychology Division of the American Psychological Association and a member of the Society for Phenomenological and Existential Philosophy.

Tod Sloan is Associate Professor of Psychology at the University of Tulsa in Oklahoma, USA. Trained in personality psychology at the University of Michigan, he has been a Fulbright lecturer in Venezuela and Nicaragua. Currently trying to develop a critical psychology of intimate relationships, he is the author of *Life Choices: Understanding Dilemmas and Decisions* (Westview, 1996) and *Damaged Life: The Crisis of the Modern Psyche* (Routledge, 1996). His e-mail address is tod-sloan@utulsa.edu.

Eric Stewart is a doctoral student in the Clinical/Community Psychology program at the University of Illinois at Urbana–Champaign, USA. He graduated with highest honors in Psychology from the University of California, Berkeley, where he was awarded the Warner Brown Memorial Prize for undergraduate research. Stewart's primary areas of study have been gay communities' HIV/AIDS prevention and activism efforts, and relationships between discourse, community, and identity. He is currently doing collaborative, qualitative research of women's strategies and resources for reauthorizing identity narratives and establishing community after traumatic brain injury.

Charles Studer gained cross-cultural experience through over forty years of work and study in developing and developed societies around the world, with particularly fruitful periods in India and Australia. He has designed and implemented a number of successful training programs for managers working in culturally diverse contexts, and has researched extensively (with Fathali Moghaddam) the pervasive nature of illusions of control in personal, professional and many other domains (to be published).

Sue Wilkinson is the founding and current Editor of the journal *Feminism & Psychology* and the book series *Gender and Psychology: Feminist and Critical Perspectives* (both from Sage). She was a founder member and first elected Chair of the British Psychological Society's "Psychology of Women" Section. Her books include *Heterosexuality, Feminism and Discourse* and *Representing the Other* (all with Celia Kitzinger) and, most recently, *Feminist Social Psychologies: International Perspectives* (Open University Press, 1996). She is currently teaching social psychology and women's studies at Loughborough University, UK, and is researching threatened sexual identities and women's experiences of breast cancer.

Preface

The two of us met a few years ago after discovering each other's published articles, which presented overlapping and complementary critiques of psychology and of society. Like many of the authors in this book, we each had criticized psychology for supporting social institutions that perpetuate injustice and promote selfishness. Although we had varied a bit in our emphases, the way we approached our work had something in common beyond the substance of our parallel critiques: rather than writing only in obscure political journals primarily for people who already agreed with us, we did most of our writing for mainstream psychology journals. We hoped to stimulate critical reflection by psychologists who don't usually read journals critical of the field's basic assumptions and norms. We saw this reflection as crucial if psychology is to outgrow its political innocence and become a more enlightened and responsible participant in public life. Our goal was not just to grumble on the sidelines but to change the status quo.

Another thing the two of us had in common was that we generally cited the work of older, more established critical psychologists who had demonstrated how societal institutions hinder social justice. Although certainly not a universal trend, there seemed to be a tradition of long-time leaders of organized psychology reflecting on their careers and concluding that the norms they had followed for most of their lives could not bring about social change. Thus, because we were not starting from scratch, we could always resurrect and build on earlier critiques.

Once we noticed the similarity in our approaches, we began to wonder if we could do more than present older arguments to the same mainstream audiences that dismissed them the first time around. Grumbling from within had its advantages, but it didn't seem quite enough. Not surprisingly, the minor tradition of respected mainstream psychologists criticizing the mainstream was matched by another tradition, this one followed by the majority: listening politely to the critics and sometimes even publishing their critiques and giving them awards, but still going about business as usual. We wondered how we could actually change things, not just write about the need for change.

Our musings led us to arrange a meeting at the 1993 convention of the American Psychological Association, a discussion session called "Will Psychology Pay Attention to its Own Radical Critics?" The two dozen psychologists who attended – many of them graduate students – founded the Radical Psychology Network (RadPsyNet), which the two of us have coordinated ever since. The group remains small, a hundred or so members around the world. We have a newsletter, and an Internet discussion group and World Wide Web site (http://uts.cc.utexas.edu/~neilands/radpsy/). The group enables like-minded critics of psychology's mainstream norms to meet one another, share concerns, and propose projects for members to work on together.

It became clear as RadPsyNet developed that our student members in particular had a strong interest in figuring out how to meld their political values with their interest in being psychologists. Many had hoped psychology would enable them to make a difference in the world, but were frustrated by the traditional demands of their professors, supervisors, and potential employers. Some said they wished RadPsyNet had existed when they began their studies, to help them pick a subspecialty or graduate school with more of a social change focus, or to expose them to the critical literatures that their coursework omitted.

The two of us realized that critical psychologists needed to try harder to reach students, as well as other psychologists not yet established in main-stream careers. Although we had written for mainstream audiences, we realized we had not done enough to get critical perspectives into the hands of students and others who don't read journals. *Critical Psychology: An Introduction* grew out of this realization. As Chapter 1 explains in more detail, the book presents an overview of critical psychology for readers with little exposure to critical perspectives. We have tried to produce a book that students can comprehend. This is the kind of book we wish we could have read when we began our own studies in psychology many years ago.

In addition to students, we think two other audiences will find the book useful: working psychologists who wonder about the relevance of critical psychology to their own work, and those who already consider themselves critical psychologists and want to see what critics are up to in other areas of psychology. By covering a broad range of areas and issues, the book points out connections and common themes that otherwise might be missed in more narrowly targeted (and more complexly written) academic articles.

A point we emphasize in Chapter 1 is that personal values, assumptions, interests, and backgrounds affect the decisions psychologists make about how to go about their work. This is certainly true in our own cases. We each bring a passion and a history to the cause of critical psychology.

For me (*Dennis*), growing up relatively privileged in working-class and middle-class Brooklyn neighborhoods, I was embarrassingly unaware for many years of social justice issues. When very young I merely accepted the "fact" that being white, Jewish, and middle class was better than being black or Hispanic and poor – the only categories of people I encountered with any frequency – just as I knew that being an American and a male was better than being anything else. As I grew a little older, my acceptance of this common-sense knowledge slowly turned to suspicion. I remember John Kennedy's call to young people to think beyond themselves, the fear of annihilation as we practiced nuclear survival techniques in school, the murders of early civil rights workers. As a teenager, I embraced the call of socialist Zionists trying to create collective settlements in Israel based on humanistic, egalitarian principles while seeking to avoid oppressing Palestinians. Over time my Zionism faded, but I remained forever aware of how difficult it is to sort out conflicting values and interests. I also remained influenced by my experiences on Israeli kibbutzim. The kibbutz system's utopian vision – the commitment to working toward a fundamentally better world even while knowing the effort can never fully succeed – inspired my later efforts in an array of social movements opposing varying forms of elite power. It directed much of my writing and teaching in psychology and, more recently, in interdisciplinary legal studies. And it led me to suggest to Isaac that we organize the Radical Psychology Network. Today, I struggle in my different roles of activist, professor, father, and husband to avoid the complacency all too common in middle age, trying like Isaac to resolve issues of my own power and hypocrisy despite my inevitably limited vision, capabilities, and sensitivities.

For me (*Isaac*), wanting to be a critical psychologist also has a lot to do with personal background. Argentina is a good place to develop a social conscience. Israel, in turn, is a wonderful place to feel torn between values of self-determination and justice. That's where I grew up, worlds apart. Canada, on the other hand, is a great place to experience privilege. That's where I'm growing old. Places and personal history fuse to propel ideals and projects. Dictatorships and disappearances in Argentina made injustice and impunity very palpable, whereas living in Israel forced me to struggle with dual national identities: oppressed and oppressor. Settling in Canada sharpened the contrast between "First" and "Third" worlds – galaxies apart. As a Jewish child in Argentina, others made sure I wouldn't feel welcome there for too long, while as an immigrant in Canada I could sympathize with other immigrants who, like me, were not always welcome. But the sensitizing effect of these experiences is sometimes forgotten amidst instances of privilege. I am aware of the privileges I have by virtue of my education. As a professor, I am aware of the power I have over students. As a father, I am aware of the control I have over my son. As a community psychologist, I realize the influence I have in community settings. But much as I would like this awareness to prevent me from abusing power, I don't always reach the level of integrity I expect of myself and others, a realization that humbles me every time I have the courage to face it. But there is no escape from questioning my own morality, a painful exercise at the best of times. I believe in disclosing hypocrisy. Professionals and governments who profess honorable values but act in oppressive ways are dangerous because they hide their own interests under a veil of self-righteousness. I see my work in critical psychology as helping to unveil hypocrisy in relationships, in the profession, in public life – and in myself.

Our backgrounds, values, and limitations are reflected in the choices we made in organizing and editing this book, choices we describe in Chapter 1. When we first discussed editing a book, others warned us about a variety of potential pitfalls. It would stretch the imagination too far to claim we never encountered any. Anyone who has ever edited a book will know that not every deadline was met and every request for revisions warmly received. Our efforts to fully cover all central areas fell short, as pointed out in Chapter 19 in connection to issues of race and ethnicity, a failure that editors of future editions should consider. But these shortcomings not-withstanding, we did avoid most serious complications. And despite the inevitable hassles of editing (and while learning a few things we might do differently next time!), we are pleased that this book serves the purpose we initially proposed: to expose the unholy alliance between psychology and social norms that benefit the powerful and harm the powerless, and to offer emancipatory alternatives. We are especially pleased that our own friendship has not only withstood our occasional disagreements and differing styles but has actually deepened throughout the process of working together. Both the book as a whole and the introductory chapter reflect this mutual process rather than "primary" efforts by either one of us as implied by the necessity of listing authors in one order or the other.

We could not produce the book we wanted without the help of many others. We owe the most to the authors who wrote the individual chapters, not only for what they wrote but also for their enthusiastic response to our original proposal and for their continued cooperation and suggestions. Most of the authors have written or edited their own books, and we especially appreciate their tolerance of our sometimes clumsy efforts to keep things on track. Except for the final chapter, all the authors wrote two or more drafts of their own chapters, taking into account our picky requests for revisions with almost universal good grace. We thank even the ones who gave us a hard time.

Ziyad Marar's enthusiasm was the primary factor that led us to choose Sage as our publisher. His instant agreement that such a book was needed confirmed our own somewhat-biased assessment and led to a congenial working arrangement. The assistance of Pascale Carrington, Brian Goodale, Lucy Robinson, Kiren Shoman, and Jackie Griffin at Sage made working with a publisher an ocean away much less of a problem than it might have been. At Wilfrid Laurier University in Canada, we'd like to thank Linda Potter, Administrative Assistant at the Department of Psychology, for her help with manuscript preparation.

We acknowledge the financial support of the University of Illinois at Springfield, which (when it was still called Sangamon State University) granted Dennis the time to work with Isaac on the book proposal. More crucially, the university provided a sabbatical leave that allowed Dennis to work on the book full-time for a full academic year.

To ensure that the book would be understandable, we asked several students to read the individual chapters and identify material that was unclear, repetitious, or in other ways in need of revision. Stephanie Campbell, Milo Fox, and James Taylor gave us excellent feedback, which we incorporated in the revisions we asked the chapter authors to make. We especially admire the students' willingness to tell us when they didn't understand something we ourselves had written, forcing us to look at our words anew. That some portions of this book remain difficult to read is a result of our not always following their suggestions.

We are also indebted to our spouses, Elizabeth Caddick and Ora Prilleltensky, for reading and commenting on never-ending chapter drafts and other material. Most of all, we thank them for allowing us to share with them the pains and excitements associated with this project. It's not possible to focus intently on an undertaking of this magnitude without inconveniencing families in many ways. So we are grateful that our partners were willing to put up with our schedules, our obsessions, and our lives in front of the computer screen – and grateful that they sometimes made us stop.

This book seeks a better world. We dedicate it to our children, who could use a better world. Observing the older ones already out on their own, Avram Safran Fox and Milo Safran Fox, reminds us that we have not yet found the solutions we were already seeking when they were young. Interacting daily with the young ones at home, Emily June Fox Caddick and Matan Prilleltensky, renews our commitment to keep on trying.

Dennis Fox
Isaac Prilleltensky

PART I
CRITICAL OVERVIEWS

1

Introducing Critical Psychology: Values, Assumptions, and the Status Quo

Isaac Prilleltensky and Dennis Fox

Editors' note *Critical psychology and traditional psychology differ in fundamental ways. In this chapter we explain what we mean by "critical psychology" and describe the subject matter of* Critical Psychology: An Introduction. *We contrast mainstream psychology's values, assumptions, concerns, and objectives with those of a critical psychology that emphasizes social justice and human welfare. As the chapter explains, we believe that psychology's traditional practices and norms hinder social justice, to the detriment of individuals and communities in general and of oppressed groups in particular.*

The chapter identifies controversial issues that later chapters develop in several ways. There is no way around this sort of controversy, because critical psychology is inherently value-laden, not value-free. It aims to change society just as it aims to change psychology. But, as you will discover throughout this book, mainstream psychology is also inherently value-laden. It seeks to maintain things essentially as they are, supporting societal institutions that reinforce unjust and unsatisfying conditions.

Psychology is not, and cannot be, a neutral endeavor conducted by scientists and practitioners detached from social and political circumstances. It is a human and social endeavor. Psychologists live in specific social contexts. They are influenced by differing interests and complex power dynamics. Mainstream psychologists too often shy away from the resulting moral, social, and political implications. This book asks you to think about these implications as you make your way in the discipline of psychology.

The word *critical* has several dictionary meanings. As used in *Critical Psychology: An Introduction*, the term describes an approach that challenges many theories and practices common in the field of psychology. The twenty-five chapter authors differ from one another in important ways, yet we share something in common: we evaluate the theories and practices of psychology in terms of how they maintain an unjust and unsatisfying status quo. As we do so, we pay particular attention to the welfare of oppressed and vulnerable individuals and groups. We believe that psychology has the potential to help bring about a significantly better world, in keeping with its ethical mandate to promote human welfare. Yet too often we settle for too little.

Throughout this book, we contrast approaches taken by critical psychologists with those followed more typically by mainstream psychologists. By *mainstream psychology* we mean the psychology most often taught in universities and practiced by clinicians, researchers, and consultants. It is psychology portrayed as a science, with objective researchers and practitioners who uncover the truth about human behavior and help individuals adjust to the demands of modern life. Some mainstream psychologists, recognizing the societal sources of much distress, propose minor reforms of social institutions to help individuals function more effectively. In general, when people become psychologists they expect to do some good. And often they do.

Yet critical psychologists see things a bit differently. As the contributing authors emphasize throughout this book, mainstream psychology reinforces Western society's unacceptable status quo, even when psychologists propose tinkering with social institutions. Indeed, the field of psychology itself is a mainstream social institution with negative consequences of its own. Of course, if existing institutions ensured social justice and human welfare, minor alterations to smooth out the rough edges might be good enough. In our view, however, the underlying values and institutions of modern societies (particularly but not only capitalist societies) reinforce misguided efforts to obtain fulfillment while maintaining inequality and oppression (Fox, 1985; 1996; Fox and Prilleltensky, 1996; Prilleltensky, 1994a). Because psychology's values, assumptions, and norms have supported society's dominant institutions since its birth as a field of study, the field's mainstream contributes to social injustice and thwarts the promotion of human welfare (Albee, 1986; 1996; Baritz, 1974; Chesler, 1989a; Jacoby, 1975; Kamin, 1974; Sarason, 1981).

We acknowledge that ours is not the only approach that might be termed "critical." Critical psychologists use the term to describe a variety of approaches that differ in philosophical justifications, terminology, political strategy, and ultimate priorities. To complicate matters, many critical psychologists do not even use the term *critical psychology*. Consequently, when we invited scholars to participate in this book, we did not select a single narrow perspective that "deserves" to be called critical. Instead, we cast a wide net, focusing on the central themes of pursuing social justice, promoting the welfare of communities in general and oppressed groups in particular, and altering the status quo of society and the status quo of psychology. Other editors might have used a different organizing principle. In this book critical psychologists approach these issues in different ways, but retain a central focus on altering the status quo in fundamental ways.

Something else we acknowledge is that, for a variety of reasons, many readers will resist this book's arguments. Mainstream psychology courses typically do not scrutinize the social, moral, and political implications of research, theory, and practice. Partly because this book rejects perspectives taught in these traditional courses, the whole critical psychology critique will strike some as too "political" or "ideological." It can be uncomfortable to contemplate fundamental criticisms of institutions we were taught to regard as basically sound. Unfortunately, psychology's increasing fragmentation and overspecialization reduce exposure to fields such as political theory, philosophy, and anthropology, where critiques of the status quo and examples of alternatives are more common. Reading critical perspectives is especially uncomfortable for students planning to work as psychologists, and for psychologists already in practice, who may feel that our criticisms of mainstream norms are directed at them. Ironically, the acceptance of our institutions as they exist, and the justification of our own role and future in those institutions, reflect political or ideological values that are part of the overall problem that critical psychology examines.

We hope you will work your way through the book with an open mind. You will discover that critical psychologists do not claim to have all the answers, and that we disagree even among ourselves about how to resolve significant dilemmas. You will also discover that most of us occupy traditional roles in psychology as therapists, evaluators, consultants, researchers, teachers, graduate students, and advocates. But in our work, as in this book, we try to raise questions about what we and others are doing, to be agents of social change rather than agents of social control. We do so with the understanding that we cannot always succeed, or even always know for sure what outcome would constitute success. Our efforts are fraught with contradictions. For these reasons and others, we could use your help to resolve our dilemmas and, more importantly, to make psychology more of a catalyst for social change and less of a hindrance.

In this chapter, we first explain briefly the central concerns of critical psychology addressed in *Critical Psychology: An Introduction*. We then describe in general terms our own vision of critical psychology, pointing out themes discussed in more detail elsewhere (references to chapters with numbers refer to chapters in this book). Finally, we tell you more specifically what to expect from this book, explaining what we asked the contributing authors to do and how we arranged the book's chapters.

Central Concerns

Critical psychologists challenge dominant societal values and the institutions that reinforce them for a variety of reasons, in a variety of ways. Amidst this diversity, though, you will see the chapter authors address three kinds of concerns in particular.

Individualism and Meaning

One general concern is that *mainstream psychology strengthens values and institutions that prevent many people from living meaningful lives.* In

Westernized societies, for example, social and economic institutions encourage people to seek meaning through individual pursuits such as advancing in careers, watching television or a computer screen, mowing lawns, and shopping. These pursuits provide economic benefits to those who control the institutions of corporate capitalism and to members of relatively privileged groups (Galbraith, 1996; Korten, 1995; Saul, 1995). But they interfere with the kinds of interaction, communication, and caring that are missing from too many lives – including the lives of those who enjoy these individual pursuits and who have everything they think they need. They hinder efforts to bring people together to resolve community problems, thus allowing political and economic elites to make decisions for the rest of us. And they blind us to the effects of our actions on those who remain oppressed as well as on the environment and on ourselves (Fox, 1985; 1993a). As described below and throughout this book, mainstream psychology's emphasis on individualism compounds this problem.

Oppression and Inequality

A more specific central concern is that *the negative consequences of societal values and norms do not fall equally on all segments of the population.* Members of relatively powerless groups typically suffer more, and in more ways, than members of more powerful or more mainstream groups. In other words, we believe that inequality and oppression are more common than supporters of the status quo claim. Despite formal guarantees in many countries of political and legal equality, most societies remain divided along power lines. Sometimes the resulting oppression is obvious, making it relatively easy to identify and (at least for those at a safe distance) to oppose. Other times it is institutionalized in subtle ways, making it harder both to understand how it operates and to combat its presence (Prilleltensky and Gonick, 1996). In either case, dominant individuals and groups maintain their power at the expense of others in their families, in the workplace, in the political and legal systems, in education and religion, and in other institutions. This is the case even when they think their actions are merely "normal" and "traditional" rather than unfair or oppressive. After all, in many societies inequality and oppression themselves are "normal and traditional." Thus, oppression is a central concept in critical psychology and in this book because it is a pervasive phenomenon that undermines the well-being of countless people around the world.

Intentions, Consequences, and Dilemmas

Just as many oppressors do not consider themselves oppressors, *mainstream psychology's traditions reinforce oppressive institutions even when individual psychologists have no such goal in mind.* Psychologists generally want to help. True, some knowingly use their skills and their status as professionals to help elite segments of society retain control, thus making sure the oppressed stay oppressed. More commonly, though, a large part of the problem is that they identify their task in overly narrow terms: seeking to help individual clients on an individual basis or to increase acceptable forms of scientific knowledge using traditional research norms (Doherty, 1995). They may support relatively minor reforms they consider "responsible" and "practical," as when their professional associations enter the political arena to advocate public policy. With this mainstream orientation, psychology shares a common failing with professions such as teaching, law, and medicine: its norms typically reflect the values, assumptions, and interests of middle- and upper-class professionals, particularly those who are white and male. It is no surprise that psychology supports a status quo that reflects psychologists' own values.

Thus, we don't dispute the fact that many psychologists have good intentions. But good intentions are not enough. For critical psychologists, the primary concern is not intention, but the consequences of actions. So we ask: does a traditional stance mislead people into identifying problems as purely individual? Does restricting interventions to those that are immediately practical hinder more significant benefits for the individual as well as for the society? Does the failure to pursue more fundamental solutions become a self-fulfilling prophecy by discouraging efforts to bring about more effective change? Authors grapple with difficult questions such as these throughout this book.

Critical psychologists face ironic dilemmas. We criticize psychology's mainstream norms for reinforcing an unjust status quo, but we sometimes use those same norms to benefit members of relatively powerless groups (see especially Chapters 13, 14, and 16). And although questioning psychology's norms can be risky for those who challenge their teachers, supervisors, and employers (Chapter 5), critical psychologists do frequently obtain the privileges – and the accompanying restraints – of a professional identity. A critical perspective may help us resolve certain issues, thus, but it raises others that are equally difficult.

A Vision for Critical Psychology

In this section, we present a conception of critical psychology founded on basic core values and assumptions related to the specific concerns noted above. Our view is generally compatible with the varying approaches in the book's remaining chapters despite differences in terminology, style, and philosophical framework. True, the book's authors have not sat down together to reach a consensus. If we did, we would not agree about every detail. Even the book's two organizers have somewhat different approaches. But these differences do not detract from our shared interest in challenging a status quo that benefits the powerful and works against the powerless. To do so, we believe it is necessary to advocate certain values and forms of political action rather than try to appear objective simply to retain legitimacy (Fox and Prilleltensky, 1996). We agree with Jean

Pettifor's comment in her presidential address to the Canadian Psychological Association:

> The discipline of psychology is moving beyond the myth of detached neutrality to discover virtue and to recognize politics as forces which determine ethical behaviour . . . The concept of personal individual ethics needs to be extended to the social and cultural environment, because the environment influences the ethical behaviour of psychologists and the quality of life of all citizens. A morally responsible perspective includes a political role for psychologists which encompasses strategies to shape that environment. (1996: 1)

Basic Values

Critical psychologists generally consider certain values primary, either explicitly or implicitly. Some analysts focus on a single primary value deserving concentrated attention, such as social justice or empowerment. Others emphasize the interplay between two or more conflicting values, such as between individualistic self-determination and mutuality or caring. No single listing of values will meet the concerns of all critics or the needs of people in varying cultural and historical settings. Yet many critical psychologists agree that values such as those laid out in Chapter 11 are of key importance. These include *social justice, self-determination and participation, caring and compassion, health,* and *human diversity* (see also Prilleltensky, forthcoming; 1994b; Prilleltensky and Gonick, 1994). Values such as these guide our critiques of current social structures and our visions of a better society. They direct our attention to institutional barriers that maintain oppressive practices.

Up to a point, you may not find these values particularly controversial. After all, caring, diversity, health, self-determination, participation, and social justice all sound pretty good. Difficulty arises, though, when we try to define and implement these values. In the real world, individuals and societies must make choices among competing values. Thus, any society seeking to enhance both self-determination and distributive justice will have to decide whether it is better for people to share relatively equally in the rewards the society has to offer, or better to let some members of society get rich at the expense of others who remain poor. Similarly, a high value placed on collaborative decision making conflicts with norms that let powerful individuals abuse their ability to affect the lives of others. Those who believe that their own cultural norms and values are best and that others should adopt what is "clearly" superior lack respect for human diversity.

Three basic considerations apply to our treatment of values. *First, we need to advance values in a balanced way.* Societal institutions that foster one value at the expense of another hinder human welfare. Social critics have long argued that, in the Westernized societies in which most readers live, a particularly significant imbalance is common: self-determination, which includes a focus on the individual, is overemphasized, while values such as collaboration, caring, and social justice are underemphasized. As we noted above, and as many chapters in this book demonstrate, mainstream psychology contributes to this value imbalance by endorsing *individualism* and deemphasizing values related to mutuality, connectedness, and a psychological sense of community (Bakan, 1966; Doherty, 1995; Fox, 1985; 1993a; Sarason, 1974; Wallach and Wallach, 1983). Similarly, with respect to health, psychology attends primarily to those who can afford individual, family, or small-group therapy, excluding many with fewer resources. By and large, psychologists fit comfortably within a capitalist system that gives lip service to both freedom and equality but in practice supports the freedom of the free market over the equality of distributive justice (Baritz, 1974; Fox, 1985; 1996; Pilgrim, 1992). Of course, a society that eradicated self-determination would overly restrict personal freedom and fulfillment. The goal is to achieve the right balance. In Westernized societies this means enhancing values related to mutuality and social responsibility.

Second, the particular configuration of values required for human welfare changes from society to society, group to group, and time to time. Members of a particular group may experience so many restrictions on their personal freedom and demands for personal sacrifice that they need more options for self-determination and autonomy. Others may experience so much individualism that their sense of community is completely eroded and they become isolated. Experiences of oppression and discontent come from various sources, determined in large part by the sociopolitical context. As conditions in society change, remnants of older value patterns in political and legal institutions hinder the creation of improved institutions more suited to changed circumstances (Prilleltensky and Gonick, 1996).

Third, some values have more potential for transforming society than others. Although caring and compassion is a fundamental value, its application on an individual basis is not enough to change a society that constantly undermines compassion by promoting competition. Distributive justice, on the other hand, ensures that our caring reaches those who are oppressed and marginalized: a fair and equitable allocation of burdens and resources helps people enjoy good health, promote their unique identities, and pursue their own goals. In related fashion, we may need to enhance the self-determination of the powerless while we decrease the self-determination of the powerful, as in feminist efforts to enhance the power of women in their interactions with relatively more powerful men.

As we become better educated about the consequences of our choices as individuals and as psychologists, we are in a better position to reduce oppressive practices and enhance human welfare. But the choice of actions, even when we educate ourselves about values, is not always obvious. There is no ready-made solution to our moral and political dilemmas. As clinicians, we may express concern for our clients, but how do we extend caring and compassion to oppressed communities? We devise psychological interventions to enhance people's mental health, but how do we avoid creating dependency on professional expertise? How can we promote people's autonomy without eroding a sense of community and mutuality? (See Doherty, 1995, and Mack, 1994, for a discussion of these dilemmas.) These questions require thoughtful consideration of the needs of all the people involved in a particular action, and awareness of which values our actions promote or hinder. Competing interests among oppressed populations and our own limited resources complicate our task. We must remind ourselves that a different combination of values may be required with diverse populations at different times as we maneuver our way through the moral maze of value implementation (Kane, 1994).

Basic Assumptions

Consistent with differences over value priorities, critical psychologists also differ from the mainstream in a variety of basic assumptions or beliefs. Again, not all critical psychologists emphasize each assumption equally. By the same token, mainstream psychologists similarly vary among themselves, though we believe that most share basic presuppositions. Although it does not do justice to the subtleties present in both mainstream and critical psychology, Table 1.1 presents objections to mainstream psychology's assumptions and implications as well as critical alternatives. It details our position in six areas: *knowledge, the nature of problem definitions and solutions, conceptions of the Good Life, conceptions of the Good Society, issues of power,* and *professional ethics.* The chapters that follow concentrate on one or more of these dimensions, as noted in the table. Here, we elaborate on the political implications of two of the central assumptions, those relating to problem definitions and solutions and to conceptions of the Good Society.

Defining the Level of Problems and Solutions   Mainstream psychologists often explain that psychology examines the individual, unlike other social science disciplines such as sociology and anthropology that examine larger groups. While this explanation makes some sense, its oversimplification both of psychological study and of human behavior has negative consequences, especially for relatively powerless segments of the population (Caplan and Nelson, 1973; Hall, 1983; Ryan, 1971).

   An individual's behavior can only be understood in the context of interaction with other human beings within socially created institutions. Psychologists who seek to understand why an individual behaves in a certain manner inevitably confront the impact of other people on that individual. It is this interaction with others throughout our lives that shapes our values, our goals, our very views of our selves. Any effort to identify the sources of significant behavior entirely within the individual neglects interaction's causal role. Equally important, it neglects the causal role of the larger social institutions in which those interactions are embedded (see especially Chapters 6 and 7).

Table 1.1 *Critical objections to mainstream psychology*

Assumptions regarding (with especially relevant chapters)	Objections to mainstream psychology	Critical psychology's alternatives
Research and knowledge *What conceptions of knowledge are espoused?* *What is the goal of research?* (2, 3, 6, 7, 8, 9, 10, 11, 13, 14, 18)	Knowledge viewed as accumulation of objective facts devoid of personal and political interests. "Value-free science can solve all human problems."	Knowledge viewed as infused with political uses and embedded within subjectivity of its creators. Research used at the service of moral values to help oppressed populations.
Problem definition and solution *What does problem definition include and exclude?* *What levels of intervention do solutions address?* (6, 7, 10, 11, 14, 15)	Problems defined in terms of intrapersonal or interpersonal deficits. Power arrangements in society typically excluded from definition. Typical interventions address individuals, neglect social systems, and blame the victims of oppression.	Problems defined holistically in terms of psychological and social factors related to disempowering and oppressive circumstances. Interventions address personal and social dimensions, try to equalize power, and strive to achieve distributive justice in access to resources.
The Good Life *What conceptions of the Good Life are promoted?* (14, 15, 17)	Good Life based on individualism and accumulation of wealth and material resources.	Good Life based on reciprocal self-determination whereby people promote their interests in consideration of other people's needs.
The Good Society *What conceptions of the Good Society are advanced?* (2, 12, 14, 17)	Good Society based on capitalist principles favoring the advancement of the powerful.	Good Society based on mutuality, democracy, and distributive justice.
Power in relationships *What constitutes legitimate power and how should power be shared?* (4, 7, 8, 9, 11, 13, 15, 16)	Power acquired through professional training and knowledge is deemed legitimate. Expert stance leads to minimal concern for sharing power.	Power should be shared equally. Legitimacy comes through a democratic process that professional psychology and society both lack.
Professional ethics *Whose interests do professional ethics serve?* (4, 11, 17)	Ethics are framed in language that serves primarily the interests of the professionals, fails to challenge their authority, and excludes the voice of clients and research participants.	Recipients of services and research participants should participate in defining ethical behavior and determining whose interests ethical guidelines serve.

Focusing only on the individual has important consequences, both for the individual and for society as a whole. We see this perhaps most clearly when we look at the problems that bring people to psychologists. An individual may experience job-related stress, for example, and seek help from a clinician. What is the job of the psychologist here? How should he or she analyze this stress? Is the goal to teach the "client" or "patient" stress-management techniques? To investigate what it is about the client that causes an apparent inability to cope with normal job requirements? Or is it, perhaps, to examine the nature of the job setting, in an effort to alter workplace demands? These approaches differ from one another. The psychologist providing assistance (or conducting research, or teaching students about this topic) makes a choice about which aspect of the problem deserves primary attention. Clearly the psychologist's role and the demands of the situation affect the choice. Is the psychologist in private practice, assisting an upper-class professional having problems with subordinates? Or does she or he work at a clinic, providing therapy for a harried working-class secretary with relatively few options? Or at a factory, hired by the corporate owners to help workers adjust to the fast-moving assembly line? Different roles lead to different interpretations of the problem, and thus to different solutions.

Critical psychologists take a different stance. In the example of job-related stress, a critical psychologist might step back from the immediate situation and ask why so many people in our society have the same problem in the first place. After all, it is not only the individual client who experiences job-related stress, but also the client's co-workers – and perhaps even the client's therapist! Perhaps the nature of work in our society inevitably leads to stress. When thousands and even millions of people experience essentially identical problems, defining these problems as "individual" oversimplifies to the point of absurdity (Albee, 1990).

Beyond the absurdity, of course, lies the politics. A philosophy of individualism, explaining problems as purely individual, leads to a search for purely individual solutions. This search may help some people up to a point. But it leaves many others on a lifelong quest because, if problems are inherently social and societal, the search for individual solutions ultimately fails. Not surprisingly, the insistence on individual solutions most harshly affects segments of the population historically defined as inferior (Albee, 1986; 1996; Bulhan, 1985; Prilleltensky and Gonick, 1996). Encouraging women, people of color, the poor, and the working class to define their problems as individual ensures that they work to change themselves rather than society. The result is reduced effort to alter the status quo, a state of affairs that benefits the privileged (Fox, 1985; Prilleltensky, 1994a). US Judge David Bazelon once made a similar point to a group of psychologists working in prisons: "In considering our motives for offering you a role, I think you would do well to consider how much less expensive it is to hire a thousand psychologists than to make even a minuscule change in the social and economic structure" (cited in Caplan and Nelson, 1973: 210).

Determining the level at which we define problems and aim solutions forces us to consider the role of *ideology*. Ideology has different meanings in different contexts (see Chapters 6, 14, 15, 17). Historically, the term first referred to beliefs imposed on the masses by political elites in order to justify societal arrangements. For instance, beliefs that people always get what they deserve, that the government only goes to war for good reasons, and that people are poor because they don't work hard are examples of ideological beliefs that blunt criticism of the status quo. Many critics have examined the negative consequences of this *false consciousness*, the widespread belief in inaccurate cultural assumptions that maintain the existing system. Over time, however, use of the term "ideology" broadened and even reversed. It became associated in public discourse with any statement that seemed to have critical political overtones, thus allowing those defending the status quo to dismiss challenges from the left as "ideological." Later, social scientists broadened the term even further by using it to refer to *any* system of beliefs and values, no different from a general "world view." According to this even-handed, depoliticized version of the term, *everyone* has an ideology.

It is not our purpose here to select one of these definitions as correct. It is important, however, to understand the different meanings of "ideology" in order to interpret conflicting uses of the term. Many critical psychologists, of course, use the term in its original critical sense, believing that false consciousness is a common phenomenon. We believe that traditional institutions such as schools, religious bodies, courts, political parties, and the media very successfully direct public opinion away from fundamental criticism of the status quo by teaching that problems are inherently individual in nature rather than societal and political. Our making this claim, however, frequently brings charges from the mainstream that our criticisms are ideological, and thus somehow suspect and illegitimate, even though the mainstream's focus on individualism is at least equally ideological.

In Search of the Good Society   Our vision of critical psychology begins with the belief that the promotion of human welfare requires an effort to create a better society – what philosophers and others sometimes refer to as a "Good Society" (Galbraith, 1996; Sandel, 1996). As described throughout this book, mainstream psychologists generally accept society as it exists, have a comfortable relationship with societal institutions, and seek to do good within the confines of the status quo (Anderson and Travis, 1983; Braginsky, 1985; Danziger, 1990; Dawes, 1994; Fox, 1985; 1993b; Herman, 1995; Howitt, 1991; Napoli, 1981; Prilleltensky, 1994a; Samelson, 1979; Sampson, 1983; Sarason, 1981; Sullivan, 1984). Psychology's increasingly influential role in public policy both reflects and reinforces this relationship (Herman, 1995; see Chapters 2 and 14).

Of course, writers across the political spectrum present their own versions of a better world, much as liberals and conservatives may all say they favor "freedom," or "family values," or "equality" yet disagree about how these concepts should be defined. A political conservative's free-market utopia where pure capitalism reigns, supposedly to the benefit of all, is very different from the version presented by radical egalitarians seeking fundamental economic equality. Some people even claim that Westernized, technologized, materialistic society is already ideal and they reject suggestions to the contrary as unpatriotic or threatening (Sandel, 1996; Saul, 1995). Critical psychologists, freed from the assumption that current societies are either ideal or inevitable, can begin to imagine better societies organized to advance the values critical psychology considers central.

Still, setting out in advance all the details would be difficult, even impossible. Critical psychologists differ among themselves concerning the details, and most do not explicitly refer to a Good Society in their analyses. But we share an emphasis on changing the status quo in fundamental ways, an emphasis often stimulated by other disciplines such as philosophy, anthropology, and political theory. Anthropologists, for example, have shown that human behavior is tremendously variable. Different cultures create different behavior patterns and social institutions. Childrearing, resource distribution, kinship networks, political decision making – all these and more vary so much that very little about human interaction seems inevitable. As we see it, a primary task for critical psychologists is to identify the consequences of the many possibilities and to advocate alternatives. Although mainstream psychologists frequently dismiss this kind of speculation as hopelessly starry-eyed utopianism, even "impractical" speculation serves two crucial purposes: it directs us toward long-range goals, which we can use to evaluate the potential worth of interim arrangements; and it leads us to examine what it is about our own societies that prevents us from making things better (Fox, 1985).

We cannot forget that differing cultures, philosophical traditions, and circumstances will require different visions of a Good Society, just as inequality and oppression take different forms in different societies. One hallmark of a Good Society might even be a refusal to assume it ever really arrives, thus requiring constant reflection and continued social change. The enterprise must proceed in a democratic and collaborative manner together with the members of society rather than being something that psychological experts advise political elites to foist on the public. But critical psychologists remain committed to weighing different approaches and establishing priorities even when we disagree about which aspects of the Good Society, and which aspects of psychology, deserve primary attention. What remains crucial is resisting dominant views that restrict our imagination and hinder our efforts to create a better society.

On Subjectivity

You will notice throughout the book that critical psychologists are more likely than mainstream writers to acknowledge the subjective nature of our efforts. You will see how the theory and practice of critical psychology relate to the authors' notions of appropriate values. This contrasts with traditional texts in which psychologists often minimize or ignore the degree to which their moral values, political and professional allegiances, personal experiences, and similar factors affect the choices they make and the positions they present. The traditional stance conforms to the *appearance* of objectivity central to mainstream views of science.

Part of critical psychology's agenda, on the other hand, is to demonstrate that these choices are never entirely objective or free from values, assumptions, and biases. By acknowledging how our own values and experiences affect us, we expose our work to a kind of scrutiny that more mainstream work avoids. When it comes right down to it, we believe that psychologists *should* engage in morally defensible work. This "should" is itself a moral statement. Just as clearly, however, the view that psychologists "should not" take values into account and "should" conform to the norms of "objective science" is also a moral position.

In our own cases, our approach to organizing this book is consistent with past life experiences that shaped our values long before we became psychologists and read material that supports our views. This is the case even though the two of us grew up on different continents in different decades, speaking different languages in different cultures. Isaac's experiences in Argentina, during a dangerous period of intense political repression, differed greatly from Dennis's exposure to the antiwar movement and counterculture in the United States in the 1960s and 1970s. Yet we also share a common heritage. We are both descendants of European Jews who left the lands of their birth to escape life-threatening repression. And we each came in contact with the Israeli kibbutz system, settlements based on communalism, economic collectivism, and a search for social justice.

No doubt the history of our people has much to do with our individual critiques of modern society. Those who occupy marginal or minority positions frequently confront mainstream injustices sometimes unnoticed by members of the majority. Similarly, our experiences in a movement reinventing social institutions affected our vision of what kind of society is possible – and also introduced us to the ambiguities of conflicting claims to justice and differing views of history. But our critiques, our vision, and our effort to sort out ambiguities are not unique; they are similar to those of many others of our generation, from very different backgrounds, who have come to more or less the same place: a commitment to resist institutions that protect the powerful by oppressing the powerless, especially institutions that we ourselves are part of.

Using this Book

Reflecting the varied ways critical psychologists have analyzed issues and dilemmas such as these, the chapters in *Critical Psychology: An Introduction* complement one another. Each presents a different piece of the puzzle or a different way of looking at the whole picture. For example, some of psychology's discriminatory norms are easier to grasp when focusing on issues of sex and gender, making a feminist analysis particularly fitting. Indeed, feminism has provided much of the impetus for the emergence of critical psychology (Fine, 1992a; Unger and Crawford, 1992; in this book, see especially Chapters 3, 4, 7, 9, 13, and 16). On the other hand, neo-Marxist psychology is sometimes more directly relevant to issues of economic class and power (Nahem, 1981; Newman, 1991; Sloan, 1996a; Tolman, 1994), issues particularly noted in Chapters 2, 5, 10, 11, and 14. Other intellectual traditions include German critical psychology (Tolman, 1994), South American liberation psychology (Martín-Baró, 1994; Montero, 1991; Chapter 15), social constructionism (Gergen, 1985a; Chapter 17), discursive psychology (Parker, 1992; Chapter 18), postmodernism (Kvale, 1992; Chapter 17), and post-positivist approaches in general (Sullivan, 1984; Chapters 17 and 18). All find a place within critical psychology as we define it to the extent that they aim to eliminate oppression, promote social justice, and redirect society's values.

Just as we do not have a monopoly on defining critical psychology, we have not fully covered all the meaningful critical work that preceded our efforts (see, for example, Braginsky and Braginsky, 1974; Bulhan, 1985; Cohen, 1990; 1994; Dryden and Feltham, 1992; Prilleltensky, 1994a; Sampson, 1983; Sarason, 1981; Sullivan, 1984; Wallach and Wallach, 1983). Frankly, we had to make difficult choices to keep the book from becoming too expensive to buy, too dense to read, and too heavy to carry. Thus, the book lacks chapters on important areas such as race and ethnicity, industrial-organizational psychology, cognitive psychology, and learning theories. These topics are addressed as relevant in other chapters. For other sources that provide critical perspectives on these issues, see the references throughout this book, as well as in Prilleltensky (1994a). Ultimately, we chose to create an accessible work that enables readers to participate in critical psychology debates and points them in the direction of the extensive literature. We include both traditional and newer fields of inquiry that raise issues likely to confront both students and practitioners.

We know that delving into new literatures marked by sometimes confusing and unfamiliar language can be intimidating. Frankly, one of the problems in spreading critical psychology's message has been our tendency as authors to write for other scholars accustomed to the jargon and style of academic debate. While useful, such work reaches a relatively small number of readers. In our view, one of critical psychology's goals should be to raise awareness more widely about the effects of psychology's status quo. Unless this message spreads, particularly to students, it will remain the property of a handful of academics with limited influence within the discipline as well as within society. Consequently, in this book we have tried to reduce obscure language to a minimum in order to make the substance as clear as possible. We admit that we sometimes found it impossible to remove specialized terminology without altering the substance as well. New or specialized terminology sometimes communicates specific ideas more precisely than any alternatives. Thus, some chapter authors use terms that may be new to some readers, and a few chapters remain more challenging to read than others. The chapters vary as well in theoretical approach, breadth of coverage, and style. (See Chapter 5 for some basic definitions.)

Within this diversity, however, there are common goals. In making your way through the book, it may help to keep in mind what the authors are trying to accomplish. We asked some of the authors to examine broad themes running through psychology as a whole and others to analyze a relatively narrow segment. We did not, however, ask the authors to present a comprehensive review of their entire subfield or a complete history. Instead, because of space limitations, we asked them to identify and clarify the field's central issues, providing a broad critical overview that readers might use as a basis for further investigation. We asked five general questions, questions you can ask yourself regarding your own field of interest:

1   Does the field promote the status quo in society?
2   Does the field promote social justice or injustice either for its particular population of interest or for society at large?
3   Is there an awareness of the societal repercussions of the field's theories and practices, or is the field oblivious of its potential negative effects?
4   Do researchers, theorists and practitioners declare their values, or do they assume what they do is value-free?
5   What are your own cultural/moral/value commitments, and how do they affect your critique?

We then provided the authors with a longer list of specific points to consider, primarily related to the assumptions listed in Table 1.1. We asked them to provide specific examples not only of how the field's mainstream strengthens the status quo but of how the field might contribute to meaningful social change. Thus, despite varying approaches, focuses, and terminologies, all the authors grapple with the same fundamental questions.

As the point about providing positive examples makes clear, we believe that many things can be done to change society and make the discipline more progressive. Because critical psychology is an approach that permeates all our functions as psychologists, in every job we do we can do critical work. We can give more voice to students, to clients, and to research participants; we can stop assuming that our training makes us experts on other people's problems; we can design research to advance the interests of powerless groups; we can write letters and help organize direct protests to counter erroneous beliefs and policies. These are all *critical* tasks that promote critical psychology. You will see specific examples throughout the book, including suggestions for research and action that students as well as practitioners can follow (see especially Chapter 5).

Our main message here is that it does not take years of training in critical psychology to begin practicing it. The myth that we cannot speak before we are "all-knowing" about a field and the mainstream's insistence that "more research is needed" frequently prevent constructive action (Fox and Prilleltensky, 1996). How much more research on oppression's destructive effects do we need before we try to end oppression? We believe we know a great deal about oppression, and about how consumerist societies erode a sense of community and personal meaning. A century of manipulating variables in laboratories and the field has not challenged the status quo. What we need instead is research that can teach us how to change real societies in fundamental ways. And we need action that goes beyond research.

Organizing Matters

We have organized this book to make it useful for professors, students, researchers, and practitioners. The first part, "Critical Overviews," introduces general issues, defines basic concepts, and offers a glimpse of how students and others new to critical psychology might proceed. The second part, "Critical Arenas," describes in some detail the place of critical psychology in specific subfields. The third part, "Critical Theories," explores differing theoretical perspectives within critical psychology. The final part, "Critical Reflections," assesses critical psychology itself. Such an organizing strategy has certain advantages. One is that professors can use the book as a course supplement in introductory courses, or as a main text in critical psychology courses. Another is that readers looking for material relevant to their immediate interests can read single chapters rather than the whole book.

On the other hand, this organizing strategy has a serious disadvantage as well: it maintains distinctions between different areas of psychology that critical psychologists argue are artificial. Dividing the field into subfields that seem distinct on paper makes it difficult to see real connections among different areas, such as between social psychology and developmental psychology, or between research methods and professional ethics. Because of this somewhat arbitrary boundary setting, we had to make hard choices in selecting our authors and defining the scope of our chapters. We hope you will keep this issue in mind throughout the book, especially as you notice different authors addressing similar themes across the field as a whole.

In the rest of Part I, four chapters set the stage for the material that follows by focusing on psychology's background and philosophy. In Chapter 2, Benjamin Harris examines how mainstream psychologists interpret psychology's history. Harris claims the mainstream pays too little attention to the profession's conforming social role and to the sociopolitical context in which the discipline developed. Traditional histories of psychology, thus, accept myths about science's supposed value neutrality and celebrate the field's supposedly inevitable progression.

In Chapter 3, Louise H. Kidder and Michelle Fine look at research methods in psychology. Psychological research has traditionally used *quantitative* experimental methods to demonstrate its status as a science. Yet, Kidder and Fine argue, *qualitative* methodology is more suited to understanding the differing perspectives of populations whose voices have not been adequately heard. Strongly influenced by feminist approaches to knowledge, qualitative methodology enables critical psychologists to challenge an unsatisfactory status quo in psychology as well as in society.

As Laura S. Brown notes in Chapter 4's examination of professional ethics in psychology, mainstream psychologists traditionally define ethics in legalistic and procedural terms, precluding an in-depth analysis of power dynamics both within and outside psychological practice. As a consequence, professional codes of ethics typically offer more protection to the professionals than to the clients or consumers of services. Brown challenges fundamental assumptions guiding codes of ethics in research and practice and shows how issues of oppression, discrimination, and social change are systematically excluded from discussions of ethics.

In the final chapter in Part I, David Nightingale and Tor Neilands link critical psychology theory to critical psychology practice, defining in the process some of the terms that other authors use throughout the book. In exploring some of the barriers faced by academics, practitioners, and students who try to live the values of critical psychology in the real world, the chapter considers the pragmatics of adopting and maintaining a critical perspective within mainstream institutions holding power over our lives.

The authors in Part II explore ten subfields within psychology. These include the traditional fields of personality theory (Tod Sloan), abnormal and clinical psychology (Rachel T. Hare-Mustin and Jeanne Marecek), intelligence research (Zack Z. Cernovsky), developmental psychology (Erica Burman), and social psychology (S. Mark Pancer). Chapters also examine newer subfields: community psychology (Isaac Prilleltensky and Geoffrey Nelson), cross-cultural psychology (Fathali M. Moghaddam and Charles Studer), lesbian and gay psychology (Celia Kitzinger), psychology and law (Dennis Fox), and political psychology (Maritza Montero). Each chapter critiques mainstream treatment of a substantive area, demonstrating connections between psychology's business as usual and society's unsatisfactory status quo. Authors focus their critique on one or more of the basic assumptions presented in Table 1.1. Thus, some explore the conservative uses of research, others examine the repressive dimensions of labeling and some forms of therapy, and still others discuss how issues of power and equality are erased from psychology's agenda. Many writers in this section criticize their subfield's allegiance to individualistic conceptions of the Good Life. The authors suggest both the promises and the dilemmas of critical psychology.

In Part III, we return to psychology as a whole. The three chapters describe differing theoretical perspectives, each of them reflected in earlier chapters. Each offers critical psychologists an alternative to mainstream approaches. Sue Wilkinson notes the potential of *feminist psychology* to reconstruct the discipline along critical lines, and clarifies the distinctions among different influential traditions within feminist psychology. Frank C. Richardson and Blaine J. Fowers examine the terrain of *critical theory, postmodernism,* and *hermeneutics,* suggesting the importance for critical psychology of approaches based on interpretation. And Ian Parker advocates an approach called *discursive psychology* to help psychologists interpret discourse, the ways in which culture conveys meaning.

Finally, in Part IV, Julian Rappaport and Eric Stewart review the state of critical psychology as presented in *Critical Psychology: An Introduction.* They point out continuing challenges we all must meet if critical psychology is to live up to the possibilities suggested in this book.

Note

Thanks to those who made specific comments after reading early drafts of this chapter: Elizabeth Caddick, Stephanie Campbell, Milo Fox, Ian Parker, Ora Prilleltensky, Tor Neilands, Alan Tomkins, and Sue Wilkinson.

2
Repoliticizing the History of Psychology

Benjamin Harris

Editors' note   *Critical historians remind us that historical accounts are not neutral. That is, historians* select *which events to recount and they* choose *among competing analytical interpretations. They make subjective choices about what is significant and what is not, choices that affect how people view the present as well as the past. For example, the history taught in schools focuses attention on some historical details and interpretations while omitting or explaining away others. This process typically strengthens mainstream beliefs in the larger society's values, myths, and current public policies.*

As Benjamin Harris demonstrates in this chapter, traditional histories of psychology play a similar role: they strengthen psychology's status quo and discredit challenges to dominant views. By celebrating psychology as a strictly scientific discipline, progressing in linear fashion to help society through value-free research, these histories ignore the role of ideological and political factors in psychology's evolution. Using illustrative case examples, some of which appear again in other chapters, Harris presents the other side of the story. He shows how research and knowledge are infused with political interests, how the social context shapes research topics, how conceptions of the Good Life and the Good Society inform practice, and how power dynamics influence the evolution of the discipline.

In a cautionary note, Harris warns critical psychologists against over-simplifying in the other direction. Although it is tempting to blame specific individuals for psychology's injustices, particularly psychologists whose influential work deserves criticism, injustice results from social forces more powerful than any single individual. Fortunately, recent histories typify what Harris calls the New History of Psychology. *This scholarship includes crucial contributions by feminist thinkers critical of traditional histories that discount women's experiences. Similar influences of feminism on critical psychology are noted by other authors throughout this book.*

Most students have two significant encounters with the history of psychology. At the beginning of their studies, students are given a historical introduction to the field of psychology. As with a welcoming handshake, teachers use history to usher students into the discipline and convey the seriousness and sincerity of those who work within. Like a quick tour around the lab or shop, a historical overview also marks the boundaries of the field and shows the research topics and methods that are legitimate and profitable.

Years later, students in psychology have a second important encounter with history as they complete their undergraduate careers. In a course titled "history and systems," students learn about the theoretical disputes that have divided psychologists into warring factions: behaviorists, Gestaltists, phenomenologists, and so on. To study these debates taking place in the nineteenth and early twentieth centuries, students read the no-longer-fashionable writing of figures such as Hermann Ebbinghaus, William James, Edward Thorndike, and John Watson. For the critically minded student, exposure to earlier generations' views of psychology has the potential to subvert the ideology of consensus that today's undergraduate courses convey. For the vast majority of students, however, courses in history and systems serve to strengthen rather than weaken the dominant paradigm in psychology.

For the history of psychology to serve the status quo, it is first turned into a narrowly *intellectual* history. Dissociated from national and world events, the history of psychology becomes the history of the intellectual discussions within elite groups such as university professors. Further removed from everyday life, the discoveries of psychologists are presented as products of individual inspiration, motivated by a timeless quest for knowledge.

As the typical history and systems course surveys the roughly 100-year history of psychology, students learn how the genius of great psychologists allowed them to design great experiments and construct great theories from the experiments' results (Roback, 1961). When such theories conflict, students are told, the result is a competition for the most scientific accuracy, which is settled on logical rather than ideological or political grounds. If social context is allowed to intrude into this story of psychological discoveries, one or another scientist might be inspired by a social concern to conduct certain experiments. The design and success of those experiments, however, are portrayed as determined by intellectual and logical criteria, rather than by factors such as social class, gender, or politics. There may be reference to a line of research fitting the *Zeitgeist* of the day, but that world view is said to act through the genius of the individual scientist, in a process resembling telepathy more than social psychology (Schultz, 1969).

Celebratory History

Implicit in such histories of psychology is the reassuring idea of gradual progress from ignorance to enlightenment. In the terminology of professional historians, this type of history is "Whiggish," "presentist", and "celebratory." Like political histories written in England when the Whig

Party was in power, Whiggish histories of psychology assume that the current status quo is a preordained result of historical progress. Guided by this false assumption the Whiggish historian views events according to the values and biases of the present, creating an essentially nonhistorical, presentist view of the past.

Most relevant to critical psychology, Whiggish histories of psychology fail to appreciate the validity of earlier scientific trends if they conflict with today's orthodoxy. Instead of appreciating past versions of psychology by the standards of their time, Whiggish historians categorize them as either helping or hindering the ascendance of currently accepted psychological theories. The resulting history views the past according to categories that are currently dominant, reinforcing today's orthodoxy and providing its practitioners with a celebratory account of their inevitable rise to power (Samelson, 1974).

Little Albert and the History of Behaviorism

Twenty years ago I learned about celebratory, Whiggish history first hand, in my initial job as a university teacher. Preparing to teach a graduate seminar, I read Watson and Rayner's (1920) article describing their unsuccessful attempt to condition fear in an infant they called Albert. To my surprise, this journal account contradicted the story of "little Albert" that was told by every textbook currently in print, including the one that I was using to teach introductory psychology. According to textbook authors, Watson easily created a rat phobia in Albert, which then generalized into a lifelong fear of rabbits and other furry, white things. In reality, Albert's fear was difficult to induce, transitory, and unrelated to the color or texture of objects. Not only was the Watson and Rayner experiment a failure, but their report of it recognized that fact.

When I looked into the textbook stories of Albert more closely, I found that Watson and Rayner's work on Albert was serving as a celebratory "origin myth" for behaviorists who wanted their specialty to have a long and convincing past. Although orthodox and neo-behaviorists portrayed the Albert story with slightly different details, all versions suggested that John B. Watson had tapped into the power of behaviorism as a theory and technology. He took the first step down the road to contemporary behaviorism, they implied, with the rest of the field gradually adopting a behaviorist viewpoint as the research support mounted (Harris, 1979).

In fact, much of Watson's influence came from his ability as a salesman. He showed his colleagues how to promote psychology to those with financial and social power, regardless of its intellectual or practical merits (Harris, forthcoming). From the behaviorists' Whiggish perspective, however, the success of behaviorism was due to its conforming to the values of experimental psychology *today*: empiricism and conceptual parsimony. Excluded from the story are factors such as salesmanship, financial interest, and manipulation of evidence to create an image.

Politically Cleansed History of Psychology

Just as John Watson worked for personal gain and disciplinary advancement, many prominent psychologists have worked for social justice. Such pro-social motivation is omitted from mainstream histories of psychology, in which the desire for truth is dissociated from the desire for a better society. In textbooks and in histories of experimental psychology, for example, one can read about the "Asch effect" – the discovery that an isolated individual will conform to a group's erroneous version of reality, but a single ally will allow the individual to resist. What is missing from these accounts is the anti-fascist subtext to Asch's (1951) study: that a small group can resist the irrational consensus of a majority. Also missing from mainstream history of psychology is Solomon Asch's experience of solidarity with a small political minority – Communist faculty at Brooklyn College – and how it may have contributed to his important psychological discovery (Holmes, 1989).

Not only has the story of Asch's leftist affiliations remained untold, but textbook histories obscure the larger history of radicals and social reformers in psychology. In them, historical figures are stripped of the belief that motivated much of their research: psychology can facilitate radical social change. Students are also denied knowledge of the struggles that have taken place between radicals and reactionaries for control over the profession and for general cultural authority.

The story of radicals in psychology is easiest to sketch in North America during the Great Depression. Because psychology had expanded dramatically in the 1920s, universities in the early 1930s produced a bumper crop of MAs and PhDs, sending them into the ranks of the unemployed. Confronted by their own lack of opportunity, industrial conflict across the nation, and the rise of fascism in Europe, scores of young psychologists saw the need for radical, collective action. Inspired by the British science and society movement and by anti-fascist intellectuals in Germany and France, psychologists in North America formed groups such as the Psychologists League and The Society for the Psychological Study of Social Issues to promote a new psychology of social change.

Because socialist, communist, and Trotskyist political parties offered a militant, international perspective on the day's crises, scores of young psychologists identified with them, and with the larger circle of sympathizers and unaffiliated radicals. The result was a vibrant discussion within reform caucuses of psychologists. To combat the growing menace of fascism, radicals and Marxists organized public discussions and wrote articles about reactionary trends in the social sciences. The eugenical views of personality psychologist Raymond Cattell, for example, were denounced by the Psychologists League decades before his politics would be discussed by the mainstream press (Neff, 1938; Wojciechowski, 1994). Equally important as combating misdirected psychology was the development of a new, revolutionary human science. This was on the agenda of scientists and political activists alike, who debated the relative contributions of Freud, Marx, Pavlov, Gestalt psychology, and other intellectual trends (Harris, 1990; 1993).

Exemplifying the use of psychology for social reform was research on the psychology of race, intelligence and personality performed by members of The Society for the Psychological Study of Social Issues. In the 1930s and 1940s, figures like Otto Klineberg used his research to debunk ideas that Blacks were inherently less intelligent than whites. This was followed by the research on Black self-esteem by Mamie and Kenneth Clark (Klineberg's former student) which provided the US Supreme Court with the scientific justification for banning racially segregated education (Kluger, 1976).

Cleansing such political content from the history of psychology, often done with subtlety, becomes blatant when performed by an institution threatened by a critical perspective. A recent example of this was the production of two histories in celebration of the 100th anniversary of the American Psychological Association. In those histories, the shaping of psychology by social forces such as the Great Depression, racism, and anti-Semitism is nowhere to be seen. Even more striking is the invisibility of those psychologists who studied these forces and who contributed to social reforms such as the *Brown* v. *Board of Education* Supreme Court decision (Harris, 1994).

Revisionist History of Psychology

As psychology has become repoliticized over the last three decades, so has its history. Beginning at the time of the Vietnam War, critics of mainstream psychology have looked to history for evidence that the field has gone astray. Finding such evidence in the scientific literature of 1890–1930, a few individuals have written accounts that are openly revisionist. That is, the authors adopt an anti-ceremonial perspective and include the unflattering details that mainstream histories omit.

Because the United States contains the vast majority of the world's psychologists and is a highly psychologized society, the development of psychology there has offered much to revisionist historians. Also, academic psychology in North America is an enterprise large enough to support hundreds of amateur historians within its ranks – revisionists included. For these reasons, the history of psychology in the United States has been the intellectual terrain most contested since the 1960s. Similar discussions have focused on psychology in other countries, however, including Germany, Austria, the former Soviet Union, England, and France (Ash and Woodward, 1987; Samelson, 1992). Parallel discussions have also taken place in the history of psychiatry (Tomes, 1994).

Leon Kamin

The most influential revisionist history to appear in the 1970s was written by an experimental psychologist at Princeton University named Leon Kamin.

Typical of scientists who have become self-taught historians, Kamin's primary goal was to discredit a contemporary trend in psychology. The focus of his criticism was the idea that intelligence tests measure the effects of heredity rather than environment. Promoted by the psychologists Arthur Jensen and Richard Herrnstein, this theory seemed to Kamin to be both unsupported by research and reactionary in its political implications.

For Kamin, the idea that psychology could be connected to politics was not new. Rather, it was something he had learned through personal experience. As an undergraduate at Harvard College in the mid-1940s, Kamin was interested in human behavior and its social context. To pursue his interests, he both majored in psychology and joined the one political party that seemed to have the size, the record of fighting fascism, and the scientific outlook needed to lead the country toward a more egalitarian, productive future: the Communist Party (CP). After graduating from Harvard in 1949, Kamin became the New England editor of the Communists' *Daily Worker* and continued to study psychology on his own. In the winter and spring of 1950, however, the CP launched a sectarian campaign against all forms of psychology not approved by Joseph Stalin, filling its publications with crude, anti-psychological polemics (Harris, 1995).

Repelled by the Party's anti-intellectualism and dogmatism, Kamin quit his *Daily Worker* job, dropped out of the CP, and returned to Harvard University to earn a PhD in psychology (US Congress, 1954). While a graduate student, however, he was subpoenaed by two different congressional committees that attacked colleges and universities for breeding subversion and dissent. Denounced by congressional witch-hunters for his refusal to testify against his former comrades, Kamin could not find a teaching job in the US despite his Harvard PhD and excellent record. In Canada, by contrast, the political climate was less hostile and Kamin became a prominent scholar and university teacher. In 1968 he returned to the US – and to the Ivy League – as Professor and Chair of the Psychology Department at Princeton University (Schrecker, 1986).

Given these experiences with the political context surrounding contemporary psychology, Kamin was well prepared to investigate the political agenda behind the development of intelligence testing in the 1920s. As reported in *The Science and Politics of I.Q.*, Kamin (1974) found that the pioneers of intelligence testing were motivated by social concerns as much as scientific fervor. Reviewing their writings during the period 1915–1935, Kamin showed them prejudiced against anyone other than prosperous, white Protestant males whose families had lived in the US for many generations. Quoting the important psychologists Lewis Terman, Robert Yerkes, and H. H. Goddard, Kamin showed them believing in the genetic inferiority of immigrants, Blacks, Native Americans, Jews, and women.

In Kamin's historical account, the prejudice of these experts was reflected not only in their academic writings but also in inhumane social policies. First were the restrictive immigration laws of the 1920s, justified by psychologists' nativist misinterpretation of First World War intelligence tests. Because of these laws, Kamin charged, East European Jews were denied entry to the US in the 1930s, perishing instead at the hands of the Nazis. Second were involuntary sterilization laws passed by many states to halt the spread of feeble-mindedness. These provisions for the mandatory sterilization of the mentally retarded, Kamin revealed, conformed to the eugenic views of Goddard, Yerkes, and the other promoters of intelligence testing. In offering this critical, revisionist history, Kamin was suggesting the potential for social injustice inherent in the new hereditarianism of the 1970s.

Stephen J. Gould

In the decade following Kamin's book, the most influential revisionist history of psychology was the aptly titled *The Mismeasure of Man*. Its author was Stephen Jay Gould, a Harvard University paleontologist and popular writer on science. Like Kamin, Gould was motivated by a long-standing concern about the political misuses of science; during the Vietnam War he had been a prominent member of the activist group Science for the People.·

In *Mismeasure of Man*, Gould (1981) suggested that twentieth century claims that intelligence was inherited were nothing new. Rather, the hereditarianism of the 1920s and 1970s echoed nineteenth century attempts to reduce human personality traits to biology. In his 150-year survey of biological reductionism, Gould showed the logic of Arthur Jensen first appearing in Europe in the period 1830–1900. There, craniometrists measured intelligence by looking at skull size, and physiognomists assessed criminality by looking at the shape of body parts. Anticipating the IQ pioneers of the 1920s, these European experts on human diversity claimed to have found quantitative evidence of the mental inferiority of women, Blacks, and non-Western nationalities.

Moving to the early twentieth century United States, Gould fleshed out Leon Kamin's history of restrictive immigration policies based on misinterpreted Army intelligence tests. He also showed how such early tests were poorly standardized, resulting in the absurd finding that half the US population was mentally retarded. To Kamin's portrayal of IQ pioneer H. H. Goddard, Gould added the story of Goddard's famous study of an allegedly degenerate, rural New Jersey family that he called the Kallikaks. Consistent with eugenic calls for the sterilization of the unfit, Goddard portrayed generation after generation of Kallikaks as feeble-minded, immoral, and criminal. Offended by the social pessimism of Goddard's *The Kallikak Family* (1912), Gould reprinted some of its illustrations and accused Goddard of retouching photos to make his subjects look demented and depraved.

In concluding his history of hereditarian errors Gould disputed the idea that intelligence was a single quality, known as "g" to its proponents. The primary mid-century advocate of that idea, Gould shows, was the elitist British psychologist Cyril Burt. Not only was Burt dishonest in dealing with those skeptical of his research, but Gould blamed his pessimistic hereditarianism for Britain's two-track educational system – in which the working classes were condemned to vocational schools and second-class careers. Although Burt was now dead and discredited, Gould equated his theories to the doctrines of Arthur Jensen, the most infamous hereditarian of contemporary psychology.

Counter-Revisionist History

For those concerned about social injustice and the oppressive use of psychology, the revisionist histories of Kamin and Gould were welcome. They challenged the consensus that psychology had developed for the good of all, free from social prejudice. They also agreed with critical histories of psychiatry and clinical psychology that the anti-psychiatry movement found so empowering.

Typical of the positive responses that these histories elicited was my enthusiastic review of Kamin's book for the *International Socialist Review*. Writing under a pseudonym – since I was a new PhD teaching at a rural university in the Southern US – I quoted the same racist statements by First World War era psychologists that Kamin had unearthed. I also repeated Kamin's denunciation of the early IQ testers for helping cause "the deaths of literally hundreds of thousands of victims of the Nazi biological theorists" (Hudson, 1977: 12).

Today I reread my review with nostalgia for its political zeal but embarrassment for its historical naiveté. What I did not know at the time is how much Kamin's historical vision shares the flaws of the celebratory histories he tried to debunk. While the political sentiments of the 1970s–1980s revisionists were emancipatory, their historical methods and perspectives actually disarm the reader who intends to challenge the status quo. They do so, first, by concentrating on a few leading men in the field, whom they see as ideologically unanimous and critically involved in deciding social policy. Their second error is to attribute malevolent intent whenever they see social injustice. Finally, they expect scientists of past eras to operate by today's standards of evidence and proof.

Such errors, it should be noted, are not unique to the work of Kamin and Gould. The anti-psychiatry and radical therapy movements of the 1970s embraced histories of mental illness that were as equally passionate and naive. Produced by figures such as Thomas Szasz, David Rothman, and Phyllis Chesler, these tendentious accounts used history to support a grab bag of ideologies ranging from libertarianism and social interactionism to neo-Marxism (Brown, 1973; Grob, 1994; Tomes, 1994).

Fortunately, a new type of critical history of psychology has arisen to supplant the revisionism of an earlier era. Its proponents are psychologists who have turned to full-time historical research, and professional historians who make psychology the focus of their studies. Together they have pioneered a historical approach that is critical of both ceremonial history and ahistorical revisionism.

New History of Psychology

This "new history of psychology" was inspired by critical currents within the history profession in the 1960s and 1970s, notably women's history and social history. As described by one of its leading advocates, the result is a history of psychology that is "more contextual, more critical, more archival, more inclusive, and more past-minded" (Furumoto, 1989: 30). In other words, its practitioners focus on nonelite groups in psychology, they look at consumers of psychological information, they use archival records to supplement the official literature of the field, and they recreate the social context in which intellectual trends develop. In dealing with the issue of gender, for example, the new history of psychology has moved beyond the simple revisionist task of replacing the "great men" in psychology with forgotten "great women." Instead of just focusing on the individual women whose careers were thwarted or who deserve to be added to history texts, the new history looks at the mechanisms by which power is exercised in the field of psychology. Those mechanisms include assigning lower status to research areas considered to be "feminine" (educational psychology), and equating scientific rigor with traditionally male attributes such as the ability to make decisions in an unemotional style. The result is a history that focuses on social context and political power as much as intellectual discovery and the warring egos of great men.

Looking at the development of intelligence testing, the new history of psychology sees that psychologists and their tests played at best a peripheral role in the passage of restrictive immigration laws in the 1920s. Racist politicians, it turns out, had decided long before that Eastern and Southern Europeans were inferior grade; they didn't need the Army IQ tests to tell them so (Samelson, 1975). Moreover, the racist unanimity attributed to psychologists by Kamin and Gould is an illusion.

As shown by more thorough studies, figures like Terman, Yerkes, and Goddard disagreed sharply on questions from the standardization of intelligence tests to the relation of IQ to crime and delinquency (Zenderland, 1987). Also, there were many lesser known psychologists who never accepted nativist and racist views of intelligence. Fifty-five years before Gould linked psychological hereditarians with nineteenth century physiognomists, for example, an assistant professor at Smith College named Margaret Curti was writing articles making the same point (e.g., Curti, 1926).

A final, prototypic error in *Mismeasure of Man* was its author's claim that H. H. Goddard had retouched photos in one of his books to make members of the Kallikak family look stupid. As explained recently by

Raymond Fancher (1988), this is not only a false accusation but one based on ignorance of Goddard's motives and methods for promoting his brand of psychology. The feeble-minded were not always detectable by surface examination, Goddard argued, and thus the services of a psychologist were needed. As a result, Goddard was one of the few people who wanted the Kallikaks to look *normal*, rather than retarded or evil. By understanding that Goddard was more interested in professional expansion than oppressing the underprivileged, one sees his role more clearly. One is also better equipped to see how psychologists have gained the power they exercise *today*: by convincing generations of institutional managers that psychological expertise will make their work more efficient.

For the nonhistorian interested in social justice today, the important point here is the frequent disjunction between motive and outcome. The world would be much easier to improve if destructive social forces could be blamed on the malevolence of a scientific elite. In the history of psychology, however, we find that psychologists rarely have a monopoly on ignorance and prejudice. Rather, the social prejudice and blindness of scientists and clinicians is usually no greater than that of politicians, popular writers, or businessmen. That is the lesson that the new history draws from the development of the intelligence test.

Those impatient for social change, however, often see their field as having unique social power – and thus a special responsibility for the sorry state of the world. Fearing their own impotence, some activists are reluctant to see their peers from earlier periods as trudging along with little ability to prevent social ills from befalling their patients and those whom they study. As Gerald Grob (1991) suggested in reviewing the history of psychiatry, such an egocentric, simplistic view of history makes it more rather than less difficult to understand social change and intraprofessional reform. Changes in the care offered by mental hospitals, for example, have often been the result of changes in patient demographics and the nature of the family – rather than the conscious decisions of psychologists and psychiatrists.

Towards a Truly Critical History of Psychology

Given this history of squabbling among historians, what is to be done? How can one fashion a critical perspective out of the competing claims of traditional, revisionist, and counter-revisionist historians? If we accept that psychologists are not inherently malevolent, how can we explain the frequent use of psychology in support of unjust social relations? If we accept that earlier psychologists' methods were no more ridiculous than those of physicians or other social scientists, do we lose our ability to criticize the often mindless empiricism of our field today? If revisionist historians misunderstood the politics of the early IQ debate, how can we hope for a political understanding of psychology in the rest of this century?

Fortunately, practitioners of the new history of psychology have produced work that is critical of the status quo, but also well researched and theoretically sophisticated. Two notable examples are Kurt Danziger's *Constructing the Subject*, covering the early twentieth century, and Ellen Herman's *The Romance of American Psychology*, which deals with the Second World War and subsequent years.

In *Constructing the Subject*, Danziger (1990) provides a revolutionary new look at the field of psychology. What is new is Danziger's focus on how psychologists have created what they study. In traditional histories, we see psychologists inventing new apparatus or new statistical techniques to study interesting phenomena – such as human aggression. What Danziger shows is that much of what seems essential to a psychology experiment is as much a social construction as a piece of lab equipment. The dichotomy between "experimenter" and "subject," for example, is a fairly recent creation. Before it became standard to psychological research, Danziger shows, there were alternative social relationships that seemed equally natural and equally eternal. Once "the subject" was created, psychological research was steered in directions that otherwise would have been impossible. Treating subjects unethically or ignoring the subject's thoughts, for example, are not possible if an experiment has no "subject."

Another creation of psychologists is the "abstract individual" that psychologists investigate and explain. That unreal but constantly studied person, Danziger shows, is "the product neither of nature nor of society but of statistical construction" (1990: 129). Furthermore, it has been the mastery of this abstract individual that has made psychological knowledge valuable to those in power. As Danziger describes it, "American psychologists scored some real successes . . . by providing knowledge products that mobilized the interests of educational and military administrators as well as the administrators of private foundations" (1990: 181). In other words, psychology has flourished by becoming a useful "administrative science" for institutions of social control. What psychology provides those institutions is not so much the secrets of behavioral manipulation. Rather, psychology has recast social relationships to yield "the human subject" – a being in need of manipulation.

Danziger's analysis of early twentieth century psychologists as "knowledge producers" is supported by Ellen Herman's recent book *The Romance of American Psychology*. Examining the period 1940–1975, Herman (1995) shows psychological experts pursuing political and cultural authority as much as scientific success. They do so by helping those in power deal with key social issues: war, poverty, race, and gender. One result is a psychological dimension to social and political policy, from the Supreme Court's *Brown* v. *Board of Education* decision to the CIA's Project Camelot and the Kerner Commission's report on urban violence. Another result is the cooptation of psychologists by the postwar political state, silencing them as political dissidents until the crisis of the Vietnam War.

Unlike the conspiratorial histories of earlier eras, Herman's perspective rejects the dichotomous view of psychology as either manipulative or freedom enhancing. Rather, she sees increasing personal freedom and social engineering are not always separable processes. Although we like to make "distinctions between democratic and antidemocratic uses of [psychology]," Herman notes, "the line separating them has a great deal more to do with social context of ideas than with factors intrinsic to knowledge production" (1995: 11). One of her goals as a historian, then, is to show how "the respective genealogies of 'control' and 'freedom' are as connected as their political reputations are disconnected" (1995: 11–12).

In looking at the rise of the psychological expert from 1940 to the 1970s, Herman shows psychology to be politically malleable, serving functions that can prove contradictory. "It has served to . . . obscure the exercise of power in recent U.S. history, but it has also legitimized innovative ideas and actions whose aim has been to personalize, and expand, the scope of liberty" (1995: 15). The former was the case in Vietnam and Chile, where psychology provided social science rationalization for political repression.

The latter, more liberatory function can be seen by looking at the creation of domestic social policies toward race relations and poverty. In the case of schools segregated by race, psychology helped outlaw this practice in the 1950s by testifying to the damaged personalities it created. In the 1960s, experts turned to the psychological harm caused by poverty and suggested reforms in the welfare state. They were persuasive, Herman explains, because "the ugliness of psychological deformation offered a justification for the Great Society that was more durable, or at least fresher, than such tired old abstractions as equality and social justice" (1995: 208).

Herman's point is not that the human sciences are ethically neutral technologies that fit the user's politics. Rather, psychology has been used repressively but contains a liberatory potential. Its liberatory potential comes from its ability to address human, subjective experience. Accordingly, psychological knowledge can add a powerful dimension to political movements, including those of the left.

The women's liberation movement of the 1960s was such a movement. As histories of that era note, a key feature of the second wave of feminism was its criticism of the male bias of traditional psychology. Less appreciated are the ways in which the same movement incorporated humanistic psychology into its philosophy and methodology of social change. Feminist "consciousness raising" groups, for example, assumed a dialectical relation between psychological and political experience, and refused to exclude either. The result, Herman asserts, was a more powerful women's movement.

Ironically, traditional histories of politics and science share with traditional histories of psychology a disdain for the subjective experience of individual actors. By restoring that dimension, Herman improves our historical vision. She also offers a lesson to activists wishing to avoid the anti-psychological excesses that have crippled the political left in its sectarian and ultra-left phases (Harris, 1995). Addressing the activists of today, Herman explains, "If psychological knowledge is to mobilize people for progressive change, rather than equip them to endure new variations on old injustices, the dichotomy between internal and external transformation will have to be rejected as false and useless" (1995: 16).

A Student's Guide to the History of Psychology

What are some lessons of my brief history of critical histories of psychology? For the psychology student, the first lesson is that methods of historical inquiry are as important to learn as research methods in psychology. Without them, those eager for social reform are easily drawn to simplistic histories. In those histories, social injustice is perpetrated by reactionaries who lack scientific integrity and are likely to harbor a hereditarian bias toward psychology. Such reductionism, I suggest, is no less dangerous in history than in psychology or sociology.

The second lesson, perhaps more reassuring than the first, is that good history can be recognized and taught. When I offer a seminar to senior students on the history of psychological testing, for example, I have them read three accounts of the development of the intelligence test. Initially, the impassioned revisionism of Stephen Jay Gould wins their loyalty. Soon, however, they switch allegiance to the more subtle accounts of Fancher (1985) and Sokal (1987); a wave of anti-Gould sentiment then sweeps through the class. By semester's end, however, many students move from anti-revisionism to an understanding of the forces that shape all histories, including the ones they like best. They realize that history, like movements for social change, is not static.

The third lesson of this chapter is that good history can be enjoyed. As exemplified by *The Romance of American Psychology*, it can be compelling reading. Equally encouraging is the fact that good history, like good fiction, challenges one's implicit ways of thinking and makes the world look different afterwards. By reading good examples of the new history of psychology, one can learn to appreciate the frequent disjunction between intent and outcome, and the role of irony in history. At the same time, one can see the field from the bottom up and from a socially informed view. The result is an appreciation of the contributions of previously neglected figures, and of the role of sociopolitical forces in shaping the work of psychologists from Asch to Zimbardo.

In the end, the critically minded reader may not find ready-made "lessons of history" to apply to today's psychological research. But through historical awareness, it will be easier to critically view what is taking place today.

3

Qualitative Inquiry in Psychology: A Radical Tradition

Louise H. Kidder and Michelle Fine

Editors' note   *Psychology's claim to be a legitimate science led it to emulate the hard sciences' laboratory methods and statistical analyses. The "positivist" goal was to identify cause and effect relations among isolated variables that the experimenter could control. Success would enable psychology to "predict and control" behavior in people defined as "subjects" to manipulate. Seeking legitimacy, psychology discarded its traditions of qualitative, interpretive, "softer" methods that examined behavior in the less tidy real world. In this chapter, Louise H. Kidder and Michelle Fine remind us of the history and potential of qualitative methods.*

As several chapters in this book point out, mainstream psychology's traditional research practices can sometimes advance critical psychology's goals, as by quantifying the existence of inequality. Yet narrowly focused hypothesis-driven research often misses sources and consequences of injustice that open-ended qualitative methods expose. Reintroduced to psychology by feminists and others over the past two decades, qualitative methods have regained some of their earlier appeal. Positivist approaches, however, remain dominant. In most areas of psychology, researchers seeking to use qualitative methods still must satisfy skeptical funding sources, hard-nosed dissertation and hiring committees, and editors who lack experience with alternative approaches.

Qualitative researchers seek not to manipulate "subjects" but to hear the voice of "participants" who join our search for knowledge and justice. They listen to what people say about their problems and, explicitly or implicitly, about the Good Life and the Good Society. By amplifying the voice of participants, qualitative researchers promote the values of self-determination and human diversity. Through dialogue with participants about the meanings of the data, they foster collaboration and democratic participation. In worrying about participants' well-being, they show caring and compassion. Thus, Kidder and Fine not only point to the merits of qualitative approaches in fully and accurately describing the human condition; they also emphasize the ethics of research, a defining feature of critical psychology.

Qualitative methods and psychology have had a long off and on relationship. It has been an intellectual flirtation, alternately secret and open, perilous and safe. Current debates about positivism and postmodernism give the impression that qualitative work is a new, quasi-scientific departure from tradition, a risky project for psychologists. Graduate students wonder whether their work will still be "psychology" if they use methods that look more like "anthropology." In this essay, we document the relationship between Qualitative methods and psychology and show how they have helped produce a critical psychology.

Qualitative methods and critical psychology are not co-terminous. Qualitative work does not automatically yield critical analyses and critical analyses do not require Qualitative methods. But they fit well together. Qualitative work helps psychologists see how class, race, and gender shape lived experience. By highlighting the subjectivities of researchers and participants, Qualitative methods bring to the fore the relations of knowledge, ethics and negotiated intimacy between researchers and the communities they study.

What Counts as "Qualitative"?

In 1987 we distinguished between two meanings of "qualitative" in ways that we still find useful:

> Qualitative work with the *big Q* is field work, participant observation, or ethnography; it consists of a continually changing set of questions without a structured design. The big Q refers to unstructured research, inductive work, hypothesis generation and the development of "grounded theory" (cf. Glaser and Strauss, 1967). Qualitative work with the *small q* consists of open-ended questions embedded in a survey or experiment that has a structure or design. The hypothesis and questions do not change as research progresses. The same questions are asked of everyone. (Kidder and Fine, 1987: 59)

Our task now is to trace the connections between critical psychology and big Q Qualitative methods. We omit the "small q" variety from this chapter because the smaller qualitative moves are not part of a radical tradition; they do not present the same opportunities for critical work.

The work we call "critical" and "Qualitative" extends back more than sixty years. John Dollard in the 1930s conducted field-based Qualitative work on race and class relations in a Southern US town (Dollard, 1937). In the 1940s and 1950s Muzafer Sherif and his collaborators immersed themselves in the rivalries of a summer boys camp to write about conflict and cooperation (Sherif and Sherif, 1953; Sherif et al., 1988). In the 1950s Leon Festinger and colleagues infiltrated a doomsday sect to observe what happens when prophecies fail (Festinger et al., 1956). In these classic studies social psychologists entered their subjects' lives without structured questionnaires, predetermined variables or research designs and no one doubted that they were doing psychological research. They were men who became known for their laboratory and experimental findings but they began their careers with field-based Qualitative work. They produced essays and books in which they explored their biases, worried about their relationships and ethics in the field, and enjoyed the texture of field work.

When they wrote, however, about these aspects of Qualitative work, they were concerned that their biases, worries and relationships were *departures* from, indeed limits on, social science. Today these very same biases, worries and relationships are being resurrected as belonging to the heart and soul, the substance, of critical social research. Over the course of the past thirty to forty years, this history of Qualitative work has been recessed, buried in the background and footnotes of research psychology. In critical tradition, we take pleasure in foregrounding this Qualitative legacy within psychology, which appears to be coming full circle.

Four features of Qualitative work facilitate critical analysis:

1   *Assuming an open-ended stance*   Beginning with a hunch, researchers tentatively form and reform hypotheses. Revising hypotheses is not only permissible but necessary. Surprises abound.
2   *Reflecting on subjectivity and bias*   Rather than treat their own subjectivity as an obstacle, Qualitative researchers take it as a datum. They examine their own subjectivities as well as their respondents' and note how both parties' biases and personal positions affect data collection and analysis.
3   *Worrying about relationships*   Even if they follow ethics guidelines and receive approval from human subjects review committees, Qualitative researchers worry about their relationships with respondents and communities. Each day in the field is another test, another opportunity for having the door closed in one's face and being asked to leave the premises.
4   *Analyzing open-ended questions and writing kaleidoscopic interpretations*   The stance begins with open-ended questions and persists in analyses that provide open-ended multiple, partial and kaleidoscopic interpretations. Like kaleidoscopic images that shift with each turn of the tube, the analysis of Qualitative work can yield multiple patterns from shifting viewpoints.

On Stance

In the early 1930s John Dollard went South from the Psychology Department of Yale University to learn how race operated within the social life of a town he called Southerntown. His stance was self-consciously Qualitative. He understood himself to be a Northern white psychologist from Yale, naive about Southern race relations. He recognized that his naiveté necessitated that he be educated by his data:

The basic method used in the study was that of participation in the social life of Southerntown. This social sharing was of two degrees and involved two roles: there was first the casual participation possible as a "yankee down here studying Negroes" and second the more intensive participation and the more specific role of the life history taker . . . The primary research instrument would seem to be the observing human intelligence trying to make sense of the experience; and the experience was full of problems and uncertainty in fact. Perhaps it does not compare well with more objective-seeming instruments, such as a previously prepared set of questions, but as to this question the reader can judge for himself. It has the value of offering to perception the actual, natural human contact with all of the real feelings present and unguarded. (1937: 18)

At the heart of what we are calling a *Qualitative stance* is, as Dollard admits, a desire to make sense of the experience with "all of the real feelings present and unguarded." Unlike the hypothetico-deductive stance in which predetermined hypotheses frame a particular set of questions, a Qualitative stance enables researchers to carve open territory about which they have vague hunches rather than clear predictions. A Qualitative stance encourages broad-based inquiry into intellectual and social spaces which may be strange to the researcher, undocumented in other studies. Propelled by a desire to know what is unknown, to unravel surprises, to be alarmed and jostled in our own thinking, Qualitative researchers embark on a sometimes quite lonely, hard to predict, intellectual adventure.

You can hear in the Dollard example how a Qualitative stance enables, but does not guarantee, a critical analysis that surfs between macro structures and micro psychologies. Because the field of variables is not pre-drawn, the intellectual harvest can move generously across the terrain. The racial, political and economic hierarchies of the South in the early part of this century and individual "Negro" and "white" personalities could be connected, woven together in theory and research. That is, Qualitative researchers have the capacity to analyze across broad territory the nuanced strategies by which power operates through individual and collective psychologies. Not constrained by a predetermined menu of variables whose main effects and interactions we track, Qualitative work first permits a broad look and then forces a narrowing of focus once the map of the field becomes clear. This way of working requires being willing to give up control, going along for the ride, not always having hold of the steering wheel – and still taking good notes.

Letting Go of Control

Qualitative researchers may fantasize being a "fly on the wall," exerting no control at all over what happens next, but documenting it all. Fortunately, both everyday realities and current ethical guidelines make being a "fly," much less a "spy," virtually impossible. But that was not true in the past.

When Leon Festinger and his colleagues became undercover researchers in a doomsday cult in 1956 they tried to achieve the status of a "fly" but they admit their failure:

> We had to conduct the entire inquiry covertly, without revealing our research purpose, pretending to be merely interested individuals who had been persuaded of the correctness of the belief system and yet taking a passive and uninfluential role in the group . . . [but] our influence on the group [was] somewhat greater than we would like. (1956: 249)

By virtue of human subjects regulations, ethical guidelines and contemporary considerations of researchers' responsibilities, researchers today who want to study a group or a site are usually required to state who they are, make their intentions known, and obtain permission to be there. They might want to be invisible but usually aren't, so they are right to worry about how their presence might affect the people they observe.

Dancing with the Data

Qualitative researchers may lose control during parts of the data collection process, but they regain it as they "dance with the data" and in the dance resume the lead. In hypothetico-deductive work control is guaranteed when only a few variables are allowed onto the stage and satisfaction comes from saying "I knew it! My predictions were right, my hypotheses confirmed." In practice, of course, researchers rarely find all their hypotheses and predictions confirmed (technically, their hypotheses are not disconfirmed, and that is the most they can celebrate). In practice, experimenters and survey researchers are more likely to find one or two of their hypotheses are "safe" (not disconfirmed); they "fail to reject the null hypothesis." The remainder of the results section in a survey or experiment often has a bewildering array of significant results that were not predicted and non-significant findings that should have been significant. Authors then perform an intricate dance in the discussion section to make sense of an unexpected three-way interaction or explain why a predicted two-way interaction did not materialize. Part of a discussion section frequently contains guess work about what the subjects might have been thinking that made the results assume these unexpected patterns. Creating a new dance in the discussion can be satisfying when it works.

In Qualitative research the dance begins early. If you are paying attention, your loss of control will be apparent sooner than you wish. The data jump at you quite unpredictably, forcing the researcher to dance – abandoning or transforming hunches, hypotheses, favorite theories. To illustrate: in a participant observation study conducted in the early 1980s, I (*Michelle*) spent time in a hospital emergency room with a young woman I call Altamese. Altamese had just been gang raped. I was a "rape crisis volunteer." She was the "survivor." We spent hours talking, with Altamese tolerating my awkward and anxious attempts at humor. In embarrassed retrospect, I was trying to "talk her into" ways of coping. Toward this end, I doused her with all that *I knew* would be "good" for her, as a feminist counselor, social psychologist, white woman academic . . . report them, tell your social worker, let your family know, don't keep it in . . .

At some point Altamese had enough of my maternal, if not colonial, advice and politely let me know that she had her own strategies. She would not press charges, or let her family know. From her community (an African American neighborhood in North Philadelphia), rarely was a woman believed by the police. If she told her brothers about the rape, they might go out and kill the accused. If she told a therapist it might help for a moment but the pain would still be within. Once I stopped talking and listened to her story, I could hear her way of making sense, that is, surviving, in a world where neither the justice system nor the streets were very trustworthy; where protecting her mother, brother and children was more important than abstract notions of justice.

I could have kept talking, or surveyed her to determine that she was "resistant" or "helpless" (Fine, 1984). But by listening I was able to unravel, partially and through my own eyes, how she saw and experienced the world and then how poorly feminist programs, drawn and designed from "our" middle-class experience, fit the needs of Altamese. The strategies and institutions I presumed could "save" me (courts, counseling, other women, family) might only prosecute or further endanger Altamese. To follow her steps I had to give up mine and recognize the extent to which race and racism, poverty and classism, personal and cultural circumstances made a difference in how we did/would respond to a gang rape. In retrospect this seems dumb, racist not to have known, embarrassing. But at the time I thought I was equipped to frame Altamese's story with the feminist and psychological categories I had available. Altamese taught me a different dance, and only then did the data make sense. Without a Qualitative stance I never would have heard her music. I would have assumed that *she* missed the beat.

Caught Off Balance

For those of us who cherish intellectual, political and emotional control, a Qualitative stance can be a curve ball, knocking a researcher into an uncomfortable sense of being off balance, ill equipped, without resources to "cope." When I (*Louise*) joined as a participant observer in a personal defense class for women I planned to discover whether the classes made women feel fearful or capable of resisting an assault – as though this were a clear dichotomous choice (I hear a 2 × 2 research design looming!). The simple answer to that simple question was that it depended on what covert messages their instructors gave. Students who took lessons from a woman and a man who unequivocally stated that no one had a right to "tamper" with their bodies felt empowered to resist. Students who learned from a man who was more ambivalent about women fighting back ended the course believing they had less right to resist. But my participant observation in the classes raised a more disturbing question which I had not anticipated: how do women learn to define "danger" when ordinary heterosexual courtship involves "aggressive initiatory activity on the part of males" (Goffman, 1977: 329)? Had I approached the study only with questionnaires I would have failed to see the confusion the women experienced. The Qualitative stance, being there, off balance, with all pores open, revealed patterns that made my original hypotheses look naively clean and simple (Kidder, 1994).

We find a paradoxical contrast between the apparent simplicity of the Qualitative stance and the power it provides to uncover meanings and reveal complex patterns. Simply being in the field, open to what happens next, following leads and hunches, revising hypotheses, following one's nose are so unlike the methods of experimental and survey design and analysis. They seem like unsophisticated and undisciplined research maneuvers, but their simplicity is illusory. Working without a structured questionnaire, without a sampling procedure or formal research design, requires daily decisions about what to observe, whom to interview, what to say next. The discipline is rigorous, severe and sometimes lonely.

On "Bias"

Built into a Qualitative stance is the explicit recognition that we, as researchers, import our lens, our "bias," to our studies. Our data are filtered through that lens, as are our interpretations, which are, therefore, always partial. We note, however, that while all research is shaped through researchers' subjectivities or biases, it is typically only in Qualitative work that these subjectivities are acknowledged, studied, interrogated and written about.

Indeed, with pride and/or embarrassment, Qualitative researchers frequently admit that they bring to the research project a package of personal identities, interests and investments (e.g. Kidder in Fine et al., 1996; Liebow, 1993). Consider an interview with Harriet McAdoo about how she became interested in her program of research:

> John [McAdoo] and I came to Ann Arbor in the Fall of 1966 and our youngest, Anna, was pre-school age. Whenever it seemed natural and playful, we always made it a point to reinforce a positive attitude about our children's racial image and it was no different with Anna. Sometimes when giving her a bath, I would let the rinse water slowly wring from the washcloth so we could trace a stream from her shoulders to her toes. Our eyes followed the stream, and we would laugh and play and I would sometimes say something like, "Look at Mommy's pretty brown girl." Shortly after arriving in Ann Arbor, Anna entered a pre-school program. One evening John and I were sitting on our bed watching television while Anna was taking a bath. Soon she rushed into the room and climbed into bed between us while saying, "Mommy and Daddy I know I'm a pretty brown girl but sometimes I wish I could be a White girl." There was no alarm, sadness or tension in her voice, but it was clear to John and me that our little one, who by every indication was a strong and healthy and happy child, was taking on racial attitudes that were far removed from how she saw herself personally – you know, her sense of self worth. Shortly thereafter I completed my first year paper

and spelled out what was to become my major focus at Michigan – the study of identity development in children, especially Black children and more particularly, the study of self esteem and racial attitudes. (reported in Cross, 1991: 78)

McAdoo's vivid story tells us about the genesis, and also the design, of her research. While some researchers "come clean" about their investments, and others note their "blind" spots or their "dis-ease," most stay silent. Qualitative researchers, in contrast, unpack their biographic baggage at the research site because they are as likely to be asked questions about themselves as they are to ask questions of their research participants. Indeed, some Qualitative researchers feel so obliged, even eager, to come clean that they devote as much time to reflecting on themselves as on their subjects (e.g., Kamala Visweswaran, 1994; Esther Newton, 1993; Jill Morawski, 1994). This self-reflection and admission of subjectivities is becoming quite fashionable in the 1990s. But it is important to remember that it was taken up by John Dollard some sixty years ago, and by Muzafer Sherif, who wrote in the early 1950s about researchers' group identifications, biases and subjectivities:

The research man [*sic*] has his own group identifications. We have noted that every group represents a point of view as it stands in relation to other groups. Every group has its own explicit or implicit premises as to the nature of human relations, as to the directions that the values and goals of group relations should take. *From the outset, research and generalizations are doomed to be deflections or mere justifications of the point of view and premises of the group or groups with which one identifies himself, if one does not start his work by clear, deliberate recognition and neutralizing of his personal involvements in these issues.* If this painful process of deliberate recognition and neutralizing of one's own personal involvements is not achieved, his autism will greatly influence his design of the study and his collection and treatment of data. (Sherif and Sherif, 1953: 11)

What Sherif called "autisms" can also form part of the data for a participant observer. This self-conscious acknowledgment of "personal involvements" and the need for researchers to reflect critically on their positions was shed from much psychological research during the 1970s and 1980s when there was a belief that researchers should be disinterested. Social science was supposed to be written, as Donna Haraway would say, from a "God's eye view" (Haraway, 1988). Such beliefs are actually quite dangerous in so far as they obscure or neutralize the typically privileged bases from which researchers write. While these biases may be unacknowledged, they are far from absent. They are simply denied and distorting.

Again, when we draw from the history of social psychology, we find those cubby holes, those methodological corners into which admissions of researchers' "biases" were stuffed, hidden, apologized for. David Rosenhan, a social psychologist who entered a psychiatric hospital under the guise of a patient, wrote in *Science* magazine about how stunned he was to experience the depths of depersonalization provoked by his short stay in a mental hospital. After he and a number of graduate assistants faked their admissions into psychiatric hospitals, Rosenhan wrote:

Neither anecdotal nor "hard" data can convey the overwhelming sense of powerlessness which invades the individual as he is continually exposed to the depersonalization of the psychiatric hospital. It hardly matters which . . . hospital. (1973: 265)

I and the other pseudopatients in the psychiatric setting had distinctively negative reactions. We do not pretend to describe the subjective experiences of true patients. Theirs may be different from ours, particularly with the passage of time and the necessary process of adaptation to one's environment. But we can and do speak to the relatively more objective indicators of treatment within the hospital. It would be a mistake and a very unfortunate one to consider that what happened to us derived from malice or stupidity on the part of the staff. Quite the contrary, our overwhelming impression of them was of people who really cared, who were committed and who were uncommonly intelligent. Where they failed, as they sometimes did painfully, it would be more accurate to attribute those failures to the environment in which they, too, found themselves than to personal callousness. (1973: 268)

Rosenhan's confession is written as a departure from, rather than constitutive of, his research. In this text he reveals his "overwhelming impression" that belies the impossibility of extracting ourselves from our research. His personal experience dramatizes the power of institutional arrangements on the otherwise "good judgement" of staff and "sanity" of residents. Without his experience inside the institution, Rosenhan's work would have lacked the passion and much of the evidence that makes his study, "Being Sane in Insane Places," compelling.

Rosenhan, Sherif, and Dollard saw their emotional responsiveness to their research as a temporary, fleeting loss of control – a threat to social science rather than part of the data of social science. They presented their experiences apologetically, as confessions of feelings out of control, which might have contaminated the data. We suggest, in contrast, that confession helps to shape, understand and interpret data. Indeed, as we will see, one woman's confessions may turn out to be another wo/man's data.

To illustrate: twenty years after writing about field work on expatriate Westerners in India I (*Louise*) can now see even more clearly my place in a former colony. The field notes that I wrote contained stories from dinner parties, shopping trips and conversations after the structured interview was formally "finished." Going back to those notes I can now write more clearly and honestly than before about the postcolonial remnants of whiteness by placing myself in the context. When I write not as a disembodied narrator but as a person who was present in "the master's house," those confessions become data:

As a first-timer I had thought I could assume a neutral social class or caste. I quickly lost that naiveté and innocence when for $100 a month my husband and I could rent a comfortable home and employ the help of a man and woman to shop, cook, carry water, launder, clean and sweep. They and we were age-mates, in our twenties, but Bob and I were "master" and "ma'm" to them and they were "Jodi" and "Sylvi" to us. They were newly married and Sylvi was pregnant. One day neither Jodi nor Sylvi came to work so I cleaned our outdoor toilet despite advice from Indian friends that I should not do jobs that were dirty, low caste, for servants. When Jodi came the next day he might have sensed my irritation and explained why he had missed work. He said simply "Ma'm, my baby died." I recall this story to place myself within the frame of what I say about other expatriates. In some of the stories expatriates tell about themselves they sound guilty of arrogance and abuse of privilege while they tacitly claim innocence. The terms "guilt" and "innocence" are not used in people's stories or explanations of their own actions, but they lie close beneath the surface of expatriate experience and the surface is fairly transparent. (Kidder, in Fine et al., 1996)

Researchers who mine their own experience can find interpretations they might have missed otherwise. Clinicians who use their own experience cautiously and honestly, as happens with counter-transference, can also arrive at interpretations they might otherwise have overlooked. But there are also risks for researchers who examine their experiences in the field or in their written texts.

Elliot Liebow's book *Tell Them Who I Am* (1993) describes how he takes a chance and benefited from being vulnerable. He entered the world of homeless women and became the object of their gazes even as he wrote about them. As he served them meals and accompanied them to courts and government offices, the women learned that his survival too was precarious because he had cancer. His telling was not an experimental manipulation but a truthful explanation for his actions and absences.

Some of the women would perhaps characterize me as a friend, but I am not certain how deep or steadfast this sense of friendship might be. One day, Regina and I were talking about her upcoming trial about two months away. I had already agreed to accompany her to the courtroom and serve as an adviser, but Regina wanted further reassurance.
"You will be there, won't you?" she said.
As a way of noting the profundity that nothing in life is certain, I said, jokingly, "It's not up to me, it's up to The Man Upstairs."
"Well," she said, "If you die before the trial, you will ask one of your friends to help me, won't you?" I looked hard at her to see if she was joking, too. She wasn't. She was simply putting first things first. (1993: xi)

Qualitative researchers may put themselves into the picture and pay attention to both their feelings and the feelings of the people with whom they are working. There are no enumerated rules for how much to focus on self versus other, how much to reveal of self and other, how to respect boundaries and "do no harm." These are ongoing considerations rather than fixed rules for Qualitative researchers. These questions surface endlessly and sit stubbornly in the foreground of Qualitative work. They can no longer be buried in footnotes.

In field work, the researcher is self-consciously part of the context. Participant observers are visible and vulnerable. Actors who cannot follow a uniform script, we act and speak spontaneously, never quite sure we made the right move. We improvise when we encounter persons or situations for whom we were unprepared. No two days or encounters are identical. Research participants are not all alike. Their differences are what interest us, and the researcher must decide in each instance how to ask questions, what to reply when asked questions and what to do next. Participant observers are vulnerable to being asked to leave or stay; being asked personal questions or ignored; being the subject of another's gaze or marginalized. We are not just actors in the field. We are acted upon and expected to be responsible. Joyce Ladner, a sociologist by training, made such a plea when she wrote:

> The relationship between the researcher and his subjects, by definition, resembles that of the oppressor and the oppressed, because it is the oppressor who defines the problem, the nature of the research, and to some extent, the quality of interaction between him and his subjects. This inability to understand and research the fundamental problem – neo-colonialism – prevents most social researchers from being able accurately to observe and analyze Black life and culture and the impact racism and oppression have upon Blacks. (1971/1987: 77)

Feminist psychologists, echoing the arguments asserted by Joyce Ladner almost thirty years ago, are today resurrecting the call for reflexivity and responsibility in psychological research. These scholars are writing about *how*, not if, our subjectivities sculpt the stories that we tell and the ones that we don't.

For psychologists trained in the positivist tradition this may be a discordant call. We have been taught that subjectivities are out of place, should be contained, monitored, whited out. Being scientific has meant being objective, detached and without passions (see Jill Morawski, 1994, for a wonderful analysis of this position). Paradoxically, however, it is argued by some, ourselves included, that researchers who reflect on rather than ignore our personal investments, thoughts, emotions and relations to those under study may find clearer visions.

On Ethics

Qualitative researchers' open-ended, question-seeking, nose-following stance and immersion in the life of a community or group engenders ethical problems that differ from those of experiments or survey work. Neither informants nor research participants in participant observation are anonymous. Their being known to the researcher (and vice versa) makes both parties personally vulnerable in a way that guarantees of confidentiality do not entirely erase (cf. Liebow, 1993). People whose communities and social relations are documented have a stake in how data are represented and they worry about the misuse of data by hostile audiences. Even if the researcher intends to help, the impact of the research is hard to anticipate and its publication can affect community residents in unpredictable ways.

Listen to the words of Kenneth Clark, reflecting on his own research findings with respect to Black children's self-images:

"We were really disturbed by our findings," Kenneth Clark recalls, "and we sat on them for a number of years. What was surprising was the degree to which the children suffered from self-rejection, with its truncating effect on their personalities, and the earliness of the corrosive awareness of color. I don't think we had quite realized the extent of the cruelty of racism and how hard it hit." The interviewing and testing proved a moving and shaping experience for Clark. "Some of these children, particularly in the North, were reduced to crying when presented with the [black] dolls and asked to identify with them. They looked at me as if I were the devil for putting them in this predicament. Let me tell you, it was a traumatic experience for me as well." (Kluger, 1975: 400, quoted in Cross, 1991: 29)

Clark worried about the impact of his research on the children and on the community in general. While his methods were not Qualitative with respect to kinds of data, his ethical concerns – printed in an interview, *not* as part of the research text – reflect the kinds of ethical concerns that are raised by thoughtful Qualitative work.

Indeed, many such questions arise in response to and in the midst of Qualitative work. "Who owns the data?" becomes an ethical question that laboratory-based participants might not think to ask. Who has veto power? What will happen to the relationships that were formed in the field? What are the researcher's post-data collection obligations? How can these data be misused against informants? Whose interpretation counts? These ethical dilemmas cannot be resolved simply by following guidelines that promise anonymity or confidentiality.

These concerns, voiced recently and eloquently by Brinton Lykes, Jill Morawski and Gail Hornstein are, however, not new to psychological research. They were raised in the decades that preceded us and even then the technical practices of masking participants' identities, obtaining informed consent and debriefing after deception were recognized as insufficient answers.

In the 1970s Philip Zimbardo wrote about his concerns for research participants in his controversial and important study of "The Psychology of Imprisonment" (Zimbardo et al., 1975). Zimbardo and colleagues asked undergraduate Stanford men to role play prisoners and prison guards for two weeks. After six days Zimbardo found the "inmates" had internalized their parts and that the role play was adversely affecting the mental and physical health of men on both sides of the bars. Zimbardo et al. wrote:

When a former prison chaplain was invited to talk with the prisoners . . . he puzzled everyone by disparaging the inmates for not taking any constructive action in order to get released . . . Several of them accepted his pastoral invitation to contact their parents in order to secure the services of an attorney . . .

We were no longer dealing with an intellectual exercise in which a hypothesis was being evaluated in the dispassionate manner dictated by the canons of the scientific method. We were caught up in the passion of the present, the suffering, the need to control people not variables, the escalation of power and all of the unexpected things which were erupting around and within us. So our planned two week simulation was aborted after only six (was it only six?) days and nights. (1975: 279)

Zimbardo and colleagues reveal quite a bit in these two paragraphs. With the hindsight of twenty years, it seems incredible that these researchers were even allowed to contemplate such a study, much less run it and publish the results. But at the time, Zimbardo's confession, like Rosenhan's, was astonishing. This admission, about the rapidity with which roles were internalized uncritically, constitute data, not an interruption of an "otherwise" scholarly text.

Qualitative work leads researchers into deep and complicated confrontations with ethical practices. Momentarily, perhaps, we have been lulled into comfort by APA guidelines, institutional review board reviews and the procedures of informed consent. But the contemporary pot of ethical troubles boils over. Qualitative researchers are at the front of these debates, although these debates should concern all researchers. Listen, at length, to the discussion that Brinton Lykes puts before us as she rethinks her informed consent form, amidst her work with Guatemalan refugee activist women:

> Concretely, the form has been a major obstacle at the beginning of each interview. Intended to "protect the subjects of the research," the women with whom I spoke experienced it as a barrier or hurdle. My conversation with one of the women is illustrative. When I presented the form she suggested that she had already agreed to talk to me (otherwise she would not be there) and that by agreeing to tell her story she had indicated her consent. Her consent meant that whatever she would tell me was a part of our public record to be used in support of the Guatemalan struggle as I understood that task. She found my choices concerning future use of the material as described on the form confusing and suggested that her signature was unnecessary, that we had already settled the question of the use of the material. When we had finally seemed to agree that she had *de facto* chosen Form A or unrestricted use and she checked this line she again refused to sign her name, indicating that she did not see why it was necessary.
>
>   By the third interview I began to discern that I was in fact misinterpreting the participants' reality *and* our relationship. I had come to this project with a clear analysis of my power as Other, with my role as a university professor with a Ph.D. and as a white North American. Yet I was also a concerned researcher who was acutely aware of the ways in which researchers have taken advantage of subjects, misinterpreted their reality, and given them inadequate access to their own labor. I recognized the many ways in which the participant both makes her/himself vulnerable in sharing his/her story and has no real control over how the researcher reconstructs that story. I had therefore designed a form that I thought would address this imbalance of power, providing a base from which the participants could assert their agenda. I would, thereby, "empower" the participants. (1989: 176–177)

While the debate has advanced, Qualitative work continues to bump into ethically messy territory. Ethics, in fact, constitutes a site in which Qualitative researchers are forging new ground that the full discipline of psychology needs to grapple with. The basic ethical guidelines or procedures which we all blithely follow do not serve research participants (Fine, 1995).

On Data and Interpretive Authority

The data involved in Qualitative inquiry are, after all, open ended. They may be observations, narratives, stories, interviews and/or focus group transcripts. They may be written by informants, written by researchers, taped or accumulated through archives. The nature of Qualitative data, however, is *not* simply that they are "not numbers," but that they are analyzed with an ear for what informants are saying rather than an eye on predetermined categories and hypotheses. Listening to Qualitative data requires that researchers be willing to change hunches or hypotheses. We may be surprised, perhaps embarrassed. We will look naive. As John Dollard admitted sixty years ago:

> The only possible conclusion from this experience was that I had the typical sectional bias to be expected of a Northerner and I thereupon set out to isolate and discount it. For one thing, I began to pay serious attention to what Southern white people told me about the interracial situation and although I did not always agree with them, I always learned from them. The discovery of sectional bias has another advantage, namely that I realized I was irrevocably a Northerner and ended my attempts to pass for anything else. (1937: 35)

Dollard was willing to listen hard to what his data were saying, and hear Southern voices. Only then could he understand that his own perspective was simply one among many.

Leon Festinger and colleagues began their social psychological research on dissonance reduction in the field. Their data were richly Qualitative. These researchers confessed to working like detectives, following leads, probing, and "nosing" about in an unstructured open-ended manner, for they did not know what would happen next in the doomsday sect they were studying. They even confessed to doing their work covertly, but that was not considered a serious breach of ethics in 1956.

> In the first place, it is clear that we were unable to rely on the standard array of technical tools of social psychology. Our material is largely qualitative rather than quantitative and even simple tabulations of what we observed would be difficult.
> We had to listen, probe, and query constantly to find out in the beginning who the members of the group were, how sincerely they believed the ideology, what actions they were taking that were consonant with their beliefs, and to what extent they were propagandizing or attempting to convince others. Later, we had to continue to accumulate this sort of data while further inquiring about what was going to happen next in the movement: when there would be another meeting, who was being invited, where the group (or individuals) were going to wait for the flood, and like questions. Our data, in places, are less complete than we would like, our influence on the group somewhat greater than we would like. We were able, however, to collect enough information to tell a coherent story and, fortunately, the effects of disconfirmation were striking enough to provide for firm conclusions. (1956: 249)

If Qualitative work entails a particular stance, subjectivities, ethics, data and interpretation, then we must come to understand Qualitative inquiry as not merely a "deviation" from a methodological norm in psychology, but a set of rich commitments, with a long history, a way of conducting research with and on, not despite, social relations and community life. It is at this point, however, that the dilemmas of interpretation emerge.

We do not believe, as others have argued (see Fine, 1995), that Qualitative work entails simply the transcription of "others' voices." Nor do we believe that narratives, observations or collected stories speak for themselves. With the arrogance of researchers (Qualitative and quantitative), we contend that psychologists have a responsibility (for some it is a desire, for others it is an anxiety, for us it is both) to assert interpretive authority over the data. Quoting again from Joyce Ladner:

> There must be a strong concern with *redefining* the problem. Instead of future studies being conducted on problems of the Black community as represented by the deviant perspective, there must be a redefinition of the problem as being that of institutional racism. If the social system is viewed as the source of the deviant perspective, then future research must begin to analyze the nature of oppression and the mechanisms by which institutionalized forms of subjugation are initiated and act to maintain the system intact. Thus, studies which have as their focal point the alleged deviant attitudes and behavior of Blacks are grounded within the racist assumptions and principles that only render Blacks open to further exploitation. (1971/1987: 77)

Ladner understood the role of the researcher as both critic and transformer of prevailing frames around social science data. For Ladner, the very point of conducting social research is to interrupt the "common sense" frames, ideologically driven by social arrangements or what she calls "the system," and to provide alternative lens for viewing social behavior.

To take this position means recognizing that Qualitative researchers are not merely tape recorders, ventriloquists or photographers (all of whom do a fair amount of editing, interpreting and splicing themselves). We are engaged analysts of social relations. By accepting such a professional stance with and upon communities and individuals, researchers select and design theoretical frames for the data, offering ever partial, temporary and kaleidoscopic interpretation(s) to readers, inviting them to generate their own.

As Qualitative workers we are intimately aware that we are the writers of record. We negotiate the data, wander through the margins of local meanings, listen to and puzzle over the words offered by informants and ultimately have the final word. While quantitative researchers are the final arbiters of which questions to ask and what the data mean, Qualitative workers enter neighborhoods, homes, nightmares, and dreams. When Qualitative workers return home with hours of field notes, voices on tapes, intimate knowledge of communities under siege, they grow uncomfortably aware of many incompatible responsibilities. There is a responsibility to *hear* what informants are saying about their lives and the meaning of their experiences and a responsibility to construct interpretations that may *or may not* conform to what informants have told us. These are the responsibilities of theorists and researchers across disciplines, across methods. But for Qualitative researchers, this often feels like a betrayal by those of us who try to research *with* people rather than *on* them.

We take the position that in our writings, research psychologists need to advance a theoretical framework around the "voices" of informants, to help analyze these voices in their historic and current circumstances. That is, we cannot merely reproduce narratives or present them as if the interpretations were self-evident. Whether we agree with the words of informants or not, whether we even like them or not, we have an obligation to surround their words with analyses for which we are the authors. Easier said than done.

This last criterion for Qualitative research is perhaps the most difficult for young scholars, especially graduate students. For a researcher who is immersed in a site, engaged with the voices of people, trusted by those who trust few, it is hard to turn the corner and impose one's own interpretation of why people are saying what they say, doing what they do, resisting as they resist, capitulating when they capitulate. But that is our task. Partial, temporary and tentative, we have a responsibility to position ourselves in relation to our data, and our position will not necessarily be the same as our informants' (have no illusions – they will not agree with each other either).

A Taste for the Field

Uncertainty about what might happen next is what some people find appealing and others find abhorrent about Qualitative work. This is part of the stance that we described earlier and what we failed to say then is that this is as much a matter of taste as it is a matter of science. We have written this chapter not only to examine the science and art (cf. Wolcott, 1995) of Qualitative work but also to give readers a taste of the pleasures and problems. We might not persuade anyone to like Qualitative work; at most we can describe how we've tried it and liked it.

We each could have conducted our work strictly as survey research projects. We did, in fact, include structured interview schedules and Likert scales, semantic differentials, and short open-ended questions (qualitative with the small q). The structured scales and interview schedule were comforting because they provided data we could "count on." But the daily encounters, the stories participants told to us, their problems, their privileges, and ours were riches we would not ignore. We wrote field notes for pleasure (and work). We have acquired the taste.

The radical possibilities that emerge within Qualitative psychology are only beginning to flourish. Some Qualitative psychologists are moving into participatory work, in which once-informants are now peers, collaborating with us as researchers (see Lykes and Mallona, cited in Fine et al., 1996; Phillips, 1995). In two urban middle schools, Michelle is conducting participatory research with young adolescent ethnographers, faculty, parents and doctoral candidates. Together, in these schools, with many different lines of vision and within a bouillabaisse of Qualitative data, we are creating a culture of inquiry. In the field of biography, Abbey Stewart and Gail Hornstein are inventing methods for feminist dialogic collaboration with living, and in the case of Hornstein (1994) with deceased informants, co-constructing lives, dialogue and biography. In cultural studies Louise has pried open the study of whiteness as a "secondary analysis" of Qualitative work done originally in India on expatriates, and British social psychologist Michael Billig (cited in Fine et al., 1996) is interviewing working-class whites about race and the royal family. In media studies, Corinne Squire (cited in Fine et al., 1996) is analyzing the representations of race, class and gender through a textual analysis of daytime television talk shows, connecting national policy, media representations and social attitudes of the white and African American viewers of these shows. In organizational and group dynamics, Linda Powell (cited in Fine et al., 1996) and Nancie Zane (cited in Fine et al., 1996) tape and transcribe, collecting Qualitative information to excavate the workings of race, gender and authority in schools and work settings. In sexuality studies, Leonore Tiefer (1994) draws from deep interviews and case studies to extract the ideological and political scaffolding upon which "good sex" is currently being constructed. In each of these instances of critical work, it is Qualitative inquiry that has enabled radical theorizing, the embroidering of structural issues with everyday psychological life, stretching the intellectual and political terrain within which psychologists do our work.

When the purposes of research are to learn what could be, to unravel what has been and to imagine the unimaginable rather than to test predetermined hypotheses, the methods available and questions to be asked are endless; the "variables" that once so securely contained our thoughts come undone like a poorly knit sweater; the ethics grow dense and need sensitive conversation; the interpretations are multiple. The methods are Qualitative. The discipline is psychology. And to those students interested in Qualitative work, welcome.

4

Ethics in Psychology: *Cui Bono?*

Laura S. Brown

Editors' note   *To the naive observer, professional ethics should be about a discipline's moral implications, about the harmful and beneficial effects of theories and practices on individuals and societies. But this is a naive view indeed. Organizations of professionals such as doctors and lawyers devise codes of ethics that protect the professional at least as much as they protect the public. As pointed out in Chapters 1 and 2, detrimental outcomes in psychology do not necessarily reflect malevolent intent by psychologists, but they are injurious nonetheless. In this chapter, Laura S. Brown clarifies how psychology's professional ethics codes primarily serve the interests of professional psychologists.*

Brown demonstrates how power and control in professional interactions are held primarily by the psychologist. Similarly, decision making processes concerning ethics are governed by professional bodies with little input from the public. Significantly, the moral dimension of ethics codes is based largely on individual ethics: the codes regulate the micro-ethics of the therapeutic relationship but neglect social ethical issues such as oppression, discrimination, and inequality. Since the codes generally assume that harm derives from the aberrant behavior of a few unscrupulous psychologists, they conveniently exclude more subtle violations such as the perpetuation of power inequalities and the deleterious effects of labeling people. This chapter challenges the notion of science as the ultimate good, denounces legitimized power inequalities, and decries ethics codes that adopt lowest common denominator values.

Disillusioned with existing codes in psychology, feminists affiliated with the Feminist Therapy Institute began to create their own code in the 1980s to explicitly and proactively address issues of oppression, exploitation, discrimination, accountability, and social change. Brown points out the benefits, as well as the difficulties, of trying to create an ethics code that takes ethics seriously.

Organized psychology in North America passed its century mark in 1992. Yet it was not until midway through this first one hundred years that the American Psychological Association (APA, 1953), still the largest body of psychologists in the world, saw fit to create a code of ethics. The energizing impetus for the creation of the code likely rests in the collective soul-searching done after World War II and the Nuremberg war crimes trials, when it became clear that principles of science and good research methodologies could also yield the horrors of fascism and the experiments of the Nazi doctors (Lifton, 1986). The introduction to this first APA ethics code sets the tone for what is to follow:

> The worth of a profession is measured by its contribution to the welfare of man [*sic*]. Psychology seeks to further our knowledge of man and to better his condition by applying this knowledge to the solution of human problems. But a profession serves mankind only in an abstract sense; upon each individual psychologist rests the real responsibility for service. (APA, 1953: 1)

Psychology, say our ethics codes, is a good profession that helps human beings, at least in the abstract. But have we been good for human welfare? Or has a limited view of humanity, and an equally short-sighted vision of what constitutes ethical behavior by psychologists, cut short the ethical possibilities of psychology?

This late attention to ethics indicates the place ethics has held in American psychology: ethics are added on, somewhat to the side, and rarely integrated into the overall context of the work of psychology. The final responsibility for the advancement of ethical psychology is placed on the individual rather than on the collective institution of the discipline. The codes construe ethical behaviors narrowly. They emphasize the avoidance of overt "sins," but pay little attention to errors of omission or covert expressions of damaging attitudes and values. They make no mention of longer-term or more subtle negative implications of psychologists' actions and decisions.

The individual psychologist is also given scant opportunity to prepare for this task of behaving ethically. This lack of opportunity itself perpetuates a less thoughtful and more poorly developed ethical sense. Most graduate students in psychology receive little formal instruction on ethics (Pope et al., 1986). This means that most psychologists have spent significantly less time learning about ethics than they have about research design or case conceptualization. Psychologists who are not preparing for careers in professional psychology practice are particularly likely to complete graduate training without formal ethics education. Research ethics are thus more often than not left open to acquisition via modeling and osmosis; they are almost never taught directly, or required for the acquisition of an advanced degree as a psychological scientist. Ethics often become salient to psychologists only when it appears they are on the verge of falling into the clearly demarcated territory of "unethical." At that point, accused psychologists offer rationalizations as to why and how this particular action still remains narrowly within the boundaries of the law, even when it has seriously harmed people or groups.

Despite this somewhat orphan position, the APA code of ethics, now in its fourth major revision (American Psychological Association, 1992), represents the rules and norms by which almost 100,000 psychologists and psychology graduate students practice research, teaching, supervision, and psychotherapy. It has influenced the codes of a number of other professional organizations, such as the American Counseling Association and the Canadian Psychological Association. As the ethical standard of the major US psychology organization, the dominant group within the discipline, it functions as the dominant norm within psychological ethics. The APA Code gives the critical reader a message about what the mainstream of the culture of psychology values, and about the manner in which that culture construes relationships of power, dominance, and responsibility.

An underlying assumption of the various APA ethics codes has been that they exist to uphold a standard for psychologists of promoting human welfare and protecting those with whom psychologists interact in their work – human and animal research participants, students, psychotherapy clients. They also create norms for civil and respectful relationships between psychologists on such matters as publication credit and "ownership" of patients. But over the past twenty-five years, a number of criticisms have been raised by various progressive or marginalized groups in psychology, as well as by the supposed beneficiaries of these ethical codes, our students and clients. These critics – most frequently from feminist psychology, mental patient liberation groups, and groups of psychologists of color – ask who truly benefits from organized psychology's formal ethical guidelines. They have inquired repeatedly into whether the dominant culture's code existed simply to uphold a certain oppressive status quo within psychology and to protect psychologists from those over whom they hold power, rather than the reverse. Attempts have been made over the years to include representatives of some of these protesting groups in the revisions of the ethical guidelines (for example, in the most recent revision of the code, by consulting groups in organized psychology representing feminists and people of color). However, critics continue to question whether these are genuine attempts to transform the meaning of ethics codes in psychology, or merely strategies to silence through cooptation.

This chapter reviews some of the critical analyses of dominant psychology ethics codes and considers the value of these criticisms. It considers who benefits from these codes, and what may be problematic about these codes' assumptions. I also consider possible alternative strategies for thinking about ethics in psychology, and about what risks and benefits, to psychologists and others, may result from incorporating alternative models.

Underlying Problematic Assumptions

Science as Ultimate Good

Among the underlying problematic assumptions of dominant ethical codes in psychology, one is particularly thorny: the assumption that what psychologists do as researchers, clinicians, teachers, supervisors and consultants is basically benign and inherently of value because it is based on "science," and that it will remain good only so long as it is firmly anchored in "science." This assumption defines "science" as knowledge derived from logical positivist "proof through disproof" controlled experimentation. It is voiced most strongly in the APA code's most recent revision, in which the opening sentences of the preamble replace a primary allegiance to human welfare with a hymn to "a valid and reliable body of scientific knowledge based on research" (APA, 1992: 1599). It can also be found in numerous current discussions of the value of psychotherapy, in which authors claim that psychotherapy is good only in so far as it has been scientifically proven to be safe and effective by means of the accepted empirical methods (McFall, 1996).

Other chapters in this volume address in detail the underlying questions of "whose science" based on "research by whom" with "what method-ologies." As Kidder and Fine ask in Chapter 3, whose gaze is privileged as one upon which our ethical behavior is founded? Other progressive psychologists have also questioned the foundations of psychological ethics (Lerman and Porter, 1990a; Payton, 1994; Vasquez and Eldridge, 1994). The various critics suggest there are serious flaws in the notion that a careful adherence to empiricism and received knowledge, called "science," will protect psychologists from abuse of their power, and protect the subjects of psychologists' actions from being exploited.

This very core assumption that science is *per se* good, and thus always constitutes an adequate foundation for psychologists' ethical action, is the first problematic concept in mainstream psychological ethics. Psychological science itself has been rife with oppressive norms. One of the founding fathers of American psychology, G. Stanley Hall, was infamous for promulgating the "scientific" belief that higher education would make women infertile and that women were intellectually inferior to men. At various times, psychological science has taught as received wisdom the "facts" that people of color or Jews were genetically inferior in intelligence; that lesbians and gay men were psychologically deviant; and that women who worked outside the home were suffering from various disruptions of normal female development (Albee, 1988; Vasquez and Eldridge, 1994).

An example of the harms that can be done by a psychologist behaving "ethically" and "scientifically" is the participation of psychologists in the involuntary incarceration of mental patients. The "scientifically based" standard of care for practicing psychologists whose patient is suicidal is to first offer, and then require, that the patient be hospitalized. Psychologists who fail to pursue such a course of action are told by risk management experts that they open themselves to lawsuits for malpractice. The underlying message here is that following the "scientifically correct" course of action will protect the psychologist (Stromberg, 1993). But what of the patient and her or his well-being? Writers from the mental patients' liberation movements have described how civil commitment strips people of their rights and humanity in the name of "protecting" the client from her or himself (Chamberlin, 1977; 1990). It exposes people at their most vulnerable to the abuses and risks found in psychiatric institutions, including forced drugging, physical restraint, and the risks of sexual assault by staff and patients alike. Here, "ethical" conduct by a psychologist can and does harm people in the name of "good practice."

Similarly, it is possible for a psychologist to conduct research that is technically ethical but still do great harm. For example, a researcher can adhere strictly to "scientific" empiricist research methodologies and give technically adequate informed consent to research participants, but still conduct research apparently demonstrating the inferiority of a particular social group. This research is harmful to that group and its individual members. Because it is conducted according to the rules, however, the question of whether it is ethical in the broader sense to pursue certain matters is left to the side. In the name of "academic freedom," the ethics codes do not proscribe certain questions as ethically problematic *per se*. The codes thus ignore the harm of generating a discourse which presumes to investigate "scientifically" the possibility that certain persons or groups are inferior, or worthy of unequal treatment. Such a discourse presumes that it is acceptable, and therefore ethical, to treat people unequally, or to view all members of a group as "less than."

Consequently, neither Arthur Jensen nor the late Richard Herrnstein were ever considered by mainstream psychology to have violated psychology's ethics by the questions they asked in their research, even though the goal of those questions was to document the alleged intellectual inferiority of African Americans. No individual person of color was harmed in this research by being given the Stanford-Binet or other tests; individual participants could even have found the tests interesting or challenging. But the manner in which Jensen and Herrnstein utilized and interpreted the test findings not only was likely to have harmed the research participants themselves. It also weakened the available social supports for people of color by stigmatizing them as genetically inferior, thus strengthening the larger culture's racist attitudes. Research ethics as currently construed by mainstream ethics codes do not require researchers to put the potential for this sort of risk into their informed consent documents (Dent, 1995; Fairchild, 1995).

This research, highlighted in the popular book *The Bell Curve* (1994) by Herrnstein and Charles Murray, has profoundly harmed people of color. It has introduced the aura and respectability of science into racist discourse about the alleged inferiority of one group in comparison to another. Ironically, many commentators in psychology have criticized the misuse of research in the book, pointing to errors in interpretations of tables or exclusion of conflicting data. But few aside from self-aware psychologists of color (Dent, 1995; Fairchild, 1995; Helms, 1995; Hilliard, 1995; Scott-Jones, 1995; Sue, 1995) have raised the more fundamental question of whether simply conducting such studies might be ethically problematic. To ask this question about the risks of certain types of inquiry challenges science's hegemony as the source of all good in psychology.

For many critical thinkers, research ethics remain problematic. Formal codes continue to focus narrowly on risks to the individual research participant, in the specific context of the experiment or study, but neglect questions about risks to the group to which the participant belongs. Even more rare are questions about whether or not certain types of research, no matter how ethically conducted, harm the culture because they directly or inadvertently perpetuate reactionary or oppressive norms. Additionally, as research methods change, ethical dilemmas expand as well. For example, the qualitative researcher develops a relationship with research participants that is not distant but intimate, one in which power is explicitly or implicitly shared. The ethical dilemmas arising from this sort of research relationship are quite different. But the norms of dominant ethics in psychology do not address them, because the norms continue to construe the research relationship as hierarchical and quantitative (Mary Crawford, personal communication, February 1996; Fine, 1992a; see Chapter 3). Thus, psychology's available ethics do not prepare a researcher to develop new methodologies and paradigms for understanding human behavior, because they fail to prepare the researcher for new ethical challenges. As long as research ethics avoid the matter of whether certain questions ethically cannot be asked, psychologists will conduct technically ethical research that violates a more general ethic of avoiding harm to vulnerable populations.

Individualism and Compartmentalization

There is another problematic assumption underlying dominant ethical codes: the artificial separation between the psychologist as psychologist and the psychologist as person in the need to adhere to ethical standards. What was initiated as an attempt to respect the privacy and personhood of psychologists has become a form of radical individualism. The person of the psychologist is split into public and private spheres, with no requirement that the two interact at the ethical level. The ethics codes also contain inherent individualistic assumptions regarding to whom the psychologist is responsible. Only the specific target of the psychologist's actions is within the psychologist's ethical purview.

Various ethical standards over the years have attempted to clarify that psychologists have a right to privacy and to conduct their personal lives in whatever manner they see fit. A meta-message of these pronouncements is that psychologists need have no personal commitment to certain ways of behaving as long as they remain within the rules while at work. The ethical code itself is thus value-free. The psychologist may privately hold various oppressive viewpoints, abuse power in her or his intimate relationships, and in general have values that are inconsistent with public welfare, with no clearly defined standard of belief regarding the rights and value of others. All this is ethically acceptable if, on the job, he or she practices restraint and follows the rules.

The inclusion of such statements in the APA codes once was truly liberatory, but it has lost its value over time. Within the context of the original APA code, published in the heyday of McCarthyism and persecution of leftists and sexual minorities in academia, these statements of freedom of belief and action had a purpose that we can appreciate. It was likely a very good thing that organized psychology supported the rights of psychologists to deviate from the community moral status quo when that standard was highly oppressive. As times have changed, the academic and social climate has become more open. But the ethical standards have become even more radically insistent on the separation of psychologists' work-related ethics from the norms by which they conduct their daily lives. They have not attempted to integrate the personal and the professional.

As Carolyn Payton noted in her critique of the 1992 APA revision,

> In at least *three* places, the reader is cautioned that the code applies only to psychologists' work-related activities. The need for such a restriction is puzzling. Does this mean that Jack the Ripper, had he been a psychologist, would not have been in violation of the code because he killed women after work hours? [And, I would add, was never caught and convicted of a felony related to his work, which might constitute a violation of the current code.] If a psychologist abuses children or batters her spouse but commits these acts at home, would no code violation have occurred? (1994: 317, my italics)

Payton's questions are not entirely hypothetical, and their answers are troubling, because in both cases, they are negative. Both Jack the Ripper, PhD and the abusive psychologist are behaving ethically by the strictest (and narrowest) definitions. Payton's questions underscore the problems inherent in compartmentalizing the person of the psychologist into worker/ethical adherent and nonworker/ethically free segments. The assumption that a person can oppress others with impunity in their private life, and then magically transform into one who is respectful of vulnerable persons – students, research participants, psychotherapy clients – when walking through the doors of the office, seems absurd on the face of it. It promotes a distance between the psychologist her or himself and psychological ethics, a somewhat cynical position.

This division can and does lead to serious harms. In the many psychotherapy malpractice cases in which I have been involved as an expert witness, I have often found a profound dichotomy, a detachment of the person of the psychologist from the meanings of the ethical codes. The psychologists in these cases often have a personal "ethics" code, as it were: as long as the letter of the law is strictly followed and no one gets caught, the spirit of the law can be violated.

As an example, in one case a psychologist began to verbally flirt with a woman client, all the while telling her that he could not have a sexual relationship with her because she was his client. A few months later, he kissed her passionately on several occasions, but continued to insist that "sex" was not going to happen because she was his client. He terminated the therapy shortly thereafter. One month after the formal termination, he had intercourse with her. When accused of ethical violations, he pointed out that at the time he had intercourse, the woman was technically no longer his client, and that the formal code did not yet ban sex with former clients. The intercourse, he insisted, had happened in his personal life, and thus, in his opinion, he was immune from sanction. He denied that either the flirting or the kissing had violated the rules because they were "not sex."

In this case, which is painfully similar in its details to many others, there was clearly no integration of the ethical guidelines' spirit into the work and life of the psychologist. The implied separations of the code had become meaningful to this man as a guide for how to proceed, as they appear to be for many psychologists. At less overt levels, such separations serve as an absence of challenge. The psychologist who is taught that she or he may hold any personal beliefs as long as they are not enacted at work may harbor racist, sexist, anti-Semitic or heterosexist values, and even actively practice them in personal life. But she or he will see no need to challenge these beliefs as part of being an ethical psychologist because the line has been drawn protecting these beliefs as "private" (Lerman and Porter, 1990b; Payton, 1994).

Lowest Common Denominator Values

This compartmentalization of the psychologist results in a third problematic assumption of mainstream psychology ethics. This is the notion, implicit in most places and somewhat explicit in the most recent revision of the APA code, that standards must be written at the level of the lowest common ethical level. This notion protects the psychologist's rights to continue in ethically questionable directions in private life and to be protected from complaints in the workplace. The 1992 code revision states in several places that the code does not constitute a standard to which psychologists should be held in legal proceedings. As one commentator who is both a lawyer and a psychologist notes, it is full of "such lawyer-driven weasel words as *reasonable* and *feasible*" (Bersoff, 1994: 384, emphasis in original). These terms protect psychologists who plead that what they did was reasonable and feasible under the circumstances, and that they cannot be held responsible for being passive in the face of ethical dilemmas.

Lerman and Porter (1990b) argue that in this regard the dominant codes are reactive, rather than proactive. They encourage passivity, existential bad faith, and the failure to be courageous when it becomes necessary to take a stand to ensure ethical outcomes. In making it easier for all psychologists to fit comfortably within the defined boundaries of being ethical, the dominant codes become enablers of the status quo. Ethics is diminished into a set of rules to be obeyed, and the vision of the psychologist as an active participant in the ethical decision making process becomes obscured.

Consequently, for example, to be an ethical APA member, one need not actively fight racism, sexism, heterosexism or other forms of oppression in the profession and the world (Brown, 1991; 1993). One merely needs to avoid being discriminatory in an overt way and break no enunciated rules. No ethical sanction is placed on the psychologist who stands by silently while oppression occurs, because there is no rule against such passive collusion.

Additionally, ethically problematic behaviors are defined in the most overt manner possible. For instance, it is clearly unethical according to the APA code's most recent revision for a psychologist to have sexual intercourse with a client, making this a class of behaviors that is relatively easy for most psychologists to avoid. A psychologist who has such intercourse will be pointed to as an ethical violator. But what of the psychologist who has persistent sexual fantasies about the client which are never voiced or acknowledged? The treatment of the client will doubtless be transformed and likely harmed by the internal experience in which the client is constantly sexually objectified. But this psychologist can stand hailed by all as fitting neatly into the ethical guidelines because no rule has been broken.

Or, we might contrast a psychological researcher who fails to give informed consent to research participants with one who fails to consider the consequences of his or her research findings. The researcher who does not submit to institutional review and does not offer research participants informed consent and refusal is clearly in violation. The researcher who collects information with all the appropriate consent mechanisms in place, and then interprets the findings so as to lead to the ridicule of a vulnerable group, is simply exercising his or her opinion about the meanings of the research. Something is missing from ethics codes that only attend to the former problem (see Chapter 3 in this book).

Ethics codes as currently written by dominant organizations are consequently laden with "thou shalt nots," rules that must be followed. They are weak on "thou shalts," the sort of aspirational goals that might make psychology ethics truly liberatory and transformative. The situation has degenerated over time in reaction to a legal ruling from the US federal government addressing "restraint of trade" of APA members. A consent decree with the US Federal Trade Commission enjoined APA from including anything anti-entrepreneurial in its ethical guidelines and even required the removal of certain long-standing rules from the code. Standards and guidelines that mandate the doing of good are potentially anti-entrepreneurial, or could create legal liability by promising to do good and then failing to deliver (Koocher, 1994). Thus, APA has become weaker than ever on this score. The revised APA code, and the entire corporate organization of APA, have shied further and further away from defining what psychologists shall do in the pursuit of good. APA remains content to say simply what constitutes bad behaviors that should be avoided, if of course this is reasonable and feasible for the psychologist to do.

In fact, on the advice of APA's attorneys, the most recent revision of the APA rules of association prohibited APA's divisions (representing concentrations of scholarship and knowledge) from promulgating guidelines or standards because such guidelines might be an illegal restraint of trade. Guidelines that promote certain proactive behaviors would only be allowed if all segments of the organization agreed to them. This requirement results in inevitable watering down of any standards until they are virtually meaningless. Under such rules, helpful and anti-oppressive guidelines, such as those for psychotherapy with women written many years ago by the Division of Counseling Psychology (Fitzgerald and Nutt, 1986), would have been forbidden because they clearly stated that certain practices, still used by many psychologists, fell below a standard for the care of women. As things stand today, to promulgate such a standard would itself be ethically problematic, because it might harm some psychologist's opportunity to make a living as a sexist practitioner. This status is more protected than ever before by the current dominant ethical rules.

Power and Power Relationships

There is a fourth problematic assumption underlying the APA code, and to some degree all dominant ethical standards: the codes define power relationships between psychologists and those with whom they work as essentially benign, as long as the rules of conduct are followed. Hierarchy is not only permissible in the ethical standards, it is valued and reified. This sort of "benign parentalism" is characteristic of most ethical standards in the helping professions and behavioral sciences. It reveals the codes' roots in the Hippocratic Oath, which itself is built upon the ancient world's rigidly hierarchical power structure in which only property-owning men had rights; all other humans (who were property, not people) required protection from the excesses of the owning classes. The ethical standards of dominant psychology do not question the value or worth of such hierarchies. Instead, they accept that hierarchies will exist, and can be handled beneficially when the powerful party, in this case the psychologist, is careful in the use of power.

Thus, we find rules in the ethical codes prohibiting sexual contact with clients, or the harassment and exploitation of students, research participants, and junior co-workers. These rules are not problematic in and of themselves. They make it more difficult for powerful psychologists to harm vulnerable people with impunity, and convey a message that this dominant group protects its weaker members. In fact, the existence of such rules and the very clear delineation of categories of persons off-limits for the psychologist's lusts are due almost entirely to the intervention of feminists. Feminists in the mental health professions were outraged by the sexual exploitation of those over whom psychologists and other mental health professionals held power (Gartrell, 1994), while feminist social scientists could no longer tolerate sexist assumptions and interpretations in research (Bronstein and Quina, 1988; Denmark et al., 1988; Fine, 1992a).

Nonetheless, the necessity for such rules underscores the power imbalances inherent in psychology between the psychologist and all with whom he or she comes into contact. The rules tell us that power imbalances are present, and they fail to question this presence. Power imbalances in research, teaching, supervision and psychotherapy have been a particular source of distress to feminist psychologists, for whom the creation of egalitarian, power-equal relationships is an important political and philosophical goal (Gartrell, 1994; Lerman and Porter, 1990a; Rave and Larsen, 1995). Some feminist critics suggest that it might be impossible to have a genuinely feminist psychology or psychotherapy because any relationship founded in psychological principles assumes the presence of a power imbalance, no matter how slight (Kitzinger and Perkins, 1993). No one has apparently raised this possibility that "feminist research" is an oxymoron.

Ethics codes as they currently stand are mostly attempts to cushion the damages done by power imbalances, rather than strategies for undermining and diminishing those imbalances. There is little evidence that mainstream psychology ethics ever sees power imbalances as problems, or the equalization of power as a goal for ethical behavior by psychologists.

Can Psychology Ethics Become Liberatory?

Critics of mainstream psychology ethics face a central question: is it possible to create ethical standards that are truly liberatory – that is, standards that promote active participation by psychologists in the creation of a more just society – rather than simply protect the public from the worst of our excesses and ourselves from complaints?

To create such standards, we must challenge the problematic assumptions at the heart of psychological ethics today and not allow them to overtake the creation of new models. This starting point can itself prove quite difficult. It asks psychologists as individuals and psychology as a discipline to move beyond self-imposed restrictions on the meaning of ethical practice to become visionary and aspirational. Psychology would no longer be construed as an abstract and empirical science apart from the political fray. Instead, it would be acknowledged as a highly political endeavor whose participation in the status quo is an actual and potential source of harm to vulnerable populations and to the soul of the profession.

More problematic still, such a revisioning requires freeing psychological ethics from adherence to legalese. Ethical codes must become meaningful, clearly voiced documents in which lines are drawn free of the careful legalisms that protect psychologists and corporate psychological organizations. The *raison d'être* of an ethics code itself requires transformation. The code would no longer be the document policing the behavior of psychologists, a trend in dominant ethics codes that created the shotgun marriage with the law. The revisioned ethics code would become a map into the difficult terrain of self-knowledge, self-criticism, self-care, and commitment to the use of psychology as a tool for making a just and free world. It would be based upon input not simply from the designated experts in psychology (the methodology guiding the latest APA code revision), or even from the entire body of psychologists (the strategy for the first three revisions). It would also include input from those affected by the behavior of psychologists – consumers, research participants, students, and other interested nonpsychologists.

The Feminist Therapy Institute Code: an Experiment in Liberatory Ethics

One organization, the Feminist Therapy Institute (FTI; 1990), has attempted to create an ethics code based on this different vision. As a member of that group, and an active participant in creating its code, I think it helpful to reflect on what we did to generate an ethics code that explicitly attempted to address what was problematic and oppressive in mainstream ethics codes. FTI's effort cannot be called entirely successful, in that it does not either address or eliminate all possible problems, and it is intentionally a work in progress. Still, it is the best example of which I am aware of an ethical standard beginning with the premise that ethics must be a part of a liberatory theory of human behavior and mental health practice. If ethics are to have true meaning, FTI insists, ethical standards must be central, rather than peripheral, to every action taken by a behavioral scientist or psychotherapist.

Feminist psychologists have been concerned with ethics since the field first invented itself around 1969. To many feminist psychologists, simply being a feminist in psychology with clearly defined values was an ethical stance, because it challenged the notion that science and practice were value-free. Feminists immediately criticized the deficits of mainstream ethical codes (Chesler, 1972). However, most feminist psychologists were initially content with attempts to reform existing codes through such documents as the APA "Guidelines for Non-Sexist Research" (Denmark et al., 1988) and the APA Division of Counseling Psychology's "Principles Concerning the Counseling/Psychotherapy of Women" (Fitzgerald and Nutt, 1986), or to more clearly define restrictions such as those against sexual intimacies with clients (Gartrell, 1994).

But it became increasingly clear that revising and reforming existing codes did not answer the needs of those who wished to practice psychotherapy in a manner that explicitly challenged the status quo. It was good to make sex with clients clearly unethical, which it had not been until the active participation of feminist psychologists in APA's 1977 ethics revisions. But this did not suffice for feminist practitioners who wished to understand how we could conduct research, teaching, psychotherapy and supervision in ways that did not replicate patriarchal hierarchies of power and dominance.

An interdisciplinary group of feminist practitioners established the Feminist Therapy Institute in 1982. The purpose was to meet collective needs for an organization of experienced feminist therapists who could meet together and offer guidance to one another. Almost immediately, ethics became a topic of discussion – including the ethically problematic behaviors that a number of feminist therapists had engaged in during experiments in transforming the status quo (Brown, 1982; 1984; 1985; Hall, 1984). It was clear to all involved that simply calling oneself a feminist psychologist did not automatically create new forms of ethical conduct. Years of socialization into oppressive norms did not respond to the simple act of renaming oneself as feminist (Brown, 1994).

At the Institute's annual meeting in 1985, the group met in a four-hour session. All of the more than forty women present talked about their own ethical dilemmas and ethically problematic behaviors in the past. Out of this exercise in self-criticism arose the awareness that FTI required its own ethics code. Thus commenced a several-year process (Rave and Larsen, 1990) of developing an ethical code that was explicitly feminist in its assumptions: anti-hierarchical, liberatory, and aspirational rather than legalistic.

The process of writing the code was itself an exercise in the ethics it attempted to codify. No one person was set up as the ethics expert; everyone was assumed to have valuable input, although not all ideas that came to the chairs of the committee that finalized the code made it into the published version. The two co-chairs solicited comments and ideas from all possible sources. Thus, many women, both members of FTI and others, had a hand in creating the code.

There was no explicit charge to the code's creators to include the input of psychotherapy consumers (and our collective failure to intentionally do this is curious, in retrospect). But it emerged during many of our discussions that FTI members had gone home and talked to their clients about what needed to be in a code. Thus, in its development the FTI code challenged the notion of a clear and precise dividing line between "us," the psychologists/psychotherapists, and "them," the people who are served. Instead, it was written by and for a community, in which some members practiced feminist therapy, supervision, research, teaching and training.

An example of this interactive and inclusive process can be seen in the manner in which the code incorporated anti-racism. During the 1986 FTI meeting, members of the organization were powerfully confronted about their covert racism and inattention to issues of racial and cultural diversity (Kanuha, 1990). This happened at the same meeting where there was a lengthy process to discuss input into the code, with people debating and discussing whether certain ideas were or were not expressions of feminist ethics. One of the several organizational responses to this challenge was to decide as a group to include in the code a commitment to anti-racism, as well as to develop a number of action projects aimed at making this ethical commitment come alive. The immediacy of the organizational response to this issue is striking; in one weekend, consciousness raising happened, and then was integrated into practice.

The process of creating the FTI code was emotionally intense and intimate, requiring all the members of this small organization to be honest with ourselves and one another about our failures and foibles. Some of the behaviors that we were now calling ethically problematic were ones that many of us had attempted at one time; some of our knowledge that they were ethically shaky came from those experiences, both as clients and as therapists. Such honesty, and the willingness to hold that information with care and compassion, is an essential component of people coming together to "do ethics." Had any of us set herself up as the expert, the judge, or the one who had never had any ethical dilemmas, the process that led to the creation of this code would not have worked.

The respect for the diversity of experiences within the group reflected the feminist ethical norm of respect for differences; the challenges and confrontations that we offered one another grew out of our shared commitment to identifying and ending abuses of power. This is also a core characteristic of doing ethics together. For people to become empowered as ethical thinkers and decision makers, as were the entire body of the FTI membership, there must be a shared recognition of values about interpersonal conduct. The idea that "the personal is political" became a guiding principle. In this case, our personal experiences as therapists, clients, supervisors, and students informed our decisions about feminist therapy ethics.

The FTI code consistently stresses the notion that feminist practitioners are responsible, accountable, and active. The relationship between the work of the professional and the struggle for social justice is explicit: "Feminist therapists assume a proactive stance toward the eradication of oppression in their lives and work toward empowering women" (FTI, 1990: 38). The therapist is defined as never being neutral or value-free: "Feminist therapists adhere to and integrate feminist analysis into all spheres of their work . . . Feminist therapists recognize that their values influence the therapeutic process and clarify with clients the nature and effect of those values" (1990: 37–38).

The organization of the FTI code highlights the manner in which the code attends to questions of integrating ethics into personal as well as professional life and into the political process. It underscores themes in which professional, personal, and political are interwoven. The five sections of the code are titled "Cultural Diversities and Oppressions," "Power Differentials," "Overlapping Relationships," "Therapist Accountability," and "Social Change." Interestingly, that last section calls upon feminist practitioners, as an ethical requirement, to "actively question other therapeutic practices in her community that appear abusive" (1990: 40). Simply doing good oneself is insufficient; calling colleagues to account is also considered an ethical responsibility. Ethical behavior is defined not as passive, but as active and interactive.

Absent from the FTI code and from FTI itself to this point have been mechanisms for policing FTI members regarding their adherence to the code. The code is thus free from legal terminology; FTI members are not asked to be ethical when it is "reasonable" or "feasible," as in APA's code. Rather, the feminist practitioner is assumed to be continuously involved in the process of ethical decision making and ethical action, in her work and her life. Ethical behavior is a process, not a static outcome. This has, from my perspective, created some dilemmas for FTI as an organization. What does it mean to have a code of ethics if we do nothing to insure it is put into practice? Are we willing, as a group, to engage the risks inherent in taking and adjudicating complaints, given the closeness of personal relationships among many FTI members?

The code is also construed as a living document, open to transformation as feminist therapists and their work transform. As of 1996 it is considered open for a formal revision process. For instance, feminist therapists in the US are struggling with the question of how to ethically practice under managed care, in which both therapist and client are disempowered by agents of the third party who pays the bills and sets limits on the number of allowed sessions. The current code has some components that indirectly address this development in the economics of psychotherapy. But it may require additions or revisions to more fully address a social, vocational, and political milieu that has changed rapidly in the decade since the code was first written.

But Can We Truly Question Ourselves?

Also absent, and potentially problematic from the perspective of some critics, are questions of whether therapy and other psychological practices are themselves ethically problematic. The FTI code challenges the notions in dominant cultural codes of the purity of science and the value of so-called objectivity and empiricism. But it does not address the question advanced by some critical thinkers (Kitzinger and Perkins, 1993) of whether psychological practice is *per se* harmful. This question is not addressed in most of the feminist commentary on ethics. The failure of feminist psychology to address this fundamental question in its single most important ethics document tells us much about the difficulty of thinking critically about ethics in psychology, because ultimately such critical analysis leads to questions of the value of the discipline itself. We have progressed to the point of asking what ethical psychotherapy might be. But we have not yet reached the point of asking whether the most ethical stance is to cease to practice therapy and thus end all collusion with dominant norms, however we reconfigure them.

Even those of us who commonly stand outside the circle of dominant psychology – feminists, sexual minorities, people of color – find it nearly impossible to imagine that the world would be better served by an ethic of not practicing psychology at all. And because no parallel group of feminist psychology researchers has attempted to create their own code of research ethics, questions regarding the value of certain sorts of inquiry remain absent from the discourse as well (although there are ongoing debates about whether a particular research methodology might itself be inherently feminist, read as "ethical"). FTI, because it is an organization composed almost entirely of practicing psychotherapists, thus reflects in its code the limitations of vision deriving from the code's origins.

Despite these limitations, the FTI code is an exciting development. It illustrates the possibilities for what can happen when people come together to "do ethics" with a critical perspective. The code, and its process of development, provide a model for other, future attempts at re-envisioning ethics in psychology.

Conclusion

Behavioral scientists and mental health professionals need documents that inform us ethically, that challenge our taken-for-granted notions about the value of our work and its impact on the larger community and the people we touch directly. But dominant ethical codes, as exemplified by APA's, fail us in this struggle. They lack responses to basic and important questions about the relationship of ethics to power, dominance, and the upholding of both the social and the professional status quo.

Ethical standards that empower psychologists as ethical thinkers and as decision makers with personal agency, who co-create ethical actions each day in concert with students, research participants, and therapy clients, are just beginning to be envisioned. Many psychologists, even those within psychology's mainstream, have begun to voice dissatisfaction with what we have created so far (Bersoff, 1994). To accomplish this task will require us to work both individually and collectively within our professional organizations. We must ask and re-ask the questions of for whom, and for whose benefit, our ethical standards are written, and we must continue to search for the hidden hand of dominance in each line that is written. As demonstrated by the FTI Ethics Code, it is possible to write ethical standards that move our profession towards a greater affinity for social justice, and towards the integration of the personal and the professional for psychologists.

We must also call upon the scientists of psychology to become more invested in the development of critical research ethics. It is interesting and troubling to turn to the documents of the American Psychological Society, an organization set up in opposition to APA and for the preservation of psychology's science base, and find no ethics code, no ethics committee, and nowhere for those who are aggrieved by psychological science and psychological scientists to bring their concerns. Critical thinkers in psychology clearly have made efforts to address the underlying ethical dilemmas inherent in research (Fine, 1992a). The time is well past due for codifications of that awareness.

Ultimately, psychologists and consumers of psychology must refuse to allow the discipline to rest comfortably within our current parameters. We must simply begin to insist that nothing less than an integration of personal and professional, and nothing narrower than a focus on the entire domain of psychology, will fit our definitions of the words "ethics in psychology."

5

Understanding and Practicing Critical Psychology

David Nightingale and Tor Neilands

If you give a person a fish, that person is fed for a day. If you teach a person to fish, you have fed that person for a lifetime.

Ancient Chinese Proverb

Editors' note Becoming involved in critical psychology is not just an intellectual endeavor, but a personal one as well. How do I nurture critical impulses? How do I cope with opposition from colleagues and friends whose views I challenge? Where can I find support for my critical views? In this chapter, David Nightingale and Tor Neilands help us connect the personal and the political.

Criticizing the institutions where we work and study is not easy. Changing those institutions is even harder, as those who depart from mainstream norms often find out rather quickly. Being critical can lead to resistance, opposition, and isolation. But as Nightingale and Neilands point out, others often share our reservations about the mainstream, even if they keep their views to themselves. Drawing on their personal experiences as volunteer organizers in organizations of critical psychologists, the authors offer the newcomer helpful hints about how to find and work with others toward becoming critical psychologists.

One of the practical barriers to understanding critical psychology is language: critical psychologists often use complex philosophical concepts to explain and justify their departures from the mainstream. In this chapter, Nightingale and Neilands clarify the significance of key concepts such as ontology, epistemology, methodology, empiricism and positivism. Understanding this terminology can help us understand why critical psychologists object to psychology's view of the world, of knowledge, and of how we should examine the world. The chapter, thus, provides a framework that helps place in context discussions in other chapters.

What is critical psychology? The answer to this question dictates how we facilitate its practice in our day-to-day lives. At its most general level, critical psychology is a response to an inadequate theory or practice in the field. A psychologist decides that current theories and practices are, at best, not helpful. At worst, they may harm disenfranchised members of society, such as women, individuals with different ethnic backgrounds, and so on. This conclusion may happen as a result of the psychologist's careful examination of his or her own values in relation to his or her daily actions. The would-be critical psychologist then undertakes two tasks: critiquing the status quo and offering an alternative to the status quo.

In different ways, the authors of the chapters in this book encourage you to step back and ask yourself a number of questions: "What am I doing and why am I doing it? What are my primary goals and values? Are my activities consistent with these goals and values?" In this chapter, we suggest how you might go about integrating the material in this book with your own studies and practices. As you do so, we have further questions. Is what you are doing now compatible with your primary goals and values and with what drew you to psychology in the first place? From where did the information you are learning from lectures and mentors come? How long has this information been around in your area of psychology? Are there competing perspectives or viewpoints that challenge the universality and applicability of this information?

To help you answer these questions, we first discuss our view of the critical psychology process in relation to psychology's status quo. Next we describe a number of philosophical considerations that will help you make sense of how critical psychologists analyze their field. Finally, we give examples of how psychology students and practitioners can begin to incorporate critical perspectives into their work. Our primary concern throughout this chapter is to help students of psychology use critical perspectives while they are still students, rather than waiting until they are practicing psychologists.

Critical Psychology: an Overview of the Process

Mainstream psychology courses typically teach *the status quo*: the currently accepted methodologies, assumptions, and theories. The process of critical psychology is inextricably tied to that status quo, because critical psychology and the status quo coexist in a yin–yang relationship: critical psychology would not exist without a status quo foil, but mainstream psychology would not grow and change for the better without critical input leading to improved methods and practices. Still, the process is not a smooth one.

Sometimes critical ideas are incorporated into an improved status quo only to become the focus of future critical perspectives. Commonly, however, the mainstream rejects developments within critical psychology as too radical or challenging to existing practices and interests. In this case, critical ideas exist in parallel to mainstream approaches, offering an alternative. Usually critical ideas are met with some measure of resistance; the greater the challenge to mainstream psychology, the greater the (initial) resistance.

Psychology's Status Quo: an Exercise in Conformity?

The first step to practicing critical psychology is to identify and learn about your field's status quo. Only through understanding the current methodology and thinking in your area of psychology will you be able to construct the best criticism of it. By becoming conversant with the material you critique, you gain more credibility as a critical reviewer of it. Once you clearly identify the limitations of that area, you can turn your attention to critiquing them.

Moving from the topic-specific to the general, it helps to understand the status quo's organizing purpose. Both undergraduate and graduate psychology programs frequently demonstrate a herd-like approach to education: certain traditions of studying human behavior and carrying out applied psychology take on an almost iconic status. Note that these traditions need not be overt. Many are subtle, passed on from one generation of scholars and practitioners to the next. For example, many psychotherapists believe the only effective way to help clients is to "cure" them within the framework of a medical model, which calls upon them to pathologize their clients. A critical approach might suggest instead that they focus upon the social origins of mental distress.

An additional complication is information overload. Mainstream psychology's sheer volume of facts and figures can overwhelm us, leaving us little time for critical reflection on what we study and do. Therefore, it is important to take a moment to evaluate critically what is taught in your courses and your research programs and what happens in your applied training. What assumptions do your supervisors and instructors make about the people you interact with and the objects you study? What assumptions do your teachers make about how to measure and quantify human behaviors? Are people treated as objects? Are you supposed to remain as distant as possible from the individuals and groups you work with?

When you evaluate these questions and their answers, you may find some of your instructors' and supervisors' assumptions to be wanting, while others may not trouble you. Psychology, like the society it studies and services, is organized in systematic ways. As such, certain assumptions, rules, and traditions help the discipline remain organized, coherent, and focused. Without some form of rules, traditions, and assumptions, psychology would degenerate into a chaotic, confused cacophony of discordant voices without a common language. While this position might lead to some radical and positive changes through advancing previously unheard-of ideas, it cannot be maintained indefinitely. A discipline in total chaos has little to offer anyone either inside or outside of psychology.

On the other hand, all these assumptions, rules, and traditions are open to critical scrutiny. Thus, the iterative process of criticism and modification actually *strengthens* psychology as a whole, making our practice of critically examining assumptions and methods an inherently positive endeavor.

Power, Politics and Resistance

We have stressed our belief that critically examining psychology's assumptions and practices ultimately strengthens and develops the discipline. However, this is not always how it works out in day-to-day practice. Theories, assumptions, and methods do not exist independently of those who use them in their daily activities. Mainstream psychologists, and others whose activities depend upon psychology's status quo, often have a personal and professional interest in maintaining and supporting particular forms of knowledge. For instance, psychometrists (people who measure personalities) are unlikely to accept a social constructionist perspective that denies the existence of a measurable personality, because the only way for them to do this would be to abandon their current profession. On a larger scale, grants from governments, large corporations, and military organizations support well established research traditions. Those who stand to lose something from changes to the status quo will vigorously resist critical analyses and actions. This resistance is not due to a lack of thought or blind adherence to tradition, but because a critical approach can threaten livelihoods, jobs, reputations, and whole professions. In this sense, being critical means challenging not only the accepted knowledge, but also those who have an investment in this knowledge. In other words, critical psychology is inherently political. Particular forms of knowledge are supported by particular societal and psychological practices. These practices are in turn reinforced by particular distributions of power.

Critiquing the Status Quo: Philosophical Arenas

We have discussed in general terms how psychology, either implicitly or explicitly, supports the status quo. In this section we demonstrate how critical psychologists address some of these issues in more specific ways. Initially, it may seem as though a discussion of academic (and often theoretical) issues moves us away from our aim of understanding how psychology can disempower particular groups within society. This is particularly true if we wish to discuss how this process implicates everyday practices of psychologists. However, it is important for those entering the critical field for the first time to understand both the assumptions of mainstream psychology and the responses of critical psychologists.

We include this information for two purposes. First, as you see elsewhere in this text, discussions and debates concerning the nature of psychology have generated important critical, yet practical, approaches. For example, Kenneth Gergen's (1973; 1976) academic reinterpretation of "social psychology as history" became a foundation for narrative and collaborative psychotherapy approaches, not only in terms of content, but also in terms of *method*. Gergen's reinterpretation of social psychology's findings demonstrated that a similar critical approach might be useful in the therapy office, and indeed it is (McNamee and Gergen, 1992).

To make use of critical psychologists' insights, however, we need to understand them. Unfortunately, discussions of these issues are often complex and confusing, featuring esoteric terminology. Adding to the confusion is that critical psychologists sometimes disagree about what is the best alternative to the mainstream for any given area of psychology (Prilleltensky, 1994a). Although this book strives to be accessible to newcomers to the field, it inevitably contains terminology and perspectives that are sometimes confusing. We hope that this section will help place in context the discussions in some of the other chapters as well as in other reading you do in critical psychology.

Second, although we couch what follows in philosophical and theoretical terms, these issues, and the methods we use to approach these issues, are inextricably tied to critical psychology practice. As demonstrated throughout this book, one way psychologists reinforce society's status quo is through supporting common-sense knowledge of the world. In turn, mainstream psychology reflects society's dominant values and mirrors its accepted practices. By contrast, critical psychology demands that we question both our psychological *and* our everyday beliefs. For this reason the theoretical debates within critical psychology are not isolated academic discussions. They can inform us about our lives and about what we take ourselves to be.

If psychology and the status quo are so intertwined, where does one begin to unravel the complexities of critically evaluating psychology? Critical psychologists have asked three broad kinds of questions in their attempts to reduce this problem to a manageable scale. *Ontological questions* relate to the nature of reality or being: what is the nature of the world and the people who inhabit it? (What sort of things exist? What are things really like?) *Epistemological questions* relate to our knowledge of the world: what can we know about the world? (What sort of knowledge can we have of the world? Can we assume our knowledge is a reflection of an objective reality or is it a more subjective or socially determined phenomenon?) *Methodological questions* relate to how we study the phenomena we wish to investigate: how should we go about finding it out? (Which methods do we adopt in our investigations of the world?)

Ontology: What Is the Nature of the World and the People Who Inhabit It?

Questions relating to the nature of the world are often considered the province of philosophers or theologians. What is our fundamental nature, what does it mean to be a person? As you see in other chapters, mainstream psychology predominantly concerns itself with an analysis of the individual in isolation from her or his environment. Importantly, it assumes that an analysis of this individual needs no reference to such an environment. This approach differs from that of disciplines that examine larger social groups. However, it is not just that other disciplines choose not to focus upon the individual *level of analysis* (different, multiple ways of defining and investigating the same phenomenon). Each, in its own way, is critical of assuming either that the "individual" level exists at all (at least in the way that mainstream psychology presupposes), or more modestly, that it should be investigated as though it were the single most important level of analysis.

Initially, this position may seem confusing, but the basis for it can be summarized as follows:

> In a culture steeped in psychological forms of thought, the idea – widely accepted in sociology – that "the individual" is a modern invention, seems barely comprehensible: what *do* they mean? It seems to be enough to point to yourself – maybe do a little twirl – and anyone in their right mind would have to agree. I am an individual, it's obvious isn't it? (White, 1989: 117)

This quote illustrates what has often been referred to as mainstream psychology's *individualism* (Sampson, 1977; 1989a): a belief that the individual is psychology's proper object of study. White contrasts psychology's position with that of sociology, which views the nature of personhood or the individual not as some already existing entity, but as something much more closely related to, shaped, and formed by the social world. Others make the same point in relation to anthropology:

> The Western conception of the person as a bounded, unique, more or less integrated motivational and cognitive universe, a dynamic centre of awareness, emotion, judgement, and action organised into a distinctive whole and set contrastively both against other such wholes and against a social and natural background is, however incorrigible it may seem to us, a rather peculiar idea within the context of the world's cultures. (Geertz, 1979: 229)

Both quotes challenge psychology's conception of the *individual* as an isolated and discrete phenomenon existing in its own right, to be explained without reference to anything external to itself. Notice also that these quotes challenge the everyday beliefs of members of the Western world. While we cannot delve deeply into it in here, we want to ensure that this point is not misunderstood. It forms much of the basis for critical psychology (for more on this topic see Burr, 1995; Sarbin and Kitsuse, 1994; Shotter and Gergen, 1989).

By contrast, critical psychology generally views the individual and society as so fundamentally intertwined that they cannot be separated from one another in any way that makes sense. Individuals and the social world they inhabit are one and the same thing, two ways of looking at the same phenomenon. The problem then becomes explaining this reality, not in terms of a *relationship* between two separate phenomena, but in terms of some sort of totality or whole.

For those new to critical psychology, these issues are often obscure and unintelligible. This is partly because of the unfamiliar terminology. But more importantly, this perspective challenges the way we look at the world on a day-to-day basis. For example, you could explain a person's severe depression in terms of the individual's "constitution" (for example, a particular neurochemical imbalance) or as the result of living under unbearable social conditions. Our explanations depend on where we look for causes of human behaviors. Do we look to the individual or to society? Do we look inside people's heads or to the social world they, and their heads, inhabit? Mainstream psychology's assumption that an individual exists independently of the social world forces psychologists to craft both their questions and their explanations of human behaviors to fit this rule, even when it may not be warranted (Breggin and Breggin, 1994).

Thus, critical psychology offers alternative ways to frame our questions, starting out with a different set of assumptions. It's not that critical psychology gives us different answers to the same old questions. Instead, it forces us to rethink the very questions we ask, allowing us to reformulate our questions, answers and practices simultaneously.

Epistemology: What Can We Know About the World?

As noted above, critical psychology's knowledge of the nature of reality differs radically from the world views of both mainstream psychology and the everyday Western world. A different ontology (that is, a different view of reality) necessarily gives rise to different knowledge about this reality. This difference can be quite disturbing.

If this is all there was to gaining knowledge then we would need to go no further with this section. However, epistemological questions relate to our knowledge of the world not simply in terms of the knowledge that we have, but more specifically in terms of the knowledge we *can* have. What assumptions underpin mainstream psychology's view regarding the *acquisition* of knowledge? To a large extent, mainstream psychology is carried out under the names of *science* and *experimentation*. Although we return to the latter in the next section, here we consider the idea of a scientific basis of psychology and critical responses to this notion.

Mainstream views of science rest upon an acceptance of two philosophical traditions, *empiricism* and *positivism*. Empiricism is the belief that what we see is what there is: the categories, differences, and similarities we perceive in the world are the way the world really is. Positivism is the belief that the world can be revealed by observation: if we look at the world carefully enough (using the right techniques) it will "give up" its nature to us and we will have an objective (and bias-free) view of it.

Thus, we might perceive that there are different races of people in the world, or that there are different genders, or children and adults, or the mentally ill and the mentally well balanced. However, critical psychology is as critical of taken-for-granted, everyday knowledge as it is of institutionalized psychological knowledge. Thus, it cautions against the assumption that just because something appears a certain way it necessarily *is* that way. This is not to say that differences don't exist. Rather, it warns us against believing these differences are naturally or objectively that way. For example, it seems *natural* to those of us in modern Western cultures to assume that children are different from adults. But it is only relatively recently that children ceased to be considered miniature adults (Aries, 1962). What appears natural to us – a qualitative difference between children and adults – is instead the product of a particular culture at a particular time in history.

What critical psychology emphasizes, given this realization, is that knowledge is not an objective reflection of reality, but depends on varying historical social arrangements. Thus, in contrast to mainstream psychology, critical psychologists trace the development of particular forms of knowledge (Foucault, 1972) and look at how knowledge, once it has arisen, is maintained and elaborated. Whose interests does it support, and who has the power to legitimize a particular form of knowledge over and above any other? A good example of this approach put into practice is much of the feminist writings on psychology and science demonstrating the male bias of Western scientific practices. For instance, Sandra Harding (1991) discusses how science legitimates and supports a male world view while simultaneously silencing the views of women.

As both everyday folk and as psychologists (whether critical or otherwise), our ways of knowing the world are tied to the world in which we live. To privilege one particular way of knowing the world over any other is a difficult venture. Mainstream psychology's view of science, for example, is one of gradual progress towards an ultimate truth, the gaining of more and more accurate information, the generation of more sophisticated and accurate theories. Critical psychology questions this perspective. It demonstrates that psychological knowledge, like all other forms of knowledge, is not something people *have* inside their heads, but is something they *make* between them in their everyday interactions with one another. The task for critical psychology is to question this knowledge, understand how it arose, and demonstrate whose interests it serves and whom it oppresses. In addition to being concerned with how we acquire knowledge, a critical epistemology also concerns itself with the applications and implications of this knowledge, examining which practices it favors and which it disallows.

Methodology: How Should We Go About Finding It Out?

Newcomers to critical psychology are generally more familiar with methodological issues than with ontological and epistemological questions. Most are no doubt aware of a number of different research methods (interviews, attitude surveys, participant observation, various psychometric measures, and so on). Many are familiar with the differences between qualitative and quantitative methodologies, the former comprising such techniques as open-ended interviews and observations, the latter based more on statistics and hypothesis testing (see Chapter 3). However, methods courses are often taught as though particular techniques are nothing more than different tools that researchers can take up as they see fit, blend in any combination, and use for any sort of investigation. We suggest instead that the critical stance we take towards the nature of the world (ontology) and our considerations of our knowledge of this world (epistemology) have particular implications for the methodology we adopt.

If we accept the social rather than individual nature of psychological phenomena, we can see that the methods of traditional psychology are not adequate. For example, it makes little sense to conduct attitude surveys if we question the reality of attitudes, at least in the sense of viewing them as relatively stable internal phenomena (Potter and Wetherell, 1987). To understand the origins of critical psychology's methods we need to remember that knowledge exists in interaction *between* rather than *within* people. We see that language, perhaps the primary form of social inter-action, is more than just a way of reflecting the world and our thoughts. It is not a mirror we hold up to our social activities, reflecting and describing our actions. Rather, language is a form of social activity in its own right, an action we perform.

Thus, critical psychologists view language as a primary medium that creates, maintains, contests, and transforms social reality. Different approaches within critical psychology emphasize different facets of the language/social-world relationship. Some focus on the *performative* aspects of speech and language, such as conversation analysts who focus on particular interactive sequences (see Chapter 5 in Smith et al., 1995). Others choose a more structural approach, concerning themselves with the concepts of *discourses* and *discourse analysis* (a discourse refers to any set of texts, images, and beliefs that construct a particular phenomenon in a particular way; see Chapter 18 in this volume). What they share is a concern with how language can be seen as a form of activity or action.

Our key point is the interrelationship between the methodology we adopt and the ontological and epistemological assumptions underpinning our choice. Our methods must fit the nature of the world and what we can know about it.

From Theory to Practice in Critical Psychology

As we have seen above, decisions we make at an ontological level about the nature of our world determine both the forms of knowledge we hold and the methods we use to analyze that world. These methods, in turn, strongly influence how we practice and apply our psychological knowledge, as well as how we live our day-to-day lives. Therefore, asking critical questions is no simple matter. It involves challenging not only our accepted psycho-logical beliefs but often our personal beliefs as well. But despite the difficulty, it is crucial to ask these questions if we are to understand how mainstream psychology maintains itself and how critical psychologists might turn our alternative perspectives into action.

Once you've successfully identified the status quo of your area of psychology, studied its assumptions and methods, identified its limitations, and read the critical literature, what next? Oddly enough, you need not immediately do something with this knowledge. Simply having the knowledge can be a liberating experience and a confidence-builder. You might continue to practice what you do currently, but your view of what it means and what it is changes significantly.

For example, one of the authors took a course on cognitive psychotherapy. Prominently featured was the work of David Burns (1989), which discussed the negative impact of black-and-white thinking on self-esteem. The course instructor explained that an absolute thought such as "I am worthless if everyone does not like me" comes from an "irrational" set of beliefs, which could be "fixed" through the application of cognitive therapy. Without a critical perspective, one might accept both the pathologizing label of "irrational" and the attendant cognitive explanation as hard, unchangeable facts. With a critical viewpoint, on the other hand, one might agree that absolute thinking patterns can be a problem area for people to explore without labeling these thinking styles "irrational." Indeed, a black-and-white thinking pattern could be socially learned in childhood or result from other unidentified factors. It is also conceivable that such a thinking style is useful under many circumstances. The ability to make a yes–no decision under time pressure can be an adaptive behavior.

This example illustrates a critical review of an assumption and a label used by a graduate course instructor. At this point, the critical student may overtly accept this mainstream perspective while tacitly holding an alternative viewpoint, which the student can put into practice at a later date out of the immediate classroom situation. Of course, while some students are comfortable with this cautious approach, others want to apply their critical thinking immediately. What follows is a variety of suggestions for outlets, audiences, and resources for those who seek to discuss critical ideas and practice critical psychology. Although there is some overlap, first we consider options for those in academic settings, and then options in nonacademic settings. As both of us work within academia we have chosen to focus on what we know best. However, this does not mean we think academia is the only (or the most important) setting.

Other Students and Colleagues

For every person who voices a question or complaint, there are likely others with the same concern, including some of your fellow students or colleagues in an applied setting. As was the case in the preceding example, you have the flexibility to tell others as little or as much as you like about your critical concerns regarding a topic of study or practice.

Of course, you may also find that your colleagues do not share your concerns. Even if they do, they may feel they cannot discuss these issues openly. Unfortunately, some co-workers or fellow students may verbally attack you for holding critical ideas. Experiencing this form of attack can be painful and surprising. But it often helps to recall how closely interwoven psychology and ordinary living are. By questioning the status quo, you may inadvertently bring into doubt a colleague's theory-laden belief structure, practical livelihood, and so on. You may find it helpful to put yourself in the place of the other person in such debates, imagining what it feels like to have your own belief structure and lifestyle brought under scrutiny. This does not mean you should give up critical inquiry. Quite the contrary. However, increasingly polarized debates characterized by *ad hominem* attacks serve little purpose and may actually do more harm than good in the long run; they can reduce your credibility and divert your attention from other, more important matters.

While *ad hoc* debate may work in an informal way, establishing some sort of structure for your critical debates is also useful. One way to do this is to establish a critical issues discussion group within your academic department or work setting. Such a group helps in a number of ways: It provides a focal point for those who are interested in these issues; it lends greater credibility to your activities, in that skeptical or hostile colleagues will find it harder to dismiss or undermine an established group than to isolate a single individual; and it provides a forum for inviting guest speakers and other interested parties with whom you would not normally come into contact. Another benefit comes from the fact that critical psychology welcomes the contributions of nonpsychologists and psychologists alike. For instance, the Prozac Survivors Support Group (Breggin and Breggin, 1994) was founded by direct victims of psychotropic medications and now has active chapters in several states of the US.

Instructors, Courses, and Research Projects

Despite mainstream norms, you may find that some instructors and supervisors are open to critical thinking and new methodologies. On the one hand, the superordinate–subordinate role can constrain freedom of expression, but on the other hand academic values supposedly encourage intellectual debate. If you are careful to phrase critical thinking as questions stemming from an overall interest in the material, many instructors and supervisors will discuss their methods openly and honestly. You may even be able to negotiate alternative course assignments that approach the subject matter in a specifically critical manner.

Similarly, students can also use dissertations, theses, and other research reports as a proving ground for critical thinking skills. For example, many such reports include a section discussing "Limitations of the Current Research and Directions for Further Study." You can use this opportunity to critique your own research and, by extension, current theories and methods in your field of study.

Courses taught outside one's specialization offer the opportunity to view old problems with new frameworks. For example, does thinking one thought following another happen as a result of Freudian free association, cognitive spreading activation theories, or neural connectionist networks? Or are these simply three different metaphors from unique subareas of psychology which describe the same phenomenon? The answer to this question may depend on the specific course in which the question is raised. An added bonus of taking courses broadly rather than narrowly is meeting new and interesting colleagues outside one's home department.

Conferences and Other Organizational Meetings

If your institution does not furnish you with enough like-minded colleagues you can travel further afield. I (*David*) first attempted to voice my critical concerns in public at a British Psychological Society (BPS) annual conference. As this is largely a mainstream conference, I had my doubts as to the reception the paper would receive, despite being convinced (at the time) that it represented a major and unique contribution to psychology. However, despite most of the delegates being politely bored, I came across a small number of people doing similar research with whom I have collaborated since.

Conferences of mainstream organizations such as the BPS and the American Psychological Association (APA) attract not only the stalwarts of traditional psychology but also people working at the fringes of the discipline, people in related areas of enquiry, and practitioners who do not whole-heartedly endorse the discipline's dominant norms. Specific divisions of these organizations (e.g., the "social section" of the BPS) also attract critical people to their events.

The Internet

Those who hunger for discussion with like-minded colleagues beyond the classroom or work setting can scan the Internet for e-mail discussion lists, World Wide Web (WWW) sites, and other repositories of discussions and critical information. Critically thinking students can debate scholars, practitioners, and other students who disagree with their critical views, without the possible social sanctions they would risk by strenuously debating a colleague, friend, or instructor. Students as well as practicing psychologists can publish their own information on the Internet and invite feedback from interested readers to start a dialogue.

Many e-mail lists, File Transfer Protocol (FTP) archives, and WWW sites are related to critical psychology, with more coming online all the time. For example, the Social Theory list (social-theory@mailbase.ac.uk), the Radical Psychology Network (radical-psychology-network@mailbase. ac.uk; http://uts.cc.utexas.edu/~neilands/radpsy/), and the psychology graduate students PSYCGRAD list (psycgrad@acadvml.uottawa.ca) often feature discussions of critical psychology topics. And if you have a topic you believe the current Internet sites do not cover adequately, you can start your own mail list or WWW site. For example, I (*Tor*) published a variant of my dissertation on self-esteem on the World Wide Web. Subsequently I received e-mail feedback from a number of readers who commented that the dissertation helped them work through their own self-esteem difficulties (Neilands, 1993).

Printed Texts and Articles

Beyond reading critical texts and articles, you can also write your own critical missives. These can often take the form of brief articles or book reviews for academic journals or the popular press, book chapters such as those in this text, or organizational newsletters and similar outlets.

In an ideal world critical psychology would be welcomed as a positive contribution to psychology. However, as noted previously, psychologists oftentimes do not adhere to this ideal when reviewing and evaluating critical ideas – and those who hold them. Thus, mainstream reviewers sometimes subject journal submissions with critical analyses to unwarranted attack, seeking to reshape the manuscripts into less critical conventional formats. To address this problem, a number of publishing avenues friendly to critical approaches have arisen (e.g., the *Journal of Philosophy and Social Criticism*). Unfortunately, however, many of these alternatives primarily serve a small community of critical psychologists, leading to the problem that many critical psychologists "preach to the converted." Similarly, critical psychologists often convene at small gatherings and conferences apart from the mainstream.

Nonetheless, these alternative publications and small conferences serve an important purpose: They inform critical psychologists of what their critically oriented colleagues are thinking and doing. They also provide a consensual base for critically oriented readers who may feel alienated or alone at their workplaces or universities. One of the challenges for today's critical psychology student is to invent creative ways of carrying the message of critical psychology beyond the confines of esoteric publications and into the mainstream. To some extent, this book represents an attempt at such a project. We look forward to soon seeing other such efforts from critically motivated scholars and practitioners.

Teaching

Teaching and mentoring students, supervisees, and research assistants offers a unique opportunity to share critical ideas with others. As the quote at the beginning of this chapter illustrates, teaching the *idea* of critical thinking, that a critical literature and a critical psychology even exist, may be the single most important thing you can do to advance a student's or supervisee's training. As an additional benefit, teaching critical ideas not only forces you to learn the critical literature well; it also forces you to learn the status quo literature on which the critical literature rests.

Advanced graduate students can frequently teach their own courses rather than simply serve as another instructor's assistant.

One of the highest forms of flattery one of our advisors ever received was at the conclusion of his "Critical Issues in Social Psychology" course. He had been especially concerned about one young woman who sat quietly during the entire course, not saying a word for the whole semester. Several days after the last class session, she dropped by the instructor's office and thanked him for teaching the class. She told him, "This class has fundamentally changed the way I think about psychology and about what I am doing." This feedback reassured the instructor that he had at least some success in conveying the concepts of critical thinking to some of his students. Furthermore, his efforts positively helped another human being practice her profession.

Internships

Some psychology programs (e.g., clinical and counseling) require that students apply the skills they have learned in *practica* and *internships*. Practica are part-time and usually occur while the student concurrently completes coursework; internships are usually full-time and take place after completing coursework. The opportunity to apply classroom-taught mainstream knowledge, as well as critical thinking, abounds in these settings. This is particularly the case if the student intern has the good fortune of working with a supervisor or mentor who is open to discussing these issues and applying critical thinking to the student's projects.

As an intern or practicum student, you also have the opportunity to observe a wide variety of professional psychologists in action. You can note the relative use of critical thinking skills and mainstream approaches in their work. Finally, an internship or practicum provides you with the opportunity to interact with the clients and others who receive the services you and your supervisors provide. You can interact with clients and ask them their thoughts and feelings about the services you and your supervisors offer, soliciting critical feedback of both yourself and the settings in which you practice.

Volunteer Work and Social Change

No less important is volunteer work, whether for a charitable organization or for minimal pay with other sacrifices. Examples of the latter are crisis intervention counselors and telephone hotline operators who help suicidal individuals cope with pressing issues during the late night and pre-dawn hours. One particular benefit of volunteering is that because your income is not directly dependent on your volunteer work, you have the freedom to speak out about issues that concern you. You also meet other volunteers likely to share similar interests. Perhaps they have some critical ideas to exchange with you about mainstream psychology, ideas that motivated them to volunteer. Regardless of the colleagues you meet on the job, you stand a high chance of directly benefiting someone through your actions. After all, critical ideas are important, but so are critically motivated actions.

You can also join social change or other activist, political, or service organizations such as anti-racism or environmental safety groups. Although these organizations are not about psychology *per se*, they may appreciate and benefit from your skills as a psychologist. As a psychology student, you might have expertise in social influence, statistics and number crunching, witness testimony, memory, neurochemical processes, child psychology, negotiation/mediation techniques, social skills training, and other topics that organizations find useful. In addition to providing needed resources, you can raise psychology-related issues as they are relevant to the group's goals.

Some Further Thoughts for Practitioners

The points we make above are as relevant to practitioners as they are to those within an academic or research setting. This is particularly the case in terms of viewing the individual as a constituent part of a wider social fabric, not as a naturally occurring and isolated phenomenon. However, while this perspective provides a substantive focus for academic psychology (e.g., analyses of identity as constituted through social practices), it is perhaps best seen as a starting point rather than as an end in itself for practitioners in this field. It provides a conceptual framework to reassess the processes of understanding and helping people with their difficulties. Critical psychologists seek to integrate critical ideas with their day-to-day activities.

Traditional approaches to mental health care emphasize individualistic forms of intervention: the treatment of symptoms through personality or behavioral change (Freeman et al., 1990) and/or the administration of psychotropic drugs (Breggin and Breggin, 1994). In recognizing the social, environmental, and material aspects of personal distress we can see that the process of helping people lead better and happier lives should not center solely around a treatment of symptoms that reside within the individual. Feminist therapy, for example, is often based on a critical awareness that "individual symptoms" frequently result from power imbalances, societal expectations, and similar factors (see Chapters 4, 7, and 16). Similarly, community psychology endeavors to uncover social aspects of personal distress, such as limited access to resources, lack of power to effect change, poverty, poor housing, and inequality and discrimination (see Chapter 11). Having identified these, the community psychologist's aim is twofold: first, to enable individuals to recognize and understand the material and social circumstances that cause or contribute to their distress; and secondly, to work towards changes in their environments to minimize these circum-stances. While one might achieve this process in the confines of the psychologist's office, it need not (and most often does not) end there. Involvement with anti-poverty groups, self-help groups, housing aid projects and similar organizations can have a direct impact upon the material and social circumstances of service users and thus facilitate their mental well-being.

Thus, a knowledge of local need and demand (particularly in terms of practical and social resources) is essential for developing appropriate therapeutic practices. We see the community psychologist not as a remote and objective "expert" concerned with psychological processes residing within a client's head. Instead, he or she is a committed member of the community, working to resolve social problems that generate the difficulties that people face in living out their lives. The critical psychologist understands locally available resources, channels them towards those who most require them, and works towards greater availability of such resources where necessary. The "Statement of Philosophy" of Nottingham Adult Community Psychology Services (based in the UK) summarizes this approach:

> Whilst remaining aware of the fact that in a society where inequality, poverty and limited opportunity exist, some are going to have greater access to resources than others, community psychology seeks to enable people to utilise what resources are available to them, and to draw local attention to the absence of resources. In developing this approach, the index of psychological well-being is not the absence of "symptoms", but the availability and utilisation of resources which may provide circumstances where the individual is able to develop security, autonomy and self-esteem. (Nottingham Community Health NHS Trust)

Conclusions

Every psychological theory has political and social implications. Whether implicitly or explicitly informed by such theories, every act we perform has political and social consequences. Our critical thoughts regarding the nature of the world (ontology), our knowledge of this world (epistemology), and our methodology and practices acknowledge and act upon these recognitions.

The actual avenues for engaging in critical psychology are numerous and change rapidly. This makes it impossible to provide an exhaustive catalog of critical psychology resources and opportunities beyond the general recommendations noted above. Instead, we emphasize here the *process* of facilitating critical psychology – how critical psychology happens – so that you can creatively make it happen for you. In this spirit, we hope to hear from students, practitioners, and others who read this chapter and subsequently pursue critical endeavors inside or outside psychology. We also hope to receive critical feedback from you, the reader, as to what we can do to update and revise this chapter and its ideas. We wish you the best of success and enjoyment in your critical psychology endeavors and look forward to hearing your own critical feedback of our work.

Note

We gratefully acknowledge the comments, suggestions, and feedback provided by Alicia Betsinger, Viv Burr, Dee Dempsey, Dennis Fox, Steve Melleish, Isaac Prilleltensky, and Arthur Travis during manuscript preparation and review.

We note that authorship duties in preparing this chapter were shared equally; the order in which our names appear was decided by who would benefit the most. As the first author is more likely to pursue a career in academic psychology, he has the most to gain from first authorship (*thanks Tor – Dave*).

PART II
CRITICAL ARENAS

6

Theories of Personality:
Ideology and Beyond

Tod Sloan

Editors' note   *When the public thinks of psychology, often what comes to mind first is the concept of personality. Likewise, many of psychology's subfields implicitly or explicitly incorporate one personality theory or another. Theories of personality, thus, offer fruitful ground for beginning our critical examination of psychology's substantive areas.*

In this chapter, Tod Sloan questions mainstream personality theory's basic assumptions. He urges us to examine choices that theorists make concerning how personality is defined, how it develops, what image of the Good Life and the Good Society the theory assumes, and what counts as validating evidence. Like Maritza Montero (Chapter 15), Sloan looks not only at what is present in theories, but also at what is absent. He demonstrates how dominant theories support the societal status quo and how a critical theory of personality can foster both personal empowerment and social justice.

Sloan explores the central dialectic between self-determination and false consciousness, a topic examined elsewhere by Fathali M. Moghaddam and Charles Studer (Chapter 12) and Dennis Fox (Chapter 14). On the one hand, critical psychologists wish to expand people's autonomy. But on the other hand, we cannot ignore societal ideologies that endorse choices such as frivolous consumerism as a means to personal fulfillment. Sloan's lament that many therapies restore "people to correct functioning within their ideological chains" is echoed in other chapters. The resulting dilemma for practicing critical therapists is not easily resolved.

Whereas traditional personality theories seek either technical control or interpretive understanding, for Sloan a primary concern is emancipation. Sensitive to diversity and social context, a critical personality theory would help change not just persons but societies as well "by showing how personal concerns and social justice are intertwined." Such a theory would be a significant step toward resolving the critical therapist's dilemma.

Human nature. Individuality. Experience. Self. Character. Identity. Psyche. Each of these terms overlaps considerably with at least one definition of "personality." Within psychology, few terms encompass so great a scope.

Few concepts are as fundamental. Concepts of personality not only shape the thoughts one can have about the phenomena of human existence, but also inform one's views on what life is about and how society should be organized. It is therefore with a certain urgency that we ask in this chapter: how have theories of personality operated in mainstream psychology? What concepts of personality might serve the purposes of critical psychology? How can we theorize about personality in a manner that contributes to the construction of a humane and just society?

In its essence, a theory of personality is a set of concepts for understanding the actions and experiences of human individuals. Most theories of personality attempt to provide a comprehensive and integrated general psychology of motivation, development, individual differences, psychopathology and mental health, as well as an account of more specific phenomena such as dreams, creativity, aggressiveness, or social conformity. In other words, a personality theory aims to provide an understanding of people at both the general and the particular levels. If a set of concepts happens to fall short of this comprehensiveness, we call it a mini-theory, a model, or simply a theory of motivation or a theory of development. The immense challenge of producing a full-blown personality theory has only been met by a dozen or so individuals. These are the figures whose work was sufficiently original and comprehensive as to merit separate chapters in textbooks on personality theory: Freud, Jung, Adler, Fromm, Horney, Erikson, Murray, Allport, Skinner, Kelly, Maslow, Rogers, and a few others. Personality theories, however, are not always the products of single individuals. Several approaches to personality theory have managed to coalesce without being identified with a single theorist, for example, cognitive-behavioral theory or existentialist theory.

Personality theories vary widely in scope, intent, and style. Nevertheless, they all tend to address several enduring questions about human nature and differ primarily according to the positions they adopt on these issues. For example, theories can be either optimistic or pessimistic about the possibility of personality change. Does personality remain roughly the same throughout life or can it change in significant ways? Theories also differ on the issues of determinism, nature versus nurture, and the degree to which persons should be viewed as unique. Throughout this chapter we will see why theoretical stances on these issues should not be considered merely matters of personal preference.

Despite wide divergence among personality theories on such issues, they share the characteristic of being theories, sets of concepts designed to help us understand or explain human nature. Thus they tend to be lumped together in textbooks designed for the survey course on personality theory, which remains one of the more popular courses in the standard psychology major. Strangely enough, this course generally contains little about *how* to theorize. Students are only expected to memorize the main points made by various theorists and perhaps to compare their positions. Even in courses in which critical thinking is encouraged, students are usually taught neither how

theories should be constructed nor how they should be assessed *as theories.*
Instead, in keeping with general practice in mainstream psychology, future
psychologists are taught that the validity of theoretical concepts is to be
ascertained by operationalizing them for experimental or correlational
studies. In conjunction with this practice, they are trained to describe
personality mechanistically with an impoverished vocabulary, reducing the
complexity of personal experience to a few quantifiable dimensions or
dichotomous categories. Psychologists are thus unable to reflect critically on
theory construction and its implications for practice. From this deficit in
training stem many of the problems that plague all sorts of applied
psychology.

Put simply, mainstream approaches have systematically reduced our
capacity to understand personality. Psychologists need to know *how* to *think*
about personality in order to understand it. The consequences are serious
and not only because we end up befuddled. Theorizing about personality or
the self within the context of mainstream psychology has generally served to
maintain the societal status quo (Venn, 1984). This happens in many ways,
two of which are mentioned here to illustrate this point.

First, concepts of personality always reflect a "historical form of individuality" (Sève, 1978) associated with a particular social order. Mainstream approaches tend to generalize this view to all societies and historical
periods. One quickly jumps to the conclusion that since people will always
be more or less the way they are (e.g., greedy, aggressive), one need not
bother with improving society.

A second form of status quo maintenance occurs when views of personality present individualistic perspectives on human development. Mainstream personality theories lead their consumers to define problems in living
as private matters to be solved by personal growth or self-actualization
(Holzkamp-Osterkamp, 1991). This diverts attention away from seeking
collective solutions to problems that are typically social in origin. Individualistic theories also forget that the luxury and leisure to be concerned
with personal growth is available only to the privileged classes in modern
societies. Massive social change would be necessary before the vast majority
of citizens could dedicate themselves to psychological well-being in the
manner implied by many theories. In short, individualistic perspectives tend
to blame the individual and leave social inequality unchallenged.

To flesh out these and other critical points, I discuss in this chapter the
historical development of the field, factors affecting theoretical choices, and
the purposes served by personality theories. In the final section, I propose a
few guidelines for theorizing about personality in a critical mode.

Historical Background

A glance at the contents of any textbook of personality theory shows that
the field defines itself as having started in Central Europe at the turn of the

century with Sigmund Freud and psychoanalysis. Of course, human cultures have always had ways of talking about individual character and notions about why individuals are the way they are, but these were not full-blown theories, nor did they pretend to be scientific. By the time of Freud, there were major theories of psychopathology and even some fairly well developed systems of "characterology," particularly in France. But before Freud, most thinking about personality was primarily theological, philosophical, and speculative in nature. Freud, like all personality theorists, also had his philosophical and speculative moments, but he also sought to derive his concepts from systematic observations in the consulting room. Over four decades, he energetically elaborated and illustrated dozens of concepts through case studies, wove his notions together, sought new evidence, and revised basic principles. The result was psychoanalytic theory and the practice of psychoanalysis itself, both of which constantly undergo further revision by theorists and practicing analysts. Inspired by Freud, Carl Jung also labored for decades and accomplished roughly the same feat albeit with different objectives and results.

As the standard textbook shows, the center of gravity in personality theorizing soon shifted from Europe to the United States. This happened in part because important European theorists emigrated before and during World War II, but also because the modern scientific world view had weakened theological concepts of personhood in the US just as it had in Europe. Psychologists began turning to secular models of personality for answers to their questions about human nature. The details of the ensuing search fill the pages of personality textbooks.

The main contours of the search derive from various reactions to Freud, who in turn embodied the central contradictions of European modernity. On the one hand, Freud's pessimism about change and his questionable scientific methods were not well received by hard-nosed, down-to-business psychologists in the United States. Behaviorists insisted on concepts that referred to observable and measurable phenomena. As pragmatists, they also wanted to see results; they had little patience for interventions that implied years on an analyst's couch. On the other hand, humanistic psychologists sought visions of human nature that offered more hope for individuals and society than Freudian perspectives (Jacoby, 1975). They also preferred to avoid deterministic approaches that overlooked individual uniqueness, consciousness, and agency (*agency* refers to a process in which one reflectively determines personal needs and interests and then acts to fulfill them). Most of the major theories proposed since Freud and Jung reflect these general concerns, but recently, in attempts to overcome obvious ethnocentrism, textbook authors have begun to include chapters on the elaborate concepts of self in traditional Hindu and Buddhist thought. Simply put, the history of personality theory is the history of a European and North American debate about the nature of human individuals and the sort of science that would be appropriate for understanding them.

To conclude this necessarily brief history, one might note that roughly a quarter century has passed without seeing the addition of an original major theory to the textbooks. What this means for the field is not exactly clear, but perhaps it indicates that we finally have enough theories and have shifted our attention to evaluating them in research and practice. Since the 1970s, researchers have preferred to work on mini-theories relevant to specific topics, and practitioners eclectically seek techniques that work, often with little regard for their theoretical justification.

Theoretical Choices

Mainstream psychology expects theories of personality to synthesize or integrate knowledge produced by the various subdisciplines of psychology such as social, developmental, abnormal, cognitive, and so forth. Although some cross-fertilization occurs between subdisciplines, only personality theorists claim the task of synthesis as their own.

Personality theorists are thus generalists who stand back to get the big picture on human nature. A certain grandiosity may motivate this pretension to omniscience, but the move toward synthesis and integration is problematic for other reasons. As theorists seek concepts or findings to incorporate in their general perspective, they necessarily make assumptions about the nature of human nature and about how it should be studied. Even when a theorist makes these assumptions explicit, a great deal of unnecessary baggage is imported in the process. Among the baggage that sneaks into personality theories as they are developed and employed, one finds (a) choices about how to frame personality, (b) choices about how personality develops, (c) choices related to world view, and (d) choices about what counts as knowledge about personality. Each of these deserves further discussion.

Choices about How to Frame "Personality," the Object of Inquiry Itself

Some theorists think of personality in terms of dimensions on which individuals can be said to differ. Most trait theory takes this approach. Others see personality as the stable core of character that produces a person's relatively consistent behavior. Psychodynamic approaches adopt this definition. Personality can also be construed in terms of uniqueness, temperamental dispositions, social aspects of individual behavior, qualities of emotional experiences, an ideal to be achieved – the list could go on and on. Thus, in the very first act of theorizing, in decisions about how personality is to be defined, numerous assumptions enter into the construction of the object of inquiry. In other words, to varying degrees, personality theories tend to stack the cards in their favor before the game even starts. For example, a theorist who has things to say about unconscious processes has nothing to lose by defining personality in a manner that highlights unconscious processes. A psychologist who wants to prove that personality is inherited will define it in terms that relate to temperament. Such preferences stem from factors ranging from professional training in a particular school of thought to religious background and personal concerns. Obviously, such initial framing of the object of inquiry directs attention to certain aspects of human behavior or experience and not to others. This is problematic because personality theories are presented as comprehensive systems. Their advocates rarely suggest that we look elsewhere for understanding. Furthermore, as we saw above, definitions of personality are also likely to reinforce implicitly a model of society that justifies the status quo and the fates of persons within it. In critical social science, this is known as a form of *ideology*. If we define ideology as ideas or images that sustain unjust social relations, then we must expect that concepts of personality may be ideological constructions (Sloan, 1994; 1996b).

Choices about How "Personality" Develops

Theorists tend to have biases about whether the behavioral phenomena they observe are due to social learning, inherited temperamental factors, long-term evolutionary processes, aspects of the present situation, a combination of the above, or an individuality that transcends all determinants. As with definitions of personality, these biases can stem from training, sociocultural context, political assumptions, and other influences. Of course, theorists' positions on the question of development direct their attention to specific spheres of behavior or experience. These positions shape subsequent thinking about the meaning or function of any aspect of personality. Again, the consequence is not only that important aspects of development may be overlooked; ideological functions may be served as well. For example, if personality is viewed as mostly inherited, it follows that changing social institutions to foster healthier personality development would be less important than improving genetic screening for desired or undesired psychological types.

Choices Stemming from the Theorist's World View

Every psychologist has ideas about the purpose (if any) of life, the goals that people should have, notions about right and wrong behaviors, sociopolitical notions regarding the Good Society, right government, the nature of history, and so forth. Each of these ideas represents a particular value stance. A few theorists have made serious attempts to link their ideas on personality to values grounded in an overarching cosmic vision – Unger (1984) and Holzkamp (Tolman and Maiers, 1991; Tolman, 1994) come to mind. The majority, however, have insisted that they are *value-free* scientists describing human reality as it is. Psychologists have been exceptionally slow in catching on that it will never be possible to be value-free in the human sciences (Fox, 1985; Howard, 1985). Yet, our embeddedness in value systems is not necessarily a problem, as many would quickly assume.

A meaningful science of personality is still possible. But to be meaningful, a science must adjust to the nature of its object as well as to the nature of the subjects who conduct scientific inquiry. This means making value stances explicit.

Choices about What Qualifies as Evidence or Knowledge

Philosophers may never resolve the basic issues about human knowledge. Personality theorists reflect this lack of resolution in the stances they take on how to study personality. At one extreme, one finds theorists who have been content to trust their intuitions, experience, or common sense. At the other extreme are a few theorists who prefer to derive their conceptual frameworks exclusively from data gathered in laboratory experiments or correlational studies. These epistemological and methodological preferences may be the product of professional socialization, personal inclination toward speculative philosophy or empirical science, requirements for publishing in scientific journals, and developments in the philosophy of social science itself. Many of the ongoing arguments between proponents of different personality theories have little to do with substantive issues; instead, they flow from different choices about what counts for knowledge. For example, to prove the validity of a concept, a Freudian might submit an account of how a patient's dreams changed after hearing an interpretation of her transference reaction. A cognitive theorist might want to see that reaction times to certain stimuli had changed as a result of the interpretation. A phenomenological theorist would probably put a lot of weight on what the patient had to say about the matter.

Despite a vague recognition of these four relatively *arbitrary* components of any theory of personality, mainstream psychology insists on dealing with theoretical propositions about personality as if they were statements about hypothesized relations between mass and energy or about the functioning of organisms such as frogs or amoebae. As a result, partisans of whatever theory scurry to amass sufficient empirical evidence to prove that their favorite theory is indeed the most accurate, valid, fruitful, practical, insight-laden, all-encompassing, or deserving of research funding. Since choices regarding the criteria and methods for evaluating a theory depend on the litany of factors we visited in the four points above, the entire science of personality gets caught in a vicious circle. Simple ideas with nonscientific origins become scientific variables used ubiquitously to account for behavior (e.g., "self-esteem", Jungian types). Complex ideas that are perhaps very useful in understanding personality but not operationalizable are neglected or rejected as unscientific (e.g., defense mechanisms, individuation). Years are spent to prove that a certain theory is valid only for it to be forgotten by the next generation or displaced by a theory that says roughly the same thing with different terminology.

In general, mainstream psychology imports its criteria for evaluating theories of personality from those used in the natural sciences: empirical validity, verifiability, internal consistency, parsimony, etc. Criteria such as these have limited relevance for studies in psychology in general. They have been especially irrelevant to the advance of personality theorizing. Critical psychologists must take this irrelevance very seriously. Instead of rushing to find isolated empirical justification for concepts associated with a particular theoretical framework, we must first engage in extensive critiques of the ideological underpinnings of basic psychological concepts. In part, this implies becoming hyper-aware of how the factors listed above enter into our thinking about personality. The point of doing so will become clear if we back up a few steps and ask why we need theories of personality in the first place.

The Purposes of Personality Theory

Here we will focus not on the motivations of the grand theorists, but on the purposes fulfilled by personality theory in everyday psychological practice. This strategy takes into account the fact that consumers of theories rarely use them as their authors intended. Furthermore, what ends up having a direct impact on individuals and societies is the way ideas are adopted and implemented.

Within mainstream psychology, personality theories are primarily used to guide attempts to change behavior, to predict future action, or to understand individual lives. Although these purposes overlap somewhat, we will address them separately.

Intervention

A personality theory can serve as a source of descriptive concepts or categories to help explain a problematic aspect of an individual's behavior and guide intervention to change it. For example, repetitive hand washing might be understood by relating it to the category of obsessive compulsiveness. Once the category is applied, various treatments would be indicated. Or, a therapist might determine that a student's test anxiety is due to fear of success linked to his Oedipus complex, and again a specific course of intervention would be specified. In such cases, one assumes that correct assignment of a category will aid a psychologist in knowing how to change the problematic behavior. Knowing how a particular behavioral manifestation is linked to a more general feature of the individual's personality guides intervention toward causes and not just effects. From this perspective, the purpose of a personality theory is to provide concepts linking symptom to syndrome, behavior to trait, effect to cause, etc. A theory is judged to be a good one if interventions based on these linkages actually work. Note that the main purpose of a theory in this case is to produce successful interventions, that is, to achieve a desired effect at the level of individual behavior or experience.

Prediction Based on Assessment of Individual Differences

A personality theory can also serve as a source of concepts or categories that chart the basic ways in which individuals differ from each other in enduring ways. The practical aim here is to use assessments of an individual's personality to predict future behavior, as in personnel selection or clinical screening. Subjective human judgments are supplemented or replaced by supposedly objective personality descriptors. The interest in individual differences is also relevant to research in mainstream personality psychology. In that field, debate still continues on the question of which traits are the most central to human personality in general and which traits make the best predictors of future behavior (Sloan, 1986). The field has also tried to determine the importance of personality relative to situational determinants of behavior. Eventually these concerns come around again to issues of prediction, since according to mainstream philosophy of science, one should be able to predict future behavior if one has explained it correctly in the first place. Note that in this case as well the main purpose served by theory is to suggest a technical intervention to produce a desired outcome.

Biographical Understanding

The first two purposes of personality theory fall clearly within the general expectations of mainstream psychological science. A good theory is expected to increase our ability to explain, predict, and control behavior. But psychology is not monolithic (Kimble, 1984). Thus, a third purpose of personality theory meets expectations that come from other quarters, in this case, the educated public and humanists. People want to *understand* why people, especially famous individuals, do what they do. Understanding differs significantly from explanation in terms of cause and effect in order to predict. The aims of understanding are multiple, and on occasion the ability to predict is desired, but even if it were possible, it would have little impact. For example, there would be no point in trying to predict Nixon's or Madonna's future behavior, but one might attain a certain enlightenment about politics or pop culture through studies of their lives. Biographical understanding requires a mustering of numerous perspectives on a person's life: childhood, family, friendships, contacts, influences, cultural trends, social institutions, historical period, and so forth. One never attains a sense of understanding a person totally, but one does begin to comprehend the struggles, the joys and disappointments, and the "meaning" of the person's life. Biographical understanding also requires a related empathic identification on the part of the person who seeks understanding. Biographical understanding necessarily involves an *interpretive* moment based on the subjective expressions of the person being understood (diaries, letters, interviews, creative works, etc.). Thus the issue of how to study lives *scientifically* is often raised and personality theories are often called upon to support a biographer's argument. An entire subfield known as the *study of lives* has arisen to address such issues and continues to inspire important contributions to our understanding of personality (cf. McAdams and Ochberg, 1988; Rosenwald and Ochberg, 1992).

It is no coincidence that the purposes served by personality theories in mainstream psychology coincide with two of the three primary interests served by knowledge-seeking in general. Following German social theorist Habermas (1971), we may refer to these as the interest in *technical control* (typical of the physical and natural sciences) and the interest in *interpretive understanding* (the hermeneutic interest characteristic of historical and humanistic studies).

In light of this, we may begin to differentiate between the purposes of mainstream theorizing and the interest to be served by critical approaches. Critical psychology seeks knowledge in order to serve a third sort of purpose. Habermas contrasts the interests in technical control and interpretive understanding with an *emancipatory* interest that motivates critical social science (cf. Fay, 1987; Held, 1980). As prototypes of emancipatory scientific inquiry, Habermas cites psychoanalysis and Marxist social theory. Both modes of inquiry not only attempt to explain and understand, but also seek to *enhance human agency in order to modify conditions of systematic suffering.* Psychoanalysis invites the patient to move away from neurotic and ideological structures toward awareness, responsibility, and desire. Marxist social theory urges oppressed social classes to be cognizant of their situation and to work for social change. Both approaches also focus on how people can overcome the obstacles to effective action in their own interest: unconscious "resistance" or alienation and false consciousness. As these examples indicate, the emancipatory interest differs from the other two in that it requires the self-reflective involvement of the persons who hope to bring about change in their own situation. In other words, rather than intervening in people's lives as if they were objects to be manipulated toward desired outcomes or simply interpreting lives out of mere curiosity, emancipatory modes of inquiry depend on the conscious participation of individuals and groups in articulating their needs and working toward their fulfillment. The emancipatory interest overlaps considerably with several other terms: liberation and deideologization (Martín-Baró, 1994); conscientization (Freire, 1981); empowerment (Cowen, 1991; Rappaport, 1981); the enhancement of subjectivity (Rosenwald, 1985; 1988).

Strangely enough, while the emancipatory interest is relatively inoperative in mainstream psychology, it is this interest that the general public expects the field, and personality theory in particular, to serve. When readers go to counselors and therapists or pick up books by Freud, Rogers, or Skinner, they seek exactly the sort of enlightenment that follows when the emancipatory interest of science is being fulfilled. They have problems in living; they are perplexed, alienated, and confused (Rosenwald, 1985; 1988). They do not seek merely to be fixed by an expert. If they were offered the chance, they would want to understand their situations, articulate their needs more concretely, and move forward with a greater sense of agency, autonomy, and meaningful relatedness to others.

How did mainstream psychology happen to deviate so far from this fairly obvious *raison d'être*? As many chapters in this volume insist, the field managed to get so far off track partly because it has been trying so hard to be respected as a science. This meant adopting various methods associated with positivism. But given that psychology's subject matter is people, positivist criteria for scientificity are inappropriate and not even based on a correct understanding of positivism (Phillips, 1987). People do not need to be studied as if they were plants or crystals, unable to communicate about their desires, needs, hopes, and sufferings. People do not need a set of universal principles or laws of behavior. Instead, people need to be invited by psychologists and other social scientists to participate in an ongoing process of reflection on our personal and collective problems in living meaningfully.

One senses that personality theories could play a very important role in the process of social transformation and human betterment, in particular by showing how personal concerns and social injustice are intertwined. Occasionally, personality theories have painted pretty pictures of what the Good Life might be like (the fully functioning person, the self actualizing individual), but they tend to end up simply exhorting us to change without empowering us to do so. Some theorists, such as Fromm (1955) and Skinner (1971), even wrote tracts on how society should be changed. Nevertheless, a theory of personality with well articulated links to a theory of modern society has yet to appear. Since critical psychologists have their work cut out for them, let us turn to the question of how we might go about the task of theorizing in a different manner.

Critical Theories of Personality

To this point, the values that guide my critique of mainstream approaches to personality theory have remained relatively unspecified. In this final section, I will move gradually toward an explicit statement of the criteria that should be met by critical theorizing about personality. What I present here is my own formulation and should not be construed as representative of a critical psychological approach. Nevertheless, the particulars of my formulation will show that I am indebted to the influence of various authors who provide key elements for critical theorizing about personality. Georges Politzer (1928), Lucien Sève (Sève, 1978; Sloan, 1987), and Klaus Holzkamp (Tolman, 1994) worked out the core principles of a dialectical-materialist psychology of personality, providing a strong corrective for both the individualism and the asocial character of mainstream psychology (*dialectical materialism* is the basic philosophy underlying Marxism, which views change as the transcendence of contradictions or oppositions in the material world). Russell Jacoby (1975), W. R. Earnest (1992), and Barnaby

Barratt (1993) show how the integration of ideology criticism and psycho-analytic theory can radically subvert mainstream notions of personhood. Edward Sampson (1989b) and John Broughton (1986) demonstrate how our concepts of self are shaped by historical contexts in ways that serve ideological functions. Herbert Marcuse (1955) and Jessica Benjamin (1988) critique patterns of socialization and social structure that interfere with our capacities for enjoyment and meaningful relatedness to others. As an aside, I urge serious study of these and other works to reduce redundancy as we go about constructing critical psychology. Many of the elements of a critical theory of personality in social context have already been worked out. Unfortunately, all I can provide here is a sketch of how some of those elements might come together.

First, critical psychology needs a definition of personality that guides our attention to the aspects of personhood that have something to do with both systematic suffering and emancipation from it. Instead of thinking of personality as simply a system of enduring dispositions or a set of personal characteristics that make one unique or different from others, we might consider personality *as a problem,* in the sense that "character structure" is generally viewed as a problem because it indicates rigidity or lack of boundaries, impaired awareness, automatic behaviors that increase one's suffering, etc. We should hasten to add that, seen this way, personality is not only a problem but a *social* problem with social origins. The aspects of personhood that concern critical psychologists are those that are systematically produced by social relations characterized by domination and oppression. A critical definition of personality might thus refer to *socially produced aspects of identity and affective experience that impede self-reflection, agency, autonomy, mutuality and other capacities that charac-terize meaningful living.* In this view, personality is something to be transcended and a critical theory of personality would help us individually and collectively to accomplish this transcendence. The capacities toward which we would want to strive could be lumped together under the term *intersubjectivity* (Habermas, 1984; 1987). (The term derives in part from a notion of full communication between self-determining subjects.)

Given this rough definition of personality, we need some idea of how personality develops. Here several varieties of psychodynamic theory suggest themselves, because these models focus on ways that early rela-tionships limit our capacities to experience our needs and to reflect on and communicate them adequately to others (Sloan, 1996a). As a consequence of early socialization, we each become unable to experience and understand our lives as fully as possible. How we label this deficit (the terms "neurosis" and "alienation" work fairly well) is less important than correctly analyzing its origins. For this task, standard psychodynamic theory is insufficient because it focuses primarily on intrafamilial factors. The processes that restrict our capacities for meaningful living derive not only from regular interaction patterns peculiar to family members and caregivers, but also from other sociocultural factors operating through the family and other socializing institutions (Münch, 1988). I have in mind factors such as social class, gender, ethnicity, and other social realities that always mediate personality processes throughout the lifespan (Gregg, 1991).

To the extent that all these factors can combine to restrict capacities for self-reflection and meaningful activity, they may be called *ideological processes*. As mentioned above, critical approaches define ideology as a system of representations and practices that sustain and reproduce relations of domination within a given social order (Thompson, 1984). In this light, personality is a crystallization of ideological processes. Power and powerlessness move not only through social institutions but also through personality as reflected in high aspirations or lack of hope, assertiveness or passivity, well-being or discontent. We have thus seen that mainstream concepts of personality are ideological constructions to the extent that they are individualistic and asocial in character. Moreover, personality itself, as it is lived, is an ideological construction. Freud had something like this in mind when he coined the term "compromise formation" to refer to the symptoms or character structures that form at collision points between nature's impulses and the constraints of civilization in the individual psyche (Marcuse, 1955). Much of the work of the Frankfurt school of critical social theory, in particular Adorno and Marcuse (cf. Elliott, 1992; Held, 1980; Sloan, 1996a), makes this basic assumption. More recently, Habermas (1987) and Foucault (Rabinow, 1984), working from different critical angles, have detailed the ways in which capitalist modernization invades the structure of identity, disrupting possibilities for intersubjectivity and fulfillment. Familiarity with these approaches is essential to the critical psychologist.

Keeping in mind the emancipatory interest as the primary impulse for theorizing, we should seek some form of nonobjectifying epistemology (theory of knowledge) and allow our methods to flow from it. Personality, even as defined here, has objective features that could be described, assessed, studied, and manipulated objectivistically. This fact explains the partial success of mainstream psychology in predicting "some of the behavior some of the time." But we need not conclude that the stability of ideologically fixed patterns of experience and action justifies interventions that treat people as mere objects and totally bypass individual capacities for self-reflection and self-determination. Nor must we run to the other extreme, as some phenomenological approaches do, of idealizing personal narratives as avenues to subjective truth when they are in fact also saturated with ideology. To the extent that self-reflection and self-determination are possible, they will occur in a difficult and challenging process of dialogue (in the broadest sense). This is so because personality itself, as defined here, is the product of failed intrapsychic and interpersonal communication (Habermas, 1971). Through dialogue, our identities and experience are reshaped to allow for the construction of fuller meaning. As Barratt (1993) argues, such critical, deideologizing activity is exactly the aim of psychoanalysis properly understood. He demonstrates that, unfortunately, much that passes for "psychoanalysis" and most psycho-therapy simply shores up crumbling identities and restores people to correct functioning within their ideological chains.

In conjunction with dialogue that challenges and undercuts impediments to capacities for meaningful living, I see a great deal of promise in an epistemology known as *negative dialectics* (Adorno, 1973; Held, 1980). Put simply, an approach to personality grounded in negative dialectics would note that our attempts to capture behavior with models, concepts, and theoretical systems tend to obscure more than reveal the object of study. Any concept necessarily aims to establish an identity or a complete corre-spondence between itself as a representation and the object it intends to portray. But something is always left out of the concept because of limitations of language, cognitive biases, complexity, etc. Thus, it can be held that concepts are always false, and especially so when they claim to have fully represented their object.

Now, in the case of concepts of personality, critical psychologists can make enormous progress by simply examining what it is that widely used concepts ignore or exclude as they pretend to capture the essence of a particular phenomenon. For example, one could look at trait theory, which reduces personality to a system of specific enduring behavioral dispositions. It would be fairly simple to show that although two people have identical profiles on a trait inventory, the meanings or intentions typically fulfilled by the actions related to those trait dimensions are so different that to say they have similar personalities would be ridiculous. The aggressiveness of the first person, for example, might be directed toward finding housing for the homeless, while the same trait in the second leads him to get into fights in bars. The supposed comparability of the two people on the trait dimension breaks down as soon as we consider what the concept left out. The objectivism of trait theory turns out to be yet another ideological trap (Sloan, 1986). This judgment may be made even before one considers the various questionable uses to which trait inventories are put by psychologists working in administrative settings (for selection and screening in courts, schools, clinics, and corporations).

To illustrate a second negative dialectical move, we could consider how mainstream concepts of personality fail to capture the ways in which personal characteristics are hardly personal at all. The *sociality* of per-sonality is erased by individualistic concepts that see the person as not only the container but also the origin of enduring characteristics. In a critical view such as the one proposed here, personality is not asocial; instead, it can be viewed as a congealed moment of social process. For example, my "shyness" and your "confidence" are manifestations of a complex inter-twining of social class, ethnicity, socialization, life experience, identity development, and so forth. What we think of as "individual" and "social" are, in the final analysis, the same. An epistemology suitable for critical theorizing about personality would consistently take this into account and attempt to transcend individual/society dualism in a dialectical manner.

The point of revealing the social in the individual, the general in the particular, is to denaturalize phenomena of personhood that are taken ideologically as innate, unchangeable, and only matters for private concern (Sloan, 1996b).

To be fair, I should bring the same negative dialectical strategy to bear on the definition of personality I proposed above. One should ask, what would be neglected if we were to view personality as those aspects of a person that interfere with capacities for meaningful living and which can be transcended through critical dialogue? First of all, this view could be faulted for remaining quite individualistic. Individual persons appear to remain the locus of ideological processes, when one could just as well look at obstacles to full communication that exist because of institutional structures. For example, state-sponsored terrorism, union busting tactics, issueless political campaigns, and suburban isolation do just as much to prevent productive communication about human needs as do features of personality. Our concept thus needs a clear anchoring in social structure and institutional arrangements. To some extent, this anchoring comes with a critical use of the term "ideology" (Earnest, 1992; Thompson, 1984), for it emphasizes not only ideas and images but also concrete practices. Nevertheless, the critique is a valid one that could perhaps be leveled at any position that puts too much weight on features of individuals rather than on sociohistorical conditions that produce phenomena observed at the individual level. The issue deserves the serious attention of critical psychologists.

A second weakness of the definition I have proposed is that it highlights communication processes both in the production of impediments to meaning and in their transcendence. In other words, the absence of capacities for self-reflection and relatedness that are essential for meaningful social living is interpreted primarily as a communication problem. Similarly, the route toward improved capacities is characterized in terms of fuller communication about needs and interests. This emphasis on communication derives in part from the work of Habermas (1984; 1987) and is meant as a corrective for mechanical and cognitive views of self-transformation. The latter see growth as a matter of manipulating oneself toward change or of thinking more realistically about oneself without addressing the emotional obstacles to change. But it could be that the interest in communicative competence is still too rationalistic in that it ignores other equally valid modes of expression that also lead beyond ideologized personality structures toward social transformation. I have in mind, for example, certain aesthetic and affective experiences that are clearly important forms of expression but are not well captured in terms of dialogue and democratic consensus formation in groups.

This brief critique demonstrates how the primary dynamic of critical personality theorizing derives from the dialectical play between concepts and experience. This process will never end. There can never be, therefore, a personality theory that will do the trick for any problem it encounters. Yet, personality theories in particular have suffered from a totalizing impulse, a desire to explain everything once and for all. They thus provide maps of human reality that try to indicate all the essential landmarks and connections between them. But they can only be maps. They may indicate that the terrain includes such things as Oedipus complexes, introversion, or self-actualization, but they will never begin to capture the lived essence of your Oedipus complex, your partner's introversion, or your client's process of self-actualization. The totalizing impulse must be resisted in all psychological theorizing as part of a larger political move against technical control of human subjectivity. The interests in pinning us down, labeling us, locating us on basic trait dimensions – and often in the guise of helping and increasing self-understanding – are part and parcel of contemporary ideological processes related to social administration and the efficient functioning of the market economy. The state and the market now cooperate to distort our own concepts of who we are and what is possible but also to negate our possibilities for becoming something else within a more humane social order (Sloan, 1996a).

In summary, the central task for personality theory is to disengage itself from the outset, in its most basic principles, from any participation in the continuing oppression of humankind by social forces that systematically reduce capacities for meaningful living. This goal implies intimate engagement with core issues related to the quality of life of diverse groups at the levels of both understanding and concerted action. As we move into the twenty-first century, some of the most pressing questions to be taken up by critical psychologists interested in personality are the following:

1   How can deep-set patterns of gender inequality be addressed at the psychological level? What institutional changes (in marriages, families, work settings) will be necessary to bring about true relational equality?
2   What sorts of processes will help individuals and groups distinguish between real needs and artificial needs manufactured by the culture industry?
3   What can psychologists do to support social movements that are likely to bring about greater social justice and equality?
4   What can be done to increase empathy and subsequent action to help people who suffer from poverty, war, natural disasters, and illness? What sorts of prevention can be accomplished without simply reinforcing the status quo?
5   How can alienation and ideologization be overcome? What psychological factors interfere with self-reflection, democratic decision making, and sense of community?
6   In the modern and postmodern social contexts, what are the possibilities for meaningful living? What social arrangements seem to be working for individuals, families, and communities? What constitutes meaningfulness in the first place?

These questions are, of course, just a few of the possible directions that might be pursued. Nevertheless, they indicate that theorizing about personality in a critical mode may inspire not only changes in psychological practice but radical transformation of the social order as well. I would add that being a critical psychologist also implies an ongoing willingness to call our own practices into question and to link our own local and global concerns as directly as possible to what we do professionally. This usually implies taking risks, breaking new ground, and enduring isolation. There is some consolation, however, in knowing that at least we are not part of the problem. We can also derive sustenance from the knowledge that we are not alone but are in fact participating in a vast collective effort – humanity's historic struggle for social justice.

7

Abnormal and Clinical Psychology: The Politics of Madness

Rachel T. Hare-Mustin and Jeanne Marecek

Editors' note   *Testing. Attention deficit disorder. Eating disorders. Self-esteem. Diagnosis. Treatment. Cultural sensitivity. DSM. Therapist. These terms are very much a part of our common discourse as abnormal and clinical psychology penetrate culture in countless ways. Reinforced by media portrayals of psychologists as therapists, many people assume that all psychologists are clinicians, and that a clinician's primary job is to "treat those whose behavior or personality is not "normal." Pressured in many countries by government and insurance company regulations, and influenced by the prestige of medical doctors, many clinicians adopt a medical "disease" model of psychological functioning. In this chapter, Rachel T. Hare-Mustin and Jeanne Marecek explore the meanings of these common terms and trends as they dissect the theories and practices of abnormal and clinical psychology.*

Using social historical evidence, Hare-Mustin and Marecek show how psychological diagnoses and interventions reinforce unjust social conditions. They analyze the place of values such as autonomy, human diversity, collaboration, and social justice in clinical psychology's discourse and practice. Paralleling arguments made elsewhere in this book, they question mainstream assumptions that norms based on white, middle-class North Americans should apply universally to other populations, and that dominant notions of the Good Life and the Good Society such as rugged individualism are the route to salvation for all.

Abnormal psychology's role in the oppression of women is one key example. Drawing from the fields of family therapy, feminism, psychoanalysis, and social constructionism, the authors expose clinical psychology's unreflective support of the status quo. Addressing the cultural origins of many so-called disorders, Hare-Mustin and Marecek help us see the connection between lack of political power and problems conventionally (and conveniently) defined as psychological rather than as political or social.

More than one hundred years ago a great man fell in love with a young actress. The problem was that he was married and had ten children. His solution was to insist that his wife was mentally ill, take away their children, and put her in an asylum. The man was a famous champion of home and hearth in his day, the author Charles Dickens.

In this same era, a mental disorder called neurasthenia afflicted large numbers of women, including many prominent social reformers and writers. A widely acclaimed "cure" for female neurasthenia, a pattern of behavior combining aspects of what today would be labeled chronic fatigue syndrome, premenstrual syndrome (PMS), and hysterical personality disorder, is described in Charlotte Perkins Gilman's autobiographical novella *The Yellow Wallpaper* (1892/1995). The treatment involved forced bed rest, deprivation of mental stimulation, isolation from adult company, and constant heavy feeding, leading to weight gains of fifty pounds or more. Gilman's heroine, rather than being restored, is made mad and driven to suicide.

When we look at abnormal and clinical psychology at the end of the nineteenth century, we can see how the fields reflected and reaffirmed the values of that historical epoch. We will argue that abnormal and clinical psychology today reflect the values of our time and place. Both fields are constituted not only by their social practices and academic ties, but also by the norms and values of late twentieth century European and North American culture. Although the modern era of treatment has been hailed by some for its humanitarian ideals and sensitivity to the rights of individuals, it falls short of such ideals when viewed from the perspective of women and other marginalized groups (Marecek and Hare-Mustin, 1991).

Social Construction of Psychological Knowledge

In this chapter, we use the framework of social construction to develop a critique of abnormal and clinical psychology (Berger and Luckman, 1966; Gergen, 1985b). Social construction holds that knowledge rests heavily on social consensus. Our social experiences and interactions shape what we take to be reality and what we regard as truth. Social construction emphasizes that language is not simply a mirror of reality or a neutral tool. Language has the power to structure social reality. It highlights certain features of the objects it represents and the situations and experiences it describes. Once a term becomes accepted in common use, it influences how we perceive the world. Consequently, in communicating with others and in generating ideas, the terms available to us constrain what we say and what we know. We not only use language, it uses us. How people talk about their experience determines what their experience is. Thus, a diagnostic label, such as "neurotic", has a profound influence on what we think of people so labeled and how they think about themselves.

The social context in which we live shapes knowledge, including psychological knowledge. The theories and practices of the mental health establishment at the turn of the century reflected and furthered certain cultural ideologies, as the opening examples show. Psychology today is an institution of late twentieth century culture; it reflects and reinforces the dominant cultural themes, ideologies, and preoccupations of our day.

Whose ideas and interests are reflected in diagnosis, treatment and practices, standards of mental health, and priorities for research? Who can speak authoritatively both within abnormal and clinical psychology and for those fields in the public arena? Who can decide what is the truth? Whose work is published and whose voices are heard? Language, as Roland Barthes (1972) has said, is a sign system used by the powerful to label, define, and rank. Meaning-making and control over language are important resources held by those in power, resources not distributed equitably across the social hierarchy. Meaning-making through language is concentrated within certain groups because of their preeminence in society and their influence on the print and electronic media. The meanings put forth can only be partial, because they exclude the experiences of many other groups. The dominant meanings maintain the status quo and justify the existing hierarchies of power and status (Hare-Mustin and Marecek, 1990).

In the fields of abnormal and clinical psychology, the power to determine what is normal and what is pathological contributes to a disciplinary regime (Foucault, 1980a). Categories of normality and abnormality define ideals of behavior, as well as which behaviors and actions are to be avoided in oneself and stigmatized in others. In this way the dominant meanings of "normal" and "abnormal" influence and constrain everyone's behavior. Dominant meanings are not the only meanings, although they may be the most visible and legitimated ones. There may be alternative ways of understanding experience, alternative interpretations of behavior, and alternative meanings put forth by groups such as working-class and poor people, women, and members of other nondominant cultural groups. These alternative accounts are key resources for developing a critical psychology. They are crucial both for challenging the status quo and for formulating new knowledge and improved practices. An important task of critical psychology is to bring such accounts forward to the attention of colleagues and students.

As you have already seen, "critical psychology" is a term that embraces many forms of critique. Both of us came to our stances as critics of the discipline initially through our engagement with feminism. We continue to be centrally concerned with psychology's knowledge base about women and gender and about problematic aspects of its relation to women, whether as workers in the field, as clients in therapy and counseling, or as students. Many of the examples and instances we describe in this chapter reflect these concerns. This is not meant to indicate that women constitute the only social group worthy of attention, or that the experiences of all women have been uniform or uniformly negative.

Diagnosis: Judging and Naming

Nearly all encounters with the mental health system start with an assessment of the client's difficulties. This assessment often results in a formal diagnosis. The central element of that diagnosis is the standardized name (or names) for the client's condition(s), for example, schizophrenia, panic disorder, or post-traumatic stress disorder.

The significance and import of a client's diagnosis depend on many things. For many psychotherapists what is important for treatment is their knowledge of clients' feelings and experiences; formal diagnosis is not of central importance or interest. However, when treatment recommendations involve the use of medications or the possibility of hospitalization, they are likely to be based on the formal diagnostic classification. Recently, as mental health care has become more routinized and corporatized in response to economic pressures, bureaucratic systems such as managed care have required clinicians to assign formal diagnostic categories. These diagnoses serve as the criteria for deciding "medical necessity," that is, which individuals deserve mental health treatment, what type of treatment they shall receive, and how much reimbursed treatment, if any, they shall receive.

The Diagnostic and Statistical Manual of Mental Disorders

At present, the *Diagnostic and Statistical Manual of Mental Disorders* (*DSM*) of the American Psychiatric Association (1994) is the standard compendium of diagnostic categories in the United States. Much of our analysis of the *DSM* would apply as well to other widely used diagnostic systems, such as the *International Classification of Diseases* (World Health Organization, 1978). As Mary Sykes Wylie puts it, the *DSM* "has become the official *lingua franca* for the entire culture and economy of the mental health establishment" (1995: 25). The first edition of the *DSM*, published in 1952, contained 198 categories of disorder. The second edition, published in 1968, listed 221 categories. The third edition, published in 1980, marked a dramatic shift in content and format, a shift that has been sustained through two subsequent revisions, 1987 and 1994. The number of diagnostic categories increased markedly, reaching 340 in 1994. In addition, the style and language of the manual became more medicalized. The text implies that psychological disorders are closely akin to physical disorders, and that they exist apart from the life situations and cultural backgrounds of those who experience them. We shall return to both these issues later, but for now, let us acknowledge some advantages of a formal and uniform diagnostic system.

Categorizing clients into diagnostic groups allows for the accumulation and integration of knowledge and experience over time, permitting generalizations to be drawn. Moreover, research on the causes and treatment of psychological problems requires some means of selecting a group of cases for study that are similar. For example, if we wish to study the family environment of adolescents who have suffered a schizophrenic breakdown, we must have a systematic and agreed-upon way of deciding which adolescents do and do not belong in our research sample. Furthermore, diagnostic categories provide workers in the field with a common language, so that they can communicate their ideas and the results of their research to one another.

Much care has gone into setting the criteria for diagnosing particular disorders. In the *DSM*, these criteria usually involve lists of symptoms. These typically consist of observations made by the diagnostician, as well as thoughts, feelings, and behaviors reported by the individual. To be useful, a diagnostic system must be reliable. That is, different diagnosticians using the system must agree in their diagnostic judgments. There have been extensive efforts to ensure the reliability of diagnostic assessments, but research reveals that clinicians often do not agree on diagnosis (Tavris, 1992). For example, American clinicians often make a diagnosis of schizophrenia for the same behaviors that in Britain are diagnosed as bipolar disorder (sometimes called manic-depression).

From the standpoint of social construction, we emphasize the extent to which diagnoses are products of their time and place. The relation of psychiatric diagnoses to culture, societal structure, and historical circumstance is readily apparent if we look at times and places other than our own. Before the emancipation of slaves in the United States, for example, the term "drapetomania" was promoted as a diagnostic label for slaves' uncontrollable urge to escape from slavery (Stampp, 1956). Another example is the diagnosis of kleptomania, which refers to an irresistible compulsion to shoplift or pilfer. The diagnostic term "kleptomania" originated in parallel with the emergence of large department stores in European cities at the turn of the century. These stores afforded shoppers – who were mainly women – anonymity, an array of tempting merchandise, and the freedom to touch and handle items for sale. This created not only incentives to purchase, but also temptations to steal. Shoppers of all social classes stole, but authorities used social class to distinguish criminal acts of theft from those purportedly reflecting mental pathology. To put it bluntly, ordinary women were regarded as thieves, but upper-class women's acts of theft were explained as a product of mental illness. The diagnosis of kleptomania excused their behavior, shielded them from criminal prosecution, and allowed the upper classes to maintain a posture of moral superiority (Camhi, 1993).

Both of these instances illustrate how what is taken to be a psychological disorder reflects the cultural and material conditions of the times. Moreover, these diagnoses reflected and furthered the interests of those in power (slave owners, the upper classes). In more recent times, the inclusion of homosexuality as a category of mental disorder in the *DSM* reaffirmed cultural and moral sanctions against nonheterosexual behavior. Homosexuality remained in the *DSM* until the 1980 revision. Another example is a category of diagnosis more or less equivalent to premenstrual syndrome (PMS), which is among the disorders added to the 1994 edition of the *DSM*. This category was included despite lengthy and strenuous opposition from many researchers, therapists, and pressure groups. They argued that the scientific rationale for including the diagnosis was flimsy at best, pointing to the lack of a clear-cut and consistent symptom picture, the difficulty of making reliable diagnoses, and the paucity of evidence on both causes and treatment (Parlee, 1989). There were also strong concerns that categorizing premenstrual difficulties as a mental disorder served to stigmatize women. Ultimately, the decision to regard any set of behaviors or experiences as a psychological disorder – rather than a medical disorder, an eccentricity, a criminal act, or a response to an oppressive and intolerable environment – is not and cannot be a scientific one. It is a political and moral decision, a judgment grounded in cultural perspectives as to which behaviors are acceptable or not acceptable.

Apart from the nature of specific categories, the proliferation of categories of mental disorders raises another concern. As categories of disorder multiply, more and more forms of behavior come to be seen as aberrant and in need of remedy. One effect is that more and more of our behavior is brought under critical scrutiny and regulation – both self-scrutiny and the scrutiny of expert authorities. Everyday unhappiness and ordinary shortcomings may come to be regarded as pathological, and possibly as indications of a need for professional treatment. Moreover, when individuals come to think of themselves in terms of a diagnostic category, they take on identities grounded on presumptions of deficiency and deviance. The popular misapplication and overuse of diagnostic labels (such as multiple personality disorder, post-traumatic stress disorder, and attention deficit disorder) have interpersonal and societal effects as well. In some instances, they may serve to excuse individuals for anti-social behavior (e.g. "I couldn't help it."). In other cases, the use of diagnostic labels serves little purpose other than to mystify everyday experience. Diagnoses may convey the impression of precision and scientific authority when, in fact, they do little more than substitute arcane professional jargon for everyday speech.

A further concern is that diagnostic labels locate the causes of the problem within the individual; this may foreclose consideration of the societal context and interpersonal relations as sources of unhappiness or dysfunction. A major goal of critical abnormal and clinical psychology is to redirect attention toward the social context, particularly to consideration of how the unequal distribution of resources and power across social groups contributes to personal distress and disability. Critical psychologists do not deny that biological factors contribute to some psychological problems. Rather, whether or not biological factors are involved, we insist that such problems are always situated in a social context. That is, the meanings attached to them, the moral evaluation made, and their consequences are inextricably linked to cultural, social, and historical circumstance. This is why the scholarly agenda of critical psychology emphasizes understanding disorders in their broad context. A good example of this is current feminist scholarship on eating problems, such as anorexia, bulimia, and compulsive eating and dieting.

From a feminist perspective, some key issues are why eating problems are gender-specific; why they are so prevalent in Europe and North America (especially the United States) but not elsewhere; why the number of women and girls experiencing eating problems has skyrocketed in recent years; and which groups of women and girls are at risk (cf. Striegel-Moore et al., 1986). To address these issues, feminists have looked closely at cultural and social views of women, the body, and heterosexual desire. One line of work documents how thinness has become a standard of feminine beauty in portrayals of women in the mass media and popular entertainment. Another line of analysis points out that women's bodies serve as vehicles for displaying the wealth and social power of the men to whom they are connected. A trim body – no less than expensive jewelry and apparel – serves to signify the upper-class membership or aspirations of a husband or father. Other scholars point out the persistent misconception that body size and weight are wholly a matter of individual will and self-control. Thus, women are enjoined to engage in continual surveillance over what they eat and how they look; to regulate, suppress, and master bodily appetites, rather than enjoy them. This emphasis on self-denial echoes traditional feminine virtues of sacrifice for others, modesty, and sexual restraint. Interested readers can explore these ideas further in recent works by Susan Bordo (1985), Carol Bloom et al. (1994), and Becky Thompson (1995).

Are Clinical Judgments Biased?

Concern for the rights and welfare of those in less privileged positions in society leads us to ask whether clinicians carry out assessments and make diagnoses without prejudice or bias. There are large disparities in apparent rates of many diagnoses across gender, ethnic, and social class lines. Of course, these disparities do not necessarily indicate biased diagnosis. They may reflect genuine differences in the distribution of these disorders in the population, differences stemming from different life experiences and access to economic and social resources. Nonetheless, some studies found that clinicians evaluating identical case protocols altered their diagnostic judgments in response to information about the gender, social class, racial identity, or lifestyle of the presumed patient (cf. Dumont, 1987; Landrine, 1989; Robertson and Fitzgerald, 1990). Moreover, given similar diagnoses and case descriptions, clinicians may make different treatment recommendations depending on the social characteristics of an individual. Thus, for example, many clinicians have been taught that individuals from lower-class backgrounds are unlikely to participate in or draw benefit from psychotherapy; hence such clinicians might overlook psychotherapy as a treatment option. In contrast, women from the middle class are over-represented among individuals referred for psychotherapy.

Both overdiagnosing and underdiagnosing have negative consequences. Overdiagnosing may occur because experiences and behaviors that are normative for a particular social group are regarded as signs of psychological disorder by the mental health professions. For example, feminist critics in the 1970s pointed out that the symptoms of so-called hysterical personality disorder closely resembled patterns of behavior and feeling that matched prevailing norms of femininity (Chesler, 1972).

Underdiagnosing refers to overlooking or minimizing a psychological condition. For example, distress and unhappiness may be labeled as "just a developmental phase" for an adolescent, or written off as hypochondriacal complaining for an elderly person, when in fact that individual is experiencing serious depression. Underdiagnosing may also occur when calling attention to an individual's condition would bring embarrassment or shame. For instance, alcohol abuse and drug abuse are likely to be underdiagnosed among women and middle-class individuals. This is especially true when the drugs of abuse are legal ones, prescribed by a physician. Underdiagnosing, of course, deprives individuals who are suffering of needed treatment that could bring relief.

How might psychologists work to counteract tendencies toward biased diagnosis? Because the biases that we point out are not simply individual acts of error or ill will, we think that individual efforts to be fair and unbiased will not suffice. Rather, we look to solutions that involve collective efforts. For example, if individuals from all cultural and social backgrounds were represented within the ranks of the mental health profession, challenges to biased beliefs and stereotypes would be mounted more readily. Thus, efforts to recruit such individuals to the profession are important. Kiwi Tamasese and Charles Waldegrave (1996) have developed an accountability model in their clinical work in New Zealand; it involves a dialogue in which those in dominant gender and cultural groups listen to the collective voices of the other groups.

Mental health professionals have often been dismissive of self-help efforts and at loggerheads with self-help and other lay groups. Yet the experiences and grassroots understanding of such groups could provide valuable insights and a perspective not otherwise available. Finally, critical psychologists' efforts to reconstruct psychology are aimed not only at altering its knowledge base, but also at reshaping its foundational assumptions. Many critical psychologists have strong doubts about psychology's presumptions of universals of human behavior that transcend time, place, and circumstance. Such doubts open the way for more particular, context-sensitive forms of knowledge to emerge. In this way, psychologists may come to regard the experiences of individuals from nonprivileged and nondominant sectors of society as an important part of their knowledge base.

The Ideological Pull of Diagnoses

Diagnoses are not just neutral labels. They constitute a system of interpretation and meaning that directs attention to certain issues and relegates others to the periphery. Current diagnostic systems are based on a medical model. They use the language and assumptions of medicine metaphorically to describe and understand psychological and psychosocial difficulties. As in physical medicine, the focus is on the individual in isolation; disorders are defined in terms of symptoms and syndromes within the individual. Thought of as symptoms, the behaviors, thoughts, and emotions that characterize a disorder are viewed as outward manifestations of an internal, underlying problem, akin to a disease. Treatment efforts in such a model focus narrowly on reducing symptoms.

We note that the *DSM*'s shift to a medicalized frame of reference coincided with the shift to conservativism in national politics in the United States and elsewhere that began in the 1980s and continues to the present. By framing psychological disorders as counterparts of physical illness, the *DSM* focuses clinicians' attention on the individual separated from the social context. It downplays the potent negative effects of discriminatory treatment, urban disarray, widening social and economic inequalities, and the growing impoverishment of the poor and working classes. In this way, the mental health professions help conceal the costs incurred to society when wealth is concentrated among a privileged few and when the state relinquishes its commitment to the welfare of the least fortunate members of society.

Some alternative voices have been heard, voices that advocate a classificatory system that includes attention to the social context of people's lives. Many family systems therapists (e.g. Bloch, 1988) have long favored a psychosocial model highlighting the interaction of individual personality factors with social groups and social conditions as the basis for understanding behavior. For example, considerable research has focused on the ways families influence the health and well-being of their members (cf. Ransom and Fisher, 1995).

Nevertheless, the *DSM* has become the preeminent organizing rubric not only for diagnosing patients in the mental health system, but also for textbooks of psychiatry and psychology, for deciding on insurance reimbursements, and for much government-funded mental health research (cf. Marecek, 1993). This reliance on a single point of view, which has come to have the status of law, should raise concern, no matter what its content. Such apparent unanimity seals off opportunities for intellectual debate and dialogue from which new ideas flow and deeper insights are generated.

Psychological Interventions

A teenage girl with a persistent cough and headaches says her father's friend has been making sexual advances to her when she has accompanied her father on his visits to the other family. No one believes her. Her father takes her to a therapist and tells him to bring her to her senses. The therapist was Sigmund Freud, the founder of psychoanalysis, and the patient, Dora (Freud, 1905/1963). The case of Dora is one of the most frequently cited cases in the psychoanalytic literature (Hare-Mustin, 1991; 1994).

The Case of Dora

Dora's father often took her along to the K. household where he was having an affair with Frau K. The husband, Herr K., had been making sexual advances to Dora since she was fourteen, apparently encouraged by Dora's father. Dora's mother maintained the standards of housekeeping expected of a Viennese *hausfrau* of her day, and although Freud never met Dora's mother, he did not hesitate to diagnose her as having a "housewife's psychosis." It is a "diagnosis" not included among the standard categories.

Freud, from his patriarchal perspective, assumed that any young girl would appreciate the attentions of a man like Herr K., be flattered by them, and accede to them. Freud regarded Dora's symptoms as signs of hysteria resulting from her aroused and disguised sexual desire. When he tried to press his views on Dora, she quit therapy, leading Freud to label her as not only disturbed, but also disagreeable, untruthful, and vengeful. The adults involved acknowledged some time later that her claims about Herr K. were true.

Some of Freud's ideas have persisted among clinicians to this day, especially notions that the seduced girl is the seducer, that the seduced female is aroused and flattered by male advances, that women are untruthful, and that the female is a psychologically defective male. Historically, when theorists within psychoanalysis attempted to raise contrary views, their ideas were not well received. Karen Horney, for example, took issue with Freud's accounts of female development, pointing out how the ideas put forth by psychoanalysts resembled the naive assumptions of small boys (1926/1967). She was publicly castigated and permanently expelled from membership in professional institutes (Garrison, 1981). Fortunately, today, feminist scholars within and outside psychoanalysis in the United States, France, and the United Kingdom are engaged in vibrant efforts to reassess and reconstruct a psychoanalytic psychology of gender. Prominent among these scholars are Jessica Benjamin (1988), Nancy Chodorow (1994; 1995), Virginia Goldner (1991), and Luce Irigaray (1985).

Focus on the Individual

Traditional psychotherapies involve a client meeting with a clinician in an ongoing one-to-one encounter. The goal is to relieve distress and disability, often by transforming the meanings a client ascribes to events or altering a client's behavior. The aim is to mute the pain of everyday life.

Conventional approaches to treating psychological problems – whether psychotherapy or drug therapy – focus on the individual as the locus of problems. This focus deflects attention away from the role of societal conditions in generating some problems and in exacerbating or even

ameliorating other problems. Moreover, conventional approaches unreflec-
tively incorporate certain ideals and norms of contemporary culture,
including its focus on autonomy, the importance of personal identity, and
self-fulfillment through individual achievement and material acquisition
(Cushman, 1995). Autonomy has been regarded as an indication of maturity
and psychological health in Western societies, and as such, has been a goal
of much of psychological treatment. Yet not all members of society may
hold to these ideals and goals. Such ideals may be antithetical to the
communitarian values of the working class in some societies and to traditions of interdependence, family solidarity, and mutuality of many cultural
groups (Hill Collins, 1990; Stack, 1974). Moreover, the life circumstances of
some individuals may render such ideals unattainable or detrimental. When
therapists wittingly or unwittingly impose such ideals on their clients, they
run the risk of doing harm (Hare-Mustin and Marecek, 1986).

Clinicians' judgments about effective ways of coping with crises and
adversity too often presume that middle-class privileges of social power and
resources are available to all. Those in professional classes may hold an
unquestioned belief in societal benevolence and social justice, a belief that
the experiences of poor people and people on the margins of society do not
always confirm. For individuals with little claim to material resources and
social power, many ways of coping available to middle-class and upper-
class people may be unavailable or even counterproductive (Belle, 1994;
Fine, 1992b).

The presumption underlying most forms of treatment is that what is
wrong lies within the individual, and external conditions do not need to be
addressed or modified. Traditional treatment approaches take as their task
helping people adjust to their circumstances rather than transforming those
circumstances that contribute to and are part of the problem. For example,
therapists may view the stress many workers experience from the demands
of greedy occupations and the alienating structures of advanced capitalism
as an individual problem. They may offer workers such stress-reduction
techniques as exercise, relaxation, meditation, and medication.

Similarly, many marital therapists assume that nothing is wrong with the
institution of marriage. When couples come for help, therefore, they
presume something is wrong with the partners in the marriage. However, in
our era the institution of marriage has become burdened by exaggerated
visions of romantic fulfillment and self-enhancement. Marriage is also
expected to cushion and be an outlet for frustrations in the public arena,
such as economic problems, a sense of social powerlessness, and lack of
recognition and affirmation from the community. These conditions contribute to the tension and violence in marriage, including wife battering and
child abuse. Violence in the family is such in the United States that it is
safer for women and children in the streets than in the home (Goldner
et al., 1990; Roesch et al., 1990; Yllo and Bograd, 1988). Moreover,
marital therapists sometimes overlook the problems caused by the con-
stricting roles of both men and women in marriage and the gender

inequality in which women have less domestic, economic, or political power than men (Goodrich, 1991). Instead therapists may content themselves with teaching clients how to "communicate" with their partners.

The Power Hour

Within the therapy situation, the therapist is the authority and thus wields the power of expertise. This has led some to ruefully label the therapy session "the power hour," and to criticize therapy as a form of social control (Green, 1995). Therapists who are sensitive to power imbalances in therapy have sought ways to share power with clients, and to check the tendency to regard the therapist as the authority (e.g. Zimmerman and Dickerson, 1996).

Some feminist therapists have argued that being in a one-down position *vis-à-vis* a therapist stifles opportunities for women in therapy to develop assertiveness and self-confidence. If women's empowerment is a goal of therapy, they reason, then the process of therapy should itself be empowering (e.g. Avis, 1991). To this end, some feminist therapists have worked to heighten their awareness of the operation and deployment of power in therapy, and to modify their approaches as much as possible (Perelberg and Miller, 1990). Some make efforts to diminish the social distance between themselves and their clients. For instance, some take care to make the therapy setting relaxed and informal. Some have challenged older strictures against personal disclosure by responding to clients' requests for biographic information or by occasionally offering accounts of their own experiences. Others have taken strides to position the client as an informed consumer, rather than a patient who submits to the doctor's orders (Hare-Mustin et al., 1979).

Psychotherapy necessarily involves a relationship in which an individual who is unable to relieve his or her pain seeks the help of a culturally sanctioned expert. As such, the therapy relationship is inevitably characterized by differences in expertise, authority, and power. Nonetheless, therapists can be vigilant about limiting the extent of power differences, encouraging clients to recognize and exercise what power and authority they do have. Notable advances in this direction have been made by Michael White and David Epston (1990) in Australia and New Zealand. In addition, the therapeutic professions, acting through their ethical boards and training committees, can call attention to and condemn abuses of power in the therapy setting (e.g. Hare-Mustin, 1992).

Alternative Approaches to Treatment

Some approaches to treatment have tried to situate psychological problems in the broader social context and address that context (see McLean et al., 1996, for work with men). Such approaches include forms of feminist therapy that question the social norms and demands of conventional femininity and masculinity (Brown, 1994; Mirkin, 1994; Worrell and

Riemer, 1992). Among family therapists, feminists insist on two further points: that therapists should stop blaming mothers for a multitude of problems (Caplan and Hall-McCorquodale, 1985) and that clinicians should ask men to change as much as women.

Family therapists work with entire families. They utilize theories of change and strategies of therapy that regard the problems as arising from the family as an interacting system rather than from a single member. Within family therapy, critics have tried to shift away from theories that blame families for their problems (McGoldrick et al., 1989; Walters et al., 1988). Some clinicians working with African Americans, Hispanic Americans, and Asian Americans have attended to cultural values and the social context of such families. For example, Insoo Kim Berg and Ajakai Jaya (1993) have pointed out the importance of Asian values of negotiation and "face saving." José Szapocznik and William Kurtines (1993) have made explicit the family and cultural context in working with Hispanic youth. Nancy Boyd-Franklin (1989) has identified the place of fictive kin as family members for many African American families.

Another alternative to traditional therapy is the psychoeducational model of intervention, which positions the clinician as more of an educator and collaborator with the client than an expert in a one-up position (Anderson et al., 1986). The model regards the client (or in some cases his or her family) as a collaborator in the intervention rather than as part of the problem. In the treatment of severe and chronic mental illness, psychoeducational programs aimed at family members and patients focus on such features as the importance of taking medication as prescribed, management of relapses, and coming to terms with the prospects of permanent diminished functioning. Even for conditions that appear to have a strong biological component, these programs emphasize the significance of the social environment in determining the course of the disorder, as well as the crucial role that supportive and knowledgeable others play in the individual's well-being and equilibrium (Goldstein et al., 1978; McFarlane, 1983).

Social change efforts were prominent in the community mental health movement of the 1960s and 1970s. That era saw the establishment of storefront clinics and other mental health resources in poor urban locales that had been underserved. Prevention of problems was the aim: early intervention strategies such as family education and childcare, as well as political action and community organizing, were directed at reducing the risk of mental disorders. In that period, numerous self-help groups, as well as client advocacy and consumer rights groups, also appeared. With community-based care available, it was often possible for individuals with chronic mental illnesses to remain in the community rather than be confined in mental hospitals. Unfortunately, when government funding for community mental health programs was withdrawn, deinstitutionalized mental patients often found themselves without treatment and among the homeless and destitute. Chapter 11, which discusses community psychology, describes in more detail the community mental health movement, its promises and its problems.

Questioning Values in Treatment

Therapy as a resource for those in distress is not distributed equally across social groups. Because it involves time and money, therapy is reserved for those with the economic means and a lifestyle sufficiently unchaotic to meet regular weekly appointments. Managed care approaches, which emphasize limitations on cost, typically support forms of treatment that are brief and can be administered by individuals with limited training (Wylie, 1994). Such treatments can have only limited goals. Moreover, they are not designed to – and cannot – address the complexity of the social situation.

Clinical psychology has not escaped the demand for cost savings and the medicalization of the mental health field. This can be seen in the recent push by some psychologists to be allowed to prescribe medication. Drug treatments for psychological problems can be useful interventions, but their goal is often limited to getting people back on their feet in order to return to their customary level of functioning. This leaves problematic interpersonal situations and societal conditions unchanged.

Assumptions of Knowledge

Traditional standards for knowledge production in abnormal and clinical psychology are based on the conventional notion that the researcher is and can be an unbiased, disinterested, and value-free observer. Social construction, however, argues that such a stance is impossible to attain. Every researcher is guided by implicit and explicit rules and assumptions about what is considered a reasonable and legitimate way of interpreting the world. The questions asked, the populations studied, the methods used reflect these rules, which appear objective and thus avoid critical scrutiny. By seeking a single best account of reality, and by searching for single causes of psychological disorders, researchers may selectively disregard diverse accounts, disconfirming evidence, and alternative views of human experience. Furthermore, when a single authoritative standard is enshrined in the *DSM* and in textbooks and journals of clinical psychology, alternative knowledges are closed off (Marecek, 1993).

Much of the knowledge in abnormal and clinical psychology is couched in universal terms. That is, theories are presumed to pertain to everyone, irrespective of social group membership, cultural background, and life history. As in psychology generally, the goal is to establish universal principles of behavior, not to identify group differences. Furthermore, researchers tend to avoid studying individuals who are difficult to locate, who are presumed to be unreliable informants, or who may not be forthcoming or cooperative respondents. Thus, studies of white, middle-class, urban-dwelling, educated individuals are overrepresented as the basis for psychological knowledge. The results of such studies are generalized to "people in general." In contrast, when individuals from other social groups are studied, such studies are automatically regarded as studies of "special populations," and wider generalizations are not attempted.

A further problem in the acquisition of psychological knowledge is the neglect of everyday experiences and identities. Instead research focuses on abstracted categories and measurements. Psychology as a field has privileged ahistorical and decontextualized investigations of behavior, ideally conducted in laboratory situations. Although the applied nature of clinical psychology pulls researchers toward consideration of real-world events, the disciplinary demands of psychology exert counter-pressures. There is little psychological research concerned with broad social and economic conditions that function as stressors. Nonetheless, some promising starts have been made. For example, Deborah Belle (1994) has addressed the effects of poverty on low-income single mothers in the urban United States. Pamela Reid (1993) has drawn attention to the way poor women's experiences are excluded from attention in psychological research and practice. A number of researchers, such as Constance Ahrons (1994), have studied the impact of divorce on individuals and families. Ignacio Martín-Baró (1991), before he was murdered by those he accused, documented the effects of political repression and torture in Central America. Oliva Espin (forthcoming), herself a Cuban immigrant, has written about the experience of immigration and exile. Lillian Comas-Díaz and Mary Jansen (1995) have drawn attention to the oppressive conditions of women throughout the world, including the effects of war and state-sponsored violence. Arlie Hochschild (1989) and Lucia Gilbert (1993), among others, have written about the stress experienced in the home with two working parents. Other researchers have studied the effects of unemployment and layoffs on personal well-being and family stress (see Osipow and Fitzgerald, 1993, for a review of this literature).

As we have pointed out, different segments of the population may have different values and standards of behavior, and judgments of normality and abnormality may not be universally shared. Indeed, ways of acting and thinking that are adaptive and perhaps even imperative for survival under one set of social and economic circumstances may appear pathological or deviant to those living in other circumstances. One's social location influences patterns of behaving, relating, and coping. This leads us to question what the standards of normality and abnormality should be and also the wisdom of setting universal standards at all.

Toward Becoming a Critical Psychologist

Critical psychology is less a matter of mastering a body of knowledge than mastering a set of practices that reflect a critical and skeptical attitude. We offer some guidelines that may help you hone your critical skills as you pursue your studies of abnormal and clinical psychology.

1 When you read about disordered behavior or its treatment, ask yourself about generalizability. That is, how widely do the authors' statements apply? Who were the participants in the research on which a statement is based? Are individuals from other cultural backgrounds and with other social characteristics likely to be different? What are the differences that might occur because of factors like age and gender?

2 Look for gaps in coverage of a topic. What issues are not considered? For example, does a discussion of a mental disorder include a consideration of the social, political, and economic circumstances that are likely to affect the risk for the disorder or the outcome of treatment?

3 Do not attend to deficit and disorder to the exclusion of human resilience and ability to cope. Can symptoms be better understood as an individual's efforts to cope or as a way of managing a difficult life transition or situation, when other avenues are closed off?

4 Ask whether deficiencies or qualities described as individual characteristics might better be explained as behaviors emerging out of a particular situation or context. Instead of asking "What groups are at risk for mental disorders?" a better question might be "What are the life circumstances that are shared by people at risk?"

5 Raise questions about psychological interventions. Are they, should they be, can they be value-free? Do the goals of treatment reflect the perspectives of a relatively homogeneous group from privileged backgrounds? Do treatments uphold the status quo, while masquerading under the guise of value neutrality? To uphold the status quo is as value-laden as to challenge it.

6 Ask how the well-being of *all* members of society can be achieved. What social arrangements are needed? Who participates in constructing the vision of normality and the good life? Who is left out? What personal values and ethical commitments must prevail if those who are disabled or unable to function because of mental disorders are to have a decent and humane life?

Conclusion: Toward the Future

Many abnormal and clinical psychologists think that mental health care is at a crossroads. Issues facing the field concern human welfare and the public interest, as well as the future of the profession. Cuts in public and private funds have placed treatment out of the reach of many needy individuals. Moreover, managed care systems infringe on clients' privacy and on therapists' professional autonomy and professional judgment as well. Many practitioners feel betrayed by the systems in which they work. In their judgment, they can no longer provide clients with adequate care.

At the same time, the mental health establishment is under pressure from various directions to substitute reliance on medication for more expensive forms of treatment, such as hospitalization and psychotherapy. Clinical psychologists – who historically have not been licensed to prescribe medications – have registered a range of reactions to these pressures. Some have sought prescribing privileges alongside psychiatrists, physicians, and allied health professionals. But others argue against succumbing to pressures to medicate. They question the adequacy of medications as the sole treatment for most disorders. In addition, they argue that it is important to preserve and further the distinctive knowledge of human behavior that psychology has developed, as well as its approaches to therapy and assessment. The issue is a bone of contention among clinicians.

The burgeoning influence of popular psychology and the expansion of professional activities into many areas of private and public life is another area of controversy. Some critics argue that psychology has oversold itself. The extravagant claims on behalf of psychotherapy in some quarters have led to an overblown faith in it. Others are dismayed by the growth of radio and television talk shows, self-help books, and pop-psych sloganeering, as well as the willingness of some psychologists to make dubious claims of expert knowledge and authority. The focus on personal life and self-advancement dominates today's popular discourse.

The immediate future is likely to see both dissent and political mobilization among abnormal and clinical psychologists. We hope that both dissent and activism go beyond narrow self-interest and guild issues. Times of ferment, disagreement, and challenge can be important moments for self-reflection, change, and progress. In crafting this chapter, we hoped to add impetus to movements in psychology for self-scrutiny and reassessment. Our goal for a critical abnormal and clinical psychology is to shift the terms of the dialogue to encompass debates about the profession's role in promoting the common good, its responsibilities for civic life and social welfare, and the role of the mental health professions in achieving social justice.

8

A Critical Look at
Intelligence Research

Zack Z. Cernovsky

Editors' note   *In this chapter, Zack Z. Cernovsky brings up to date the debates over the science and politics of IQ described by Benjamin Harris in Chapter 2. Cernovsky offers the study and measurement of intelligence as a case study of the gap between critique and practice.*

Anyone working in clinical settings knows the pervasive use and impact of intelligence tests. Scientific-sounding "intelligence quotient" scores are used to expand or limit educational opportunities, place children in special education classes, and justify hiring and firing employees. Policy makers use IQ scores to blame the victim: they point to racially biased results as proof that social interventions fail because "it's all in the genes." Although, as Cernovsky details, there is little scientific basis for measuring intelligence in a valid way, psychologists continue to do so. This causes immense damage to individuals and groups who are stigmatized as intellectually inferior by psychological tests that are given more credibility than they deserve.

A challenge for critical psychologists in clinical settings is to learn how to resist institutional practices perpetuating the use of discriminatory assessment tools. Even when results are used for benevolent purposes in the short run, labels have a life of their own, triggering self-fulfilling prophecies and perpetuating negative stereotypes. Beyond the implications for the individual, psychologists should weigh the moral repercussions of legitimizing definitions and tools that are ultimately oppressive, even when they help individual clients obtain needed services.

Focusing on the pursuit of knowledge, Cernovsky exposes the biases and errors of influential researchers as they collect and interpret their data. As emphasized in other chapters, subjectivity and political interests permeate research – just as they permeate the public's willingness to accept certain results and reject others. Cernovsky helps us uncover these factors in intelligence research and policy from the days of the eugenics movement, when IQ tests categorized Southern and Eastern European immigrants to North America as feeble-minded, to today, when books like The Bell Curve *resuscitate racist impulses in an increasingly conservative era.*

Psychology's support for an unjust status quo has taken many forms over the years. As noted in several chapters in this book, one important form is the use of psychological tests to explain – in effect, to justify – a lack of societal equality. Administering and interpreting intelligence tests are primary examples of how the routine work of mainstream psychologists can hinder progress toward social justice. Because psychological tests are "research tools," the public often assumes that their results or interpretations are infallible. This assumption is a mistake, one with serious negative consequences for members of groups seen as "genetically inferior" as "proven" by "science."

Psychologists, educators, psychiatrists, and the lay public often misunderstand intelligence as consisting exclusively or primarily of the skills assessed by modern tests of intelligence. These IQ (intelligence quotient) tests have an excessively narrow focus on skills and tasks acquired and rehearsed in the process of formal or informal schooling. The narrow focus prevents these tests from detecting other crucial ingredients of intelligence such as creativity or social intelligence (the ability to understand, accurately perceive, and influence emotional states and social behavior of others).

These IQ test limitations have historical roots. The first generally accepted intelligence test was devised for school settings by Binet and Simon in France at the dawn of the twentieth century. This test assessed skills expected of school children of different ages. Its purpose was to serve as an objective criterion for sifting out children considered retarded (to be placed in special classes) and for placing other children at their appropriate grade level (see historical background in Fancher, 1985). Binet's test items were later extended for use with adults.

Today, the items of adult IQ tests still remain pervasively based on school-related skills. The test taker and the test administrator usually follow roles analogous to those of a school teacher and a pupil at exams. These roles encompass various implicit requirements specific to Western culture, as noted below.

In this chapter, I discuss underlying conceptual and methodological issues in contemporary research on human intelligence. A major obstacle in intelligence research is the use of *inadequate measurement tools*. Another obstacle is the frequently encountered static view of intelligence as biologically transmitted via genes and *relatively immutable* (unchangeable) during the lifetime. Many psychologists also treat intelligence as a *unidimensional* phenomenon, reducible to a single IQ measure. This unidimensional approach fails to adequately explore creativity, one of the most vital aspects of intelligence. Contemporary fashionable "academic" trends such as J. Philippe Rushton's and Richard Lynn's reports on genetically based "racial differences" in intelligence are often based on an archaic or *incompetent methodology*. Those who follow these trends will miss the opportunity to more fully use the human potential for economic and emotional benefit of all involved.

Misinterpreting Intelligence Test Scores

The intelligence test interpreter typically assumes that the test taker is motivated to make the best possible effort. However, this motivation to succeed and excel may be relatively weak or even absent in some segments of our society. In addition, test items traditionally are imbued rather exclusively with the mainstream culture of the country where the test was developed. In some cases, intelligence tests measure the extent to which the individual is familiar with that particular cultural tradition rather than the test taker's cognitive talents *per se*. For instance, questions such as "Who was the American president during the Second World War?" have limited validity for assessing intelligence outside North American mainstream culture. Items assessing arithmetic skills or rote memory (memorizing series of digits comparable to telephone or fax numbers or postal codes) may also be less relevant in cultures where numeric coding is less pervasive.

Some psychologists misinterpret tests such as the Raven's Progressive Matrices as measures of fluid intelligence, relatively independent of formal schooling. Yet the Raven's Matrices obviously contain items that can be solved more easily by persons trained in geometry or in algebraic formulae involving negative and positive numbers. These tests are of dubious value if administered to persons raised within a dramatically dissimilar culture. The traditional Eskimo, the rural Chinese, Tibetans from remote and relatively inaccessible villages, disadvantaged South African blacks, or US blacks and Latinos isolated in a ghetto would likely perform better on items whose content is more consistent with their well rehearsed normal daily activities.

Multiple subcultural discrepancies between the test taker and the test developer or test interpreter often prevent IQ scores from adequately reflecting human intellectual potential. Some of these discrepancies were extensively discussed by Dalton Miller-Jones (1989). Noteworthy is the particular use of language in specific sociocultural environments. For example, in response to the item "What is a hat?," the child raised in a poverty stricken ghetto subculture may reply with action-related elementary words such as "you put it on your head." This response is more adaptive in the particular subculture than a dictionary or encyclopedia style definition expected by IQ tests. The dictionary style response could lead to misunderstandings or provoke the disapproval of significant others.

Classical textbooks of psychological testing have warned that "it is unlikely that any test can equally be fair to more than one cultural group" (Anastasi, 1988: 357). Numerous academic psychologists still misinterpret IQ scores from other cultures as indicating genetic inferiority of these groups. For example, Richard Lynn extensively relies, in his postulate of racial inferiority of blacks, on tests such as the Raven's Matrices used in African settings (see critique by Leo Kamin, 1995). Those who defend Lynn's position may argue that blacks are in poverty stricken ghettos because of their genetically inferior intelligence and that their lifestyle and economic condition are a consequence of inborn intellectual inferiority.

This circular reasoning ignores the value of high-quality formal schooling or the impact of conveniences available rather exclusively for the upper socioeconomic class, such as CD-ROM equipped computers or frequent travel to other countries.

These misinterpretations of scores on IQ tests have a long history. Some of the psychologists involved in assessing immigrants on their arrival to the United States in the first half of this century interpreted low test scores as a sign of feeble-mindedness. The prominent psychologist Henry Goddard reported extremely high rates of mental retardation for several immigrant groups (Jews, Italians, and Russians) and concluded that "One can hardly escape the conviction that the intelligence of the average third class immigrant is low, perhaps of the moron grade" (1917: 243). Similar misleading claims typically have been associated with a reliance on poor methods and blatantly nonrepresentative samples. For example, Goddard himself admitted that his data were only from six small highly selected groups. Many of these immigrants were not sufficiently familiar with English or psychological tests to comprehend what was happening during the assessments. Psychologists naively considered nonverbal instructions for these IQ tests as adequate, on the untested assumption that nonverbal communication does not differ from culture to culture.

IQ Scores as Indicators of Criminality?

As mentioned by Evans and Waites (1981), American psychologists often misinterpreted IQ scores as an indicator of criminal potential. According to Terman, "all feeble-minded are at least potential criminals. That every feeble-minded woman is a potential prostitute would be hardly disputed by any one. Moral judgement, like business judgement, social judgement, or any other kind of higher thought process, is a function of intelligence" (1919: 11). Goddard's (1917) article on feeble-mindedness among non-Anglo-Saxon immigrants to the United States may have contributed to the subsequent application of very restrictive immigration quotas. Countless refugees and dissidents in German Nazi or Soviet dominated territory perished during World War II and the postwar decades as a result of these quotas.

Heritability of IQ Scores?

Both genetic factors and environmental factors may determine the level, style, and content of adult intellectual functioning. The environmental influences include both psychosocial influences (such as parental stimulation, formal education, peer pressure) and biological influences (such as nutrition, climate, bacteria, and environmental toxins). There have been numerous attempts to determine the relative contribution of the genetic and environmental factors. Despite these efforts, no scientist has succeeded so far in offering a generally accepted theoretical solution for determining the extent of heritability of intelligence. Published estimates of its heritability vary between the statistically feasible extremes. However, the underlying procedures are based on false premises and dubious statistical methodology (see Crusio, 1990; Roubertoux and Capron, 1990a; 1990b; Schonemann, 1989; 1990; 1992; 1995; Taylor, 1980). The case of the British psychologist Sir Cyril Burt is instructive.

During and after World War II, Burt was revered as an authority on the question of heritability of intelligence. Favoring hereditary over environmental explanations, he supported his opinion with data from studies comparing IQ score similarity of monozygotic (i.e., identical) twins with their genetically less closely related siblings. Burt's particular merit seemingly consisted in gathering the largest set of data on identical twins who were raised separately. According to Burt, these twins were separated in early childhood and raised in different socioeconomic environments. His data, if credible, would have helped to tentatively explore the relative contribution of environments and of genes to adult human intelligence (for historical background, see Fancher, 1985; Hearnshaw, 1979).

Burt's methodology was generously and uncritically praised by several politically influential figures within academic psychology such as Hans Eysenck and Arthur Jensen. After Burt's death, however, closer scrutiny of his work by Leon Kamin (1974; 1981) suggested carelessness and fraud. For instance, Burt was so negligent in his research reports that he even failed to indicate which intelligence tests he used to measure intelligence. Burt also published his papers with co-authors ("Miss Conway") who could never be located. These "co-authors" were totally unknown in the institution listed as their place of employment. They were also unknown to members of the scientific community of that time. They were probably invented by Burt to render his research claims more plausible.

Burt also reported findings of almost identical (and in some cases identical) correlation coefficients for twin samples of gradually increasing size. Since IQ tests are not a precise tool, it is unlikely that an identical IQ will be obtained even when retesting the same person over time. The likelihood of repeatedly obtaining the same or almost identical coefficients while increasing the sample size in Burt's studies is extremely small. Burt also reported that the socioeconomic status of the adoptive households for the twin pairs (supposedly rated by Burt on a six-point scale) was uncorrelated. This would indicate that the twins were distributed rather randomly to families from various socioeconomic strata. This is a methodologically improbable situation: under normal circumstances, separated twins are likely to be placed into at least partly comparable adoptive environments. These methodologically and statistically suspect aspects of Burt's data (see more details in Kamin, 1974; 1981) as well as Burt's reluctance to let other researchers inspect his raw data strongly suggest an uncomfortable conclusion: Burt may have fraudulently manufactured the data to support his belief that intelligence is largely inherited.

Burt's charismatic impact on British social policies adversely affected millions of children in the United Kingdom. According to Fancher, Burt testified to British government committees that children's intelligence levels were largely fixed by the age of eleven or so, and were accurately measurable by standard tests given at that age. Thus Burt's was one of several influential voices which helped produce the so-called "eleven plus" examination system in Britain, under which all eleven-year-olds were given a series of academic and intelligence tests, the results of which streamed the top-scoring minority into intellectually demanding "grammar schools" and the majority into the less challenging "modern schools." It was virtually impossible for a child to move from a modern to a grammar school, and grammar school training was required for eventual acceptance into a university. (1985: 176)

Ironically, Burt was promoted to prominent positions within British academic psychology, including chair at the University College of London. As editor of the *British Journal of Statistical Psychology*, he was able to fill the journal with his own numerous articles, some of which were extremely lengthy and had not the remotest connection with statistical or any other branch of mathematical psychology (Hearnshaw, 1979). His various academic and editorial positions provided him with ample opportunities to selectively promote students with similar hereditarian views: if he were likely to select and promote his protégés on the basis of their personal political views rather than on the basis of their methodological skills, we now may have an aging generation of academic psychologists artificially promoted by his charismatic influence as well as subsequent generations of those similarly promoted by Burt's former protégés. These underlying phenomena could partly explain the contemporary boom of sociobiological or behavior genetics publications in which "heritabilities" are calculated for a wide range of behaviors on the basis of dubious statistical models and unrealistic methodological assumptions (see criticisms presented by Crusio, 1990; Flynn, 1987a; Roubertoux and Capron, 1990a; 1990b; Schonemann, 1989; 1990; 1992; 1995; Taylor, 1980; Wahlsten, 1994).

Thomas Bouchard has been represented by journalists in the last decades as one of the most prominent investigators into heritability of behavior and intelligence. However, both his hereditarian views and his reluctance to submit his twin data from heritability studies to an independent inspection by peer scientists (see Horgan, 1993) are largely reminiscent of Cyril Burt. Without peer scrutiny, research data have very little scientific value.

Environmental Influences

It is important to emphasize that the static concept of intelligence as primarily genetic in origin conflicts with evidence of a massive increase in IQ scores from one generation to the next. According to Flynn (1987b), data from fourteen economically advanced nations indicate IQ gains ranging from five to twenty-five points in a single generation. This intergenerational increase suggests there are powerful environmental influences that affect performance on tasks typically included in IQ tests. This increase is frequently ignored both by authors of contemporary introductory psychology textbooks and by researchers who study human intellectual potential.

There are other examples of environmental factors in IQ differences. For example, low brain weight found in some old data on blacks from hot African countries could be related to relative infant malnutrition rather than to genetic racial differences. The detrimental impact of malnutrition on brain development has been documented by Monckeberg (1973). Malnutrition affects not only brain and head size but also intelligence. For instance, the quality and quantity of nutritional intake in 153 Egyptian infants aged between eighteen and thirty months was found to be correlated with their intellectual performance at twenty-four months: infants with more adequate nutrition fared better (Wachs et al., 1993). Recent studies on adults suggest that even skipping breakfast may result in relatively inferior performance on subsequent cognitive tasks such as those from Cattel's Culture Fair test (Spring et al., 1992).

At present, black parents tend to be younger than white parents at the birth of their first child. Black parents also more frequently have larger families, thus having more later-born children. Statistical reviews by Storfer (1990) show that, on average, children of younger parents have lower IQs than those of older parents and that later-born children from large families have lower IQs than those born first. According to Storfer, these and related factors could explain a large part of IQ discrepancies reported in some comparisons of black and white children.

Unidimensional View of Intelligence

Measuring intelligence in IQ points is *reductionistic* in the sense that it reduces an individual's intellectual ability to a single number. This is a common practice in clinical, industrial, and school settings. The underlying assumption is that all (or most) facets of intelligence have the same underlying common factor, often labelled "g". The g factor theory has generated lengthy academic debates.

According to Schonemann (1995), the belief in a unitary g factor is irreconcilable with modern statistical methodology. Contemporary mainstream research has not adequately mapped human intelligence. As noted above, this research has mostly been restricted to school-related numerical, verbal, and spatial skills and to the culture-specific information disseminated in public and private schools. To the extent that these tasks require similar skills, reductionist psychologists may find illusory support for the unitary g factor theory, at least in some studies. Traditional IQ tests tend to be the epitome of the school routine. Test takers and test interpreters implicitly share the beliefs that there is only one correct solution for most items (as in convergent thinking), that all viable solutions are known to the test psychologist, and that these correct solutions are only reiterated by the test taker. The reductionist approach fails to include items assessing creativity (as in divergent thinking; see discussion in Cohen et al., 1992). These creative aspects of intelligence are crucial for scientific and economic progress, human adaptability, and the long-term survival of our species.

Greatly stimulating for pioneers exploring neglected aspects of human intelligence is the intuitive monograph by Howard Gardner (1983). Gardner discusses seven intelligences: linguistic, logical-mathematical, spatial, musical, bodily-kinaesthetic (as in dancers, actors, and competitive athletes), intrapersonal (knowing oneself), and interpersonal (knowing others). In sum, defining intelligence as whatever is measured by IQ tests (a definition proposed by some psychologists in the past) unduly restricts the concept of human cognitive functioning.

Reliance on Poor Research: the Examples of Rushton and Lynn

Recent comparisons of intelligence in different racial groups by J. Philippe Rushton (University of Western Ontario, Canada) and Richard Lynn (University of Ulster, Northern Ireland) are remarkable examples of pseudobiological focus (see Lynn, 1993; Rushton, 1988). Unfortunately, their research has had more influence than its quality deserves. In this section I summarize methodological objections to their conclusions about human intelligence.

Head Size Measures as Indicator of Intelligence

Both Rushton and Lynn use head size measures as a convenient substitute for IQ scores, on the inaccurate assumption that these two variables are sufficiently closely related. Rushton (1990a) listed correlation coefficients from twenty studies of head size and intelligence to document the existence of a statistical relationship between the two. The average correlation in Rushton's list (as calculated by Cernovsky, 1991) was only 0.18. This is too low to support Rushton's and Lynn's interpretation of head size differences as differences in intelligence. Classical introductory psychology textbooks warn about similar overinterpretations of low correlation coefficients. For instance, Atkinson et al. state: "Correlations between 0 and .20 must be judged with caution and are only minimally useful in making predictions. One should be suspicious of investigators who make strong claims that are based on correlation coefficients in this lower range" (1983: 24).

As reported in more detail elsewhere (Cernovsky, 1994), Bouchard defended Rushton's reliance on low correlation coefficients. He argued during the question period following Cernovsky's (1992) paper at the International Congress of Psychology in 1992 that weak correlation coefficients should not be underestimated. As support, he referred to Rosenthal's recent work on this issue. But this is a misuse of Rosenthal's work on meta-analysis.

Rosenthal and Rubin (1985) argued that small statistical trends are frequently invaluable even when they fail to reach traditional criteria of statistical significance ($p = 0.05$ or 0.01). They provide the following example:

> Suppose that, of 20 critically ill patients in a small, randomized experiment, 10 are assigned to a treatment condition and the other 10 are assigned to a control condition. If none of the control patients survive and 3 experimental patients survive, our results will not be significant at $p \leqslant .05$ by a chi-square test or a Fisher exact test. However, we believe it is essential on scientific as well as ethical grounds that such results should be published. (1985: 528)

In Rosenthal's example, Type I error (use of an ineffective drug to treat a patient who is going to die very soon anyway) has only minor negative consequences compared to Type II error (failure to use treatment that might save 30% of the critically ill patients). The majority of us, if critically ill, would still opt to receive the treatment. That is, we would choose a slight chance of survival even if it is not a "statistically significant" chance, because without the treatment we would die anyway. There are no negative consequences from taking the drug unnecessarily.

This is not at all comparable to claiming, based on weak correlations, that head size is an indicator of intelligence. Type I error, underlying Rushton's speculations, leads not to minor negative consequences but to the defamation of blacks, promotion of racial hatred, and even unnecessary loss of life in racist mob activities. Rosenthal and Rubin defend an experimental use of weak trends in situations where ignoring these trends may result in clearly aversive consequences. But Rushton and Lynn go far beyond this statistical context: they treat two weakly correlated variables as sufficiently identical to rely on the first as the indicator of the second.

Rushton and Lynn also occasionally refer to modern brain size studies. The relationship of brain size to IQ score may be somewhat closer than that found for head size. However, this relationship is also too low to justify substituting one variable for the other. For example, the correlations found by Andreasen et al. (1993) ranged from 0.26 to 0.56, indicating from 12% to 31% of shared variance. Yet, Andreasen and her colleagues emphasized the modest nature of these relationships. Even 31% of shared variance certainly does not justify using one variable as a viable measure of the other. Rushton and Lynn also ignore clinical case studies by Lorber on British adolescents with an extremely small cortex (see summaries in Lewin, 1980). Some of them had IQ scores at or above 120 and were academically successful in high school and subsequently at university, including in areas such as mathematics.

Obsolete Data Sets

Rushton (1988; 1995) and Lynn (1993) frequently rely on antiquated data. As pointed out by Weizmann et al. (1991), old skull collections may have peculiar social histories. For example, both Rushton and Lynn marshalled the skull size data from the famous Morton's collection as evidence of racial inferiority of blacks. Yet the skulls from Morton's collection were originally collected by George Glidden (Stanton, 1965), a supporter of slavery. Glidden may have pre-selected the skulls for each racial group on the basis of skull size in order to support his political position. His motivation was to prove that the creators of ancient Egyptian civilization were white and that blacks existed only in subservient positions.

Misrepresentation of Conclusions of Other Scientists

Both Rushton (1990a; 1990b; 1990c; 1991; 1995) and Lynn (1993) misrepresented statistical analyses by Beals et al. (1984) as supportive of their racial theory. According to Rushton,

> Beals et al. (1984, p. 306, Table 2) computerized the entire world database of 20,000 crania gathered by 1940 (after which data collection virtually ceased because of its presumed association with racial prejudice), grouped them by continental area, and found statistically significant differences. Sex-combined brain cases from Asia averaged 1380 cm³ (SD = 83), Europe averaged 1362 cm³ (SD = 35), and Africa averaged 1276 cm³ (SD = 84). (1990b: 791)

The table with cranial data averages for the continents indeed exists in Beals et al.'s article. However, Rushton and Lynn neglected to mention that Beals et al. explicitly warned readers, on the same page, that these data confound genetic influences with the effects of climatic zone: "If one merely lists such means by geographical region or race, causes of similarity by genogroup and ecotype are hopelessly confounded" (1984: 306).

Within a given racial group, cranial capacity varies depending on the climatic zone. For example, the American Indians are spread over a wide variety of climatic zones and show a corresponding variation in skull size: those from warmer climates have smaller cranial capacity. This pattern is also true for other racial groups. Beals et al. concluded, on the basis of extensive statistical analyses, that correlations of brain size to race are spurious: smaller crania are found in warmer climates, irrespective of race. In fact, Rushton's own tabular summaries of cranial data, based on Herskovits (1930), clearly show these trends. In Rushton's summaries (1990b: see Table 2), the average cranial capacity for North American blacks (1622 cm³) is similar to the average for Caucasians (1621 cm³) from comparable climatic zones. Caucasians from warmer zones such as Cairo (1502 cm³) were similar to some of the black Africans, for example, the Masai (1508 cm³). It is only by "pooling" the black North American data with data for blacks from countries within hot climatic zones (notorious for famine and infant malnutrition that impede brain growth) that Rushton obtained an illusory support for his "genetic" postulates.

Rushton (1988; 1995) also misleads his readers to assume that Tobias's (1970) survey of cranial data supports his theory. Rushton selectively reported only those data from Tobias's monograph that were consistent with his theory. He failed to mention the data sets, also reported by Tobias, showing that cranial size and number of "excess neurons" of North American blacks exceeded those of the French, the English, and American whites (1970: 9, Table 3).

Another example of misrepresenting the work of others: Lynn (1993) reanalyzed old data from a study of physical characteristics of Philadelphia school children in the decades preceding 1970, collected by Krogman (1970). He concluded that head sizes are larger in whites than in blacks and also larger in men than in women. According to Lynn, given the positive association between brain size and intelligence, "there should be corresponding race and sex differences in intelligence" (1993: 92). But Lynn misled his readers with respect to the social background of the children in Krogman's study. Allegedly quoting directly from page 4 of Krogman's monograph, Lynn described the blacks as being from the middle and upper-middle class and the white children as being from the middle class. However, on that page Krogman (1970) described the sample of black children as being from the lower-middle and middle-middle class and the white children as being from the middle-middle and upper-middle class. The two racial groups differed with respect to socioeconomic class in the opposite direction than sketched by Lynn. According to Krogman, the whites were largely from the white collar and skilled labor population with a few from a professional and academic level. The blacks were from the blue collar and semi-skilled labour population. Since the data were collected in the decades preceding 1970, these class differences in urban settings could well be associated with a major difference in quality of child health care, nutrition, educational stimulation by parents, and other factors with a potentially adverse impact on the central nervous system and intellectual development.

Several types of brain size measures can be used when comparing samples grouped on the basis of gender or skin color. Some researchers consider it important to correct the absolute brain size for body height, weight, or surface, on the assumption that larger bodies require proportionately larger brains for the control of various motor and physical functions. Rushton's and Lynn's uncritical interpretation of these measures of brain/body size ratio as a valid indicator of biological intelligence is misleading: some lower animals such as squirrel monkeys or house mice have more favorable brain/body ratios than humans without demonstrating a corresponding intellectual superiority (see a review of Rushton's theory by Cain and Vanderwolf, 1990). Both Rushton and Lynn almost always rely only on absolute brain (or cranial) size data. Significantly, they resort to corrections of cranial size data for body size only when convenient to defend their dogma of black inferiority. For example, Lynn (1993) built almost his entire article (and his thesis of blacks' intellectual inferiority) exclusively on the review of absolute cranial size data. Yet he then suddenly switched to the cranial size "corrected" for body height when the absolute cranial capacity in black girls was greater than in white girls.

Meta-Analysis of Rushton's Data by Gorey and Cryns

A recent meta-analytic study provides additional evidence of methodological weakness in Rushton's procedures. Gorey and Cryns (1995) indicated
that the mean correlation coefficient in data sets listed by Rushton for
black–white intelligence differences was only 0.23. Gorey and Cryns also
found that Rushton's work has an unbalanced overrepresentation of references to supportive data. When they recalculated the data for the same
variables based on a computerized random literature search, the mean
correlation coefficient dropped to 0.15. Similarly, the mean coefficient
based on data sets chosen by Rushton to document black–white differences
in personality and temperament was 0.37. But with data based on a
random literature search, this coefficient dropped to –0.02. Gorey and
Cryns examined eight variables. On all eight, Rushton's "data" were more
supportive of his hypotheses than the data based on a computerized
random literature search.

Preferential Publication of Supportive Data

Some researchers (and also journal editors) may hesitate to publish data
not supportive of their personal beliefs. Or, while gathering the data, their
data can somehow be distorted to match personal expectations. For
instance, Rosenthal's (1991) statistical work suggested that about two-thirds
of observational errors made by investigators are in the direction of
supporting their hypothesis. These biased errors occasionally push a result
over the magic 0.05 cliff, leading to "statistically significant" confirmatory
findings.

   In some cases, political bias or political pressure may lead to a pre-
ponderance of published findings that are unfavorable to blacks. For
example, the editor of *Canadian Psychology*, the leading Canadian
psychological journal, published a lengthy article by Rushton defending
his racial research and expounding his racial theory. Subsequently, the
editor declined to publish a manuscript describing methodological and
statistical deficiencies in Rushton's work. He said that "each new salvo
against Dr. Rushton's position inevitably requires that he be permitted the
right of response, and his views – which do not seem to change – are
trotted out again and again" (letter from Patrick O'Neill, editor, *Canadian
Psychology*, June 20, 1991). The editor's letter admitted that the submitted
criticism of Rushton may present original methodological information. Yet,
these methodological considerations were less relevant for the editorial
decision than "academic politics" in Canadian circles.

   Until recently, black students were systematically prevented (often by the
brutality of the white mob) from entering US universities. Some who
persisted paid for this with their lives. For this reason, most data are from
studies prepared by white psychologists only, some of whom are notorious
for their bias against blacks. Their biased research style is exemplified by
Arthur Jensen's work. His findings of racial differences in reaction time to

complex tasks (interpreted as a relatively culture-free measure of intellectual functioning) have been artificially manufactured by his selective publishing of confirmatory results only. He has failed to publish his own disconfirmatory data (see documentation by Kamin and Grant-Henry, 1987).

Conclusion

The critical psychologist may deal with a wide variety of topics in intelligence research. The issues raised here partly overlap those discussed by Kamin (1995) in his critique of the highly publicized controversial book *The Bell Curve* (Herrnstein and Murray, 1994). Herrnstein and Murray erroneously treat Lynn's and Rushton's work as a reliable scientific source. They fail to discuss the numerous methodological flaws in Rushton's and Lynn's methodology as known from various reviews (Cain and Vanderwolf, 1990; Flynn, 1989; 1990; Kamin, 1995; Weizmann et al., 1990; 1991; Zuckerman and Brody, 1988).

The widespread promotion of the works of Rushton and Lynn and recent attempts to rescue the scientific reputation of Cyril Burt (see Jensen, 1992) are alarming academic developments. These trends may discredit American and Canadian academic psychology on an international scale. Research funding could be channelled more constructively into more methodologically adequate research on personality factors and on strategies that enhance economic or scientific creativity and productivity.

9

Developmental Psychology
and its Discontents

Erica Burman

Editors' note   *An entire lexicon of supposedly benign words makes human development seem independent of social and political context. Terms such as "natural," "progress," "growth," "body," "health," and "evolution" make children's "development" look like an unremarkable, universal, inevitable progression. We all have notions – reinforced by the media and by our own ~~hazy memories of childhood~~ – of how children are "supposed" to develop. Dominant political forces use these notions to reinforce their own conceptions of childhood and related concepts such as "family values."*

In this chapter, Erica Burman discusses absences in developmental psychology, such as the absence of social context. As pointed out by Tod Sloan (Chapter 6) and Maritza Montero (Chapter 15), absences are worth noting. They have implications for defining and solving problems. For example, because development is supposedly about innate striving towards maturity, not about power struggles, developmental psychologists overlook power dynamics among parents and children, fathers and mothers, teachers and students, and rich and poor. As in other areas of psychology, the failure to notice that behavior norms are ethnocentric, androcentric, and patriarchal serves the interests of dominant groups. So "instead of poverty, unemployment and frustration," Burman says, "we have evil children, bad mothers, absent fathers and broken homes." Burman shows how popular discourses and metaphors conceal normative prescriptions under the guise of scientific descriptions: what dominant groups prefer as the desirable way to rear children is portrayed as the natural way for everyone to rear children. The consequences are severe for those whose lives do not match dominant cultural expectations.

But few things are "natural" about childrearing practices, most of which are socially constructed and culture-specific. Burman advocates a developmental psychology more sensitive to the needs of children in differing contexts as well as to the needs of their primary caregivers, mothers. Studying children and women in real-life sociopolitical contexts and stopping the export of Anglo and US assumptions to other countries would be crucial steps in the right direction.

Developmental psychology is usually considered to be that area of psychology dealing with children and child development. In principle, it also concerns change processes throughout people's lives. The recent resurgence of "lifespan" developmental psychology is a corrective to the individual, child-focused orientation that has preoccupied the mainstream. I will not focus on this here, although some of my arguments apply also to "lifespan" reworkings of developmental models (see Lichtman, 1987).

Rather, in this chapter I question the assumptions that inform the theory and practice of mainstream developmental psychology. While this chapter cannot detail specific criticisms of particular models (for this see Burman, 1994), it provides a more general critical framework for their evaluation, with signposts for following up particular issues. As we shall see, one of the enduring features of developmental psychology is its capacity to claim expertise over a wide range of psychological practice. Like the child it studies, developmental psychology demonstrates an adaptability that renders attempts at exhaustive critique futile. As such, all we can aim for is an informed basis on which to recognize and, where appropriate, counter its claims.

The Scale of the Problem

Where does developmental psychological knowledge come into play? While often seen as a subdiscipline of psychology, as a particular and separate specialty, this view underestimates developmental psychology's influence both inside and outside psychology. Varieties of developmental psychological theories infuse discussions about children's natures and qualities, about processes of psychological growth and change, and about family life. Such theories do not confine themselves to laboratory study or textbooks. Instead, they form a key resource for a wide range of welfare professions which have arisen in industrialized countries to supervise, evaluate and "support" children and families. Health visitors, social workers, community psychiatric nurses and teachers, as well as others who receive a distinctly "psychological" training such as educational psychologists and psychotherapists, have all been steeped in developmental psychology. In this sense, all professional talk about relationships, about parenting skills and styles, as well as about attachment, bonding, cycles of abuse and the like, rely upon forms of developmental psychology.

More than this, such talk is not the sole domain of professionals. It circulates in the ways we frame and understand our experiences, as children, as parents, as family members – and as psychologists (Burman, 1991). Women's magazines, self-help books and toy shops, no less than criteria for referral to educational psychologists, or for child custody, or for qualification for state benefits, all draw upon ideas about children's natures and the conditions in which they should be reared. This transformation of expert into everyday knowledge hints at a paradox at the heart of developmental psychology: what the mystifying jargon of the experts and the language of scientific neutrality obscure is that developmental psychology itself is shot through with cultural-political assumptions.

This chapter indicates the oppressive consequences of developmental psychology's unwillingness to own up to its culturally situated, partial claims to truth. In particular we will see how the appeal to the child and the story of children's development operate in powerful ways to change statistical descriptions into societal prescriptions. The shift from a descriptive to an evaluative rendering of what is normal introduces a moral "ought" into an account of "what is." Current social arrangements of, for example, class, gender and cultural inequalities appear as natural inevitabilities, unamenable to social reform or change (see Lieven, 1981). Developmental psychology has therefore been mobilized to support a thoroughly conservative social agenda. This is why we need a critique of developmental psychology. But beyond this we also need to consider how the rhetorical powers of developmental psychology can be harnessed to envisage more useful ways to conceptualize growth and change.

We all have memories of being children. Such recollections invest the domain of childhood in all kinds of politically charged ways, as nostalgia for a lost past or as hope for an improved future (Burman, 1995a). In contemporary modern societies children cannot function as just themselves, but figure as symbols of ourselves, as projections of our hopes and fears. The challenge for developmental psychology, as for society generally, is to focus on the needs of real children in specific cultural-political contexts, rather than study areas that represent our own projections of what it is to be a child.

A Slippery Subject

Conventional developmental psychological writings are littered with references to "the baby and the bathwater": which to keep, and which to throw away. The baby is the quintessential subject of psychology, the unit of development, the developing individual. Here we see elaborated Western psychology's traditional dualism between individual and society. The baby is constituted as the privatized, individualized domain of the psychological. The bathwater is its sociocultural milieu, an optional overlay that surrounds or supports it but does not fundamentally infuse or construct it. This prior integrity of the developing organism as separate from its environment reiterates a liberal bourgeois conception of the individual–state relationship that is enshrined in modern legal systems (Henriques et al., 1984). According to this conception, individuals exist prior to sociality, and relationships are only formed by exchanges between these already-enclosed individuals. There is no scope here for an account that tries to address our culturally defined construction of forms of experience. Rather, we have apparently developmental accounts that cannot account for development. We talk about development as if it all happened within the individual child, uninfluenced by the social milieu.

Moreover, the failure to theorize the social production of this asocial conception of the child cannot allow for difference. Like the singular baby suspended in its bathwater, traditional developmental accounts portray the directions and goals of development as unitary. Never mind who bathes the baby, or the temperature of the water, or even if it is water, or whether the cleaning agent is liquid (shampoo) or solid (soap), whether the baby is soaked or scrubbed, whether s/he floats or swims, whether s/he is sung songs to or told stories. What the metaphor promotes is a representation of development as a natural, universal process. As we shall see, the consequence of this is that difference can only be envisaged in terms of deviation, deviance or inferiority.

Body Politics

Lest all this seem a trifle overinterpretive of an innocent figure of speech, let us pause to recall the history and potency of metaphors of the body in relation to forms of social organization. The earliest theorists of modern politics drew parallels between the workings of the physical body and political processes. Indeed the notion of the role and function of a state was formulated in terms of "the body politic."

Such organic metaphors relating the state to a "natural body" are hallmarks of modern, male, Western Enlightenment thinking of the eighteenth century onwards. They highlight the connections between the Enlightenment as an approach to knowledge and knowledge generation and as a theory of social order and disorder. With its faith in reason and science the Enlightenment created the conditions for the emergence of psychology alongside other modern social and natural sciences. The rational body of man thus gave birth to the developing, progressive baby of psychology and Western culture. If the state is conceived as an integral self-organizing and maintaining body, then its strategies for maintaining social order and efficiency are "naturalized," or rendered as natural. The interests of the state determine what counts as healthy or unhealthy functioning. With such prescriptions centered on the body, there is no scope for competing interests, contradiction or struggle. The modern metaphor of "the body politic" thus eclipses the social assumptions constructing its particular representation of a single, health-seeking, self-organizing body. Similarly, the metaphor of the baby to signify the task of development naturalizes the work of culture in making (rather than discovering) its subjects.

In essence, then, metaphors of the state as an organic body lead us to think of it in terms of health and pathology, according to which challenges to the so-called "natural order of things" are viewed as "unnatural" and "unhealthy." If a healthy state is seen as functioning smoothly and in harmony, its strategies for maintaining social order and efficiency are rendered invisible or treated as natural: expressions of competing interests, contradiction or struggle are correspondingly disallowed except in terms of pathological deviations from the "natural." In the case of developmental psychology, we adopt a similar "natural" metaphor and view deviations from socially constructed norms as "unnatural." We forget that our views about development and growth are not natural but are saturated with politically charged rhetoric about power and social arrangements.

Developmental psychology, while it currently functions as a separate subspecialty of psychology, is intimately connected with other areas of psychology. Indeed it owes its origins to the domain of "individual psychology" emerging in the late nineteenth and early twentieth centuries. At that time, new nation states and empires of the West were consolidating their central and colonial power bases, and in need of techniques to classify and segregate individuals and populations. The topics of such classification ranged from mental ability to social adjustment, and the institutional arenas requiring such demarcation ranged from prisons, to mental asylums for the insane, to distinguishing educable children from ineducable (Ingleby, 1985; Rose, 1990). But first and foremost was the elaboration of criteria for the mental and physical fitness of recruits to fight colonial wars (Rose, 1985).

Thus developmental psychology, far from being some rarified academic conceptual hobby, has always been informed by dominant social agendas. Just as intelligence tests originated in the demand for some means to determine criteria for exclusion from mainstream schooling at a time when primary education was becoming compulsory for all children across Europe and the US, so theories of "maternal deprivation" became prevalent in Britain, and less so in the US, precisely because of their different economic climates. In Britain, such ideas were associated in the period after World War II with the exclusion of women workers from the public sphere to vacate their jobs for the men returning from war. Such theories formed at least part of the rationale for closure of the day nurseries in Britain that were provided during the war. Even now these theories bolster rationalizations for the failure to provide adequate day care or the moral panics about "latchkey children" (Riley, 1983). In the US context, where women were beginning to work outside the home, Harlow's experiments on monkeys were overtly concerned to show how maternal contact was more important than mere presence. But, as well as legitimating a further spurious rationale for imprisoning and torturing generations of monkeys, this still functioned in coercive ways to evaluate the "quality" of the care provided by women (see Haraway, 1989).

Developmental Fallacies

A range of logical fallacies, including androcentric (male-based) and imperialistic "phallacies," structure developmental thinking. Just as the pregiven baby remains outside culture, so its surroundings are presented as undifferentiated. We talk of "the environment," but this term is applied loosely, sometimes meaning physical contexts of climate or conditions, other times familial organization and emotional qualities. Inadequate though it is, terms such as *environment*, like *adaptation* and *function*, all bear witness to the legacies of evolutionary theory that framed the formulation of psychological, especially developmental psychological, questions. The preoccupation with "survival of the fittest" is a particular reading of Darwinian theory that significantly devalues Darwin's original emphasis on the species advantage of variability (Morss, 1990). The study of children was of interest to the first psychologists because they subscribed to a framework which saw each child as repeating in its development the developmental processes of the species (as in the slogan "ontogeny recapitulates phylogeny").

This naturalization of development collapsed psychology more and more into biology. Psychologists rushed to identify the earliest moment of emergence of a particular quality or capacity, presuming that the closer they could trace it back to the moment of birth (or more recently of conception), the more biological it must be. This is a classic developmental fallacy: it treats biology as culture-free and therefore ignores the social shaping of experience that selects both the exhibition and the interpretation of "the biological." The literature on sex differences is the classic expression of this style of reasoning, standing as an exemplar of poor research practice and interpretation. It amalgamates and compares diverse studies conducted to answer different questions, and on noncomparable samples (see Henshall and McGuire, 1986). Further, it is easy to see that claims about "the development of sex differences" (in, for example, aggression, or the distribution of verbal versus visual-spatial thinking) legitimize differential access to, and occupational statuses allowed, men and women. Perhaps in these days of biological revivalism – with claims of pre-sexed brains and minds predisposed to crime – the appeal to psychology to explain such outcomes is redundant. Nevertheless, vigilance on the uses of developmental psychology to support such accounts is necessary.

Thus the focus of developmental psychology has been not on specific children developing in particular sociohistorical circumstances, but on a generalized and abstract child as exemplar. In this vein, Piaget embarked on his celebrated analyses of the structure of children's thinking because he saw this as equivalent to the study of the growth of logic. For him, children's growth of understanding repeated the history of modern science in its shifts from concrete to abstract thinking, or from egocentrism to detached objectivity. For Piaget, biology met philosophy in his project of "genetic epistemology," the study of children's thinking.

Piaget was not alone in such reasoning. Sociologists and anthropologists as well as psychologists partook of such reductionism. People deemed "less developed" were considered psychologically equivalent to one another, so that parallels were readily drawn between children, women, "neurotics" and "primitives." By means of such developmental phallacies the dominance of powerful social groups was viewed as natural. Moreover, the attribution of developmental status functions as an index of power relationships, justifying practices of patriarchal and colonial subordination of women and black and minoritized people. Think here of the political use of terms like "underdeveloped countries." Again, the term makes it look as if these countries are behind developed ones in some natural progression. The term does much to obscure the oppression of poor by rich countries. In this light the project of development becomes a tautology, self-serving and self-maintaining: if the more developed possess what the less developed lack, then not only do those in power define what development is, they also obscure the exercise of such power within the naturalizing language of development. The convergence between ageist, sexist and racist themes within the notion of "paternalism" structures the interpretation of "development" to make this far from "culture-free". Development is not a self-evident, or self-enclosed, entity, but requires agents, objects and values. It is always *of* something, *to* somewhere, as evaluated *by* someone.

"Progress" is the key term that binds together claims to natural, individual and societal development. We need to ask: who judges, according to what criteria, and to what effect? In other words, we need to be suspicious of the agendas that research on children can be mobilized to fulfill. Not only are gross injustices and interventions inflicted on families and cultures "in the name of the child" (Cooter, 1992), but historical and actual practices of child development research, by depicting the child as the precultural raw material for development, act as a crucial forum to legitimize such injustice.

Objects and Subjects

Of course, "the environment" in which children develop is far more specified than the naturalized evolutionary account suggests. On the one hand, according to the asocial, naturalized model, whether the baby in the bath is regularly bathed by a person of a particular gender, or even the same person, is irrelevant. But we know that the world over it is almost always women who are primarily involved in the regular and intimate care of children. Similarly, developmental psychological interventions are principally directed at mothers, who thereby become the focus of scrutiny. In an ever enclosing spiral, women, as much as children, have been the objects of developmental psychological study – of how they mother, how they have mothered, and how their own experiences of being mothered affect how they mother. Once again, we see how, by such analytical slips, women's capacities for childbearing lead to concern with their adequacies at child-caring. This works to endorse cultural prescriptions that equate femininity with motherhood and thus either ignore or stigmatize women who cannot, or do not wish to, have children.

Significantly, until recently men as fathers have attracted little interest in developmental psychology. Perhaps this was a function of structuring research around opportunity samples of (middle-class) women who were available to be studied at home with their children, while men were out at work. The developmental literature has largely considered fathers in terms of their absence (e.g., Shinn, 1978), which has been considered a problem only in relation to sex role development, particularly for boys, except where themes about discipline connect with broader issues of social order. Thus, "fatherless families" not only suffer societal marginalization, but are deemed further "at risk" as sites for the development of homosexuality owing to the absence of a strong male figure with whom the boy can "identify." In their provocatively titled book *The Abuse of Women within Childcare Work*, O'Hagan and Dillenburger (1995) explore how the invisibility – and sometimes avoidance – of men in social work interventions further pathologize women (and correspondingly exclude men). Aside from media presentations of "new men" holding babies as indices of new-found depths of intimacy and vulnerability, dominant representations of childcare treat "parent" as equivalent to "mother."

Since industrialization prompted the growth of nuclear family organization in the West (and appears to do so in currently industrializing countries), the responsibility for children has fallen upon an ever more isolated mother. Her maternal successes and failures form an intense topic of interest not least because where she "fails" the state is expected to step in and pay up in the form of providing services, including "care." Welfare "help" is always at the expense of increased scrutiny. Such is the mixed blessing of a welfare state apparatus which constructs mothers as responsible not only for children's current welfare, but for their future moral actions.

Here we can note the limited conception of the social even within "new social developmental psychologies" (e.g., Harré, 1986; Shotter, 1984) that treat development as originating from an initially undifferentiated mother–child unit. This is a significant improvement on the isolated, presocial child as the unit of development. But the study of the mother–child dyad is always in danger of maintaining the doubly familiar ideological distinction between state and family. It reduces the conception of "the social" to a relationship within the home between child and primary caregiver (assumed to be singular and female). This reintroduces the private–public split, and ushers in a new variety of individualism and liberal humanism to exonerate the state from its role and responsibilities in helping children.

A further, key developmental fallacy is evident in the ways themes of social order and disorder are linked to mother–child experiences when the baby is young. Based on these interactions, negative outcomes are claimed to be predicted, leading to "preventive" interventions for the social good. The title of Denise Riley's (1983) book *War in the Nursery* conveys how dominant themes from the world outside the home come to govern conceptualizations of what goes on inside it. What Riley calls the "desert island" view of the context of children's early development so beloved of developmental psychologists – of mother and child portrayed in a cosy, private space of the home – naturalizes a particular historically and culturally specific arrangement. Separating this profoundly ideological representation from the social structures that produced it allows social problems to be treated as individual deficits. Instead of poverty, unemployment and frustration, we have evil children, bad mothers, absent fathers and broken homes.

It is therefore debatable whether children or their mothers form the central focus for developmental psychology. Moreover, mothers are subjects of developmental psychology as well as its objects. As Marshall's (1991) and Urwin's (1985) interviews with mothers suggest, we feel evaluated and regulated by how children's rates of progress through various developmental milestones reflect upon us.

Normalized Absence/Pathologized Presence

So far I have talked in general terms about the scrutiny instigated by developmental psychology's practices, but not all mothers, children and families are positioned equally in relation to psychology. Ann Phoenix (1987) has coined the phrase "normalized absence/pathologized presence" to describe how the experience of black people is typically excluded or ignored, only to appear as associated with "social problems" such as early and single motherhood. As such, black people's experiences and development either are invisible or are presumed through assimilation to the white, middle-class norms that structure the models. Even where they do gain attention, as in cross-cultural psychology, cultural differences in childrearing norms, practices and goals tend to be treated as variations on an assumed common theme, rather than as throwing into question the entire set of culturally embedded assumptions that infuse the models. An emerging literature documents the diversity of cultural practices around caring for children within Europe and the US as well as elsewhere (Dawes and Donald, 1994; Everingham, 1994; Nakano Glenn et al., 1994; Phoenix, 1991; Ribbens, 1994).

A similar story structures attention to class issues in developmental psychology. Class differences are only addressed in terms of inferiorities or deviations from the middle-class norms presumed to be better. Notions of sensitive mothering, like child-centeredness, are profoundly connected with theories that became prevalent after the Second World War (the so-called "war against fascism") linking the production of the democratic citizen to patterns of family relationships. The links between childrearing and the broad themes of social order and organization were forged through psychological theories of play and parenting styles. To be strict or punitive to your child was tantamount to inciting them to become amoral, lacking in internal rules and boundaries, and vulnerable to authoritarianism. The same threats attended being permissive – a fine double bind. In addition to these powerful cultural prescriptions, a further consequence of the advent of "progressive" or "child-centered" education was the recasting of childcare into education. Altogether, this collection of practices produces a huge prohibition on mothers who argue with their children, refuse to play with them, or use inconsistent disciplinary practices. Moreover, these mothers are popularly associated with black and working-class mothers. This is not surprising at least in part because, as working women (both inside and outside the home), they (like other middle class working women) have less time to engage in child-centered, "democratic" negotiations with their children. Walkerdine and Lucey (1989) have usefully highlighted these points in reinterpreting Tizard and Hughes's (1984) analysis of class differences in mother–daughter conversations. They point out how the prevailing sanctification of "sensitive mothering" works to pathologize working-class women who fail to exhibit the requisite behaviors.

The same dynamic of presence and absence (under conditions of pathology or invisibility respectively) characterizes the positions of other oppressed groups. Lesbian mothers rarely figure in psychological accounts except in terms of discussions of who is deemed "fit to parent." Developmental psychological knowledge is deployed in custody cases in relation to children's purported needs for a father figure, with lesbian mothers much more likely than heterosexual mothers to lose their children (Chesler, 1992). Black and lesbian mothers challenge normative conceptions supported by developmental psychology about what families are and should be like. Once again these are not simply textbook topics. They have material effects on the conditions of people's lives and the "choices" they are allowed to make. Gay men and lesbians in many "overdeveloped," industrialized countries are excluded or devalued as foster parents, while lesbian mothers and heterosexual women not married or in "stable relationships" are denied access to fertility services, including donor insemination. As Alldred (1996) argues, the issue for critical psychologists is how both to repudiate psychology's stigmatizing role in such issues and to reinterpret existing literatures to support more progressive agendas.

From Old Problems to New Agendas

Psychology has trouble recognizing that the implicit gender informing its models is the Western world's culturally normative masculine subject. In developmental psychology this norm is given new life in the trajectories it traces: development is structured to mark a move from the culturally feminized qualities of attachment, relationship, concrete connectedness and context dependency, to autonomy, detachment, and dispassion. The gendering of the term "mastery" that characterizes developmental psychological accounts of progress is apt (see Broughton, 1988; Walkerdine, 1988). In this developmental hierarchy, rationality is a quality possessed culturally by white middle-class men, with all others infantilized, or rendered into the position of children. Girls occupy a particular position in this complex of ideas, since they are doubly excluded from reason. That this is so, and that developmental psychological knowledge contributes to making them so, is graphically illustrated by research in primary schools. Walkerdine et al. (1989) document how (female) teachers evaluated girls as being less clever than boys because they were good and worked hard, and therefore were considered to lack the flair and spontaneity that boys exhibited and that the teachers saw as characterizing true ability. Thus the active, discovering, problem-solving child of developmental psychology, like Piaget's (1957) model of the child as mini-scientist, is a boy. That the teachers in Walkerdine et al.'s study maintained these views even where the girls were outperforming the boys on tests is sobering testimony to the potency of such assumptions.

Social categories and identities are not additive, but intersect in complex ways. Practices of social marginalization and subordination that developmental psychology participates in may well overdetermine the oppression of particular individuals and groups. This occurs where "race" and class positions intersect because histories of racial exclusion mean that black people are economically disadvantaged, and it is intensified for black single and black lesbian mothers who as women are further economically disadvantaged. Nevertheless, we should not get so caught up in stacking up piles of oppressions that we fail to acknowledge the impact of their combinations. Because what it means to be a white woman is different from being a black woman, we need to examine "race"-specific gendered identities (Afshar and Maynard, 1994; Mama, 1995). Taking these questions seriously means that we have indeed to throw the baby out with the bathwater. We must arrive at a new metaphor to visualize the historical emergence of the multiple and fluctuating forms of subjectivity that comprise who and what we are.

Attention to the normative cultural assumptions structuring developmental psychology brings forth new questions for a critical psychology. So as well as responding to the social inequities maintained by developmental theory, we can begin to use such apparent "deviations" and previously pathologized experiences as a resource to inform us of the limited conceptions the theories so far allow. If we take seriously the notion that children do not necessarily have a single primary caregiver, but may be brought up by a number of family (including extended family) figures including siblings as well as older women, what might this mean for psychological development and future relationships? Beyond exposing the injustices developmental psychology colludes with, exploring these issues in a positive way offers new insights into the limitations of our existing models.

So, for example, anthropological work has been used to critique the culturally specific and purportedly general status of psychoanalytic approaches to child and gender development (Kurtz, 1992). If, instead of ignoring their existence, we took seriously the relationships developed by women who are not the biological mothers of the children, but who care for (and are paid to care for) children, what could we learn about alternative and diverse ways of envisaging intimate relationships (see, e.g., Nelson, 1990)? If, instead of presuming, as developmental psychology textbooks do, that language development is about children learning to speak a single language, we took as our starting point how most children in most of the world learn at least two languages (and often many more), what does this do to our understandings of communicative and symbolic roles of language? Rather than treating "bilingualism" as a supplementary issue, an optional extra for some children, we could start to address what this current exclusion indicates about dominant forms of developmental psychology. Moving from a unitary model of language to exploring the emergence of multiple languages could enrich our understanding of the varieties of what "growing up" means, in diverse times, places and positions (Skutnabb Kangas and Cummins, 1988).

Powerful Designs

There is a final absent presence that we must comment upon before we move on: the absence of children in developmental research. We have already seen how the focus on the abstract notion of "the child" has precluded study of particular children. There is another paradoxical absence: children's participation in developmental psychology's topics and agendas.

Rarely are children themselves invited to give consent to participate. Rather, their teachers or parents are the presumed agents to give consent on their behalf, and children themselves are less likely to refuse to participate if they know that their parent or teacher has already consented (Abramovitch et al., 1991). The current international attention to children's rights similarly invokes varieties of cultural knowledges about children that, as critical psychologists, we might want to question. This should also teach us a salutary lesson on our poor record on soliciting children's active participation in research, and on the actual or potential exploitation of specific children in the name of generating research about children in general. It is no less a challenge for developmental psychology than for any other agency or model to theorize and implement participatory approaches that involve children rather than subject them to its interventions. Once more we might speculate about what inviting children to participate in the formulation of developmental psychological questions might teach us, rather than merely treating "participation" as a matter of securing consent to our procedures.

This brings to the fore the issue of power in research, in matters not only of conceptual definition but also of research practice. Developmental psychology has only really addressed the power of children as "child effects" on caregivers (Bell and Harper, 1977). Psychology, with its individual focus, has particular difficulty understanding power relations as socially structured frameworks that may be expressed by individuals, but are created in larger social contexts. Questions of power in research are generally addressed only in terms of "influences" on the "data."

This is currently illustrated in the developmental psychological literature on children's suggestibility. While this topic has achieved new media attention because of legal issues posed by interpreting children's testimony, the issue has long been accorded significant attention. However, it has been conceptualized only in the individualized terms of internal states or competences that undergo distortion according to social circumstances, rather than in terms of the ways social conditions give rise to varying accounts (Burman, forthcoming). Thus, what children say or the competencies they show are influenced by their status in power relationships (Burman, 1992; 1993). However, this is not the way this work is usually interpreted (see, e.g., Brainerd, 1973; Donaldson, 1978). It is an irony that power relations are not seen as a structural dimension of all developmental psychological research. The discipline is structured around the asymmetrical relationships between adults and children, still further intensified by that of researcher and researched (more typically of experimenter and subject). Developmental psychology could have much to offer in promoting an understanding of power (Burman, 1992; forthcoming).

In part this situation arises not only from the personalizing framework of psychology, but also from a scientific model that tries to avoid admitting its intervention in what it studies. Perhaps developmental psychology, with its focus on the messy feminized and domestic arena of child concerns, has been especially subject to the lure of masculine science. Certainly, both its subject matter and the visibility of women as researchers in it have prompted justifications of its scientific rigor (Murchison, 1933). Moreover, such claims to dispassionate, disinterested reason give rise to a rhetoric of "social relevance" that confirms both developmental psychology's efficacy and its expertise in commenting upon social issues.

Towards a Critical Developmental Psychology

What else might critical developmental psychologists do to counter the current abusive and oppressive practices reproduced and meted out in the name of development? The "towards" of the above heading signals both a provisionality and a sense of movement without defining its endpoint. As we shall see, it is hard to get into the business of critical alternatives to developmental psychology without reproducing some of the same assumptions and orthodoxies at issue.

Morss (1995), in his analysis of critical and uncritical varieties of developmental psychology, distinguishes three positions. Firstly, there are social constructionist approaches, including the work of Shotter, Harré and

Gergen. Morss argues that these retain residues of individualist frameworks in their emphasis on the development of mutuality through mother–child interaction. Secondly, there are accounts that call for a critical psychology of development (Broughton, 1987). Although these accounts are more sensitive to social and cultural definitions of development, they risk reproducing the "natural" developmental narratives of mainstream theories. The third position Morss identifies is "anti-developmental" in the sense that it formulates explanations of change without recourse to notions of underlying, natural regularities. Such approaches therefore refuse to subscribe to coherent unitary models of development; instead, they engage piecemeal, introducing elements to critical dispute in a critical way, without commitment to an overall alternative model.

While this, broadly speaking, is the position I have adopted here (see also Burman, 1994), I want to end by offering some examples of key areas of intervention for critical developmental psychologists and/or critics of developmental psychology.

Arenas for Intervention

Below I outline five preliminary examples indicating key issues for critical work.

Investments in Children

One way of trying to comprehend the significance of developmental psychological theory and its practices is to connect it with broader cultural representations of childhood – their historical specificity, their gender polarizations, the emotive and evaluative functions of the appeals to children's "best interests." Similarly, we need to explore what is at stake for adults in efforts to recover "stolen childhoods," for either adults or children. By asking such questions we can begin to contextualize forms and functions of developmental psychological knowledge. We can further understand what it draws upon, what cultural practices it recirculates as expert knowledge, and thus start to limit the powers it wields through its claims to scientific knowledge. This is not simply an abstract, academic exercise. It can help us to recognize and listen to the needs and wants of children.

Practicing the Everyday

A second strategy that wards off the burden of generalized and abstract models of development is to focus on the everyday. There is a Northern European tradition of developmental research (see, e.g., Andeneas, 1995; forthcoming; Solberg, 1990) drawing on feminist sociology (e.g., Smith, 1987) that sets out to document the concrete and specific details of children's lives, in varying circumstances. The approach focuses on "life history" and accounts of daily and weekly activities, rather than setting out to discover deep truths about children's qualities or conceptualizations. The topics concern, for example, how children spend their time when unaccompanied by adults in their homes, and how this relates to their sense of themselves as autonomous, independent agents as well as arising through their parents' changing condition of employment (Gulbrandsen, 1994). The complexity and diversity of the pictures of children's lives built up in this way puts into practice the call to move away from unitary developmental models to elaborating multiple developments. If close attention to the lives of a relatively homogeneous group of children reveals such diversity, then how much more open should we be to multiplicities across broader geographical and cultural contexts?

Women and Children

Thirdly, we have seen how the subject of developmental psychological enquiry shifts from child to mother, with girls invidiously positioned in between. A key issue both for feminist analysis and for those who champion children's rights is how to represent both conceptually and politically the current relatedness of women's and children's issues without either collapsing these into each other, or treating them as absolutely separable (as existing rights legislation does). Currently, presumptions about wanting, bearing, caring for, and knowing how to care for children enter deeply into definitions of normative femininity. Feminists have been correct to locate children as a source of women's oppression, and this chapter has shown developmental psychology's contribution to this. This is not all children do for women, however, as feminist work indicates (Rich, 1980; Riley, 1987). What critical developmental psychologists need to be wary of is the ways other agendas (of social hygiene, social control or cultural imperialism) can be performed by virtue of interventions either "in children's best interests" or in the name of women's emancipation (Burman, 1995b).

Development in Development

Fourthly, attention to the colonizing (that is, appropriative) and homogenizing (reducing of differences) impetus of unitary developmental models brings a new critical light to bear on the ways developmental psychology is exported from its Anglo-US arenas of production to non-Western contexts of consumption (Boyden, 1990). The developmental psychology available in Africa and Asia is largely Anglo-US in origin, although there are efforts to make these models appropriate and relevant to their new contexts of application (see, e.g., Dawes and Donald, 1994). There are resonances between economic models of development that prescribe the Western model of industrialization as the only route to progress, and psychological approaches. The commonality arises through the shared theoretical and political commitment to progress, seen as a unitary endpoint exemplified by the "more developed" and to be aspired to and emulated by the "less developed." If psychology is not to reproduce at the level of psychological regulation the injustices of economic structural adjustment, we need to counter equivalently coercive assumptions about its goals and directions (Burman, 1995b).

Rights and Wrongs

More obviously, developmental psychology forms a key resource for national and international policies promoting children's rights. In elaborating legal entitlements of children, programs for child protection, and strategies for ensuring children's participation in decisions concerning their welfare, notions of child development operate both explicitly and implicitly, as expertise and as common sense respectively. We need to be prepared to highlight the consequences and limitations of these dominant conceptualizations. We have already touched on some issues relevant to the delimitation of the notion of "rights," such as the artificiality of the separation between interventions on behalf of women and children, and the paradoxical position of "the girl child." In debates about parental fitness we need to address, and challenge, how the discourse of "children's needs" can be mobilized for reactionary ends in depriving women of custody of their children (Alldred, 1996), or how teaching mothers how to play with or "stimulate" their children will not change the broader contexts of social and economic deprivations that are largely responsible for children's "failure to thrive." In other words, while maintaining the importance of work with and for children (rather than on them), we must work to ward off the psychologization of political problems.

Resources for the Suspicious Developmental Psychologist

Finally, there are a number of quite readable critical accounts of developmental psychology that should help critical psychologists to keep going, and growing, critical.

Bradley, B. (1989). *Visions of Infancy*. Oxford: Polity, Blackwell.

Broughton, J. (Ed.). (1987). *Critical Theories of Psychological Development*. New York: Plenum Press.

Burman, E. (1994). *Deconstructing Developmental Psychology*. London: Routledge.

Morss, J. (1995). *Growing Critical: Alternatives to Developmental Psychology*. London: Routledge.

Stainton Rogers, R., and Stainton Rogers, W. (1992). *Stories of Childhood: Shifting Agendas of Child Concern*. Hemel Hempstead: Harvester Wheatsheaf.

Note

Thanks to Diane Burns, Juliette Coleman, Brenda Goldberg, Michele Moore, Tina Miller and Ian Parker for their comments on an earlier draft – they've made all the difference.

10

Social Psychology: The Crisis Continues

S. Mark Pancer

Editors' note   Many critical psychologists are social psychologists who believe their field fails to take the word "social" seriously. This is especially so in recent years in Europe, as it was in the United States two or three decades ago. Similarly, many chapters in this book are at least partly "social psychological" even when they are not labeled as such: their authors insist that human behavior must be understood in a social context, paying attention to socioeconomic, historical, and political factors whether the immediate concern is child development, psychotherapy, personality theory, or political behavior. But ironically, unlike the social psychology growing out of sociology, social psychology within psychology has become increasingly asocial, as S. Mark Pancer emphasizes in this chapter.

Pancer focuses specifically on mainstream social psychology in North America, which continues to dominate the field despite efforts to devise alternatives. He contrasts the reform-oriented aspirations of social psychology's pioneers with the field's limited accomplishments. While such key figures as Kurt Lewin strove to make the discipline socially useful, subsequent generations adopted approaches that do little to advance human welfare. Pancer emphasizes that social psychology has become even less social under the increased influence of the "cognitive revolution," a problem identified in Chapters 12 and 14 as well.

A redirected, critical social psychology could help us understand why people acquiesce to conditions of oppression. It could teach us to collaborate with one another. It could discover how to distribute resources fairly and how to share power equally. But the narrow methodologies criticized in this chapter, along with an excessive focus on the psychology of the individual, make these possibilities look rather illusory. It is too early to tell whether the critical social psychology emerging in Europe (e.g., see Chapter 18), or the use of more qualitative and value-explicit approaches (Chapter 3), will enable social psychology to live up to its potential.

The most commonly accepted definition of social psychology describes the discipline as "an attempt to understand and explain how the thought, feeling, and behavior of individuals are influenced by the actual, imagined, or implied presence of others" (Allport, 1985: 3). This definition, in one variation or another, is found in most current social psychology textbooks. An informal survey of the tables of contents of these texts would likely provide a somewhat richer appreciation for what concerns and interests social psychologists. These tables of contents typically include topics such as social perception and cognition, attitude formation and change, prejudice and discrimination, aggression, altruism, interpersonal attraction and relationships, social influence, and group behavior. Most texts also contain chapters which examine the way social psychological theory and research have been applied in areas such as health, the environment, law or politics. A perusal of the major journals in the field would reveal a similar array of topics, but a greater concentration of research in the areas of attitudes and social cognition, particularly in the American journals which comprise the majority of journals in the field.

In this chapter, I first briefly recount the history of social psychology, highlighting the field's connection to social and political issues. I then describe significant critiques raised during the discipline's "crisis of confidence" in the 1960s and 1970s. Following this, I evaluate social psychology's current state in the aftermath of that crisis, and suggest that many of the issues that contributed to the crisis remain unresolved. Finally, I offer some suggestions as to how social psychology can address these issues, in part by reaffirming its role in promoting social change and human welfare.

A Brief History of Social Psychology

Modern social psychology began at about the turn of the century. Triplett (1898) conducted the first social psychology experiments, examining the way in which the presence of other individuals appeared to enhance performance on certain tasks. The first books titled *Social Psychology* were written in 1908 (McDougall, 1908; Ross, 1908). While Ross's text dealt with topics such as mob violence that continue to attract the attention of social psychologists, neither book had a research base on which to draw, and neither really defined the newly emerging field (Hilgard, 1987). It was Floyd Allport's 1924 text titled *Social Psychology* which helped define the discipline of social psychology, and established it as one of the standard course offerings in American psychology departments.

The first great boom in social psychological research occurred in the period from 1920 to 1940. Much of social psychology during this period was driven by the burning social issues of the day. The early 1900s, for example, were a time of massive immigration to North America from Eastern Europe. It is not surprising, therefore, that social psychologists began to study attitudes toward and within national and ethnic groups at this time. Bogardus (1925), for example, developed one of the first attitude scales (the "social distance" scale), to assess attitudes toward various racial and ethnic groups. Katz and Braly (1933) conducted their famous study of stereotypes, in which they assessed the impressions that Princeton first-year students had of individuals from a variety of national and ethnic backgrounds.

The rise of authoritarian regimes during this period stimulated research into topics such as leadership and the influence of group norms on individual behavior. Lewin et al. (1939) conducted their classic study of autocratic, democratic and *laissez-faire* leadership at this time. Sherif (1936) began his exploration of the impact that group norms and standards can have on individuals' behavior. In 1939, Dollard et al. published their study of the causes of human aggression.

One of the key influences on social psychology during this period was the Depression (Finison, 1976). Up until the Depression, psychologists had worked almost exclusively in university settings. In the 1930s, employment opportunities for psychologists were disappearing, as they were for the population at large. In January of 1935, a group of psychologists met at Bellevue Psychiatric Hospital in New York to discuss employment issues. A number of those who attended this meeting expressed the view that there was a need in the community for trained psychologists. This group expanded and, later that year, became the Psychologists League, which, along with psychologists belonging to other groups such as New America, advocated an expanded role for psychologists in the community. In 1936, at the American Psychological Association Convention in New Hampshire, social psychologist Ross Stagner chaired a meeting in which the Society for the Psychological Study of Social Issues (SPSSI) was founded. SPSSI was the first organization dedicated to using psychological research to advance the cause of human welfare. Its objectives were twofold:

1 To encourage research upon those psychological problems most vitally related to modern social, economic and political policies.
2 To help the public and its representatives to understand and to use in the formation of social policies, contributions from the scientific investigation of human behavior (Krech and Cartwright, 1956: 471).

Another key influence on social psychology was the Second World War. Cartwright suggested that the war, and the political turmoil in Europe in the years preceding the war, were "the most important single influence on the development of social psychology up to the present" (1979: 84). One important source of this influence came from the individuals who emigrated from Europe in the years preceding the war. The rise of anti-Semitism in Nazi Germany in the 1930s resulted in the exodus of some of Europe's brightest scholars and scientists. One of those who came to North America at this time was Kurt Lewin, who was to have a seminal impact on social psychology. It was Lewin, the "practical theorist" (Marrow, 1969), who championed an approach to social psychology which blended science with humanitarian values. This blending was most evident in Lewin's (1946) ideas about "action research" and "field experiments," in which research was tied to social action designed to improve the lot of the less fortunate in society. One of Lewin's other major contributions was in the study of social interaction within group settings. It was Lewin who coined the term "group dynamics" and founded the Research Center for Group Dynamics, which carried out the first systematic work on behavior within groups.

When the war began, the army recognized social psychology as an area of specialty, and recruited social psychologists to conduct research on a wide variety of topics relating to the war effort – morale in both civilians and soldiers, military administration, international relations, the public's attitudes toward and support for war-related policies and activities. By the end of the war, social psychologists had come to see themselves in a new light, not just as academics, but as the progenitors of a new social psychology which had a key role to play in producing a new and better society.

The end of the war, however, also marked the beginnings of a reaction to the applied orientation of social psychology that had been building throughout the prewar and war years. Critics decried the atheoretical and unscientific nature of social psychology, and pushed for a more scientific discipline, built upon theories that were tested under rigorous laboratory conditions. With the sudden and premature death of Kurt Lewin in 1947, there remained few strong voices for the integration of theory, research and social action. Consequently, "a split developed that widened into a chasm" after his death (Deutsch, 1975: 2). Conferences in Bethel, Maine in 1947 and 1948 failed to bring the scientist and practitioner factions together, and contributed to the development of an academic social psychology which held application and action in relatively low esteem.

In the two decades following the war, the academic laboratory approach quickly established its dominance over the field. A perusal of the major social psychology journals of the 1950s and 1960s reveals a concentration of research on topics such as attitudes, communication processes, group processes and leadership, almost exclusively within a laboratory setting. The study of attitudes, one of the major areas of investigation during this period, was dominated by the persuasive communication work of Hovland and his associates, and Festinger's cognitive dissonance paradigm. Very little of this work was directly related to important social issues, and almost all of it occurred in university laboratory settings: "By 1965, the experimental approach was the queen of methods. In fact, in some quarters it was vaguely disrespectful to even consider using any other method" (Hendrick, 1977: 20).

The Crisis of Confidence in Social Psychology

By the mid 1960s, social psychology had grown out of its adolescence to become a mature and thriving discipline. There were some, however, who began to wonder about the kind of discipline it had become. Beginning with Ring's 1967 article, titled "Experimental Social Psychology: Some

Sober Questions about Some Frivolous Values," and continuing through the late 1970s, a series of articles posed serious questions about the values underlying social psychological investigation, the way in which research was conducted, and the relevance of the discipline to social behavior in real-world settings.

Ring's article distinguished three types of social psychology: a humanistic, action-oriented psychology, deriving from the Lewinian tradition; a scientifically oriented social psychology, which emphasized the laboratory experiment and eschewed any attempt to make the discipline socially relevant; and a "fun-and-games" social psychology, which stressed clever experiments that produced counter-intuitive findings, but contributed little to the advancement of knowledge. Ring argued that the "fun-and-games" approach dominated, and anguished over the impact that this was having on the field:

> Social psychology today, it seems to me, is in a state of profound intellectual disarray. There is little sense of progress; instead one has the impression of a sprawling, disjointed realm of activity where the movement is primarily outward, not upward. We approach our work with a kind of restless pioneer spirit: a new (or seemingly new) territory is discovered, explored for a while, and then usually abandoned when the going gets rough or uninteresting. We are a field of many frontiersmen, but few settlers. And to the degree that this remains true, the history of social psychology will be written in terms not of flourishing interlocking communities, but of ghost towns. (1967: 119–120)

Others suggested that laboratory methods, and the hypothesis-testing approach to understanding social interaction, were inadequate to achieve an understanding of the complexity of human social behavior. McGuire (1973) decried the use of manipulational laboratory experiments, advocating instead correlational, multivariate studies designed to generate theories and hypotheses, rather than only testing them. Silverman (1977), in his article "Why Social Psychology Fails," also argued against the laboratory manipulational approach, and suggested a more descriptive, naturalistic, discovery-oriented approach to research, with laboratory experiments providing only a supplementary role. Cartwright (1979) and Smith (1972; 1973) offered similar criticisms.

Other critics during this period argued that social psychology was too individualistic in its approach (Sampson, 1977; Steiner, 1974). Sampson suggested that social psychology was based on American ideals of "self-contained individualism" in which "a substantial burden of personal and social responsibility for success and failure is placed on the individual within an individualistic perspective" (1977: 779). Such an approach, he argued, neglected to consider the impact of the community and the society on behavior, placed the burden for resolving problems on the shoulders of the individual (see also Caplan and Nelson, 1973), and justified social programs that matched the "isolating, atomizing, individualizing, and alienating function" of this perspective. To replace this approach, he argued for an "interdependent" perspective, which located the responsibility for behavior within the context of community, society and a system of mutually influencing relationships.

One of the most damning criticisms of social psychology during the "crisis" period was that it was irrelevant. Social psychological research, without being grounded in significant social problems and social issues, risked losing its sense of direction. Smith, in his review of the first volumes of the *Advances in Experimental Social Psychology*, bemoaned the fading of Lewin's legacy, and longed for a return to the kind of social psychology that Lewin had envisioned: "For Lewin, basic and applied research, laboratory and field research, were complementary, not opposed. I hope that as systematic social psychology emerges from its present 'crisis,' it may regain something of the Lewinian synthesis" (1972: 95).

Twenty Years Later – the Crisis Continues

What has happened to the crisis in social psychology in the twenty or more years since it developed? Some, like Augoustinos and Walker (1995), have suggested that the crisis has merely faded away, not because the issues were resolved, but because the discipline has lost interest in pursuing them further. Others, like Reich (1981), have argued that many of the issues that precipitated the crisis have been resolved with the development of a more applied and methodologically sophisticated social psychology. Finally, there are those (e.g., Jones, 1985) who have suggested that there never really was a crisis, and that social psychology should go on with business as usual.

In what follows, I plan to revisit the issues that were raised by the crisis literature of twenty years ago, in an attempt to take stock of the current state of the discipline. My focus will be on the who, what, where, why and how of today's social psychology. Who does social psychological research, and who is being studied? What is (and what is not) being studied? Where does social psychological research take place? What are the primary methods used in studying social behavior? At the base of all of these questions is the question addressed by all of the chapters in this book on critical psychology: what relevance do the theories and practices of social psychology have with regard to our knowledge of human social behavior and the promotion of human welfare?

Who Does Social Psychology, and to Whom?

In his 1979 paper on the historical context in which social psychology developed, Cartwright suggested that "due to the social conditions of the time in which they entered the field, they [social psychologists] are predominantly white, male, middle-class Americans, and thus reflect the interests and biases of this segment of the population" (85). To what extent does this description hold for the social psychologists of today? There can be no doubt that certain elements of this description have changed. One element which has shown the greatest amount of change is the gender of those practicing social psychology. There are now more women social psychologists than ever before, and these women have made major contributions to every area of social psychology. They have not only added significantly to the body of our knowledge about human social behavior; they have begun to make some profound changes in the way social psychology is practiced. It is not surprising, for example, that women social psychologists have been at the forefront of those who have examined topics such as gender differences in social behaviour or intimate social relations, which were formerly neglected in the male-dominated era of the discipline. Feminist theory and research methods are also beginning to produce fundamental changes in the way in which social psychologists view the world and conduct their research (Griffin and Phoenix, 1994; Reinharz and Davidman, 1992; Wilkinson, 1986).

Somewhat less change has occurred in other aspects of Cartwright's (1979) description of the demography of those practicing social psychology. Social psychology is still predominantly an American enterprise, although it has become somewhat less so over the years. This is not surprising, given the fact that the United States has what has been described as a "veritable army [of psychologists] supported by the world's most extensive research infrastructure" (Moghaddam, 1987: 914). Of the twenty or so major journals which publish primarily social psychological research, only a few are based outside of the United States. This has produced a decidedly American perspective in the development of theory and research on human social behavior, a perspective limited by the cultural context in which American social psychologists practice: "Social psychologists are not merely students of society, they are also participants in it, and despite their best efforts to attain a detached objectivity in their research, their thinking is affected by the particular culture in which they live" (Cartwright, 1979: 85).

Social psychology still appears to be practiced primarily by individuals who are white and middle class. The great majority of those who teach social psychology and conduct social psychological research do so within an academic setting. Most of these individuals have PhDs. Relative to the general population, they are well paid, and extremely well educated. They also appear to be mostly white. A recent edited volume titled *The Social Psychologists: Research Adventures* (Brannigan and Merrens, 1995) contains the accounts of how sixteen prominent social psychologists came to be involved in their respective research areas. The page which faces the beginning of each chapter presents a photograph of the researcher; in every case, that researcher is white.

What of the "subjects" of social psychological investigation? To what extent do they represent the ethnic, national, cultural, socioeconomic, age and gender groups found in society at large? Several examinations of participant characteristics over the last twenty-five years indicate that social psychological research has been very restricted in terms of who is selected as the subject of investigation (Higbee et al., 1976; 1982; Higbee and Wells, 1972; Sears, 1986). Sears, for example, found that three-quarters of the articles published in three major social psychological journals in 1980 and 1985 were based on investigations which used American undergraduate students as the sole research participants. Only 17% of the studies published in 1985 used nonstudents. Sears suggests that the narrow participant population on which social psychology is founded poses some serious questions about the validity of the picture of human social behavior that emerges from this research. University students come from a much higher socioeconomic level than do individuals from the population at large; their attitudes toward social issues are less crystallized than are those of older adults; most have not yet formed stable peer group relationships; they tend to be compliant to authority; and they are more cognitive in their orientation than the general population. Sears draws a caricature of the undergraduate research population and contrasts this with the kinds of individuals who are not studied by contemporary social psychologists: "contemporary social psychology . . . presents the human race as composed of lone, bland, compliant wimps who specialize in paper-and-pencil tests. The human being of strong and irrational passions, of intractable prejudices, who is solidly embedded in tightly knit family and ethnic groups, who develops and matures with age, is not that of contemporary social psychology" (1986: 527).

What Is Studied?

The social psychologist of the 1940s, transported to the present and given the chance to skim through some of the major journals in the field, would be profoundly surprised and rather disappointed. She (or more likely, he) would find a social psychology which is much more concerned with the individual than with the way in which individuals relate to one another, and would likely agree with Baumeister's assessment of the field:

> There is a paradox in the way social psychology is practiced today: It isn't always all that social. Ironically, most social psychologists think of people as largely self-contained units, conceding only that occasionally these units come into contact with each other. Perhaps this is not too surprising. The United States is the nation of rugged individualism, and so American thinkers turn out to be oriented toward individuals. (1995: 75)

In part, this state of affairs is the result of the cognitive orientation which has come to dominate thinking in social psychology today. Some have suggested that this perspective is more cognitive than social, and that "the only thing social about social cognition is that it is about social objects – people groups, events" (Augoustinos and Walker, 1995: 3). One of the leading articles in a recent issue of the *Journal of Personality and Social Psychology*, for example, described a series of studies in which research participants attempted to recall Chinese ideographs projected for brief intervals onto a screen (Murphy et al., 1995). The "social" feature of these experiments involved interspersing pictures of either happy or angry faces with the ideographs presented during the recall phase of the experiments.

With the dominance of the cognitive approach, social psychology has retreated deeper and deeper into the heads of the individuals who are studied. Even topics such as intimate relationships are studied from the perspective of the individual. This makes it difficult to conceive of social interaction from a more "contextual" perspective that places greater emphasis on interpersonal and cultural processes (Pepitone, 1981; Senn, 1989). Consequently, topics such as collective behavior, intergroup relations, and social conflict receive much less attention from social psychologists than do topics such as the self, social inference processes and person memory. While researchers outside the United States (and particularly in Europe) have given greater attention to the former kind of topic (Moghaddam, 1987), they often do so using the same kind of cognitive, individual-centered analysis. Thus, it seems that the individualistic approach that Sampson (1977) described during social psychology's crisis era has not dissipated, but, indeed, has become even more pronounced with the so-called cognitive revolution in social psychology.

Many of the theories originating during social psychology's pre-crisis era were motivational in nature. The forces that motivated social behavior came from both within and outside the individual. People were seen as being motivated to obtain rewards (from the groups to which they belonged and from others), to see themselves and their groups in a positive light, to achieve desired goals (both group and individual). A sense of what some of the key forces were that motivated social behavior was drawn from observing the interaction of individuals in real social settings. With the advent of a more cognitive social psychology, theories are more likely to come not from the observation and analysis of social interaction, but from cognitive psychology, and they are more likely to focus on intrapsychic processes than on motivation. Consequently, theory and research have become more individual-centered and even further detached from social behavior in social environments.

One of the solutions offered for dealing with the crisis of the 1970s was to ground social psychological research and theory in the significant social issues and social problems of the day. One result of the call for more relevant social psychological research was the establishment in 1971 of a journal specializing in the application of social psychological research and theory to social issues. Reich suggested that the establishment of the *Journal of Applied Social Psychology* was "the most significant symbol of the final arrival of applied social psychology" (1981: 65). Questions have been raised, however, as to just how applied the research published in the journal is (Helmreich, 1975; Mark et al., 1976). Moreover, most of the research published in the journal involves applying theories that were developed primarily in the laboratory to social issues and problems in real-world settings. Relatively few articles appear to use applied research or social action to inform the development of theory (a recent paper by

Reicher, 1996, shows how this can be done, however). The dialogue envisioned by Lewin, between theory and laboratory research on the one hand, and field or action research on the other, in which each contributes to the other, remains largely unrealized. Additionally, the presence of an "applied" journal of social psychology reinforces the notion that there is a distinction between basic and applied social psychology, and allows for the continuation of a basic or "pure" social psychology that is not grounded in social issues and concerns, or tested in settings outside the laboratory.

Where Is Social Behavior Studied?

In the years surrounding the Second World War, when social psychology experienced its first great burst of activity, researchers conducted their empirical work in a wide variety of settings. Cantril (1940) studied radio listeners; Hovland et al. (1949) conducted research on soldiers in training and combat settings; Bettelheim and Janowitz (1950) looked at veterans in the communities to which they had returned when the war ended. After the war, research was carried on in factories (Coch and French, 1948), housing projects (Deutsch and Collins, 1951; Festinger et al., 1950), and summer camps (Sherif, 1951; Sherif and Sherif, 1953; Sherif et al., 1955). Even Leon Festinger, whose cognitive dissonance theory was to prepare the way for the dominance of both the cognitive approach and the laboratory experiment, based his best-known book on dissonance theory on research that was conducted outside as well as inside the laboratory (Festinger, 1957).

With the deification of the laboratory experiment in the 1960s and 1970s, research outside the laboratory became more and more rare. It was the reliance of social psychology on the laboratory experiment, perhaps more than anything else, that led to the crisis of confidence that the field experienced in the 1970s, and supposedly to a more applied and relevant social psychology in the 1980s and 1990s. But has social psychology moved out of the laboratory in any significant way? An analysis of the research appearing in major social psychology journals would indicate that it has not. Sears (1986), for example, coded studies appearing in three major social psychology journals in the years 1980 and 1985. In 1980, only 15% of the articles appearing in these journals looked at adult research participants in their natural settings. In 1985, this figure dropped (marginally) to 13%. In both years, the great majority of articles published in the three journals described investigations of undergraduate students in laboratory settings.

How Is Social Behavior Studied?

During the heyday of the laboratory experiment, the majority of studies involved the manipulation of independent variables by the experimenter and the measurement of the impact of these manipulations (usually by means of closed-ended response scales) on a limited set of dependent variables. Research participants were frequently misled about the purposes of the experiment, as it was thought that if they knew what the study was about, they would respond in an unnatural manner. The research "subject" was seen as something to be studied under a carefully controlled set of experimental "conditions." Furthermore, the participants were perceived as being largely unaware of the factors that influenced their behavior (Nisbett and Wilson, 1977). Their thoughts, feelings, apprehensions and hopes in relation to the experimental procedure (or anything else) were largely ignored, with the exception of the way in which these things were reflected in responses to the scales which they were required to complete. Essentially, the research participants had little or no "voice" in the empirical process, no means by which to express their own thoughts and feelings about how the experimental environment was affecting them.

The laboratory experiment appears still to be in its heyday, accounting for the great majority of investigations published in social psychology journals (Sears, 1986). While useful to assess the impact of a limited number of variables on a limited set of responses, the laboratory is a very poor representation of the rich, multifaceted and complex environment in which social behavior occurs. It is similarly impoverished in terms of its ability to represent the many and varied ways in which individuals respond to their social environment. Methodologies which are more suited to representing the complexities of the environments in which social behavior occurs, and their impact on the individuals living in those environments, are used infrequently in social psychological research. It would seem that the call of Silverman (1977) and others for a more descriptive, naturalistic and inductive approach to understanding social interaction has gone unheeded. This has occurred despite the availability of a wide range of qualitative methods, such as interviews, case studies, and naturalistic observation, that allow for a more adequate representation of social life in its natural setting. Ironically, such methods were used by social psychologists in the earlier years of the discipline, but fell out of favor when social psychology became infatuated with the laboratory experiment.

The Current State of the Field

Social psychology as it is practiced today seems not to have changed very substantially from its "crisis" period of the 1960s and 1970s. Many of the concerns of that day apply to the social psychology of today. In some respects, the difficulties have become more pronounced:

1   In 1979, Cartwright stated that social psychologists were "predominantly white, male, middle-class Americans." Even with the increase in the numbers of women entering the field, and the greater attention paid to research outside of the United States, a statement describing the current state of affairs wouldn't be very different. Present-day social psychologists are predominantly white, male and female, middle-class Americans. How can individuals with these demographic characteristics

develop a social psychology which is relevant to individuals and groups who may be nonwhite, poor, and/or living in a very different cultural and political environment?

2   The "subjects" of social psychological investigation continue to be predominantly undergraduate students who are better educated, more cognitively skilled, less attached to their groups, more compliant, less diverse in age, and wealthier than the general population (Sears, 1986). How can a social psychology developed from such a narrow data base represent the general population, and what can be done to expand this data base?

3   The individualization and cognitivization of social psychology has led to a social psychology which is no longer driven or informed by the significant social issues and social problems of the day. In many instances, what passes for social psychology is not even social, in that it has little to do with the way in which individuals interact with one another.

4   The majority of social psychological research still involves individuals acting in isolation in academic, laboratory settings. Social interaction, however, does not occur in a laboratory or in a person's mind. It occurs in schools, neighborhoods, workplaces, libraries, shops and homes. It happens at concerts, football games, meetings, and celebrations. Social psychologists need to be more determined to look at social behavior in the places where it actually occurs.

5   The methods employed in the majority of social psychological investigations have involved the testing of hypotheses by manipulating a limited set of independent variables and assessing their impact on a limited set of dependent variables. While newer analytic techniques such as structural equations modeling (Bollen, 1989; Hayduk, 1987) have spurred a greater use of correlational methods, these methods are still more suited to hypothesis testing than to the naturalistic description of social behavior and social settings. In addition, these methods do not give research participants a voice in the research process.

The picture of social psychology that emerges from this analysis is of a discipline that has lost touch with its subject matter. In its push for legitimacy as a science, social psychology has detached itself from its roots, from the social problems and concerns that were its first impetus, and from the values that made the field an exciting and relevant enterprise.

Resolving the Crisis

How can social psychology begin to regain its sense of direction and purpose? I shall try to be relatively pragmatic in my suggestions for change, and to provide some examples of practices that represent the kind of social psychology that I envision.

Research Partnerships

One way of expanding the data base of social psychology beyond under-graduate students in laboratory settings is to form research partnerships with individuals who represent the groups and live in the settings that are to be studied. Individuals interested in violence against women, for example, could form research partnerships with women who have experi-enced violence, individuals who provide services to those women, and even perpetrators (or former perpetrators). These individuals come from an experience base that gives them a special insight into some of the possible causes of violence, the factors that maintain violence, and possible solutions. They will know, likely better than the academic researcher, how best to approach research participants, what kinds of questions to ask, and how to interpret the data that result. More importantly, though, the active participation of these individuals in the research process gives them a voice that has been lacking in social psychological research, and could help to break down the predominance of a professional discourse in which "only the voice of the professional has currency, while the voices of those outside are rendered silent" (Parker and Shotter, 1990: 9). This kind of "stake-holder" involvement in the research process is a common practice in other social science disciplines, such as evaluation research (Pancer, 1996; Weiss, 1983).

Partnerships are also needed among social psychologists from different nations, to ensure the development of a body of knowledge that reflects more than just an American cultural and political context. As Cartwright has said, "Social psychology, more than any other branch of science, with the possible exception of anthropology, requires a breadth of perspective that can only be achieved by a truly international community of scholars" (1979: 85). This kind of partnership would ensure that the kind of critical psychology that has developed outside the United States (e.g., Parker and Shotter, 1990) has a greater impact on the field's mainstream.

Qualitative Research Methods

Qualitative or naturalistic research methods are particularly well suited to describing and understanding social behavior in its natural settings. Some of the most commonly used qualitative methods involve the use of in-depth, open-ended interviews, naturalistic observation, case studies, and the analysis of documents. The qualitative or naturalistic approach differs fundamentally from the hypothesis-testing, deductive approach of the laboratory (Lincoln and Guba, 1985; see also Kidder and Fine, Chapter 3 in this volume). It is inductive and discovery-oriented; it allows for the study of social behavior as it unfolds in its natural environment; it allows those being studied to express themselves more fully, unrestrained by the bounds of fixed-response questions; and it provides a richer picture of the wide range of variables that influence social interaction. An excellent example of how such an approach can be used is provided in a recent

study by Kidder et al. (1995), who used open-ended unstructured interviews to examine women's recall and reconstruction of experiences with
sexual harassment.

Unfortunately, qualitative methods are rarely used in social psychological
research, particularly in North America, though a much stronger tradition
of qualitative research exists in European social psychology (Henwood and
Parker, 1994). Henwood and Pidgeon (1994) distinguish three different kinds
of qualitative approaches that psychologists have employed in their research.
These range from the empirical approach of Miles and Huberman (1994),
through the contextualist, grounded theoretical approach of Strauss and
Corbin (1990), to the constructivist approach of discourse analysts such as
Potter and Wetherell (1987). Henwood and Pidgeon suggest that, of these
three, discourse analysis represents the most significant break with
traditional laboratory experimental social psychology (see Chapter 18).

Action Research

Over twenty-five years ago, Nevitt Sanford suggested that the separation of
science and practice that had been institutionalized after World War II had
condemned action research to an "orphan's role in social science" (1970: 7).
While the volume of action research has certainly not changed very much
over the years, this approach has had a steady, if small, presence in
the arena of social psychological research, right up to the present day. The
tradition is perhaps most evident in the area of social conflict. One of
the best examples of the action research approach is the jigsaw group
technique pioneered by Aronson and his colleagues with groups of school
children (Aronson, 1990; Aronson et al., 1978; Aronson and Gonzalez,
1988). In utilizing this technique, children are organized into small, multi-
ethnic and multi-racial learning groups. Each member of the group is
assigned one portion of the day's lesson, which he or she must teach to the
rest of the group. Thus each group member must rely on the other group
members to learn all the material. These groups have proven very
successful in promoting racial harmony in multi-racial school settings. This
kind of action research serves a dual purpose. It not only helps to promote
human welfare; it also contributes to the development of theory. For social
psychology to enhance its relevance and utility, researchers must become
more willing to develop and implement social interventions, in addition to
using theory and research to understand social problems.

Integrating Applied and Basic Research

To a large extent, applied research has been marginalized by the division of
the field into basic and applied components. The result is a body of theory
and research appearing in mainstream journals which is frequently
unrelated to social concerns, or even to social behavior. It is time for the
mainstream journals in social psychology to reintegrate the applied and

basic components of the discipline, and to begin to apply standards of social relevance to manuscripts that are being considered for publication. Social psychology *is* an *applied* social science. To hive off that portion which is applied is to render it even less relevant to social concerns and to remove it even further from the realm of real social experience.

Making Values Explicit

Because social psychology had its roots primarily in the United States, the values it took on during its formative years were largely those prevalent in the American culture. These values included a belief in democracy and individual rights, the ability of the individual to overcome any obstacles to growth and development, and the achievement of social progress through a process of rational problem solving (Cartwright, 1979). These values played a significant role in both the topics that were chosen for investigation, and the way in which these topics were studied. Later in the history of the discipline, another set of values was grafted onto the earlier set. These were the values of scientism and professionalism which continue to have a profound impact on the way social psychological topics are investigated. Parker and Shotter (1990) argue that these values, which lie at the root of social psychological theory and the "institutional apparatus" of social psychology, need to be deconstructed and replaced by a more pluralistic set of approaches.

It is certainly time for the discipline to reexamine its values, to place them in a broader cultural context, and to make them more explicit. The establishment of a set of core values, and the periodic assessment of these values, have been useful in providing direction to other subdisciplines of psychology, such as community psychology (Rappaport, 1977). Prillel-tensky and Nelson (Chapter 11 in this volume) suggest that this kind of exploration of values can lead to changes which transform a discipline rather than merely ameliorating aspects of it. This would certainly be the case if social psychology were to move (back?) to a more social activist approach in deciding upon the issues, methods, theories and activities that define the discipline.

Conclusions

Social psychology, for the most part, has had a proud history. It developed from a tradition that valued human welfare and saw the discipline as a means to bring about a more humane society. While the current emphasis on the hypothesis-testing approach, and the dominance of the field by an individualistic perspective, have somewhat diverted social psychology from its former path, the concern that social psychology has for alleviating human suffering has never been lost. It is alive in organizations such as the Society for the Psychological Study of Social Issues, in the social action tradition that continues to be practiced, and in the desire of social psychologists for a discipline that not only contributes to our understanding of human social behavior, but is useful and relevant, as well. It is time, however, for social psychology to move beyond the crisis in which it has been immersed for nearly thirty years by reexamining its core values and methods, and working to give those whose perspectives have been absent from social psychological discourse a stronger voice in its future.

11

Community Psychology: Reclaiming Social Justice

Isaac Prilleltensky and Geoffrey Nelson

Editors' note *As we shift our focus to newer, less traditional subfields that arose or expanded in the turbulent 1960s and 1970s, we are more likely to discover disillusionment with mainstream psychology's individualistic assumptions. This is especially the case for community psychology, as Isaac Prilleltensky and Geoffrey Nelson describe in this chapter.*

Mainstream psychology defines social and mental health problems as person-centered – and thus seeks solutions aimed at individuals. In contrast, community psychologists direct their efforts at systems rather than at individuals. They work in schools, churches, neighborhood and grassroots associations, mutual help organizations, and workplaces. Unlike traditional applied psychology, community psychology uses a multi-level perspective, is sensitive to social context and diversity, and focuses on people's competencies rather than deficiencies. Community psychologists act as collaborators rather than experts and prefer participatory, action-oriented research methods. Most important for critical psychology, community psychology seeks to eliminate disempowering social conditions.

All these features might lead one to believe that critical and community psychology are one and the same. Unfortunately, this is not the case. Community psychology does target systemic sources of suffering. But as Prilleltensky and Nelson point out, it does so in an ameliorative *rather than a* transformative *way. Thus, community psychology follows the same pattern as subfields such as psychology and law (Chapter 14): although it tries to reform existing structures to ameliorate harsh conditions, it does so without challenging the status quo's underlying legitimacy. Critical psychology, on the other hand, insists that we cannot eliminate oppression without transforming oppressive institutions and altering the basic premises of unjust systems. For community psychology to benefit from critical psychology's insights, Prilleltensky and Nelson emphasize, it must move social justice from the background of the discipline's concerns to the foreground.*

What a block! My block is the most terrible block I've ever seen. There are at least 25 or 30 narcartic [*sic*] people in my block – In the summer they don't do nothing but shooting, stabbing, and fighting.

H. Kohl, *Thirty-Six Children*

Many community psychologists have listened to the stories of people living in disadvantaged communities, like that of the twelve-year-old student in Herbert Kohl's grade six class in Harlem back in 1962. These stories, replete with experiences of poor health, abuse and violence, powerlessness, discrimination, and poverty, have motivated us to alleviate human suffering. We each have our own journey that has led us to this field. Yet we share in common many of these personal experiences, which have informed our values in our work as community psychologists.

In line with the main objective of this book, the primary aim of this chapter is to examine the extent to which community psychology has fulfilled its promise of advancing certain values for disadvantaged communities (Montero, 1994). Following Baier (1973), we define values as principles and practices that confer benefits to individuals and communities. Table 11.1 defines the five main values we endorse as community psychology's values, necessary to help oppressed communities and to promote a better and more just society. These are the values of *health, caring and compassion, self-determination and participation, human diversity*, and *social justice*. Our rendition of values is context-bound, imperfect, and evolving. Values conflict, and we do not always have the appropriate conceptual or practical devices to resolve these dilemmas adequately (Berlin, 1984). Nevertheless, we believe that these five values contain sufficient merit to address a wide range of human and social needs (Prilleltensky, 1994a; 1994b).

In this chapter we first describe guiding principles for actualizing the values of community psychology. We then discuss how the field's values have evolved over time in North America. Although we focus on the North American context, the one we know best, evidence suggests similar patterns in other parts of the world (Montero, 1994). Finally we outline a major gap in community psychology: the lack of attention to the value of social justice. We offer recommendations for incorporating this value more fully into our research and action.

Guiding Principles to Actualize Values

We propose five principles to guide the implementation of community psychology's values.

Principle 1   *Advancing the well-being of disadvantaged communities requires actualizing all five values in a balanced way*

We argue below that these central values are, in effect, part of community psychology's social agenda. Fundamental human needs, values, and rights must be met and upheld for a better and more just society to emerge. But

Table 11.1   *The current salience and social impact of community psychology values and their corresponding guiding concepts*

Values	Community psychology guiding concepts	Continuum of saliency Background —— Foreground		Continuum of social impact Ameliorative —— Transformative	
		Background	Foreground	Ameliorative	Transformative
Caring and compassion The expression of care, empathy, and concern for the physical and emotional well-being of others	* Psychological sense of community * Social support * Self-help		X	X	
Health A state of physical and emotional well-being that is intrinsically beneficial and extrinsically instrumental in pursuing self-determination	* Prevention * Health promotion * Pursuit of wellness		X	X	
Self-determination and participation The ability of individuals to pursue chosen goals and participate in decisions affecting their lives	* Empowerment * Citizen participation	X			X
Human diversity Respect and appreciation for diverse social identities and for people's ability to define themselves.	* Diversity * Oppression	X			X
Social justice The fair and equitable allocation of bargaining power, resources, and obligations in society	* Justice and equality * Political education * Social change movements	X			X

we also claim that the field has given some of the values more attention than others. These values are complementary and not mutually exclusive.

This is a crucial consideration in any assessment of the comparative worth of values. In isolation, these values cannot attain their objective of bringing us closer to a better society. Because each value by itself is insufficient, problems arise when we adhere too closely to one principle but neglect another equally important one. A typical case is the extolment of autonomy and self-determination at the expense of distributive justice (Fox, 1993a) or sense of community (Bakan, 1966; Fox, 1993a; Riger, 1993). We can appreciate the complementarity of values, for example, when we see how *caring* is interwoven with *justice*. There cannot be health without justice, and there cannot be justice in the absence of caring and compassion (Habermas, 1990; Kymlicka, 1990). Caring and compassion demonstrate sensitivity to someone else's well-being, while the pursuit of social justice ensures that our compassion extends beyond our immediate circle of care. This is what Kimball called the "dialectics of care and justice" (1994: 396).

However, for political, economic, and historical reasons, societies adhere to a few values to the neglect of others. Patriarchal, capitalist values such as rugged individualism, competition, meritocracy, and the amassment of wealth and consumer goods have dominated life in North America (Saul, 1995). Community psychology has not been immune to this trend. We have paid disproportionate attention to the values of health, caring/compassion, and to some extent self-determination/participation and diversity. We have neglected social justice.

Principle 2   *Within a given social ecology, some values appear at the foreground of our consciousness while others remain in the background. We must move the neglected values to the foreground to attain the necessary balance*

The social ecology influences the particular configuration of values at a certain time and place. As a result, some values are more salient than others (see Table 11.1). While the socioeconomic, cultural and political climate may favor a particular value, such as health, it is our obligation to determine which values we may be neglecting. By reworking the values to meet the needs of a specific community, we will advance more holistic and ecological theories and practices (Kelly, 1986).

Thus, for example, in Western societies the values of self-determination/participation, human diversity, and social justice currently remain in the background, while caring/compassion and health are at the forefront of our concerns. Thus it is necessary to accentuate the background values. In another location or at another historical moment, the values might be configured differently, potentially relegating some values to lower priority. This may occur under regimes that want to advance social ideals, however just in the end, without caring and concern for the individuality of its members. If that were the case, we would have to restore the suppressed values of caring/compassion and health to ensure that citizens enjoy the full range of values.

Observations from other societies illustrate how different contexts require the advancement of different values. Kibbutzim (collective settlements) in Israel used to demand of their members a great deal of personal sacrifice to meet communal goals. With the passage of time, however, kibbutz members began to feel they were compromising their privacy, individuality and self-determination for the good of the collective. Institutional practices then changed to allow members greater freedom in pursuing their interests.

The saliency and effects of values vary not only across time and place, but also across communities of peoples. Different groups may share a temporal and geographical location, but their needs may be vastly distinct. Thus, within a particular time and place two or more groups facing different circumstances may require different configurations of values to advance their well-being. For example, women and people of color may need to see self-determination/participation and human diversity advanced, while people who have experienced unexpected illness or personal tragedy may have a greater need for health and caring/compassion (Trickett et al., 1984; 1994).

Our ecological interpretation of values is a dialectical one. A series of principles may predominate at one point in time, and these ideals may indeed serve the community well. But as the social ecology changes, so does the need for alternative conceptions of the good. A value may serve us well for a while, but after a certain period of time it may lose its liberating features. We should ask ourselves what values will best advance the well-being of this community at this historical juncture (Kane, 1994).

Principle 3   *Within the present social context, the value of social justice remains in the background. By neglecting this value, we reinforce the same unjust state of affairs that disadvantaged many communities in the first place*

Neglecting social justice reinforces an unjust state of affairs (Scherer, 1992). But our historical analysis suggests that most of our work as community psychologists tries to ameliorate living conditions within the existing distribution of wealth and resources. Herein lies the main barrier for the fulfillment of our mission (see Table 11.1). For as long as we try to address only the consequences of an uneven allocation of resources, without looking at the problem's root cause, we confront only the surface of the issues. This is what Joffe and Albee (1988) meant when they said we should explore "the causes of the causes" of problems in living. Most of the issues we deal with in our preventive and community interventions are symptoms of a profound social malady: injustice.

Principle 4   *We must distinguish between ameliorating living conditions within the present social structure and transforming the conditions that create disadvantage*

We need to ask ourselves whether our persistent efforts to organize communities are directed at amelioration or transformation. *Amelioration* means change within a system, or what has been termed "first-order change," while *transformation* means changing the basic premises of a system or "second-order change" (Rappaport, 1977). To be sure, ameliorative work is important and needed. Moreover, ameliorative projects have the advantage of producing results in a relatively short period of time. But we should ask ourselves whether it is justified to invest most of our energies in ameliorative work just because it produces some results quickly. Without larger transformative efforts these gains may be undermined in the long term.

Transformative social justice work is conceptually and practically difficult (Scherer, 1992). Many are the incentives for choosing ameliorative work: it is more focused; it does not threaten the status quo; and there is by now a solid research base to support ameliorative preventive efforts. Indeed, community psychology has changed the field of mental health by supplementing clinical treatments with preventive interventions. Focusing on transformation rather than amelioration now requires that we move from person-centered to ecological interventions that span and connect several levels of analysis (Cowen, 1985; Febbraro, 1994; Nelson and Hayday, 1995).

Principle 5   *We must expand the implementation of values from micro and meso contexts to macro social ecologies*

Applied psychologists traditionally try to implement values at the micro level (e.g., family and interpersonal relationships) or, at best, at the meso or middle level (e.g., workplace, schools). Many psychologists wish to enhance the self-determination of clients or small groups, desire to respect human diversity, and show empathy and concern for those suffering from life stressors. But these micro and meso social interventions are embedded within a larger social context of inequality, oppression, and discrimination. Hence, efforts to promote collaboration and respect for diversity at the micro level are undermined at the macro level by a larger social structure that promotes inequality, supports individualism and competition, and is intolerant of diversity.

If the first four values in Table 11.1 were actualized at the macro level, the aspiration of social justice would be met, for social justice concerns the fair distribution of societal resources. Consistent with an ecological analysis, the values refer to resources (e.g., health, caring and compassion) that operate at different levels (micro, meso, and macro) (Kelly, 1986). The point of social justice is that everyone in society should benefit from these values. By pushing the boundaries of our interventions outward, to encompass the micro, meso, *and* macro levels, we promote the value of social justice. We move from community psychology's status quo depicted in Figure 11.1 toward the ideal expressed in Figure 11.2.

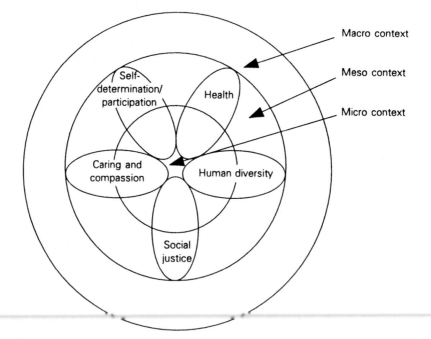

Figure 11.1   *Current scope of values in community psychology*

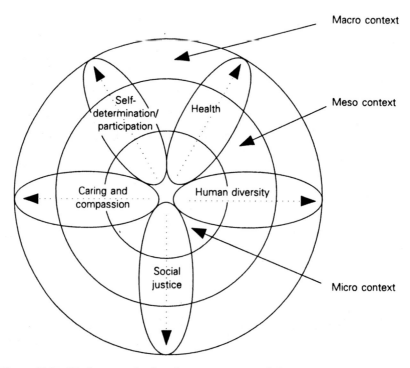

Figure 11.2   *Ideal scope of values in community psychology*

Community Psychology's Values in Historical Perspective

Throughout its three decades of formal existence, community psychology has promoted a series of important values. We show in this section their interconnections, noting which values have been emphasized in different periods of time.

Founding Values: Caring, Compassion, and Health

Community psychology's emergence in the sixties reflected the larger social discontent with individualism, alienation, loneliness, and fragmentation of the human experience (Sarason, 1988). Psychologists seeking antidotes for these social ills shifted their definitions of mental health problems, as well as their interventions, from the individual to the community. As Table 11.2 shows, community psychology reframed problems in terms of an ecological perspective that is sensitive to human diversity, at the same time that it promoted community-based solutions. The sense-of-community metaphor (Sarason, 1988) captures what we mean by caring and compassion: a shared emotional connection, common ground, trust, and feelings of belonging (McMillan and Chavis, 1986). The need to counteract isolation with a sense of community was, and to some extent still is, a potent unifying concept in the field (García et al., 1994; McMillan and Chavis, 1986; Newbrough, 1995).

The reorientation from individuals to communities signified more than a numerical expansion of the locus of intervention. It also meant that communities could handle their own affairs. Moreover, it is important to note that our need for a sense of community can never be met by professionals and human services (McKnight, 1995). While many human services agencies and professionals strive to be caring and compassionate, community psychology recognizes that informal sources of support are critical for people's sense of community.

It is hard to fathom the relevance of other moral values in the absence of caring and compassion, for they provide the basic motivation to look after someone else's health and well-being. Yet while this value's essential place is indisputable, its insufficiency becomes apparent when we realize its ameliorative nature. In our opinion, the sense of community sought in our neighborhood associations and social support groups is designed to cope with the results of existing inequities, not with their antecedents. This is why we conceptualize caring and compassion as having primarily an ameliorative effect.

The primary value of physical and mental health was, and still remains, a constitutive dimension of community psychology. In the early years, community psychologists were strongly influenced by the field of public health. Several founding community psychologists helped to import notions of prevention and health promotion and to apply them to mental health problems (Rosenblum, 1971). In an effort to increase the scope of this

Table 11.2 *Assumptions and practices of traditional applied psychology and community psychology*

	Traditional applied psychology	Community psychology
Levels of analysis	Intrapsychic or interpersonal	Ecological perspective (interdependence of individuals, families, community, and society)
Problem definition	Based on individualist philosophies that lead to blaming the victim	Based on social context and cultural diversity
Time of intervention	Remedial (late/reactive)	Prevention (early/proactive)
Goals of intervention	Reduction of maladaptive patterns	Promotion of health and well-being
Type of intervention	Treatment/rehabilitation (services)	Self-help/community development/social action (resources)
Focus of intervention	Deficits/weaknesses	Competence/strengths
Role of "client"	Passive recipient of services (focus on acquiescence to treatment)	Active participant (focus on voice and choice)
Role of professional	Expert technician (assessment and treatment)	Resource collaborator (consultation, action research, planning, community development, social change agent, advocacy)
Type of research	Applied research based on positivistic assumptions	Participatory and action-oriented research
Social ethics	Value-neutral stance and tacit acceptance of status quo	Strong emphasis on values, identification of oppressive social conditions, and orientation towards social change

approach, Cowen (1994) has recently referred to our field as the pursuit of wellness. The preventive and health promoting foci of interventions are outlined in Table 11.2.

Thus, the values of caring/compassion and health have been operative in the research and practice of community psychologists since the inception of the field (Bennett et al., 1966; Rosenblum, 1971). These two values have been evident in what Cowen (1980) has termed the *generative* and *executive bases* of primary prevention. By the generative base, Cowen means basic research that illuminates the pathways to health or dysfunction. Community psychologists have contributed to research on stress, coping, and social support for adults (e.g., Gottlieb, 1981) and risk and protective factors for children (e.g., Hawkins et al., 1992; Yoshikawa, 1994). This research constitutes much of the generative base for prevention programs.

The value of caring and compassion has also been reflected in the executive base of community interventions. Community psychologists have played an instrumental role in developing interventions that enhance social support for vulnerable adults and children (Gottlieb, 1983). In its early history, community psychology pioneered the development of programs using paid and volunteer nonprofessionals to provide support to children and youth at risk for psychosocial problems (Cowen et al., 1975; Davidson and Redner, 1988), adults with a history of psychiatric problems (Rappaport et al., 1971), and other populations. More recently, the value of caring and compassion has been extended to include collaboration with self-help/mutual-aid groups (Lavoie et al., 1994).

The notions that nonprofessional helpers and self-help/mutual-aid groups could be as effective as highly trained clinicians and that prevention could reduce the need for treatment threatened the professional status quo. For example, critics both within psychology (Jensen, 1969) and in other mental health disciplines (Lamb and Zusman, 1979) challenged the legitimacy of preventive interventions, arguing there was no evidence indicating such interventions were effective. Community psychologists have refuted many of these challenges through research and action. They have demonstrated the effectiveness of nonprofessional helpers (showing they are at least as effective as professionals for many problems: Berman and Norton, 1985; Hattie et al., 1984), self-help/mutual-aid groups (Humphreys and Rappaport, 1994), and primary prevention programs (Price et al., 1988; Rae-Grant, 1994).

The bulk of the work in primary prevention, however, has adopted person-centered intervention strategies at the micro or meso level, such as teaching life skills or building social support (Cowen, 1985). There have been few attempts at macro-level social systems change. The danger of pursuing only person-centered interventions is that unjust social conditions are ignored. Preventionists, thus, inadvertently reinforce an ideology of rugged individualism through which individuals can presumably rise above and conquer social disadvantages (Albee, 1986; Febbraro, 1994). Similarly, most of the work on self-help/mutual-aid groups has emphasized individual change rather than social change (Humphreys and Rappaport, 1994). There is no question that prevention in general, and primary prevention in particular, are concerned with the broad ecological sources of human suffering. However, while the move from intrapsychic orientations to a community- and population-wide focus is laudatory, we need to ask whether prevention and health promotion truly address the "causes of the causes," or only the surface of the causes (Joffe and Albee, 1988).

Caring/compassion and health, community psychology's implicit founding values, continue to exert a strong influence on the field today. We believe that these values, *by themselves*, do not hold the potential for transformation. We need to expand community psychology's value base.

Emerging Values: Self-determination, Participation, and Human Diversity

The value of self-determination and participation in decisions affecting one's life was articulately expressed by Rappaport in the eighties (1981;

1987). His influential articles on *empowerment* prompted the field to ponder the difference between what we call ameliorative and transformative work. Rappaport (1981) argued that empowerment, not prevention, should be community psychology's guiding mission.

As an intervention, empowerment refers to actions and policies designed to enhance the degree of control vulnerable individuals exercise over their lives. As an outcome, it refers to the feelings of control and to the actual decision making power accompanying those feelings (Zimmerman and Rappaport, 1988). Thus, the concept brings attention to the social structures that prevent people from controlling their destiny. Lack of power to change proximal as well as distal oppressive systems is a major source of disempowerment (Lord and Hutchison, 1993). The last five categories of Table 11.2 denote the attention community psychology pays to the values of participation and control. In our view, the empowerment movement has moved us closer to the transformative end of social interventions (Boyte and Riessman, 1986; Newbrough, 1992). However, it has not yet grown into a social justice movement aimed at the origins of disempowerment.

Most recently in the history of the discipline, the value of human diversity has drawn attention to oppressive social structures, thereby further politicizing community psychology. Issues of diversity and oppression address cultural and political traditions that exclude marginalized people from mainstream processes. While Rappaport (1977) recognized cultural diversity as a key value, only in the last decade has this value manifested itself in discussions of feminism and gender (Mulvey, 1988), ethnic and racial diversity (McNicoll and Rousseau, 1993; Trickett et al., 1994), sexual orientation (D'Augelli, 1994), and disability (Fawcett et al., 1994). However, most work in this area has concentrated on strategies of inclusion into existing institutions, not on rebuilding those institutions on a more egalitarian basis.

The values of self-determination/participation and human diversity have been reflected in research and action over the past ten years. Research related to self-determination/participation can be seen, among other places, in special journal issues on empowerment (Rappaport et al., 1984; Zimmerman and Perkins, 1995). This research has taken community psychology beyond the narrow boundaries of mental health. As for human diversity, while community psychology has historically ignored women, people of color, gays and lesbians, and people with disabilities (Loo et al., 1988; Novaco and Monahan, 1980; Swift et al., forthcoming), research examining the experiences of diverse people has recently begun to emerge (McNicoll and Rousseau, 1993; Trickett et al., 1994; Serrano-García and Bond, 1994).

In addition to changes in the *content* of community research and action, the values of self-determination/participation and human diversity are beginning to influence the *process* of community research and action. These values are evident in recent papers advocating participatory, action-oriented, feminist, and indigenous approaches to research (Collins, 1991;

Montero, 1994; Serrano-García, 1990; Serrano-García and Rosario, 1992; Stanfield, 1994). A goal of this approach is to amplify the voices of people lacking in power. Qualitative research methods are often used to obtain different stakeholders' social constructions of reality (see Chapter 3). Finally, participatory action research has an explicit political agenda of helping to foster social change (Price and Cherniss, 1977; Reinharz, 1992).

These same values have also influenced community psychology's practice and action arenas. Self-determination/participation and human diversity call for realignment of professional roles from "expert" to "resource collaborator" (Tyler et al., 1983). Historically, many preventive and community interventions have been driven by professionals. Instead, community psychologists can act as resource collaborators in alternative settings that are operated by service users, or they can share power and work in partnership with consumers (Constantino and Nelson, 1995; Nelson and Walsh-Bowers, 1994).

Clearly, the values of self-determination/participation and human diversity have gained in prominence. However, community psychologists have not fully embraced the implications. For example, although Rappaport (1981; 1987) conceived of empowerment as a multi-level construct that includes actual power and perceived power, Riger (1993) has argued that most research on empowerment has focused on the individual level of analysis and has neglected political power.

Similarly, while there are more women in the field, fundamental incorporation of a feminist agenda and ideology into training, research, and practice has not occurred (Mulvey, 1988; Swift et al., forthcoming). Likewise, Suarez-Balcazar et al. (1994) found that many community psychology graduate training programs do not have professors of color or courses in ethnocultural diversity. Only 23% of the directors surveyed believe that their programs successfully train students in issues related to ethnocultural diversity.

The values of self-determination/participation and human diversity in community psychology are in their nascent state of development. We need to incorporate them more fully into our training, research, and action. Examining the forces that inhibit and facilitate change could help us develop strategies to realize these values in our work (Mulvey, 1988).

The Future: the Value of Social Justice

Thus, we arrive at the last value of Table 11.1, social justice. This value refers to the fair and equitable allocation of bargaining power, resources, and burdens in society (Kymlicka, 1990; Miller, 1978; Rawls, 1972). This is the value where the discrepancy between rhetoric and action is the greatest.

Proponents of sense of community, prevention, empowerment, and human diversity typically invoke social justice as a prerequisite for the fulfillment of other values, but we somehow stop at that. Most notably, Albee (1986; 1996; Albee et al., 1988) has reminded us that by neglecting to act on social injustice we remain ineffective in our preventive efforts, as we fail to alter the "causes of the causes." Without an even distribution of social goods, other basic values, needs, and rights cannot be fulfilled. Whereas community psychology in the sixties may have been socially progressive in comparison to traditional applied and clinical psychology (see Table 11.2), it is altogether possible that in the nineties it has lost its progressive edge and become part of conservative mainstream institutions. It would not be the first time that a profession's or social movement's radical impulses faded (Chavis and Wolff, 1993).

Without social justice, an indispensable building block of the Good or Ideal Society is missing, putting the whole edifice at risk of collapse. The community psychology literature has paid very little attention to issues such as social action, advocacy and social change movements, poverty and anti-poverty organizations, grassroots community organizing, human rights, sustainable community economic development, and social policy. Moreover, as we noted above, much of the field's research and action focuses on the micro and meso levels, not on the macro level (Novaco and Monahan, 1980; Peirson and Walsh-Bowers, 1993). Finally, much greater attention is paid to research methodology than to our work's political dimensions and dynamics.

A Social Justice Agenda for Community Psychology

Key Themes for a Social Justice Agenda

As authors, our major and humbling challenge is to recommend avenues to actualize social justice. In this section, we provide an initial and incomplete framework for a social justice agenda in community psychology (see Table 11.3). We believe that three key themes provide some guidance: (a) connections between the personal and the political; (b) connections among constituents who are involved in, and affected by, social change; and (c) connections among the micro, meso, and macro levels.

The importance for social change of connecting the personal and the political has been championed by the feminist movement (Mulvey, 1988). Politics cannot be separated from everyday experiences of injustice (Smith, 1987). When women share their experiences of oppression with one another, they come to see how their experiences are not isolated incidents but part of a pervasive pattern of men's domination of women. Thus, personal experiences reflect the larger political issue of power differences between men and women in society. Making this connection is part of consciousness raising that fuels a process of personal empowerment and social change (Mulvey, 1988; Surrey, 1991).

Continuing with this illustration, the interdependence of micro, meso, and macro contexts draws attention to how sexism is manifested at multiple levels of analysis. Women experience sexism in their families and close

Table 11.3 *Key themes for a social justice agenda for community
psychology theory, research, action, education, and training*

Community psychology activities	Key themes for a social justice agenda		
	Connections between the personal and the political	Connections between micro, meso and macro contexts	Connections between constituents
Theory	* Grounding in issues and settings * Attention to subjectivity and personal experiences of oppression * The role of intrapersonal, interpersonal, and social conflict in social justice	* Interdisciplinary frameworks * Integrative theory of change * Sensitivity to interdependence of levels * Need to address implementation of values at all levels	* Balance between rights and responsibilities * Balance between individual and collective issues
Research and action	* Emancipatory research and action * Participatory action research approaches	* Multiple levels of analysis and intervention * Naturalistic case studies on effects of injustice and power inequality at all levels	* Involvement of multiple stakeholders and negotiation of power differences * Sensitivity to diversity of stakeholders
Education and training	* Recruiting for diversity * Attention to personal interests that might interfere with actualization of values * Promoting conscientization	* Addressing issues of justice within training programs * Mentoring in settings espousing social justice causes * Learning to identify contradictions at all levels	* Creating a psychological sense of community within the training program * Building long-term relationships with settings espousing social justice

relationships (the micro level) and in their work, school, and religious
setting (the meso level). Both levels are affected by the larger macro
context: social norms that objectify women, socioeconomic inequality, and
social policies that harm women and children. A social justice focus
requires changes at all three levels of analysis.

Connections among constituents are important for building a psychological sense of community among different stakeholders (Sarason, 1988)
and promoting social change through relationships (Surrey, 1991). In part,
this notion also concerns how one oppressed group relates to other
oppressed groups. While it is necessary for individuals and groups to define
and develop their own identity (Taylor, 1992), it is also important to be in

solidarity with other oppressed groups. Recognizing common ground and building coalitions, while maintaining individual identity, is a key strategy for developing a constituency for social change (Balcazar et al., 1994; Nelson, 1994).

The relationship between oppressed groups and those in power is another important dimension. For example, psychiatric consumers/survivors historically have seen mental health professionals as agents of oppression (Burstow and Weitz, 1988). However, professionals who identify with the emancipatory goals of consumers/survivors can define new roles in collaboration with such groups and assist them in realizing their goals (Constantino and Nelson, 1995; Nelson and Walsh-Bowers, 1994). The negotiation of power between unequal groups is central to promote social change. Finally, we need to develop authentic connections with members of disadvantaged communities. When power is shared, personal connections are made, and unique strengths are recognized, a working alliance for social change is formed.

We now turn to a discussion of the implications of the key themes for theory, research and action, and education and training in community psychology.

Social Justice and Theory

Because experiential grounding will inform our theoretical frameworks, we need to connect the personal and the political and immerse ourselves in issues and settings with a social justice agenda. While community psychology has gone beyond the narrow boundaries of community mental health centers to work with meso-level schools, neighborhood organizations, and self-help/mutual-aid organizations (Shinn, 1987), these settings have a social welfare orientation. Guided by the values of caring/compassion and health, social welfare settings focus on protecting and promoting health and well-being. As such, they are geared towards amelioration.

We need to become more involved in settings with a social justice, transformative, and macro-level orientation, such as labor unions, environmental organizations (e.g., Greenpeace), community economic development organizations and worker cooperatives, anti-poverty organizations, advocacy coalitions for people with disabilities, Public Interest Research Groups, feminist movement organizations, and multicultural and anti-racism organizations. Immersion in such settings – and reading more radical literature – will help us develop the political literacy about social issues that is uncommon in North American society (Macedo, 1994). It will catalyze a process of what Freire (1993) has called "conscientization": a critical awareness of how we are shaped by, and how we can shape, our political environment. This experiential base will inform our theoretical analyses of social problems and social change (Bennett, 1987).

Our theoretical analyses must move beyond the micro and meso levels to incorporate macro sociopolitical contexts. To do so, we must look to other disciplines for theoretical frameworks, as in recent interdisciplinary work by Prilleltensky and Gonick (1994; 1996) that analyzes psychological and political aspects of oppression. Similarly, resource mobilization theory, from sociology and political science, provides a useful framework for analyzing the role of social movements in social change (Morris and Mueller, 1992).

Regarding the connections between constituents, a community psychology social justice theory needs to be holistic and achieve an ecological balance between rights and responsibilities and between individual and collective issues. Although Rappaport (1981) advanced empowerment as a way of achieving balance between needs and rights, we believe that empowerment, in its emphasis on self-determination and the acquisition of power, could potentially advance the agenda of one group at the expense of another. The same is true for the concept of human diversity, which could lead to more resources, respect, and autonomy for one group, while others suffer. There is a danger that our society can become too oriented towards meeting the needs of particular sectors to the point that there is no longer any common bond or purpose.

Community psychologists should explore the philosophy of *communitarianism*, which espouses a balance between rights and responsibilities (Avineri and De-Shalit, 1992; Etzioni, 1993). While in its current form communitarianism suffers from a lack of class analysis and a clear political philosophy, as Kymlicka (1990) and other critics charge (cf. Bell, 1993), a communitarian orientation can help undermine the domination of the liberal individualist tradition. Communitarianism emphasizes social responsibilities and the collective good in the pursuit of social justice (Frazer and Lacey, 1993). This concept does not negate the need for diverse individual or group identities and self-determination. Rather it acknowledges that this need must be met in a community context in a way that the common good is upheld and advanced as well. Solidarity among diverse constituents is an important feature in the communitarian approach.

Social Justice and Research and Action

To link the personal and the political in community research and action, we should reverse the current emphasis on research over action (Chavis and Wolff, 1993). That is, action should lead and research should follow. Becoming immersed in settings that have a social justice orientation will provide us with a base to do research that appreciates and contributes to the goals of such settings. Participatory, action-oriented approaches are best suited to the goals of a social justice agenda (Reinharz, 1992; Serrano-García, 1990).

Our collaborative social intervention projects should have explicit outcome goals. As suggested by resource mobilization theory, some potential justice-related goals are changes in public policy, the politics of decision making, the distribution of socially valued goods, collective consciousness, and resources for future mobilization (Balcazar et al., 1994; Nelson, 1994). Bunch (1987) outlined similar criteria for evaluating feminist reforms: material improvement in the lives of women, enhancement of individual empowerment, the establishment of group structures for further change, heightened political awareness, and increased control by women of social institutions. These criteria reflect outcomes at multiple levels of analysis, from the micro to the macro. We need to look at processes that facilitate or impede the realization of such outcomes and at how changes at one level affect other levels.

Research that follows action, which is driven by the participants in the setting and their needs, and which examines processes and outcomes at multiple levels of analysis, will not fit neatly into experimental or quasi-experimental designs. Thus, we advocate a naturalistic case study approach as the basic methodology (Lincoln and Guba, 1985). Case studies provide a flexible way to use several methods to describe and analyze change in a particular social setting (see Bennett, 1987). Case studies of a mental health coalition and a prevention organization with which one of us was involved for several years, both of which had a social justice orientation, illustrate the type of research we propose (Nelson, 1994; Nelson and Hayday, 1995).

Social justice research should involve multiple stakeholders in the research process (Guba and Lincoln, 1989; Lincoln and Guba, 1985). One goal of bringing diverse stakeholders together is to raise awareness of the issues and of the experiences of other constituents. As Guba and Lincoln (1989) argue, part of the researcher/evaluator's role is to be a mediator and change agent. Thus, the research process provides a forum for the negotiation of power and social change among stakeholders. Examining such intergroup relationships is important for research with a social justice agenda (Wittig and Bettencourt, 1996).

Social Justice and Education and Training

Education and training in community psychology needs to help students make connections between the personal and the political. Consequently, our programs should be concerned not just with training in research and practice skills, but more broadly with education in a world view in which the value of social justice plays a central role. Just as applied and academic community psychologists need to undergo a process of conscientization (Freire, 1993), so too do students. Socialization in a social justice ethos will influence students' identities as social activists, thus linking the personal and the political (Trickett et al., 1984).

To help students make connections between micro, meso, and macro levels of analyses and to build bridges among constituents, we must also attend to social justice issues within our own graduate programs. We cannot focus on social justice issues "out there" while ignoring injustices and power imbalances in our own institutions. We need a healthy climate within our programs to provide a safe and congruent base from which we can engage in broader social change activities both on and off campus. Having diversity with respect to gender, age, and ethnocultural background will further contribute to the educational milieu for students and faculty alike (Suarez-Balcazar et al., 1994).

At the meso and macro levels, we can work with other faculty, students, and staff within our universities towards social justice goals. Some examples of this kind of work include developing policies regarding employment and pay equity, establishing policies and programs to prevent sexual assault and harassment (Bond, 1995), and organizing "teach-ins" on important social issues. And we can work in the wider community as well. Faculty who have established long-term relationships with settings having a social justice orientation and social activists from these settings can serve as mentors for students in training. The importance of such field settings, which provide a forum and support for engaging in social justice work, cannot be underestimated (Bennett, 1987).

Conclusion

For us, community psychology's main mission is to advance the well-being of oppressed communities (Martín-Baró, 1994; Montero, 1994). As we stated at the beginning of this chapter, this is why we became community psychologists. Thus, we should ask ourselves *whose interests should take priority* and *with whom we should ally ourselves*. By focusing primarily on ameliorative work, community psychologists have not paid sufficient attention to transformative efforts to help oppressed communities. Caring/ compassion and health served us well as founding values, but our singular and persistent focus on them has prevented the advancement of more contextually relevant values such as self-determination/participation, human diversity, and social justice. By identifying a few avenues for the promotion of social justice within community psychology, we hope to help the discipline bridge the gap between rhetoric and action.

But bridging this gap is a formidable process. We recognize that there will sometimes be contradictions and tensions between our professional roles and our commitment to social justice. To live the value of social justice means that we must take some risks. By becoming more outspoken advocates, our credibility as professionals and researchers will be challenged. At a minimum, those who uphold the status quo will label us "biased" or "political." In some cases, our jobs in human services, research institutes, and universities may be in jeopardy. Thus, it is important for us to find ways to protect particularly the young professionals among us who are most likely to be in precarious positions. We need to develop social support networks with like-minded people who can help us recognize these dilemmas and help us make the trade-offs that will enable us to live with integrity.

Note

We wish to thank Fabricio Balcazar, Maurice Elias, Dennis Fox, Milo Fox, John Lord, and James Taylor for offering helpful suggestions. We tried to incorporate their thoughtful and insightful feedback.

12

Cross-Cultural Psychology: The Frustrated Gadfly's Promises, Potentialities, and Failures

Fathali M. Moghaddam and Charles Studer

Editors' note *In theory, cross-cultural psychology has the potential to challenge mainstream psychology's assumptions and institutions. Cross-cultural psychologists understand, after all, that culture plays a significant role in human behavior. An explicit focus on cultures different from the Western societies dominating psychology should improve the likelihood of creating alternative methods and theories. Freed of the assumption that the West is all there is, cross-cultural psychologists should be more open to noticing and appreciating differing perspectives. As it turns out, however, Fathali M. Moghaddam and Charles Studer demonstrate in this chapter that cross-cultural psychology is not a critic of the mainstream but a fervent supporter. As a result, instead of promoting human diversity, mainstream cross-cultural psychology actually promotes cultural homogeneity.*

Along with social and political psychology, cross-cultural psychology bears the irony of neglecting the context where behavior occurs. Like these other two disciplines, cross-cultural psychology is wedded to cognitive and laboratory approaches and discounts the role of power disparities, injustice, and lack of resources. Moghaddam and Studer note that the increasingly dominant cognitive model neglects the importance of social norms and social context. Instead of seeing culture in a holistic way, encompassing the social, historical, and political background, culture is viewed as just another variable to account for. Indeed, most cross-cultural psychologists adhere to traditional positivist frameworks of analysis based on mainstream norms.

Despite the potential for psychology in (and about) other cultures to develop in liberatory ways, Moghaddam and Studer note that "mainstream cross-cultural psychology has failed to be liberating" and that it "helps disseminate false beliefs that are contrary to the interests of minorities around the world." The authors seek to reclaim the place of power, justice, culture and context in a more critical cross-cultural psychology.

Cross-cultural psychology has lived in the margins of general psychology
as a frustrated gadfly.
                    R. A. Shweder, "Cultural Psychology: What is It?"

This insightful observation, made by Shweder (1990: 11–12), serves as a
useful point of departure for our critical discussion of cross-cultural psychology. Most psychologists would agree that cross-cultural psychology has
failed to make an important impact on traditional general psychology.
Moreover, anyone familiar with the tone of discussions in the cross-cultural
literature generally, and cross-cultural conference gatherings specifically,
would readily agree that cross-cultural researchers feel frustrated about this
situation.

But as to *why* cross-cultural psychology remains a "frustrated gadfly,"
and what should be done to remedy the situation, there is considerable
disagreement. On the one side are mainstream cross-cultural researchers
whose interpretation of science and the scientific method would keep cross-
cultural psychology very closely tied to general psychology's mainstream
(e.g., Triandis, 1994). Those in this camp constitute the dominant group.
They tend to support a traditional positivist philosophy of science, sometimes explicitly. On the other side are scholars who propose a variety of
alternatives to traditional psychology, sharing a common anti-positivist
platform. This latter group is a minority.

We agree with Shweder (1990) that cross-cultural psychology remains
marginal partly because it offers no substantial challenge to the core
working assumptions of mainstream general psychology. At the heart of
these assumptions is a general hypothesis: so-called "central processing
mechanisms" lie behind, and *cause*, observable behavior, whether that
behavior is performed by a Japanese, a French, an Indian, a South African,
or any other person. More broadly, cross-cultural psychology shares with
traditional psychology the assumption that *causal* rather than *normative*
models better explain human behavior – in other words, that behavior
stems from identifiable "causes" rather than being related to factors such as
social norms. We discuss these issues in the first part of the chapter, where
we also refer to the growing literature in cross-cultural psychology.

A central feature of both mainstream general psychology and mainstream cross-cultural psychology is a neglect of ideology, power disparities,
intergroup relations, and other issues related to justice (Taylor and
Moghaddam, 1994). This neglect of ideological issues is often manifested
in *reductionism*, involving attempts to explain social behavior through
identifying causal factors internal to individuals. Or, when factors external
to individuals are cited as causes, they tend to be factors unrelated to
ideology. An example of this is attempts to explain aggression through
reference to temperature variations. Through such an analysis, riots and
other acts of collective aggression are described as being caused by high
temperatures rather than by perceived injustices, discrimination, and other
ideologically related issues.

In the second part of the chapter, we argue that human behavior is not causally determined, so that attempts to establish universal relationships between "cause" and "effect" are fundamentally flawed. Through a discussion of aggression, selected because it is a topic of both theoretical and practical importance, we argue that the most promising way ahead is not psychology as the science of observable behavior, or as the science of mental life. Rather, it is to conceive of *psychology as the science of normative behavior.* Human beings are envisaged as unique in their socially acquired skills to construct, identify, and use complex normative systems as guides to behavior. Such normative systems involve norms, rules, and other cultural characteristics that help prescribe correct behavior for people in given settings. Some patterns of normative behavior become so well established and so stereotyped that we can confuse them with causal sequences. But habits have their origin in rules and norms, not in causal mechanisms. This point becomes crucial when we examine attempts to change patterns of human action.

This emphasis on normative systems necessarily leads to a concern for power disparities. Some groups enjoy more power than others in shaping normative systems. Through such power, dominant groups can influence the behavior of minorities. Thus, psychology as the science of normative behavior is in part concerned with how dominant groups maintain and extend their favored position through manipulating normative systems.

Third, we argue that psychology conceived as the science of normative behavior is necessarily cultural in a profound sense. The normative system is a human construction, which can be reconstructed in many different ways. However, limitations in the ways normative systems can be reconstructed indicate certain universals in human social life.

Shweder (1990) insightfully assesses mainstream cross-cultural psychology's limitations as a conceptual system in relation to traditional psychology. However, we also need to examine mainstream psychology's ideological functions more broadly. Ultimately, we believe, ideological factors explain why cross-cultural psychology remains a marginal force. In the final section, we build on previous discussions (Moghaddam, 1987; 1990) to assess mainstream cross-cultural psychology in the context of power relations in the Three Worlds of psychology.

One of the points we emphasize is that psychology can be looked at as an abstract body of knowledge. But we can also look at it as a resource pool, a means by which competing groups maintain, lose, or extend their power. As a resource pool, psychology legitimizes power relations, and can be used to alter power relations. Psychology historically has been dominated by white middle-class males in the United States: over the last century they have enjoyed a monopoly as both the researchers and the "subjects" of this discipline. They constitute the core of psychology's First World (Moghaddam, 1987). By expressing the norms of their own culture as if they were universal laws of human nature, First World psychologists create a powerful impetus for other cultures to adapt their different behavior norms to what they wrongly perceive as the facts of human life.

Cross-cultural psychology, as usually practiced, does not challenge traditional psychology's philosophical foundations. But at least it attempts to include the rest of the world in psychology's domain. Even if this inclusion is only as participants in research, it does mean a foot in the door for some minorities, with the possibility of greater influence in the long term. Let there be no doubt that this issue of inclusiveness does not just concern abstract ideas in the ivory tower. It is political and bears on conflicts over real resources. Thus, we argue, the continued neglect of cross-cultural psychology is to a large part due to the threat it poses to the political status quo in psychology.

The Gadfly and Traditional General Psychology

> Cross-cultural psychology is the study of similarities and differences in individual psychological functioning in various cultural and ethnic groups; of the relationships between psychological variables and sociocultural, ecological, and biological variables; and of current changes in these variables. (Berry et al., 1992: 2)

> What is psychology? It is a field of inquiry that is sometimes defined as the science of mind, sometimes as the science of behavior. (Gleitman, 1992: 1)

Students in general psychology courses are typically offered definitions of psychology matching those presented by Gleitman. A definition that gained influence through the emergence of cognitive psychology since the 1950s is psychology as "the science of mind." This replaced the more global definition of psychology as "the science of behavior," in line with behaviorism's emphasis on overt behavior.

Texts introducing general psychology convey, sometimes explicitly, two features of the discipline. First, students learn that in the vast majority of cases psychologists conduct experiments to determine the "causes" of behavior. They manipulate independent variables (e.g., temperature) in order to measure their impact on dependent measures (e.g., aggression). Causes thus come in the shape of independent variables, and their effects are reflected in changes in the dependent variables. Students learn an advantage of such experiments: researchers can conduct them in laboratories, where it seems more feasible to bring all the variables under the experimenters' control. They learn that the world outside the laboratory, the "field," has too many "nuisance variables" to allow for the identification of causal relations.

Second, students are reminded that in the present cognitive era, causes may be located either in stimuli external to individuals, or in assumed central processing mechanisms internal to individuals, or in both (for a classic treatment of this issue, see the discussion of situational, dispositional, and interactional approaches to the study of behavior by Snyder and Ickes, 1985). Thus, traditional psychology adopts a causal model. It seeks to identify causal relations between external stimuli, internal central processing mechanisms, and behavior.

A first ideological implication of this causal model is that there is a fixed reality in the social world and an equally fixed cognitive endowment in each individual. Cause–effect relations are assumed to be permanent and part of an objective reality to be discovered by psychologists. Moreover, psychological research is seen as ideologically neutral. The model assumes psychologists use objective methods (such as the laboratory experiment) that allow them to discover truths about human behavior, independent of biases, political or otherwise.

A second ideological implication has to do with the causal model's goal of discovering universals in human behavior. This goal particularly opened an avenue for cross-culturalists to try to gain influence. In order to discover true universals, they argued, it is necessary to test the hypotheses of general psychology among different cultural groups – not just among undergraduate students in US universities, the group traditional psychology most commonly studies (see Moghaddam et al., 1993: Chapter 2). Thus, cross-cultural psychology justifies its existence in part through this "transport and test" methodology.

In a sense, cross-cultural psychology became a methodological extension of mainstream psychology because they share the same central underlying assumptions. Cross-cultural researchers would translate, adapt, and transport mainstream tests to different cultures to explore the universality of different hypotheses derived from both developed and developing societies. In this way they would "eventually discover the underlying psychological processes that are characteristic of our species" (Berry et al., 1992: 4).

Thus, the main contribution cross-cultural psychologists explicitly offered mainstream psychology has been the addition of culture as an independent variable. This vast addition has required that psychological test material be adapted for use with "subjects" drawn from different cultural groups. Since the publication of the first *Handbook of Cross-Cultural Psychology* (Triandis et al., 1980), there has emerged a growing literature reflecting the power of culture in the role of independent variable (for general reviews, see Berry et al., 1992; Brislin, 1990; Lonner and Malpass, 1994; Matsumoto, 1994; Moghaddam et al., 1993; Segall et al., 1990; Smith and Bond, 1994; Triandis, 1994).

However, despite increases in the number of cross-cultural psychology publications, this subdiscipline has remained in the margins and achieved minimal influence on traditional mainstream psychology. To understand why the impact of cross-cultural psychology remains minimal despite the growing cross-cultural literature, we must consider more closely the philosophical and methodological foundations of cross-cultural psychology. As Shweder (1990) points out, these foundations do not challenge traditional psychology. In the next section, we raise questions about the route cross-cultural psychology needs to take to establish itself as a viable alternative to traditional psychology.

Culture Incorporated in Causal Models of Human Behavior

> Cross-cultural research in psychology is the explicit, systematic comparison of
> psychological variables under different cultural conditions in order to specify the
> antecedents and processes that mediate the emergence of behaviour differences.
> (Eckensberger, 1972: 100)

Eckensberger (1972) makes explicit the idea that cross-cultural psychology
attempts to identify cause and effect relationships between culture and
behavior. We shall use research on the assumed link between temperature
and aggression, behavior intended to harm another being, to clarify two
points. First, the incorporation of culture strengthens psychological
research. Second, even when culture is "attached" as an independent
variable to traditional psychology, the causal model is still inappropriate
for explaining human behavior. Rather, we advocate the adoption of a
normative model, which allows us to avoid reductionism and attend more
fully to ideological issues.

Temperature–Aggression Links in General Psychology

The idea that hot temperatures promote aggressive behavior fits a number of
causal explanations in psychology (Anderson, 1989). The most important of
these is the *frustration–aggression hypothesis* in its original (Dollard et al.,
1939) and various revised forms (Berkowitz, 1962; 1993). The original
hypothesis stated that frustration produces a state of readiness or instigation
to aggress, and that aggression is always preceded by some form of
frustration. At the center of the hypothesis, then, is the assumed causal link
between frustration, defined as the blocking of a sequence of goal-directed
behaviors, and aggression. Subsequent research did not support the
hypothesis, because it was shown that people can handle frustration in
many ways other than aggression, and aggression can arise for reasons other
than frustration (for further discussion, see Geen, 1990; 1995).

Contemporary psychologists do not accept the frustration–aggression
hypothesis in its original form. However, the idea that increasingly
uncomfortable temperatures should prime aggressive thoughts, which in
turn increase the motive to aggress, is in line with several influential recent
models (Anderson, 1989). These include the negative affect escape models
(Baron and Richardson, 1994) and a revised frustration–aggression model
(Berkowitz, 1993). These newer models have been influenced by cognitive
psychology. They attempt to incorporate cognition and affect into the
causal chain, moving from environmental stressors (stimuli) to aggression
(response).

In line with mainstream psychology's traditions, researchers have conducted laboratory experiments to demonstrate the relationship between
temperature and aggression. The prototypic study was conducted by Baron
(1972). It involved a situation where research participants were assigned the
role of teacher, and given the task of teaching material to another
(supposed) participant (who was actually a confederate of the experimenter).

Teachers worked in hot or cool conditions (independent variable) and could administer shocks (dependent variable) to learners.

After a review of laboratory experiments investigating the temperature–aggression link, Anderson concluded that,

> On the whole, these laboratory studies of concomitant temperature–aggression effects yield more confusion than understanding. Sometimes hotter conditions led to increases in aggression; at other times the opposite occurred. Most of the studies were by the same researchers using the same general paradigm, yet even this did not result in consistency in findings across studies. (1989: 91)

Disappointed with the results of laboratory studies, researchers faithful to the causal model have turned to field research to try to demonstrate a causal link. One line of attack has been to compare acts of aggression, such as homicide, across regions varying in temperature. Research along these lines is not new (e.g., Lombroso, 1899/1911). The results generally seem to support the temperature–aggression hypothesis. For example, the homicide rate is higher in the southern (and warmer) parts of the United States, England, and Italy, than it is in the northern (cooler) regions. Given that this relationship seems to hold across different countries, the findings could be interpreted as indicating a universal aspect of human behavior. It would seem that culture is not needed to explain temperature–aggression variation across regions. Yet in warmer climates the weather permits, indeed encourages, more public social contact, an equally plausible generic explanatory concept for increases in aggression.

More broadly, an account of aggression based on temperature variations ignores the issue of ideology entirely. Consider, for example, collective riots in major urban centers of the United States. Such riots have typically involved ethnic minorities, such as African Americans and Hispanics. One interpretation of such collective aggression is that minorities are rebelling against unjust social practices, including what they see to be a corrupt and immoral "justice" system. But an alternative account is that such aggression arises because of hot temperatures, independent of ideological issues specifically and culture more broadly.

The Culture of Honor

Nisbett and his associates have challenged the idea that aggression is best explained by factors such as temperature rather than by cultural characteristics (Nisbett, 1993; Nisbett and Cohen, forthcoming). Examining differences in homicide rates between North and South in the US, these researchers evaluated and dismissed explanations for this difference based on temperature (hotter in the South), poverty (poverty more acute in the South), the institution of slavery (historically centered in the South), and the notion that Southern whites learned violence by imitating the violence of African Americans. More specifically, they dismissed the temperature-based explanation by showing that violence in different subregions of the South does not vary with differences in temperatures across locations.

Having argued against these possibilities, Nisbett put forward the explanation that "the South is heir to a culture, deriving ultimately from economic determinants, in which violence is a natural and integral part" (1993: 442). As we review the characteristics and sources of this culture to which Nisbett refers, it is important to keep in mind that although he has moved beyond the approach of traditional psychology to adopt a cross-cultural view, he has not abandoned the assumption that behavior is causally determined. But now it is culture, derived from economic determinants, that is the causal agent, the independent variable.

The culture Nisbett (1993) refers to is presumed to derive from economic determinants associated with a herding economy. (Nisbett focused on the herding culture of the South, but the implication is that his thesis may extend to herding cultures in the West of the US and elsewhere.) Herders are always vulnerable, because all their wealth, their herd, is on display in the open, and can be attacked. A lifetime of work may disappear in an instant if they allow the theft of their herd. For this reason, it is essential that herdsmen portray themselves to be manly and ever ready to fight if provoked.

Laboratory Studies on the Culture of Honor

In addition to gathering field evidence for this explanation, Nisbett and his associates conducted a series of interesting laboratory experiments to show that Southerners and Northerners respond differently to insult (Nisbett and Cohen, forthcoming). The research participants were students from the North and the South studying at the University of Michigan. In a prototypic experiment, participants in the experimental treatment were insulted (called an "Asshole!" by a confederate who posed as a passerby), and a series of measures were taken to assess their reactions. Subjects were also presented with scenarios and asked to explain how they imagined the stories would end. For example, one scenario involved a man with his fiancée at a party when an acquaintance of theirs, who clearly knows of their engagement, makes several obvious passes at "the other man's woman."

Results showed consistent differences between the two groups of research participants. The Northerners were more likely than the Southerners to be amused rather than angry by the "Asshole!" incident. And the insulted Southerners were more likely to end the scenario concerning the fiancée with some kind of violent confrontation (e.g., the man leaves the party with his fiancée, after punching out the acquaintance who had made passes at the women in question).

In general, then, Nisbett and his associates make a strong case for the idea that Southerners react to insult with greater violence. More broadly, they use the results of experimental and field studies to propose that higher homicide rates in the South are better explained by a culture of honor that characterizes herding societies, than by temperature differences *per se*. This research seems to represent an example of how cross-cultural psychology can contribute to traditional psychology.

However, if we treat culture as a causal agent and assume a deterministic link between culture and behavior, then we have not moved toward a position that is fundamentally different from that of traditional psychology. It is only when a normative explanation of behavior is developed on the basis of culture that cross-cultural psychology can offer a viable and preferable alternative. "Honor" is a code, not a mechanism. One can live up to it, fail to live up to it, and so on. One risks contempt by not responding to provocation appropriately. Of course, what constitutes an appropriate response depends on the cultural context (for a fascinating account of an honor code, see Shakur, 1993).

Causal and Normative Approaches

In order to highlight the crucial differences between causal and normative accounts of behavior, it is useful to delve deeper into what we mean by culture. The most important achievement of culture is that it prescribes correct behavior, the way people *should* do things. The details of what is correct behavior can vary considerably, depending on the characteristics of the person and the situation. For example, people vary with respect to their *positions in social space* (e.g., one can be a mother or father in kin space, an employer or employee in occupational space, and so on) and their *social roles* (the behavior prescribed for a person in a given position, such as how a mother or father, or an employer or employee, is expected to behave). *Norms* are prescriptions for behavior in particular settings (e.g., correct behavior at a funeral as opposed to a wedding); *rules* are prescriptions for behavior for people in specific social roles (e.g., how guests, priests, and so on, are supposed to behave at funerals and weddings). Positions, roles, norms, and rules are all part of a *normative system* that clarifies correct behavior for persons in situations.

During the processes of socialization, individuals become skilled in identifying and using particular normative systems. This ability develops gradually through socialization, and alongside language learning. But it is essential to appreciate that rules, norms, and other aspects of culture do not cause individuals to behave in particular ways. Rather, they provide guidelines about how people are supposed to behave.

For example, when motorists reach a stop sign at a crossroads, the sign does not cause them to stop. Indeed, some motorists choose to ignore the sign altogether and drive straight through. However, most drivers recognize the sign, and the vast majority follow the rule by bringing their car to a halt. Similarly, when a father tells his son, "If a kid hits you, then you get a stick and smack that kid over the head," he is not causing his son to behave aggressively. He is telling him what is considered the right thing to do in their family. The son could do the right thing according to his family's values, but he could also behave differently.

Thus, culture provides prescriptions for behavior in a normative manner, it does not cause behavior. A normative explanation of behavior allows room for agency, for some measure of free will and for deviations of various kinds from an acknowledged code. Also incorporated in a normative account is the idea of humans as *intentional* beings. By this we mean that the instruments of human thinking (words, signs, models, and the like) stand for things other than themselves. In a sense, behavior is always pointing beyond itself, as long as there are people to interpret intentions in behavior.

Aggression and Ideology

Causal accounts conceptualize a wide range of factors leading to aggression. Such factors include temperature, genetic characteristics, psychological traits, and the like (see Geen, 1990). The assumption underlying causal accounts is that the presence of causal factors, such as high temperatures or a certain genetic makeup, will automatically lead to aggression. By *automatic* we mean that individuals have no choice, and need not even be aware of what is going on when they act aggressively.

But consider the aggression shown by a group of workers who are on strike and trying to prevent nonunionized workers from crossing the picket line. The workers on strike may show aggression toward the police, strike-breakers, and other people seen to be acting against their collective interests. How are we to explain the scenes of fighting outside the factory where the striking workers are picketing? We contend that such behavior is best explained with reference to issues of perceived justice, collective rights, and ideology more broadly. Explanations based on temperature variations would certainly be inadequate, because they completely neglect the political nature of the behavior in question, its relation to the codes of working-class culture.

To take an even more dramatic example, consider the issue of terrorist attacks. A terrorist who places a bomb in a crowded part of the city with the intention of killing people is certainly acting aggressively, although surreptitious bomb planting is very unlike struggles on the picket line. But is such aggression to be explained by reference to temperature variations, or genetic features of the terrorist, or other "context-free causes"? Again, our contention is that such acts of aggression must be considered in political context. What is the political goal of the terrorist group? What is their ideology? More broadly, we may ask how it is they came to be labeled as terrorists, keeping in mind that one person's terrorist is another person's freedom fighter (see Taylor and Moghaddam, 1994).

The Issue of Prediction

Culture creates patterns in the social behavior of collectivities, but it does not allow prediction of any one specific individual's behavior. For example, cross-cultural research among boys in Finland, Israel, Poland and the

United States shows that early television viewing is associated with aggressiveness (Huesmann and Eron, 1986). This research reveals a broad pattern of relationships among subject samples from particular populations. But if we picked out a specific boy from that population and asked, "Can we predict the aggression of this one particular boy on the basis of his television viewing?," the answer would be no.

This brings us to two major criticisms typically leveled at normative models. The first is that they lack predictive power. In response, we reiterate that when the behavior of specific individuals is being considered, neither the normative nor the causal model enjoys high predictive power. Although patterns of behavior may be identified among collectivities, the behavior of specific individuals is not predictable.

For example, although Nisbett and his associates demonstrate a general tendency for subjects from the South to react more violently to insults than those from the North (Nisbett, 1993; Nisbett and Cohen, forthcoming), they could not predict how any one specific research participant would behave. It is not possible to predict if a particular Southerner or Northerner will be among those who behave differently from most of their regional group. This is not because of random variation in some other variable but because of different degrees of commitment to a code.

The inability of statistical trends to allow predictions about specific individuals is taken for granted in legal practices. The intellectual historian Daniel Robinson never tires of telling the following New York story that clarifies this point wonderfully. Consider the case of a robbery in New York's Harlem section, which is largely an African American neighborhood. Statistically speaking, there is a high probability that if a robbery is committed at 2:00 a.m. in Harlem, the robber is a young African American male. Suppose the police round up people they find in the vicinity of the robbery that morning, and their "net" brings in two bus loads of Japanese tourists lost on their way to the airport, and one young African American male. Why bother to have a trial? If we are willing to work on the basis of probability, then the Japanese tourists should be set free and the young African American male should be declared guilty. Of course, the legal system works in a wiser manner, and so should psychologists.

The Normative Model and Variations in Behavior

A second criticism of the normative approach is that it fails to explain variations and change in social behavior. If culture prescribes "correct" behavior, and people conform to normative systems, how can we explain the fact that everyone does not behave the same, and that behavior does not remain stable across time? In response to this criticism, we make two points.

First, there is not one culture, but many cultures. Cultural diversity is a feature of most societies, both Western and non-Western (Moghaddam and Solliday, 1991). Consequently, individuals may become skilled in the recognition and use of many different normative systems, just as they can learn different languages.

Variations in culture become particularly apparent when immigrants use a range of assimilation and heritage/culture retention strategies to integrate into their adopted societies. This is reflected in the literature on ethnic groups in North America (e.g., Lambert and Taylor, 1990; Moghaddam and Taylor, 1987; Moghaddam et al., 1987; 1989; 1995) and in Western Europe (Lambert et al., 1990; see also readings in Goldberger and Veroff, 1995). Improved communications systems allow greater movement of populations, and thus people become more aware of alternative normative systems. They learn that what their culture deems correct (e.g., how to cook food, how to entertain guests, how to conduct wedding ceremonies) is only one way of doing things, and there are many other alternatives. The availability of a variety of normative systems is one explanation for differences in human behavior.

Second, in response to the criticism that normative models fail to explain social change, it is important to note that individuals do not conform to normative systems in an absolute manner. They can, and do, flout the prescribed or correct way of behaving, and they sometimes initiate alternative normative systems that are at least partly novel. Technological advancements contribute to this process.

For example, consider the rapid spread of video games among young people, particularly in Western societies. Many video games involve players shooting at moving human targets, as well as the simulation of other types of extreme aggression (Cooper and Mackie, 1986; Zuckerman, 1987). In some important respects, youngsters playing these games undergo the same kinds of experiences as soldiers in army training: reflexively shooting at moving targets (Grossman, 1995). The increased violence among young people since the 1970s may be associated with the development of new norms relating to aggression, with youngsters regarding the streets as an extension of the killing fields they experience in video games. These norms are described by many people as anti-social. This is an apt description in the sense that they are "anti" the norms that once prevailed.

Thus, by advocating a normative model, we are not suggesting that people necessarily follow the prescribed behavior in their culture. Individuals can and sometimes do behave contrary to prescribed ways. This is one means by which social change comes about. The research of Moscovici (1985) and his associates suggests that minorities can bring about change if they remain consistent in their stand. The nature of this minority influence tends to be fundamentally different from majority influence: minorities influence more through persuasion arising out of a rethinking and a reassessment of issues, whereas majorities influence more through sheer domination and superior power. The success of the major religions that began with a small number of followers, including Christianity, Judaism, and Islam, demonstrates that minority groups can bring about cultural changes and make their own normative systems dominant.

Culture and Universals in Human Behavior

Nasrudin ran to an appointment in a near-by town, stark naked. People asked him why.

"I was in such a hurry to get dressed that I forgot my clothes."

The fate of cross-cultural psychology brings to mind this instructive Sufi story: cross-cultural psychology has been in such a hurry to put on the scientist's white lab coat that it quite forgot about culture. Of course, researchers have not forgotten culture as an independent variable, as something assumed to causally affect behavior. Rather, they have neglected culture as the manufacturer of the very "central processing mechanisms" that are at the heart of cognitive psychology.

Cognitive psychology has a central assumption, sometimes made explicit: behind observable behavior, behind the symbols of communication, behind all the cultural variations evident among human populations, lie detached central processing mechanisms. These mechanisms are the focus of social cognition research (Fiske and Taylor, 1991). Important cognitive theories, such as dissonance theory (Festinger, 1957), are assumed to reflect psychological universals. Cognitive psychologists assume that if researchers successfully strip away all the surface elements, such as those that appear as variations across cultures, then the deeper underlying cognitive processes become apparent.

Cross-cultural psychology's contribution to this traditional general psychology has been to test the universality of certain assumed central processing mechanisms. For example, researchers have pointed out that cognitive dissonance does not manifest itself in the expected way in some non-Western cultures (see Moghaddam et al., 1993: 12). Cross-cultural psychology *is* making a valuable contribution in this way.

But it would make a far more important contribution if it went one step further and pointed out that the concept of central processing mechanisms is itself a cultural construction, a point we elaborate in the final section. Culture is not "out there," to be treated as an independent variable, as something that "impacts on" individuals. Rather, the very thinking, the "deeper level" of cognition that is the focus of cognitive psychology, is constructed culturally.

However, by asserting that there is not a context-independent, culture-independent level of cognitive processes, we are not claiming there are no psychological universals. There is enough similarity in the human condition (ecology, physiology, and so on) to create some commonalities in cultures and psychological characteristics (for a related discussion, see Krebs and Miller, 1985). In order for there to be a human society, certain common psychological characteristics must be present. For example, for there to be meaningful dialogue between persons, there must be turn-taking in verbal and nonverbal speech. Irrespective of the language, ecological conditions, and other characteristics of the speakers and their surroundings, each must speak in turn. Otherwise, what is accepted as meaningful dialogue in human societies will not be achieved. However, the norms of turn-taking are enormously various, expressing the widely different rights accorded to speakers and potential speakers in different cultures.

Our contention, then, is that human thinking and all the various mechanisms cognitive psychology idolizes as reflecting deeper universals are themselves constructed through culture. This is far from being a novel position, since it has been elaborated by a number of long-standing alternative approaches to psychology (Moghaddam and Harré, 1995). These alternative approaches, including ethogenics, cultural psychology, narrative psychology, discourse analysis, and the like, challenge traditional psychology in a way that is far more fundamental than does cross-cultural psychology.

One set of reasons, then, as to why cross-cultural psychology remains marginal has to do with the lack of foundational differences between traditional psychology and cross-cultural psychology. In short, cross-cultural psychology does not seriously challenge traditional psychology's assumptions. But there are also factors related to ideology and power, which we turn to next.

Issues of "Inclusiveness"

In order to explain the nature of psychological research and why it has taken on one set of biases rather than others, we must go beyond considering the discipline as a "scientific enterprise" independent of ideology. Psychology has an important role in power relationships, both within societies and internationally. Psychologists enjoy considerable control over important resources, through their roles as experts who define and measure intelligence, sanity, mental health, normalcy in behavior and psychological functioning, and many other things that are pivotal in modern life. This enormous power is unequally distributed across groups.

Moghaddam (1987) has described the dominance of the United States, the First World of psychology, in the international arena. The US extended its domination in this arena after the collapse of communism in Eastern Europe and the former Soviet Union. This dominance allows the United States to monopolize the manufacture of psychological knowledge, and to export this knowledge to other countries around the globe. This monopoly is maintained through the control that the US has over publication outlets (books, journals, etc.), test manufacturing and distributing facilities (to publicize and disseminate major psychological tests internationally), training centers, and the like.

The Second World countries, consisting of Western European nations and Russia, have far less influence in shaping psychology around the globe. Ironically, the philosophical roots and many of the seminal ideas of contemporary psychology originated in the Second World. But it is in the United States that mainstream psychology has taken final shape. Just as the countries of the Second World find themselves overpowered by US pop culture (from Walt Disney to rock music, from McDonald's to Hollywood movies), they also find themselves overwhelmed by US-manufactured psychological knowledge.

Third World countries are for the most part importers of psychological knowledge, first from the US, but also from the Second World nations with which they historically had colonial ties (e.g., Pakistan and England; Algeria and France). India is the most important Third World "producer" of psychological knowledge. However, even in India the vast majority of psychological research follows the lines established by the United States, and to a lesser extent by Western Europe (Sinha, 1986).

The unequal abilities of groups to influence psychology internationally is paralleled by inequalities within societies. As noted earlier, psychology in the United States, the First World, has traditionally been dominated by white middle-class males who have been both the researchers and the subjects of research (see Moghaddam et al., 1993). For most of the twentieth century, this is the group that has set the agenda, defined the issues, directed the research, and interpreted the data. It is only in the last few decades of the century that women, ethnic minorities, and others outside the mainstream have had a voice in shaping psychology.

But even today, crucial resources in US academic institutions remain under the almost total control of the majority group. University presses and research funding committees still tend to discriminate against minorities, albeit in highly subtle ways. Scholarly publishing remains a largely white enterprise. University presses employ few minority staff members, and in many cases none at all. The same is true of research funding sources. In many cases they distribute money among an inner circle and reject the use of external/blind reviewers, for the avowed reason that it would be "administratively difficult" to include them. One of the consequences of such discrimination is to impede the influence of minorities in psychology and other research domains.

Cross-cultural psychology is one of the avenues through which minorities have begun to have their voices heard in psychology. First, there has been a demand that psychology make good its claim to being the science of *humankind* by including women and nonwhites as research participants. This is reflected to some extent in the contents of the more recent editions of *The Handbook of Social Psychology*. For example, the editors of the third edition explain that the chapter on sex roles reflects "issues and interests that were simply not factors in 1954, were barely on the horizon in 1968–69, but are very much part of our lives in the 1980s" (Lindzey and Aronson, 1985: iv).

Second, the question has been raised as to how valid psychological theories are when applied to minority groups (e.g., Matsumoto, 1994). In part because mainstream cross-cultural psychologists have raised such questions, even while still accepting traditional psychology's philosophical foundations, cross-cultural psychology has earned the neglect of traditional psychology. It has been maneuvered into a marginal position. However, we need to look more closely at cross-cultural psychology's role in relation to minorities.

Cross-Cultural Psychology and Minorities

Mainstream cross-cultural psychology has failed to be liberating. Instead, it has only helped extend traditional psychology's dominance. Indeed, we believe that, from the perspective of minority groups, cross-cultural psychology is in some ways even more backward looking than mainstream psychology. (By minorities in this context, we refer to all those who have less power – and this includes psychologists who are critical of mainstream psychology.) General psychology is often criticized for neglecting issues of power, justice, intergroup relations, discrimination, and the like (Taylor and Moghaddam, 1994). These issues are also neglected, perhaps even more so, in cross-cultural psychology.

Cross-cultural psychology's neglect of such issues is particularly devastating to the interests of minorities, because cross-cultural research helps legitimize psychology in the international arena. Cross-cultural psychology helps create false consciousness at the international level, because it helps disseminate false beliefs that are contrary to the interests of minorities around the world (for a discussion of the concept of false consciousness in psychology see Jost, 1995). Our illustrative example is the case of aggression; we referred earlier to attempts to explain aggression by doing "cross-cultural" studies of how variations in temperature "cause" aggression. Such theoretical orientations obviously leave little room for ideology and real differences of interests, such as those between minorities in rebellion and oppressive powers, or between traditional psychologists and heretical critics!

Concluding Comment

The academic domain should ideally be a democracy of ideas, where open competition leads to the recognition of, and support for, the very best products of the human intellect. In practice, however, academia is still far from being an open system. It continues to be monopolized by majority groups, as are disciplines such as psychology (Sampson, 1977). Traditional psychology is molded by ideological biases that reflect the culture of the United States, particularly the main normative system of the culture, and more specifically the biases of the white males who have historically dominated the discipline. They have been the researchers and the subjects, they have posed the questions and provided the answers, they have reported the findings and taken up the applications. To point out the historical monopoly in psychology of white US males is not to deny that they are also well represented in the vanguard of "anti-positivist" psychology. However, to say this is not to justify traditional psychology's continued ethnocentrism.

Mainstream cross-cultural psychology does not challenge the causal model, the assumption of central processing mechanisms, or any of the other fundamental philosophical foundations of traditional psychology. Despite this, it has still been demoted to the sidelines in the bigger academic picture. In essence, cross-cultural psychology remains a frustrated gadfly because it has called for the inclusion of minorities as participants in research so that the universality of traditional psychological theories could be tested. Traditional psychologists could not tolerate cross-cultural psychology even in this minimal role as an additional, exotic methodology – a means by which traditional psychological tests would be transported and tested among different cultural populations.

But there are pointers indicating how cross-cultural psychology could make important contributions. These are provided by vanguards of the new alternative psychologies, such as the orientations discussed by Bruner (1986) and others. Cross-cultural psychology should reject the causal model and the idea of culture as an independent variable. Instead, human behavior should be seen as normative and fundamentally cultural: if culture is integral to thinking, a decontextualized central processing mechanism is an impossibility. Cognition and culture are inseparable. Both the instruments of cognitive research and the mental mechanisms under study are cultural products. This perspective leads to a viable alternative to traditional psychology, and takes cross-cultural psychology out of the situation of the frustrated gadfly.

13

Lesbian and Gay Psychology:
A Critical Analysis

Celia Kitzinger

Editors' note *Among the newest of psychology's recognized subfields is "lesbian and gay psychology," which Celia Kitzinger defines in this chapter as a psychology that is "explicit about its relevance to lesbians and/or gay men, does not assume homosexual pathology, and seeks to counter discrimination and prejudice against lesbians and/or gay men." As Kitzinger points out, the field's very existence demonstrates that efforts to change mainstream psychology can sometimes succeed. In the process, she charts the complicated relationship among mainstream psychology, lesbian and gay psychology, and critical psychology.*

The success of lesbian and gay psychologists in replacing stigma with legitimacy raises an issue for critical psychologists well beyond this particular arena. Several authors in this volume comment on a multifaceted dilemma that Kitzinger tackles head on: what do we do when our goal of helping individuals collides with our interest in transforming society more fundamentally in the future? For example, since critical psychology rejects the mainstream's research methods and the assumptions of positivist science, are we justified in using those methods to provide tangible improvements for individuals who are oppressed and rejected? How can we proclaim that "mainstream psychology justifies equality" when doing so strengthens norms and assumptions that are harmful in the long run even if they help in the short run? Can we treat individuals without being individualistic? As Kitzinger notes, although the sources of oppression are social, it is individuals who go to psychologists for help.

These are difficult questions, for which there are no easy answers. In documenting its effective opposition to oppressive norms, Kitzinger affirms critical psychology's accomplishments in legitimizing lesbian and gay psychology and in moving the larger society toward greater acceptance of lesbian and gay individuals. In identifying the resulting dilemmas, she pushes the field forward, from critique to emancipation.

Traditional mainstream psychology presented homosexuality as a form of pathology, with lesbians and gay men characterized as the sick products of disturbed upbringings. In so doing, psychology provided a "scientific" justification for the oppression of lesbians and gay men: psychological "evidence" has been invoked as a rationale for locking us up in mental hospitals and prisons, breaking up our relationships with our lovers, taking our children away, denying us jobs, and blatantly discriminating against us in law and social policy. In the first section of this chapter, I briefly summarize some of the ways in which lesbians and gay men are oppressed, and expose the ways in which psychology as a discipline has been complicit in this oppression.

But this traditional psychological perspective is no longer the norm within psychology. Since the 1970s, there has been an important shift towards the creation of a lesbian and gay psychology that challenges the whole notion of homosexuality as pathology, investigates the reasons for prejudice and discrimination against lesbians and gay men, develops theoretical and practical responses to lesbian and gay concerns, and attempts to create effective changes in the world such that lesbians and gay men might be spared some of the injustices to which we are currently subjected. This branch of psychology is sometimes referred to as "lesbian- and gay-affirmative" psychology – especially so in its infancy – but usually just as "lesbian and gay" psychology. It is a form of "critical psychology" in the sense that it "challeng[es] a status quo that benefits the powerful and works against the powerless" (Prilleltensky and Fox, Chapter 1). As used here, the phrase "lesbian and gay psychology" means psychology which is explicit about its relevance to lesbians and/or gay men, does not assume homosexual pathology, and seeks to counter discrimination and prejudice against lesbians and/or gay men. "Lesbian psychologists" and "gay psychologists" are psychologists involved in this type of psychology: no implications are intended as to the characteristics of the psychologist her- or himself. A "lesbian and gay psychologist" can be heterosexual, just as a "social psychologist" can be anti-social, or a "sports psychologist" a couch potato. (Many lesbian and gay psychologists have, however, openly stated that they are lesbian, gay or bisexual, e.g. Brown, 1992; Kitzinger, 1987; Nichols, 1987). In the second section of this chapter I outline the achievements of lesbian and gay psychology as "critical" psychology.

In the third section I explore the *limits* of this lesbian and gay psychology. I illustrate its implicit acceptance of many of the traditional norms and values of mainstream psychology, in particular (a) its reliance on *positivist empiricist methods* and its acceptance of the grand narrative of science, and (b) its acceptance and incorporation of the taken-for-granted *individualism* of psychology as a discipline. The key question raised in this section, then, is: "Is lesbian and gay psychology critical enough?"

In the fourth section of the chapter I use the example of lesbian and gay affirmative psychology to reflect upon the dilemmas in which many critical psychologists are necessarily embroiled. As the example of lesbian and gay psychology makes clear, for psychologists wanting to change the world, the rhetorics of liberal individualism and of positivist empiricism are powerful and persuasive discourses which can be used to influence policy makers and to create social change. When critical psychologists refuse these discourses, they are often, in effect, undermining their own ability to intervene effectively in real-world politics. The chapter ends, not with solutions to these dilemmas, but with some suggestions for managing them, and considers what critical psychologists in general might learn from the specific case of lesbian and gay psychology in their efforts to create a better world.

Heterosexist Oppression and Traditional Mainstream Psychology

Lesbians and gay men are oppressed in almost every aspect of our lives. A comprehensive overview of anti-gay violence and victimization in the United States found that up to 92% of lesbians and gay men report being targets of anti-gay verbal abuse or threats, and that 24% report physical attacks (Herek, 1989). Over 75% of the thousands of women and men studied expected to be the target of future harassment because of their sexual identity (Berrill, 1992). Families of origin often refuse to accept a homosexual member (Strommen, 1993). In the workplace, gays and lesbians are often penalized by anti-gay clauses in contracts or conditions of service: pension schemes or relocation allowances that exclude a same-sex partner; denial of childcare, sports or canteen facilities to a same-sex partner; definitions of "paternity" leave which exclude lesbian co-mothers; and compassionate leave limited to the spouse and blood relatives of the employee (Kitzinger, 1991). The heterosexism of the health care services (Ryan and Bradford, 1993), and of other major social institutions such as the police force (Burke, 1995) and the education system (Epstein, 1994), have been well documented. The legal oppression of lesbians and gay men is commonplace. Oppressive legislation includes, in the United Kingdom, Section 28 of the Local Government Act which prohibits the "promotion" of lesbian or gay lifestyles as "pretended families." It is widely understood actively to endorse the removal of pro-gay literature from the shelves of public libraries, and the sacking of openly lesbian or gay teachers in schools.

Consequently it is hardly surprising that most lesbians and gay men are invisible as such – to their families, to their colleagues in the workplace, and in society more generally. Even those lesbians and gay men who are sufficiently open about their homosexuality to risk taking part as subjects in research usually take pains to conceal their homosexuality in other aspects of their lives: they report various forms of subterfuge, including introducing partners as "friends," avoiding conversations about personal matters, and inventing (or even acquiring) a fiancé(e) or spouse (Kitzinger, 1991).

Traditionally, mainstream research on lesbianism and male homosexuality has served as a justification for this oppression. From the late nineteenth and early twentieth centuries when research on homosexuality first started to appear (e.g., Bloch, 1909; Forel, 1908; Krafft-Ebing, 1882) until the mid 1970s, as much as 70% of psychological research on homo-sexuality was devoted to the three questions: "Are homosexuals sick?"; "How can homosexuality be diagnosed"?; and "What causes homosexuality?" (Morin, 1977). The vast bulk of this early sexological, psychological, psychiatric and (especially) psychoanalytic writing supported the view that homosexuality was pathological, and this view is still expressed by some mental health practitioners. In a book published in 1980 called *Overcoming Homosexuality*, a clinical psychologist advances an argument still used by some psychologists today:

> Homosexuality is a symptom of neurosis and of a grievous personality disorder. It is an outgrowth of deeply rooted emotional deprivations and disturbances that had their origins in infancy. It is manifested, all too often, by compulsive and destructive behavior that is the very antithesis of fulfilment and happiness. Buried under the "gay" exterior of the homosexual is the hurt and rage that crippled his or her capacity for true maturation, for healthy growth and love. (Kronemeyer, 1980: 7)

According to psychoanalyst Elizabeth Moberly, lesbians suffer from "a state of incompletion" (1983: 66) which does "imply pathology" (1983: 86) and lesbians supposedly exhibit "childishness; marked dependency needs; jealousy and possessiveness; a sense of inferiority and depression" (1983: 40). The main psychoanalytic training institutions in England have been widely criticized for their assumptions about homosexuality (Ellis, 1994). In 1995 the Association for Psychoanalytic Psychotherapy in the National Health Service (one of the most prominent British organizations) invited as guest speaker the North American psychoanalyst Charles Socarides, whose view is that homosexuals are sick, compulsively driven by their unnatural urges into abnormal forms of sexual behavior. He has said that homosexuality is a form of "aberrancy," and "a revision of the basic code and concept of life and biology," and he recommends conversion therapies to "cure" homosexuals by changing them into heterosexuals (Jones, 1995). Up until the last fifteen years or so, techniques designed to convert gay men and lesbians into heterosexuals (so-called "conversion therapies") were commonplace: two comparatively recent attempts at "cure" include psychosurgery on two gay men (Schmidt and Schorsch, 1981) and hypnotherapy on a young lesbian (Roden, 1983).

Critical Contributions of Lesbian and Gay Psychology

Fortunately, this approach to homosexuality as pathology is now the exception rather than the rule. The combined efforts of gay liberation and second-wave feminism have ensured change. In 1973 the American Psychiatric Association, after major disruption to its meetings by lesbian and gay activists (Alinder, 1972), removed homosexuality *per se* as a category from its *Diagnostic and Statistical Manual*. In 1975, the American Psychological Association (APA) adopted the official policy that homosexuality *per se* does not imply any kind of mental health impairment, and urged mental health professionals to take the lead in removing the stigma of mental illness that has long been associated with gay male and lesbian sexual identities. Nine years later, in 1984, the APA approved the establishment of a formal division (APA, Division 44) dedicated to the psychological study of lesbian and gay issues. Anti-gay prejudice and discrimination is still apparent within some psychological theory and practice (Kitzinger, 1990a): for example, proposals to form a parallel division within the British Psychological Society (BPS) have repeatedly been turned down by the Scientific Affairs Board and by the BPS Council (Comely et al., 1992; Coyle et al., 1995). However, it is unusual for explicitly anti-lesbian and anti-gay comments to be made by representatives of psychological bodies, or by acknowledged experts in the field, and it is rare to find overt reference, within Anglo-American psychological writing, to homosexuality as pathology (Morin and Rothblum, 1991). The majority of psychologists are not now willing to use techniques designed to change clients' "sexual orientation" (cf. Hall, 1987: 222).

Research on lesbian and gay issues has now moved well beyond simply the repeated demonstration of the "normality" of lesbians and gay men and the field is no longer devoted simply to arguing the case for homosexuality as a normal variant of sexual behavior. Recent texts outlining and defining the field of lesbian and gay studies include Gonsiorek and Weinrich (1991), Garnets and Kimmel (1993a), Greene and Herek (1994) and D'Augelli and Patterson (1995): between them, these books cover a wide range of current concerns too diverse to do more than summarize here. Some indicative "key topics," all of them covered in the four texts just cited, are listed below:

- coming out as lesbian or gay, overcoming internalized homophobia, and developing positive and healthy lesbian/gay identities;
- building healthy lesbian and gay relationships;
- the challenges of lesbian and gay adolescence, midlife, and old age;
- parenting issues for lesbians and gay men;
- homophobia and anti-lesbian/gay discrimination;
- mental health issues relating to physical health including HIV, AIDS, chemical dependence;
- cultural diversity among lesbians and gay men;
- bisexuality and questions of "choice," flexibility and flux in sexual identities;
- the development of positive psychotherapeutic models for working with lesbians and gay men.

The explicit intention behind much of this research is to bring about social change. "We have got to learn what we can about sexual orientation – and about related issues like homophobia – so we can build a better world" (Ruse, 1984: 141). In this better world people will be aware of "the fallacy of assuming that everyone is heterosexual, or that all important research questions shall be defined from the point of view of heterosexuals" (Garnets and Kimmel, 1993b: 600); they will understand that "being lesbian or gay is not a personal problem (or mental illness), but a minority-group identity" (1993b: 601); and they will be "sensitive to all aspects of human diversity" (1993b: 600). This world will be better for society as a whole. Lesbian and gay researchers have routinely pointed to the costs to society of homophobia, rigid adherence to traditional sex roles, anti-sex ideology and the exclusion of gays and lesbians from particular jobs (e.g., the military): "the emerging lesbian- and gay-affirmative paradigm in psychology can help our society evaluate the costs and destructive impact of these outdated and wrong-headed ideas" (1993b: 601). The "better world" ushered in by lesbian and gay psychology is "better" not simply for lesbians and gay men, but for *everyone*.

In pursuit of this better society, lesbian and gay psychology in the US has made important critical interventions into social policy and legislation. For example, drawing on her research demonstrating "the normal psychosocial development of children born to or adopted by lesbian mothers," Charlotte Patterson (1994: 172) comments on its implications for legal issues surrounding foster care, adoption, child custody and visitation rights. Lesbian and gay psychologists have testified in court on behalf of lesbian mothers in custody cases, provided expert witness for gays and lesbians wishing to adopt or foster children, documented and protested anti-gay and anti-lesbian violence, and provided court testimony for the coalition of civil rights organizations seeking an injunction to stop Colorado's Amendment 2, which would have prohibited anti-discrimination laws protecting lesbian and gay citizens.

In sum, if, as Prilleltensky and Fox (in Chapter 1) suggest, the hallmark of critical psychology is that it challenges many theories and practices common in the field of psychology, and that it does so in the interests of building a more just world, then lesbian and gay psychology is clearly an example of a very successful form of critical psychology. The field has even been heralded as offering a new paradigm for psychology (e.g. Brown, 1989; Garnets and Kimmel, 1993b), and it has been so successful in its challenge to anti-gay and anti-lesbian theory and practice in psychology as to have substantially reformed the discipline. Today, psychology is more often heard to speak publicly on behalf of lesbians and gay men than on behalf of those who would oppress us.

Critical Limits of Lesbian and Gay Psychology

I want now to present an alternative perspective on lesbian and gay psychology – a perspective from which it is less of a "success story" than it would perhaps at first appear. I want to suggest, in this section, that lesbian and gay psychology, while "critical" of the anti-lesbian and anti-gay bias of much traditional mainstream psychology, nevertheless uncritically incorporates, and reinforces, some very traditional ideas. I will show, first, how lesbian and gay psychology embodies traditional notions of positivist-empiricist science, in which the objective scientific psychologist investigates and uncovers "facts" about the real world. Second, I will show how lesbian and gay psychology relies upon and reinforces the individualism which pervades mainstream psychological theory in general. My argument is that lesbian and gay psychology dramatically oversells itself in claiming to represent a radical new "paradigm," given the extent to which it incorporates conventional mainstream psychological ideas. I also want to show how the incorporation of these mainstream ideas actively undermines lesbian and gay psychology's attempt to create a better world.

Lesbian and Gay Psychology as Positivist-Empiricist Science

The story contemporary lesbian and gay psychology tells about itself is a story of progress from the bad old days when (based on poor science) homosexuals were considered sick, to the current understanding that homosexuality falls within the normal range of human behavior. Once upon a time, the story goes, researchers thought that homosexuals were sick and perverted. This was because they were biased by religious prejudices and trapped by the social conventions of their time: their research lacked present-day sophistication and objectivity. Now, in our sexually liberated age, with the benefit of scientific rigor and clear vision, objective up-to-date research demonstrates that lesbians and gay men are just as normal, just as healthy, and just as valuable members of a pluralistic society as are heterosexual people. This story is told in most literature reviews and overviews of research on homosexuality: "all contemporary research discussions [of homosexuality] reiterate some version of it" (Krieger, 1982).

This story of progress is common across the social sciences: stories of changing professional views are incorporated into the mythologized history of a discipline in what has been described (by philosopher of science Richard Rorty, 1980) as the "up the mountain story." Its function is to illustrate the superiority of contemporary research over that of the past. Psychology, as a scientific discipline, is based on the idea of progress. Through uncovering the "errors" of previous research (whether these are caused by fraud, bias, social stereotypes, inadequate sampling techniques, lack of control groups or whatever) psychology presents itself as moving towards ever more adequate approximations to truths about the world (see Chapter 2 in this volume). From the point of view of critical psychology, then, the claim of lesbian and gay psychology to represent scientific progress is a conventional piece of self-interested rhetoric: "the idea of progress is a literary achievement" (Gergen, 1992: 25). Although lesbian and gay psychologists sometimes present themselves as doing something very radical in criticizing the heterosexist biases of traditional mainstream psychology, there is nothing at all radical about criticizing earlier research. In fact, continual criticism of other scientists' research is an essential part of science as an institution.

Moreover, lesbian and gay psychology is rigidly conventional in the sorts of criticisms it advances. It complains that previous research (demonstrating homosexual pathology) was not "scientific" enough – that is, that it failed to conform to the conventional scientific norms of mainstream positivist-empiricist psychology. As Mulkay and Gilbert point out, "most practising scientists regard the existence of error as a threat to the enterprise of science" (1982: 165). Confronting the "error" of mainstream psychology in pathologizing homosexuality, lesbian and gay psychologists employ an elaborate repertoire of interpretive resources to account for such "mistakes," while never questioning the traditional conception of scientific rationality itself. So, for example, one researcher complains, in a rash of alliteration, that the "sickness theory of homosexuality is shabby, shoddy, slipshod, slovenly, sleazy, and just-plain-bad-science" (Kameny, 1971: 18), and another says that, "theories which continue to purport an illness model of homosexuality represent egregious distortions of scientific information about homosexuality in the service of hatred and bigotry" (Gonsiorek, 1995: 24). It is clear that any challenge to positivist-empiricist notions of "science" is almost totally absent from lesbian and gay psychology. Rather it serves, as I have argued elsewhere, to reinforce positivist-empiricist norms:

> [R]adicals who expose the research of their colleagues as pseudoscientific are conforming precisely to the rules of scientific endeavour and, in arguing that other people are not playing by the rules, they necessarily reinforce the validity of those rules . . . [T]he recent work of radical researchers on homosexuality is politically counter-productive. Employing the rhetoric of pseudoscience in their anxiety to dismiss the "pathological" model, they serve a useful function for social science by upholding and reinforcing its institutionalised norms. Their research constitutes an impressively coherent public-relations job on behalf of positivist-empiricist social science. (Kitzinger, 1990b: 68, 74–75)

Lesbian and gay psychologists typically end their papers with calls for more rigorous adherence to the scientific method, better designed tests, and more valid and reliable results. For most critical psychologists, this call for better science is a rhetorical flourish which serves only to conceal underlying power structures. Many critical psychologists would advance arguments closer to that of the anti-psychiatrist Thomas Szasz (1981). Szasz uses research on homosexuality as a paradigmatic example of the thesis that social science reflects social norms, functions to reinforce and legitimate the ideological hegemony of the powerful (in this case, heterosexuals), and defines as "sick" those who refuse to conform with the dominant definition of reality. According to this argument, the "mental health" sciences are expressly intended to fulfill this controlling and manipulative function. It is not something that happens "by mistake" when researchers stray from the path of methodological purity; rather it is their very *raison d'être*. Calling for "better science," or arguing about the validity of tests used, or the appropriateness of control groups, serves only to conceal the power interests at stake, and to reinforce the power of an oppressive discipline.

Psychology is a disguised narrative of power, control and exploitation, a "self-celebratory monologue" (Sampson, 1993: 4) which constructs not just homosexuals but also women, non-Western peoples, black people, and people of subordinated social classes as Other – that is, as inferior and inadequate compared with the white Western ruling-class male norm (Wilkinson and Kitzinger, 1996). From the perspective of critical psychology, then, social scientific texts presenting homosexuals as sick should not be read in order to find out anything about lesbians or gay men. Rather they should be read in order to explore the ways in which this Othering is performed, to investigate the rhetorical ploys through which heterosexuality is presented as having been proved (by science) as the normal, natural, healthy way to be. For examples of how this reading may be performed, see the first two chapters of my book, *The Social Construction of Lesbianism* (Kitzinger, 1987).

According to many critical psychologists (e.g., Gergen, 1985b), our very notions of what it is to "do" science, what "count" as scientific facts, and what constitutes "good" scientific practice are the products of the particular time, place, and culture within which they are embedded. Critical psychologists focus instead on the role of power in the social making of meanings, the place of rhetoric in establishing scientific "fact," and the processes by which human experience, common sense and scientific knowledge are both produced in, and reproduce, human communities. Despite its apparent bravado, then, the positivist-empiricist commitment of most lesbian and gay psychology sets it at odds with a great deal of critical psychology and locates it firmly within the main body of the discipline. And that is, in fact, just where lesbian and gay psychology would like to be. A leading researcher in the field recently made explicit his concern to rescue the field from "politically correct foolishness" and to "repsychologize" lesbian and gay psychology: "to put our theories to empirical test; to engage in theoretical revision as necessary; and most important, to reconnect our theories and data to the main body of psychological theory, research and practice" (Gonsiorek, 1994: ix).

Lesbian and Gay Psychology as Individualistic

Lesbian and gay psychology was born out of a reaction against a traditional mainstream psychology which defined homosexuality as sick. Its reaction, not surprisingly, was to present evidence for lesbian and gay mental health – and, subsequently, to provide evidence for the pathological nature of anti-gay ("homophobic") individuals. From its nativity lesbian and gay psychology was shaped by that which it opposed: it accepted that psychology was in the business of diagnosing the mental health or pathology of individuals and it wanted only to alter the bases upon which those diagnoses were made. Like mainstream psychology, then, lesbian and gay psychology is fundamentally individualistic. Ironically, this is never more evident than when considering the oppressions to which lesbians and gay men are subjected (see Kitzinger, 1987, for a fuller version of this argument).

Lesbian and gay psychology typically talks about oppression using the term "homophobia." This word began to appear in psychological writing in the late 1960s and early 1970s. "Homophobia" was defined as "an irrational persistent fear or dread of homosexuals" (MacDonald, 1976) or "an irrational fear or intolerance of homosexuality" (Lehne, 1976). The word became widely used only after 1973 when a psychoanalyst, Dr. George Weinberg, published a popular book on homosexuality in which he used the word. Psychologists have developed scales to measure homophobia (e.g., Hansen, 1982; Larsen et al., 1980) and describe homophobes as authoritarian, dogmatic and sexually rigid individuals who have low levels of ego development and suffer from a whole range of personal problems and difficulties in their relationships (MacDonald and Games, 1974; Weiss and Dain, 1979; Hudson and Rickets, 1980). Not only does this concept reinforce the power of psychology to label people as "sick" or "mentally healthy" at will; it also depoliticizes lesbian and gay oppression by suggesting that it comes from the personal inadequacy of particular individuals suffering from a diagnosable phobia. Critical psychologists have pointed out that psychology has systematically replaced *political* explanations (in terms of structural, economic and institutional oppression) with *personal* explanations (in terms of the dark workings of the psyche, the mysterious functioning of the subconscious). The term "homophobia" imputes sickness to specific individuals who supposedly deviate from the rest of society in being prejudiced against lesbians and gay men.

Worse still, the mental health not only of *heterosexuals* but also of lesbians and gay men is threatened by homophobia. This is not simply because homophobes reject us and hurt us (behaviors which have, according to lesbian and gay psychologists, "negative mental health consequences" for lesbians and gay men: Garnets et al., 1993), but also because we allegedly suffer from something called "internalized homophobia" ("the oppressor within": Margolies et al., 1987: 229). The idea of "internalized homophobia" was recently described as a "central organizing concept for a gay and lesbian affirmative psychology" (Shidlo, 1994: 176). Instead of going to heterosexual therapists (like Socarides) to be cured of our homosexuality, now lesbian and gay men are supposed to seek out lesbian and gay therapists to be cured of "internalized homophobia" which is purported to have a "deleterious and pathogenic impact on developmental events in gay people and their psychological functioning" (1994: 180) – causing everything from generalized misery to impaired sexual functioning. Accepting oneself as lesbian or gay is characterized as a "developmental task" or as a "stressor," and the therapist's task is to help the client come to terms with their real sexual orientation (Greene, 1994: 6) – a process which is made more difficult, according to these psychologists, by "internalized homophobia." Therapists working with lesbian and gay clients are advised: "Always plan to spend a period of therapy time assessing with your client the effects of possible internalised homophobia" (Falco, 1991: 29). Of course it is true that some people are unhappy about being gay, just as some people are unhappy about being working class, or black, but these forms of unhappiness are not "phobias" or instances of individual pathology. They are perfectly reasonable responses to oppression.

The concept of "internalized homophobia" is used as an explanation for the many ways in which lesbians and gay men allegedly *oppress ourselves*. Unable to accept our own homosexuality, riddled with guilt and self-hatred, we deliberately seek out situations in which we can experience pain or failure. In lesbian and gay therapy, clients are helped "to see all the ways in which they may maintain a victim attitude or provoke and perpetuate their social isolation" (Decker, 1984: 40). As one therapist explains:

> It is also possible for the person who is not comfortable with being gay to use coming out as a weapon to hurt herself as well as those she has chosen to "come out" to. One aspect of the process of guilt on the part of the lesbian may be to develop a need for self-punishment which can be accomplished by alienating herself from family and friends. The fear of family rejection can become a self-fulfilling prophecy. (Groves, 1985: 20)

Others make similar points: homosexuals may "set themselves up for rejection with poorly planned and impulsive disclosure in an environment that is likely to produce a harsh response" (Gonsiorek, 1995: 34) and they may "abandon career or educational goals with the excuse that external bigotry will keep them from their objectives" (1995: 33). The idea that lesbians and gay men are psychologically damaged (suffer from "internalized homophobia") runs throughout the literature of lesbian and gay psychology. "Internalized homophobia" joins other recently invented forms of pathology (e.g., "erotophobia" and "merger": see Kitzinger and Perkins, 1993, for details and critiques) as psychopathologies especially liable to be suffered by gay men and/or lesbians. The focus is yet again shifted away from the oppressor and back onto the victims of oppression.

Many critical psychologists have documented psychology's disciplinary dependence on, and reproduction of, the individuated self (Kitzinger, 1992a). Individualized explanations have routinely been used within psychology to obscure structural and institutional power. The psychology of prejudice, for example, diverts attention away from the structural oppression of black people or women, in favor of examining the personality dynamics of the "racist" or "sexist" individual. The solution to racism or sexism is presented not as collective social action, but in terms of education, or psychotherapy, or different styles of childrearing. Pathological personality patterns and emotional disturbances are invoked to "explain" problems like industrial conflict (caused by individuals' "attitudinal militancy": Llewelyn and Kelly, 1980) or unemployment (caused by "state benefit neurosis": Pearson, 1975). Vast areas of human suffering are approached as problems of "individual functioning," legitimating programs designed to change individuals rather than the world in which we live.

The work of lesbian and gay psychologists on "internalized homophobia," and on other "psychological problems" associated with being gay or lesbian, unquestioningly fits within this traditional approach. If psychologists' aim is to reduce the "psychological distress" and "internalized homophobia" which results from anti-lesbian and anti-gay discrimination, do they risk losing sight of the need to change society and stop these forms of discrimination altogether? If their aim is to decrease "stress" and to increase the "ego strength" of the victim, do they risk forgetting that it is the perpetrator, not the victim, who is the real problem? What political choices are they making in focusing on the problems of the oppressed rather than on the problem of the oppressor? What are the political consequences when, instead of interrogating and challenging heterosexuality (e.g., Wilkinson and Kitzinger, 1993), they concentrate instead on mopping up the problems heterosexuals cause us as lesbians and gay men? Lesbian and gay psychology, like mainstream psychology, retains a clear focus on *individual* health and pathology and the role of social institutions and structures are only peripheral to this preoccupation.

In sum, then, despite its claims to represent a new paradigm of critical psychology, there are clear limits to the extent to which lesbian and gay psychology challenges the mainstream, and these limits seriously undermine its stated intent to create a better world.

Critical Dilemmas

Critical psychology and lesbian and gay psychology are united in their commitment to challenging oppression and to building a more just world. The question I want to address in this section is why, given this shared commitment, critical psychology and lesbian and gay psychology have adopted such different perspectives on what is needed in the struggle to get from "here" (the status quo) to "there" (the better world). Is it that lesbian and gay psychology is "not critical enough" (as implied by the "critical" comments in the preceding section), or could it be that critical psychology is "too critical"? Is it (as is often claimed: e.g., Abrams and Hogg, 1990; Ussher, 1990) "throwing the baby out with the bathwater"?

As someone who has a history of criticizing lesbian and gay psychology from the perspective of critical social constructionism and radical feminism (see Kitzinger, 1987; Kitzinger and Perkins, 1993), I want here to present the case for the "other side." The argument I advance here is that lesbian and gay psychology may well be positivist-empiricist and individualistic (attempts to argue the contrary are wildly unconvincing), *but this is not necessarily so damaging to its political efficacy as the attacks of critical psychologists suggest.* As we have already seen, there are certainly political *costs* to accepting traditional scientific norms. But equally – as I will show – there are costs to rejecting them. Similarly, there are clear political costs to individualism – but, equally, costs to rejecting it. I will explore first the politics of positivist empiricism and second the politics of individualism, and end by reflecting upon the dilemmas raised by the case of lesbian and gay psychology in deciding just what is "critical" about critical psychology.

First, then, lesbian and gay psychology retains a firm commitment to positivist empiricism. In so doing, it has established for itself a clear place within the discipline of psychology as a whole. Because it poses no challenge to the fundamental tenets of psychology, lesbian and gay psychology can be "added in" to the mainstream, and consequently can modify it in various ways – in particular, by pointing to the scientific failings of psychological accounts branding us as sick and perverted. In this way, lesbian and gay psychology has certainly been effective in entering and influencing mainstream psychology. This has resulted in important changes in the ways in which homosexuality is addressed in (for example) mainstream undergraduate textbooks and in scholarly work across the full range of topics to which lesbian and gay psychologists have contributed. What this means is that there is often now a "lesbian and gay" contribution in edited books or in special issues of journals on topics ranging from adolescent psychology to the psychology of personal relationships, from alcohol abuse to bereavement (Kitzinger, 1996). See, for example, the special issue on personal relationships of the very mainstream BPS journal *The Psychologist*, for which an article was commisioned on lesbian and gay couples (Cramer, 1995); or the special issue of the APA journal *Developmental Psychology* (Patterson, 1995) which was wholly devoted to lesbian and gay concerns.

Moreover, lesbian and gay psychology's commitment to science has proved valuable in establishing lesbian and gay civil and political rights. As long as the legal and political apparatus that governs us is (or affects to be) responsive to scientific "evidence" in making decisions about who is allowed to teach what in state-run schools, who is permitted to adopt or foster children or to use medically provided artificial insemination services, who is imprisoned, and what acts of violence count as crimes, one can argue that it is important for gay and lesbian psychologists not to vacate the field.

For psychologists wanting to change the world, the rhetoric of traditional mainstream psychology is a very important piece of legitimation. In rejecting it, critical psychologists run into problems because they are, in effect, undermining their own position as authoritative psychologists. In abandoning (and critiquing) the language of "objective discovery," in insisting that the knower is always part of what is known, and in drawing reflexive attention to the social construction of their own research and writing, critical psychologists lose the power to intervene effectively in real-world politics: they cannot issue authoritative statements (backed up by "science") on matters of public policy; they don't make credible expert witnesses in court; they become (often quite literally) unintelligible. It is hard to argue for the moral or political superiority of a refusal to attest to the mental health of a lesbian mother in a custody case on the grounds that the concept of "mental health" is a socially constructed one. At such times, critical psychologists may feel that their own "high epistemological ground" is a luxury which they can only, in conscience, sustain because their theoretical opponents, the unreconstructed positivist empiricists, are willing to enter the witness stand. In sum, critical psychologists' refusal of science leaves them without arguments acceptable to the mainstream and hence unable to influence it: they are often perceived simply as sniping at mainstream psychology from the margins. Lesbian and gay psychologists, by contrast, have entered, and in some respects transformed, mainstream psychology and consequently are in a position to influence social policy decision making in concrete and constructive ways.

Second, lesbian and gay psychology is rooted in the traditional individualism of mainstream psychology, and, as critical psychologists remind us, individualized explanations have routinely been used within psychology to obscure structural and institutional power. From the perspective of lesbian and gay psychology, however, it is clear that social oppression causes *individual* suffering. It is *individuals* who turn up in the consulting rooms of psychologists, on the wards of mental hospitals, or in the emergency rooms of hospitals. While many of the problems experienced by lesbians and gay men (e.g., coming-out concerns) are undoubtedly caused by or associated with the social conditions of oppression, they are nonetheless experienced as acutely painful *personal* problems. Often, too, individual lesbians and gay men seek help from psychologists because this seems the only way to deal with the anguish of a mother's death, the ending of a significant relationship, or problems in their relationships with lovers and friends. These problems are exacerbated by the heterosexist world in which we live, but they would be problems in any world.

Whatever critical psychologists' commitments to explicit social and political change, there is clearly a problem if, when faced with a suffering *individual*, they have nothing to offer except "waiting for the revolution" (Brown, 1992). Therapists' attempts to argue that individual person change in therapy can contribute to social and political change are unconvincing (see Kitzinger and Perkins, 1993, for discussion of this point). It seems, then, that the cost of refusing individualism is that psychology has nothing to offer people *as individuals*. This cost is not acceptable to many people, including many critical psychologists themselves – hence the desperate search (manifested by, for example, most feminist therapists) for therapies which will somehow tackle "individual" problems without being "individualistic." It may well be the case that the radical critique of individualism advanced by critical psychologists depends upon the continued existence of therapists who are willing to deal with human suffering on an individual basis, leaving critical psychologists with a clear conscience and free to concentrate on fomenting political revolution.

Overall, then, lesbian and gay psychology shares critical psychology's commitment to social justice, but also adheres to mainstream psychology's commitment to positivist empiricism and individualism. To the extent that it has been successful in promoting social justice (in social policy, in the courts, in education and in other social agencies), this can be in large part attributed to its adherence to the mainstream values of psychology as a discipline: it has used the scientific method and the humanistic concern with individuals in the cause of lesbian and gay rights. From the perspective of critical psychology, this adherence to mainstream values accounts not only for the notable *successes* of lesbian and gay psychology, but also for its notable failures. In pursuit of short-term gains, it reinforces the power of psychology as an oppressive institution, doing little more than tinkering with diagnostic criteria but leaving intact the whole rotten apparatus of diagnosis, control and domination.

14

Psychology and Law: Justice Diverted

Dennis Fox

Editors' note *Law is a particularly significant institution in societies portraying themselves as ruled by law rather than by the whims of officials or the direct decisions of societal members. Legal institutions worldwide resolve disputes among individuals, maintain order, and enforce governmental decisions; in some countries courts resolve national policy issues as well. As Dennis Fox notes in this chapter, mainstream psychologists in the new subfield of "psychology and law" share the popular but questionable assumption that the purpose of law is to ensure justice and equality. Thus, they see little danger in combining psychology's theory and practices with law's power.*

Paralleling the decreased emphasis on social change in community psychology (Chapter 11), social psychology (Chapter 10), and the "psychology of women" (Chapter 16), today's psychologists of law generally deemphasize the explicit concern for justice that motivated the field's pioneers. As Celia Kitzinger (Chapter 13) and Sue Wilkinson (Chapter 16) in particular point out, psychology's traditional practices can sometimes challenge an unjust status quo, at least in the short term. But Fox indicates that psychologists of law too often see themselves as insiders in the law rather than as challengers of the law. The result is a dangerous trend toward strengthening law's control not just over the lives of those seen as psychologically troubled or troublesome, but over the lives of everyone. Current efforts to base legal decisions on psychologists' notions of what is "therapeutic" are especially worrisome.

Fox suggests that the law uses rules, technicalities and courts to provide the appearance of justice while actually maintaining injustice. Paralleling concerns about ideology and false consciousness noted in Chapters 6 and 15, he urges psychologists of law to expose false consciousness and oppose law's unjustified legitimacy.

Mainstream psychologists contemplated legal issues long before *psychology and law* developed in the United States as a recognized field in the 1970s. Earlier in the century, European and US psychologists wrote scattered and generally uninfluential articles and books on law-related topics (Ogloff et al., 1996). Today, in contrast, members of the American Psychology-Law Society (APLS) influence policy in the American Psychological Association (APA) and other organizations. "Psycholegal" journals such as *Law and*

Human Behavior and *Behavioral Sciences and the Law* provide outlets for research and, secondarily, for theory. Additional signs of the field's growth include APA's establishment in 1995 of the theoretical journal *Psychology, Public Policy, and Law*; collections and reviews of course syllabi and textbooks (Liss, 1992; Ogloff, 1993); publication of the *Handbook of Psychology and Law* (Kagehiro and Laufer, 1992); expanded graduate training and career opportunities (Cavaliere, 1995; Ogloff et al., 1996; Tomkins, 1990); and increased research outside the United States.

APA and APLS devote considerable resources to increase psychology's influence on law-related policy issues (e.g., Heilbrun, 1995; Ogloff et al., 1996). This effort parallels psychology's increased impact on American public policy more generally (Herman, 1995). It also coincides with efforts by psychologists and legal scholars to develop theoretical justifications for the law's use of social science evidence (e.g., Monahan and Walker, 1988; 1991; 1994; Tomkins and Cecil, 1994). Oftentimes representing APA, psychologists testify in legislative hearings and submit briefs to appellate courts on issues ranging from racial discrimination and the death penalty to the rights of mental patients, women, children, and gays (Grisso, 1991; Roesch et al., 1991). They identify empirically incorrect legislative and judicial assumptions about human behavior, evaluate policy options, and suggest how psychology can help the legal system work better. Psycholegal advocates increasingly write not just for psychology journals but for the law reviews that judges and lawyers are more likely to read. APA even publishes *Psychology, Public Policy, and Law* as a law review rather than as a traditional psychology journal. Inevitably, psychologists trained as lawyers, often in dual-degree programs granting both a doctorate and a law degree (Ogloff et al., 1996; Tomkins, 1990), are especially influential within the field, as are lawyers interested in psychology.

Unfortunately, growing influence has not brought increased concern for justice. When the field began, June Tapp and Felice Levine based *Law, Justice, and the Individual in Society: Psychological and Legal Issues* on their assumption that "the union of social science and law promotes justice" (1977: xi). This assumption reflected the field's initial effort to "challenge and transform a prevailing 'judicial common sense' that had been used to keep the disenfranchised down so long" (Haney, 1993: 375). Shortly afterwards, though, Craig Haney remarked that "psychologists have been slow to decide whether they want to stand outside the [legal] system to study, critique, and change it, or to embrace and be employed by it" (1980: 152). More than a decade later, he lamented: "I believe we are beginning to lose a sense of shared purpose in psychology and law. I speak about a sense of the waning of collective effort, a loss of common goals, and an abandoning of a sense of mission – the mission of legal change" (1993: 378–379). Most recent work pays little explicit attention to the kinds of issues Tapp and Levine addressed.

Psychology-law's decreased justice focus gains significance from the fact that legal systems hinder the Good Society's creation (see generally

Bonsignore et al., 1994; Kairys, 1990; Turkel, 1996). From a critical stand-point, it is clear that the "rule of law's" purpose is not to ensure justice but to establish a rules-based social control system based on technicalities, categories, and abstract principles. "The legal system is, at its base, about the allocation of power, and the existence of power relationships" (Perlin, 1991: 111). Lawyers and judges tell us which actions and policy alternatives are technically legal (and therefore possible) and which are illegal (and therefore wrong). At least at the formal level, modern legal systems support the value of self-determination by endorsing one form or another of individual rights (such as to property and to speech). But they do so at the expense of the Good Society's other values noted in this book's introduction: distributive justice, health, caring and compassion, respect for human diversity, and collaboration and democratic participation (see Isaac Prilleltensky and Geoffrey Nelson's discussion in Chapter 11). Law, thus, fails to balance individual autonomy with the values necessary for both real community and a psychological sense of community (Fox, 1985; 1993a).

Rather than accepting law's traditional values, psychology and law should consider what kind of justice-based legal system a Good Society would have, and perhaps whether it should have a legal system at all. In this chapter, I note several topics pertinent to a central policy-related task: *challenging the legitimacy of any legal system that not only fails to seek justice but actually deflects alternative routes to social change.* First, though, I describe from a critical perspective the three overlapping but distinct components of mainstream psychology and law, each represented in psychology-law organizations, journals, and overviews of the field (Kagehiro and Laufer, 1992; Levine, 1995; Ogloff, 1992; Ogloff et al., 1996). These include *forensic psychology*, or legally relevant clinical issues; *legal psychology*, or applied empirical research; and *policy-oriented psychological jurisprudence*, or efforts to develop a philosophy of law based on psychological values. Throughout the chapter, I emphasize the legal system in the United States, the field's primary context today, though much of the discussion applies to other systems as well.

Ron Roesch clarified our task in his APLS presidential address:

Let me state my values and beliefs clearly. I believe that (1) we should place a greater emphasis on changing the legal system to make it more fair and equitable; (2) disproportionate emphasis is placed on individuals and individual responsibility rather than on system-level changes; and (3) changes within the justice system will never be sufficient to create a just society, nor will within-system changes by themselves ever have much of an impact on individuals who come into conflict with the law. The problems inherent in our justice system cannot be resolved simply by addressing problems within that system. We can make changes that will make the system more fair or more effective in dealing with individuals within the system, but, in the long term, I believe that this will not be enough because it will not change the fundamental inequities in our society at large. (1995: 329)

Forensic Psychology

Although this chapter emphasizes policy issues rather than the court-related work of individual clinicians, it is important to note that forensic concerns permeate the field. The majority of professionals working in psychology and law identify themselves as forensic/clinical psychologists. Some receive forensic training in law and psychology graduate programs, but most graduate from traditional clinical programs (Ogloff et al., 1996; Otto et al., 1990). Organizations such as the American Academy of Forensic Psychology (AAFP) provide advanced training and certification.

As described throughout this book, clinical psychologists influence decisions by legal authorities in individual cases (see, e.g., the chapters by Brown; Hare-Mustin and Marecek; and Kitzinger). Judges and other authorities frequently point to a psychologist's report to justify committing someone to a mental hospital, finding a criminal defendant not guilty by reason of insanity, declaring someone incompetent to stand trial or control his or her own money, or removing a child from an "unfit" parent. Forensic psychologists, thus, directly affect people's lives in legal contexts, often to the disadvantage of those without the resources to make their way through the legal system.

The subjective nature of clinical decision making, the law's assumptions about "mental illness" and the causes of behavior, and judges' reliance on psychological experts raise practical and ethical issues that psychologists, psychiatrists, and lawyers have addressed (e.g., Melton et al., 1987). Many of these issues relate to the fundamental distinction between the work of forensic psychologists and clinical work performed outside the legal system:

> The forensic mental health professional is not, after all, "seeing a patient" for therapeutic purposes. Instead, she is intervening on behalf of the litigation, economic or administrative needs of one of a series of third parties – an attorney, the court, a prosecuting agency, a state mental health facility, an insurance company, an army. But for these external actors, the forensic relationship would not – could not – exist. There can be no pretense, for instance, (1) that absolute confidentiality applies at the forensic interview, or (2) that the mental health professional is present to provide treatment. (Perlin, 1991: 115)

Responding to concerns over the "economic and scientific future of forensic psychological assessment" (Grisso, 1987: 831), APLS and AAFP have sought to enhance the field's status and influence. They created a formal ethics code, the "Specialty Guidelines for Forensic Psychologists" (Committee on Ethical Guidelines for Forensic Psychologists, 1991), and they urge APA to create a formal specialization in forensic psychology (Heilbrun, 1996). Unfortunately, enhancing the professional credentials of psychologists increases rather than decreases their power to intervene in people's lives. As Michael Perlin pointed out, despite the attention paid to traditional ethical concerns and psychologists' role as expert witnesses, "the basic power questions that pervade all of these relationships are still rarely explored" (1991: 114). Instead, mental health professionals "tend to view these cases . . . as involving questions of professional autonomy, 'turf' issues, public safety considerations and matters of competing fundamental constitutional interests" (1991: 113). A task for critical forensic psychologists, then, is to focus attention on the "unbalanced" forensic relationship (Perlin, 1991), working with those who are victimized by the alliance of mental health professionals and legal authorities (Petrila, 1993).

Legal Psychology: Applied Empirical Research

Unlike forensic psychology, legal psychology's core subject matter originates in experimental research in social psychology as well as in developmental psychology, perception and memory, and related areas. In the 1960s, some social psychologists used research on leadership, conformity, communication patterns, and similar small-group dynamics to help explain jury decision making. Despite criticisms of legal psychology's traditional experimental method (King, 1986), narrowly focused research, often on jury dynamics, eyewitness accuracy, and other trial-related topics, remains the norm. The goal is to develop "theories that describe, explain, and predict human behavior by reference to law" (Small, 1993: 11). Beyond research, some experimentalists serve as expert witnesses in civil and criminal trials and submit "friend-of-the-court" briefs to appellate courts, presenting data in areas as varied as eyewitness accuracy, discrimination, and rape trauma syndrome. Others help lawyers select favorable juries and prepare persuasive courtroom presentations. Although jury consultants attract public disapproval when they defend wealthy individuals accused of crimes, more routinely they defend large corporations sued by victims of corporate harms or by other corporations.

Entrenched in the moderately liberal segment of psychology's political spectrum, mainstream legal psychology retains liberalism's benefits but also its drawbacks. When psycholegal researchers choose sides, either explicitly or implicitly, more often than not they seek to make the system work a bit better for members of powerless groups. The belief that "the law is a good thing" and that "psychology is, too" (Melton, 1992) makes it seem reasonable to design research to reduce misdirected discretion or to make judges aware that their assumptions about human nature are wrong. Partly because both psychology and the law traditionally attribute problems to individuals rather than to societal faults (Haney, 1993; Roesch, 1995), psychologists can become insiders within the legal system (Melton, 1990). Even if they sometimes sympathize with more radical perspectives, their belief that there is little chance for widespread change limits them to proposing relatively minor "workable" reforms.

Unfortunately, being an insider (or believing that one is an insider) directs attention to the minutiae of the law and obscures the complete picture. The system has acknowledged past errors, the feeling seems to be – the legal justifications for slavery, women's subjugation, oppressive working conditions – and it now means well. It just needs more data to do the job right, to rid itself of residual principles and procedures that continue to restrict equality and social justice. Not surprisingly, thus, legal psychologists have a stake in believing the authorities will use the data they generate. Tocqueville (1831/1973) noted long ago that political issues in the United States frequently become legal issues. Today, psychologists turn political, legal, and moral issues into empirical ones (Haney, 1980; 1993). They resist the notion that important social problems persist because of conflicting values and competing interests rather than because the authorities lack accurate information (Fox, 1991). In practice, however, the system ignores or rejects data that challenge system goals (Perlin and Dorfman, 1993).

As is the case for psychologists more generally (Prilleltensky, 1994a), legal psychologists' own values show through in their choice of research topics and their conclusions. For the most part, though, they avoid explicit value statements. They use the guarded language that their methodology's restrictions and their desire to appear value-neutral allow (Fox, 1993b; Haney, 1993). Some even retreat from trying to make the legal system work "better" (a value judgment, after all) and investigate instead whether the legal system works "as it's intended." They leave it to others to decide what that intention should be. Researchers may spend years revealing the inequities of the death penalty, for example, clearly inspired by moral antipathy to legalized execution. They may argue, based on their view of the data, that the system can never administer the death penalty fairly, without arbitrariness and racial bias. Yet by restricting their argument to the data, they leave themselves open to challenge by competing research, or by technical criticisms of their own, or by judges who simply dismiss the data as irrelevant (see Costanzo and White, 1994).

Some have urged their peers to broaden legal psychology's scope in both substance and method. They do so in convention speeches, organizational newsletters, and the American Psychology-Law Society journal *Law and Human Behavior*. APLS officers, editors, and commentators advocate expanding the traditional material on juries, eyewitnesses, and expert witnesses that fill psychology-law courses, textbooks, journals, and convention agendas (Roesch, 1990; 1995; Saks, 1986). But despite these calls, and despite applause at conferences for those who urge change, most psychologists ignore those appeals in their research and practice. Trends in the social sciences toward methodological innovation and substantive broadening have had less impact on legal psychology than on other components of the "social science in law" movement (Haney, 1993). "The narrow focus of psycholegal research continues to be the despair of writers in the field" (Kagehiro and Laufer, 1992: xi).

Psychological Jurisprudence and Public Policy

Psychological jurisprudence refers to the development of "theories that describe, explain, and predict law by reference to human behavior" (Small,

1993: 11; see also Small and Wiener, 1993). Whereas legal psychologists may study how judges and other legal system actors make decisions in practice, theories of psychological jurisprudence tell judges and legislators how they *should* make decisions: guided by psychological data and values that suggest not just what law is, but what law ought to be. True, legal psychology and psychological jurisprudence are interdependent, and narrowly focused empirical work can sometimes expose oppressive legal practices. However, it is psychological jurisprudence that holds the most promise for stimulating a critical psychology of law. So far this promise remains unfulfilled.

Theories of jurisprudence are frameworks for directing legal decision making. Psychologists of law know that, despite the legal system's preferred image of rational, objective reasoning, judges exhibit the same subjective processes as the rest of us. As *legal realists* pointed out early in the twentieth century, legal reasoning rarely leads to a single correct decision. Judges routinely choose among competing precedents and principles. Their political views, class position, religious and philosophical beliefs, and so on influence these choices (Kairys, 1990). The realists urged judges to shape law according to broad values, guided by a better understanding of how legal decisions affect real people. Not surprisingly, psychologists have been happy to provide this understanding.

Modern critiques emphasize that law is inherently subjective, biased, and goal-oriented, even when we have good judges. Substantive legal principles and procedural rules steadily lead in one direction or another. *The policy problem is to select the desired direction.* Feminist, communitarian, libertarian, and other movements with different visions of the Good Society offer competing theories of jurisprudence. Particularly relevant are *law and economics* and *critical legal studies*. Both movements agree that law is never neutral. The law takes sides. The two movements disagree sharply, however, about whether the law's support for the powerful is a good thing. On the economic right, law and economics seeks to use law to pursue goals such as economic efficiency, often based on capitalist theory (Landes and Posner, 1987). Building on law's already strong support for the rights of individuals to control their own property despite most consequences for others, law and economics has had increasing influence. In contrast, critical legal studies efforts to reduce elite power, building on neo-Marxist and other left perspectives (Kairys, 1990; Unger, 1983), have had little impact on legal doctrine.

Where do current psychological perspectives fall amid this broad array of politically charged theories? Small (1993) describes three forms of psychological jurisprudence: an approach to *psychological jurisprudence developed by Gary B. Melton*; *therapeutic jurisprudence*; and a jurisprudence based on *cognitive science*. Psychological jurisprudence of the first kind has the potential to incorporate critical justice-based perspectives. Unfortunately, and perhaps not surprisingly, the newer jurisprudences of the second and third kind seem likely to eclipse it.

Melton's Psychological Jurisprudence

Gary Melton, a past APLS president, broadly challenges psychology-law's mainstream (Melton, 1987; 1988; 1990; 1992; Melton and Saks, 1986). Acknowledging he is "not sure that the field of psychology and law is going anywhere," Melton claimed that "to a great extent, psychologists of law still have blinders on when they look at law and the legal system" (1991: 1). Melton proposes instead a psychological jurisprudence that picks up where legal realism left off. He not only accepts the view that values play a central role in legal decisions, he reminds us that psychology has its own values to pursue. Attacking the law and economics movement's claim that economic efficiency should be the law's goal, Melton (1990) says psychology knows better: psychologists should urge legal decision makers to choose actions likely to enhance psychologically desirable values related to human dignity, such as personhood, privacy, psychological sense of community, equality, and justice. In this sense, Melton's critical psychological jurisprudence advances well beyond legal psychology's mainstream timidity. A legal system directed by the values Melton proposes would go a long way to redress the law's historical bias in favor of those who are white, male, heterosexual, and financially well off.

Unfortunately, Melton (1990) combines his call for a legal system based on dignity-related values with a view that law, properly understood, already shares these values. Rejecting the critical legal studies view that law is a tool of the powerful, Melton believes that "law is intended to promote human welfare" (1992: 383). His perspective, thus, is decidedly liberal rather than radical. He asks psychologists to use their influence as insiders to reform the law. So whereas Melton would have psychologists help the law choose psychologically desirable values, he stops short of a radical psychological jurisprudence more suspicious of law's potential (Fox, 1993b; 1993c).

Therapeutic Jurisprudence

Melton's jurisprudence at least has the potential to move psychology and law in the direction of social justice. Unfortunately, another descendant of legal realism has rapidly overshadowed it, one that may be well meaning but is potentially dangerous nonetheless. David Wexler and others propose reshaping the law – particularly mental health law – according to the values of *therapeutic jurisprudence* (Schopp, 1993; 1995; Wexler, 1990; 1992; 1993; 1995; Wexler and Schopp, 1992; Wexler and Winick, 1991; 1993; for overviews, see Perlin, 1993; Sales, 1995). In Wexler's view, "the law itself can be seen to function as a therapist or therapeutic agent" (1993: 21). Psychologists should evaluate how "legal rules, legal procedures, and the roles of legal actors (principally lawyers and judges) may be viewed as social forces that sometimes produce therapeutic or antitherapeutic consequences" (1993: 21). Judges, for example, might change the way they conduct commitment hearings, making the formal legal proceeding itself part of the therapeutic process. In response to criticisms that he never defines *therapeutic* with enough specificity (Melton, 1994; Slobogin, 1995), Wexler prefers "allowing commentators to roam within the intuitive and common sense contours of the concept" (1995: 221). Not surprisingly, many psychologists have responded enthusiastically to the prospect of judges and legislators paying even more attention to clinical advice. They have begun to apply Wexler's "therapeutic jurisprudence lens" to a wide range of issues in mental health law and, increasingly, in other legal areas as well.

Anticipating the obvious objection, Wexler repeatedly denies that his proposals will lead to a "therapeutic state" marked by paternalism, coercion, and unwarranted state intervention into people's lives. He agrees that therapeutic improvement is not the law's only goal, and insists "the law can use mental health information to improve therapeutic functioning without impinging upon justice concerns" (1993: 21). Claiming only that "other things being equal, mental health law should be restructured to better accomplish therapeutic goals," Wexler acknowledges that "whether other things are equal is often debatable, and therapeutic jurisprudence does not resolve that debate" (1993: 21)

Despite widespread acceptance of Wexler's assurances (e.g., Perlin, 1994), from a critical perspective there is cause for alarm. The legal system and the mental health system have each treated individuals poorly, and often oppressively. The prospect of the two systems working together even more closely risks increased social control disguised as mental health treatment. As demonstrated elsewhere in this volume, state coercion, paternalistic and otherwise, has fallen most harshly on women, people of color, lesbians and gays, and the working class, as well as on non-conformists and political outcasts in all segments of society. Petrila warned that therapeutic jurisprudence "reinforces the existing distribution of power in the relationship between treater and treated" (1993: 882). According to Slobogin, "the danger lies in denying it will have this effect, because doing so may foster a tendency to ignore other values or create a temptation to see the convergence of therapeutic and other values where none exists" (1995: 214).

In Melton's view, there is "little reason to expect that a bit more science will lead to more effective decision making or, more importantly, more *just* processes and decisions . . . Mental health courts – and, some would argue, the legal system in general – have been notoriously ineffective in doing justice effectively" (1994: 216). He agrees with Wexler that "justice and mental health are not necessarily in conflict" and that "doing justice well probably has therapeutic effects." But he cautions that "we should achieve a bench and a bar that do justice well before we encourage them to act as mental health professionals, too" (1994: 216). The law's failure to ensure justice, in the mental health system and elsewhere, puts a different light on Wexler's hope that "therapeutic jurisprudence may then grow tremendously in scope to embrace all, or virtually all, legal arenas" (1995: 229).

Cognitive Science and Psychological Jurisprudence

Small (1993) noted the limited but growing impact of a third form of psychological jurisprudence, based on *cognitive science*. This growth is not surprising, given the increased influence of cognitive perspectives in recent decades. Unfortunately, because it emphasizes internal mental processes and deemphasizes "affect, context, culture, and history" (Prilleltensky, 1994a: 88), cognitivism encourages efforts "to adjust the mind, and not society, in order to promote well-being" (1994a: 93; see Moghaddam and Studer, Chapter 12 in this volume). Critical psychologists of law, consequently, must be wary of efforts to demonstrate a "relationship between the behavior of law and universal processes of human rationality" (Small, 1993: 10; see also Wiener and Small, 1992).

Some believe there are already grounds for cognitive jurisprudence to develop quickly. Wiener et al. found, not surprisingly perhaps, that "85% of published [psycholegal] studies make use of information processing concepts [rather than the dignity-based perspective that Melton advocates]. Given these results, the question remains: From where does one find the meaning of psychology and law's core values?" (1993: 92–93). They answer their own question with an essentially status quo position:

> For a jurisprudential theory to have maximum impact on the legal process it will need to find its legitimacy, in part, in the values that make up the conventional knowledge of the community of scientific psychology. Psychological jurisprudence can only be as powerful as the research base that justifies its ultimate positions. A unified theory of psychological jurisprudence ought to begin with the conventional knowledge of the science of psychology and law. (1993: 94–95)

Clearly, limiting policy to whatever "the consensus of the research community" supports will not bring social change. Along with a potentially repressive therapeutic jurisprudence, the search for "universal processes of human rationality" dims the isolated calls for a critical psychology and law. To the mainstream, apparently, even a moderate justice-based jurisprudence such as Melton's is beyond the pale: "Operating outside the consensus of the paradigm, psychological jurisprudence is in danger of becoming a political platform adhered to by some members of the community but not driven by the growth of psycholegal knowledge" (1993: 93). Critical perspectives, of course, are not part of the mainstream consensus.

Challenging System Legitimacy

I have argued so far that psychologists of law too often ignore law's role in maintaining an unjust status quo. What can critical psychologists do about this? Free of traditional assumptions and sympathies, we can nudge the mainstream away from narrowly focused examination of trivial and noncontroversial topics. And we can advocate fundamental changes in the law, as well as alternatives to it. Central to this task is examining how the legal system maintains its *legitimacy*, which enhances respect for, and obedience to, law and legal authorities (Fox, 1993b).

Dictatorial governments use open force to impose policies on resistant populations and prevent demands for justice. In contrast, liberal states claiming to be representative democracies use coercion and manipulation only when necessary. More often, *the state limits fundamental challenges by teaching the population that the system is legitimate*. Thus, people obey the law not just to avoid punishment, but because they believe the authorities have the right to make demands (Kelman and Hamilton, 1989; Turkel, 1996; Tyler, 1990). It is partly for this reason that disagreement among judges confuses the public about what the law really is: it shakes our faith in the authorities' legitimacy. We may conclude that individual judges are corrupt, stupid, racist, or biased, but we often believe that the underlying law is above politics rather than part of it. We laugh at cynical jokes about lawyers and sometimes even judges, but there are few jokes about law itself.

As Tapp (1974) pointed out, inaccurate beliefs about human behavior strengthen the law's legitimacy. She described the "crippling assumption" that law is the only source of "justice, obligation, and responsibility" and warned that "if [this assumption] continues . . . then the emergence of an authoritarian repressive law is more likely" (1974: 54). In other words, we often believe that people behave justly and responsibly only because the law requires it – that we cannot be good unless we are forced to be good (Lerner, 1982). This belief may partly reflect lack of awareness that law is a recent invention. So-called "primitive" groups resolved disputes and maintained order without legal systems for most of human history (Barclay, 1982; Fox, 1985; 1993a; 1993c).

In the remainder of this chapter I note several topics particularly relevant to the crucial role of legal fictions and myths in enhancing system legitimacy. In these areas and others, critical psychologists of law should examine subjects Melton suggested are central to a values-oriented psychological jurisprudence: the symbolic impact of law, the subjective meaning of law in everyday life, and legal socialization. What does law mean to us, and how does it come to mean that, and what are the implications for justice?

Procedural Justice, Substantive Justice, and False Consciousness

"The rule of law" assumes that the procedurally correct application of general principles is best even when it brings unfair results in particular cases. By directing attention to procedures rather than trying to reach a fair result (seeking *procedural justice* rather than *substantive justice*), legal authorities deflect calls for social justice and fundamental fairness. The belief that authorities use fair procedures enhances system legitimacy despite negative outcomes (Tyler, 1990; Tyler and Mitchell, 1994). When the law insists that the rules of the game count more than the outcome, we tolerate injustice because it seems to result from a legitimate procedure.

Although concern for due process and fair procedures is important, it is not enough. After all, the system routinely gives lawbreakers, welfare clients, and political activists procedurally correct hearings before locking them up, cutting off their checks, or rejecting their calls for social change. As Haney noted,

> We are at risk of creating a perfect justice machine that grinds up the victims of societal dysfunction and disarray and deposits them into the legally sanctioned sea of oppression and human misery that is our prison system. Even if all our due process dreams came true in psychology and law, and this mythical justice machine ground away with perfect procedural precision and accuracy, much substantive injustice would still remain. (1993: 381)

Tom Tyler, the field's leading investigator of procedural justice, repeatedly notes that a procedural focus can lead to *false consciousness*: "Government leaders may find it easier to create conditions of 'perceived fairness' than to solve problems or provide needed benefits" (Tyler et al., 1986: 976; see also Tyler and Mitchell, 1994). Yet despite his awareness that the authorities may manipulate us, Tyler devotes little discussion to how frequently they do so. In *Why People Obey the Law*, for example, Tyler claimed that "the study of procedural justice is neutral about the quality of the existing legal system" (1990: 148). He added that "it is beyond the scope of this book to evaluate whether those studied 'ought' to be more or less satisfied than they are with legal authorities" (1990: 148). Tyler's approach makes sense only from a perspective that presumes the benevolence of legal and political authorities. In contrast, Haney bluntly criticized the Supreme Court's "let them eat due process" attitude and "the national obsession with process [that] has allowed us to ignore dramatic inequalities in substantive outcome" (1991: 194).

The belief in system legitimacy dampens public protest when the government uses procedurally correct coercion and manipulation to inhibit challengers (Fox, 1993b). State legislatures in the United States, for example, routinely devise procedural hurdles to exclude nonmainstream political parties from the ballot. Procedural rules raising the cost and time of litigation make lawsuits against corporations or governments difficult to pursue, but wealthy corporations can easily afford lawsuits against activists. The law limits police surveillance, infiltration, and repression of activist groups – unless the police use appropriate procedures. At trial, judges following correct procedures typically prevent defendants from presenting a necessity defense based on their motivations for breaking the law. Judges also refuse to tell juries about jury nullification, the doctrine that allows jurors to acquit despite the evidence if they believe the defendant's actions were justified (Fox, 1993a).

What can critical psychologists do about false consciousness and the failure to ensure substantive justice? We can expose procedural flaws where they exist, but we must remember that the system can always adjust its practices to reach its goals. We can also support victims of procedurally correct injustice, but here too we must remember the limitations of our efforts. Governments and corporations with far greater resources will adopt any useful methods we develop (Haney, 1980). For example, social scientists devised scientific jury selection to help the Harrisburg Seven defend themselves against Vietnam-era conspiracy charges (Schulman et al., 1973). Today, though, it is primarily large corporations rather than activists or criminal defendants who can afford to use it.

Most important is to assess substantive results as well as procedural fairness. To do so, we must consider a difficult question: which "independent definitions [of justice] . . . might 'make sense' from a psychological perspective" (Haney, 1993: 379)? Unfortunately, "Psychology and law has continued to operate without a shared conception of, or commitment to, justice. We have no clearly articulated theory of value and, therefore, no overarching vision with which to address and reform the legal system" (1993: 379). Tyler and Mitchell noted that "the important role of ideology in shaping individual reactions to experiences highlights the need to consider the sociopolitical context within which legal decisions occur" (1994: 795). But in their view, although "psychologists do acknowledge the importance of the larger society in shaping subjective reactions to particular experiences . . . they do not typically focus on social structural or cultural factors in their analyses" (1994: 795). A critical psychological jurisprudence would focus not merely on *perceptions* of fairness, but on the real consequences of inequality, oppression, and exploitation in particular sociopolitical contexts.

Law, Capitalism, and Distributive Justice

Considering the "social structural and cultural factors" affecting substantive justice should lead psychologists of law to examine *law's role in endorsing and protecting capitalism and class inequality.* Capitalist theory is steeped in unquestioned psychological assumptions about an essentially selfish human nature (Wachtel, 1983). Yet psychology-law generally ignores these assumptions. It barely scratches the surface of legal issues related to class inequality and distributive justice. Is the profit motive really the highest value of human motivation? Is economic growth really more important to individual well-being than dignity, empowerment, and a psychological sense of community? Only an understanding of capitalism's development explains the changing nature of many basic legal principles. For example, judges and legislatures in the nineteenth century transformed the law's older equity and fairness norms to suit commercial interests (Horwitz, 1977). Under the guise of applying neutral principles, the law deflects attention from substantive oppression, as when the concept of individual merit maintains racism in the workplace (Haney and Hurtado, 1994). In this context, the law and economics school's increasing influence is not surprising.

Law in capitalist countries endorses resource distribution according to social psychology's equity norm: goods are distributed in proportion to inputs of time, effort, money, and so on. A critical perspective redirects attention to competing principles of equality and need (Fox, 1993a; 1996). What can legal psychologists say about substantive justice, and about the consequences of injustice, when assessing minimum wage and similar requirements, affirmative action and its alternatives, equal pay and comparable worth, or the definition of "disability" in a job-scarce economy (Fox, 1994)? How much more than a typical worker's salary should the law allow a corporate executive to receive? Psychologists of law devote endless effort to uncovering false judicial assumptions concerning jury biases, adolescent competence, and similar topics that liberal academics find interesting. There is no comparable effort to uncover false assumptions that prop up capitalism, particularly capitalism in the welfare state version that liberal academics prefer.

When psychology-law researchers do address issues related to capitalism, they pose little substantive challenge. As an example, in recent years psychologists have begun to examine *the nature of the business corporation* (Tomkins et al., 1992). Psychologists and legal researchers examine how executives and managers make decisions and how workers carry them out. They propose methods to reduce risky and harmful decisions and enhance corporate responsibility and ethics. These approaches fall squarely within the liberal reform tradition of trying to reduce capitalism's negative consequences. Unfortunately, as with efforts by industrial-organizational psychologists to maintain managerial control over workers (Prilleltensky, 1994a), these efforts do nothing to challenge the essence of corporate dominance (Fox, 1996).

Corporate law lets enormous numbers of people pool their resources to fund large-scale enterprises. Corporate executives make decisions in the name of the corporation to maximize shareholder profit. Presuming that the corporation is a legal person, United States law grants it constitutional protections. Shareholders are not liable for damage to workers, communities, or the environment. Avoidable harm rarely leads to civil penalties, let alone criminal ones. Evidence of problems that come with large size – hierarchy, conformity, role demands, and others identified by social and organizational psychologists – is ignored. The law, in other words, has created institutions that now dominate the world economy and increasingly dominate and homogenize the world's cultures (Bonsignore, 1994). It has done so over the past century and a half, as judges and legislators reversed earlier legal principles that restricted the scope, size, and function of corporate institutions. In the face of this dominance, in the face of the law's use of a bizarre "group mind" theory as the basis of legal doctrine, psychologists devote more effort to giving the corporation a human face than to uncovering the facelessness beneath the mask (Fox, 1996).

The Reasonable Person Fiction

The law frequently uses the fictional *reasonable person* as a standard for behavior the law expects. As demonstrated by legal psychologists in a variety of arenas, the law's view of what behavior is reasonable often conflicts with the behavior and beliefs of real human beings (Horowitz and Willging, 1984). The law takes little notice of the diversity of behaviors that might be equally reasonable.

Historically, the law called the reasonable person the reasonable *man*. Although the language has changed to suit modern sensibilities, the concept itself is pretty much the same. The fictitious reasonable person is still purely rational in strict economic terms: a self-oriented, asocial individual (well off, white, heterosexual man?) motivated not at all by concern for others, and unusually aware of the law's logic and assumptions. Critical psychologists might explore the degree to which real people's views of justice and fairness conflict with the law's fiction. How should notions of what is reasonable change in the Good Society?

The Side-Effects Problem

Mainstream proposals for legal and policy reform sometimes succeed. Unfortunately, successful reform efforts often bring *unpredicted and unintended side effects* because so many seemingly separate social problems are actually related. Focusing on narrow, "manageable" problems, particularly at the individual level, rather than carrying out system-wide change can cause the resolution of one policy issue to complicate others (Fox, 1991; 1993b; Haney, 1993; Roesch, 1995).

Beyond the complications of narrowly focused individual-level solutions lies another possibility: law-based solutions to social problems may bring short-term gain at the expense of greater dependency on legal authorities, reducing people's ability and motivation to work with others to devise community-based solutions (Fox, 1985; 1993a; 1993b). Noting that the centralized state inhibits both individual autonomy and a psychological sense of community, community psychologist Seymour Sarason (1976) identified this phenomenon as the *central anarchist insight*. Although conservatives who criticize "welfare dependency" also make this argument, we should not dismiss it out of hand. Critical psychologists should acknowledge the reduced autonomy and sense of community as a serious issue. But we should also insist on structural change to revitalize communities and eliminate our economic and legal system's destructive inequality.

Conclusion

Both law and psychology have supported an oppressive status quo. If the field of psychology-law merges the techniques of psychology's mainstream with law's oppressive tendencies, the result will be even greater injustice. The appeal of therapeutic jurisprudence raises such a possibility, as does the routine empirical work of legal psychology that helps the law do its job better. Psychology and law's "client" – the legal system – scarcely needs help to retain its dominance. Tragically, psychologists help the law become even more effective at benefiting some at the expense of others. This is particularly the case when the perspectives of women, people of color, the poor, and other victims of the legal system are notably absent from the field (Haney, 1993).

On the other hand, there is a ray of hope: the historical presence in psychology-law of a focus on justice, combined with Melton's psychological jurisprudence based on values of human dignity. A critical psychology and law can seek to answer crucial questions. What would we like to see in the Good Society – not just what do we think it practical to advocate today? Can we alter law so significantly that it can become a force for justice, or does law just help those who already maintain control? As we answer these questions, we can raise public awareness about the nature of law and its consequences. Instead of helping law portray itself as a neutral seeker of justice, we can expose false consciousness and "awaken the sense of injustice" (Deutsch and Steil, 1988). Throughout, we can "aspir[e] to the role of transformers, system shakers who risk alienation but seek real substantive change" rather than remaining "content – even complacent – to serve as technicians and tinkerers in the law" (Haney, 1993: 384).

Unfortunately, if law is always an ally of the status quo, then we cannot radicalize it. As Haney cautioned, "You cannot change a system from which you seek acceptance, and the costs of making our work palatable to an inherently (and increasingly) conservative legal system may simply be too high" (1993: 385). This caution takes on added significance in light of Herman's broader question: "Does the rise of psychology herald a new chapter in the evolution of humanism or merely indicate that Big Brother is bright enough to arrive cloaked in the rhetoric of enlightenment and health?" (1995: 315). On the one hand, trying to turn the system in a progressive direction supports law's victims. This support is crucial. On the other hand, working as insiders within the law by filing appellate briefs and similar activities legitimizes legal institutions while draining energy and focus from advocating fundamental alternatives (Fox, 1993b). Can we sufficiently salvage law? Resolving this dilemma is the ultimate task for a critical psychology and law.

Note

I thank Elizabeth Caddick, Isaac Prilleltensky, and Alan Tomkins for their detailed comments on two or more earlier drafts.

15

Political Psychology:
A Critical Perspective

Maritza Montero

Editors' note *Political psychology has something in common with other disciplines whose subject matter has inherently political implications. As in community psychology, cross-cultural psychology, psychology and law, and feminist psychology, mainstream political psychologists address potentially controversial political topics in a way that avoids fundamental challenges to psychology's established norms and society's established institutions. While critical psychology is explicitly political, Maritza Montero points out in this chapter that political psychology is largely apolitical and acritical.*

Political psychology rarely explores issues of oppression and domination in Western democracies, the merits of alternative political systems, or the way in which political factors advance or hinder the Good Life and the Good Society. Instead, it focuses on highly psychologized safe topics such as attitudes toward politicians and the personalities of world leaders. Montero asks us to consider why certain topics are emphasized ad nauseam while others are shunned. Identifying the need "to bring to the surface concealed, distorted, denied or ignored aspects of an issue," she notes that we can learn from exclusions as much as we can from inclusions. Issues are neglected or declared illegitimate for a reason, typically because they threaten the status quo. In political psychology as in other areas, "absences and exclusions should be suspected, for they may serve hidden interests."

Montero's discussion of what constitutes a legitimate or illegitimate area of study parallels similar concerns in the chapters on ethics, history, and developmental, clinical, feminist, and discursive psychology. By finding out what is missing and putting it back into view, critical psychology can help redefine the contours of a field, forcing it to pay attention to fundamental concerns such as oppression, emancipation, subjectivity, and the nature of knowledge.

The concept of critique is not univocal. Typical meanings of the concept include judgments of the quality, morality, goodness, or beauty of something. Within the social sciences, "critical" means challenging the unquestioned assumptions, explanations and interpretations of social phenomena.

A critical perspective refuses to accept or discard a postulate just because it conforms to principles established or founded on authority, tradition, or common wisdom. It also adopts an open attitude towards rival or alternative explanations and postulates. Such an approach questions what the mainstream presents as universal, natural, and irrefutable.

To assume this critical position very often means taking a radical approach, getting at the fundamental aspects of issues, at the roots of problems or phenomena. In some cases, to achieve depth means to bring to the surface concealed, distorted, denied or ignored aspects of an issue. In doing so, critical theorists subvert and threaten the habitual way of looking at things. We assume a radical position not to put upside-down a certain order (although I must confess that the idea appears to me very attractive), but because of the need to reveal what is not recognized. This orientation has the potential to create new forms of knowledge.

Starting, then, from a critical perspective, I present first an overview of mainstream political psychology. Later, I hope to show that there is more to political psychology than is usually considered within the field.

The Definition of Political Psychology and Its Object of Study

There is a consensus that political psychology, as a scientific discipline, developed from the convergence of psychology and political science (Greenstein, 1973; Iyengar and McGuire, 1993; Seoane and Rodríquez, 1988; Stone, 1981). The discipline studies the effects psychological processes have on political behavior and, vice versa, the psychological effects political structures have on individuals or groups (Stone, 1981). This definition is sufficiently ample to accommodate a variety of phenomena and behaviors.

Psychological processes related to politics include perception, cognition (e.g., beliefs, values, social representations, attitudes, ideology), socialization, leadership, social identity, conflict, communication, authoritarianism, and power. Behaviors such as conformity, mass movements, voting, and political affiliation are also of concern to political psychologists. But this is not all that could or should be encompassed by political psychology. The study of political trauma (torture, exile, political persecution), political terrorism, social movements, and the power of minorities are some of the neglected areas within the mainstream. Questions we should ask upon noticing these absences include: why are these themes not present? Whose interests are being served by their exclusion? Whose welfare is being ignored?

Other perspectives of political psychology emerge from these themes and questions. Martín-Baró considered that the definition of political psychology should stress the study of "psychic processes through which people and groups create, strive for, and exert the necessary power to satisfy certain socially determined interests in a social structure" (1995: 216). This definition does not accept the concept of politics without analysis. Instead, it presents what Martín-Baró considered its central element: power, revealing its role, and making it the center or locus of politics. Indeed, power is the key to understanding the construction of most political texts.

A Short Life and a Long History

Political psychology began to be recognized as a systematic area of studies, with its own academic place, in the seventies, when the first texts defining the field were published (Greenstein, 1973; Knutson, 1973; Stone, 1974). In 1978 the International Society of Political Psychology gathered for the first time researchers and practitioners in the field. The same organization launched in 1979 the first specialized journal, *Political Psychology*. By the end of that decade, political psychology was firmly established as a professional and academic specialty. However, long before that time there were publications that clearly may be placed within the field. The name "political psychology," for instance, had been in existence since 1910 when Gustave Le Bon published a work entitled *La Psychologie Politique*. Before him, in 1780, Saint-Simon, another Frenchman, had already used the term "psycho-politics" (Munné, 1986: 20).

McGuire (1993) identified three main phases in the development of mainstream political psychology in the twentieth century. During the first phase there was interest in studies of personality and culture (1940–1950). Research examined the personality of political leaders and the political behavior of specific cultures. During the second phase research primarily focused on the study of political attitudes (e.g., conservatism, liberalism, dogmatism) and voting behavior (1960–1970). The third, and current, phase emphasizes political ideology. Ideology mainly means, in the United States, a system of beliefs. However, in other parts of the world (Latin America, Europe), ideology has been understood as the hegemony or domination of certain ideas over others. In circles where Marxist thought has had an influence, ideology has come to mean false consciousness. Thus, the overall emphasis in this phase is on social cognition.

This chronology, however, does not include important works produced at the end of the last century and at the beginning of this one. There are at least two stages preceding McGuire's chronology. The first, from 1895 to 1920, was marked by the proposal of a psychology of the masses. In Europe (Le Bon, 1895; 1910) as well as in Latin America, where a rich literature characterized by an evolutionary and positivist perspective can be found, the relation between politics and sociopsychological processes was being considered. In the second stage, from 1923 to 1940, the Frankfurt School in Germany introduced the Marxist perspective in psychopolitical studies. Linking the ideas of Freud and Marx, the Frankfurt School studied ideology as the distortion of social realities aimed to serve particular interests. Wilhelm Reich's work, such as *The Mass Psychology of Fascism* (1933/1970), can also be included within this tradition. A history of political psychology cannot and should not ignore these developments.

There is something to be learned from this historical overview. Ethnocentric perspectives presented as universally valid interpretations should always be challenged for what they ignore. Biased visions of the world and of historical processes permeate the discourse of political psychology, thereby creating only very partial knowledge. What should be regarded as a part of the discipline is portrayed as the whole discipline. This portrayal excludes and silences the achievements of other peoples. Students and researchers should be aware of the ways in which a discipline can narrow our vision and capacity to deal with social and political processes.

Absences and exclusions should be suspected, for they may serve hidden interests. Socially constructed versions of the world are depicted as natural and universal. We are taught to take for granted and accept as normal current ways of doing politics. Our unquestioned political habits serve specific political interests, the interests of those who are invested in protecting the status quo. Willingly or not, mainstream political psychology colludes with those interests by not challenging political structures and by remaining silent on alternative power arrangements. The discipline lends scientific credence to political systems that work to benefit the few at the expense of the many.

Politics in Disrepute

The condition of the human being as a social and political animal (*zoon politikon*) is unquestionable. But the very political nature of social behavior has often been ignored, both by society and by political psychology. Political accounts of social behavior are treated with a great deal of apprehension. A certain malaise seems to be attached to the concept of politics, a certain discomfort. This annoying aspect of politics derives from two sources. On the one hand, the people despise the manipulative behavior of politicians who exclude them from important decision making processes. On the other hand, politicians prefer not to be disturbed by the political actions of the people. Thus, both politicians and discontent citizens have come to treat the word "politics" with disdain.

The consequence of this is that politics is reduced to partisanship and governmental action. Citizen participation in politics is limited to voting and political affiliation. The exercise of political power, then, is limited to election times. Citizen participation is further restricted by equating politics with government, a narrow view that is often supported by political psychology. These conceptions of politics disconnect the people from the political process, forgetting that democracy is based on the very participation of citizens in public affairs.

The deconstruction of the term "politics" in Western countries reveals that the concept has lost its original meaning. It has been detached from the root which fastened it to the *polis* (Greek "city"). Politics has come to mean the actions of a specific group of people who arrogate for themselves the capacity to manage the polis.

Politics and the Individual

What makes an action or an actor political? Where does the political character of behaviors reside? Usually, what a politician does is considered political. So is what happens in a political context such as government offices or international relations. But the relationship between actors and actions and the dominant social order should also be considered political (Martín-Baró, 1995), as should the construction of political meaning in discourse.

People involved in politics are usually portrayed in mainstream political psychology as main or supporting actors. Main actors are those who exert institutionalized power and control the government (congressional representatives, presidents, secretaries of state, magistrates, and the political parties whose members fill these offices). Supporting actors are the masses, the citizens whose political activities are reduced to the ritual of voting every few years. Through elections, the people legitimize the power of the main actors, delegate their power, and ultimately lose their power. In some ways, the relationship between traditional politicians and the citizenry may be compared with that of a stage actor to his or her audience. Actors expect a price of admission, attention, applause, and silence during the performance. They also expect the audience to come back for the next show, and even to love them.

The behavior of the masses in the audience is often examined with the curious look with which we observe wild animals. Current conceptions of the masses as irrational, aggressive, and unpredictable perpetuate myths initiated in the nineteenth century by Gustave Le Bon (1895/1952). Behind this conception is the idea that ordinary people, the great majority of the people, do not know what they want, or what they need, or what is convenient for them. Thus, someone knowledgeable, be it a person or a group, should tell them, and make important decisions for them such as taxing them beyond their means, sending them to war, or relocating them. In essence, their presence in politics is circumstantial. They appear and disappear according to the convenience or interests of the main characters. On the one hand their vote is demanded and they are the object of discourses seeking their approval. On the other, certain maneuvers are hidden from them and they are excluded from decisions that directly affect them.

It is common, then, to find studies on the effects of political systems and ideas on individuals (e.g., political socialization, political attitudes, beliefs and values such as conservatism, dogmatism, liberalism, or democratization); on the effects of authoritarianism on people; and on the development of political leadership. But forgotten are those who resist and live with the consequences of political decisions made on their behalf by the main characters. The problem is that the people, as a subject of democracy, are usually reduced to statistical tendencies in surveys, the average of which is considered public opinion. Certain groups such as minors, ethnic minorities, women, low-income persons, immigrants, and elderly people are rarely considered main actors. They are reduced to mere deviations or nonsignificant results in statistical graphs. While in theory everyone is equal before the law, in reality not all people in a democracy enjoy the same rights (Boudon, 1977). Thus, for example, minors, nonnationalized immigrants, military personnel, and prisoners in some countries are banned from participating in elections. These legal restrictions alienate many people from the democratic process.

When political psychology turns to the great political figures of history, there is a tendency to emphasize their use of power and their access to it from a predominantly individualistic perspective. The governing styles of certain presidents and political parties are analyzed, as well as their discourses, in order to know their ideological tendencies and their influence on the population and on other political figures. Those ideological views are often shared by the researchers themselves, who therefore consider them unquestionable. Thus, in an analysis of presidential speeches in Venezuela between 1938 and 1992, Rodriguez (1993) found that while the people do not appear in them as main players in a democracy, the political parties, the military, and the Catholic church very much do.

Martín-Baró expressed the need to "ask oneself which are the main groups or persons involved in each political relationship, and not to settle for the positive or apparent" (1995: 229), in order to unveil power maneuvers. But I think that this should be done not only to identify who is manipulating power and resources behind the scenes, but also to identify those affected by those actions. Political psychology should study all the political players, and not just the "positive or apparent" ones studied by the mainstream. These include:

1   Traditional political actors: politicians, governmental representatives, legislators, magistrates.
2   Players whose influence is exerted from the background, not directly evident: business managers, economic and religious groups and leaders.
3   The citizenry, defined as the aggregate of individuals who have political rights and duties, and who, by exercising them, take part in the government of a nation.
4   The people, as a group comprising citizens and noncitizens who act and react to political actions.
5   Minority groups which may be the object of differential political treatment. By minority groups I refer here to groups with a clear identity, and with defined and consistent objectives opposed to those of the political majority. Although minorities often pay a price for their political involvement, they often manage to have a social impact (Moscovici, 1976; Moscovici and Mugny, 1987).

Politics and Social Identity

The relationship between social identity and politics has been the subject of study in political psychology since the inception of the field. While fundamental to the understanding of concepts such as nationality and nationalism, this line of research has reinforced dependency and legitimized interpretations that disqualify some groups from having national identities. Many people in the former colonies now considered "developing countries" in the "Third World" (that is, not yet developed according to the model of the "developed" world) have come to internalize negative images of themselves. This phenomenon, variously called "national underevaluation," "colonial ideology," or "negative national self-image," has been studied in Venezuela (Montero, 1985; 1990; Quintero, 1993; Salazar, 1983), South East Asia (Alatas, 1977), Tunisia (Memmi, 1968), Algeria (Fanon, 1968), and Argentina (D'Adamo and Garcia-Beaudoux, 1995). The research shows how groups and even entire societies develop self-denigrating images of themselves by internalizing negative attributions.

To understand this phenomenon we must understand the concept of *ideology*. Ideology refers to a system of ideas that promotes particular interests. These interests are typically upheld by fostering ideas that distort, deny, or conceal social and historical facts and processes. Thus, ideology constructs reality in such a way that people internalize negative attributions of themselves as natural and legitimate. Through a self-fulfilling process, people behave in accordance with these negative perceptions. The political consequences of this phenomenon are many. People consume imported goods with the belief that locally produced ones are inferior, they import cultural norms and fads that are detrimental to the local population, and in general they regard products coming from the First World as better. Most importantly, they believe that strong and authoritarian leaders are needed because they are not "enlightened" enough to handle democracy.

Political Participation or Political Action?

Even before political psychology was recognized as a branch of psychology there have been studies examining *political participation*. These explored voting behavior and militancy in political parties. Although the term "participation" is frequently used in the literature, authors have begun to widen its scope (Lederer, 1986; Montero, 1995; Sabucedo, 1990). This is because limiting its use to voting and to political affiliation creates a predominantly reactive perspective on what political participation is all about.

For this reason, I prefer to talk about *political action*, placing the emphasis on the dynamic character of social actors shaping societies and building social institutions. For example, Marsh and Kaase give a definition of political participation that breaks with the traditional conception. For them, participation involves "voluntary activities by individual citizens intended to influence either directly or indirectly political choices at various levels of the political system" (1979: 42). They thus include activities such as demonstrations, strikes or lockouts, taking over public buildings, removing ads and signs, and other forms of violence.

Similarly, Sabucedo defines political action as "intentional behavior by an individual or group with the aim of achieving some type of influence in political decision-making" (1990: 73). Along with this definition he points out that political action is essentially tied to the democratic system, to which it lends legitimacy. Then, for a democracy to be considered as such, it must create channels through which citizens may express their will. These channels may be conventional or alternative. Conventional modes of political action refer to activities traditionally defined as political and usually expected from society's members at certain moments (e.g., voting). Unlike alternative modes, they are foreseeable and foreseen.

Alternative Political Action

Traditional views of politics rely heavily on the *ideology of a just world*. According to this ideology, society is organized in a fair and just way, and the "professionals of politics" in charge attend to the needs and anxieties of citizens. If we follow certain rules, society will run smoothly and predictably, and we will avert conflicts. Whoever does not fit into society and behaves unpredictably is deemed abnormal or deviant.

Political protest thus is delegitimized on the basis that it does not follow the rules of the game. Protesters are considered extremists. Nevertheless, Lederer observed that "political protest in advanced industrial democracies beginning in the late 1960s reflects the politicization of mass publics and the emergence of new styles of political action" (1986: 355). These new "styles" are what we call *alternative modes of political action*, that is, nonconventional forms of action related to discontent. These new forms of politics reveal the incapacity of traditional forms to express the feelings and the needs of the masses or of specific groups who feel deprived of rights and aspirations.

Alternative modes of doing politics do not correspond to accepted standards and rules of predictable forms of political participation. They seem to sprout spontaneously in groups or by individuals. Sit-ins, graffiti, boycotts, burning of draft cards or brassieres, so popular at the end of the sixties and beginning of the seventies, as well as the hijacking of airplanes and taking of hostages, all represent alternative modes of action that threaten the established order of things. These actions can be legal or illegal. Illegal ones include violent as well as nonviolent actions, such as refusal to pay taxes, refusal to comply with military service, and other forms of civil disobedience.

Many of these actions have succeeded in forcing laws to be amended to satisfy the needs of marginalized or radical groups. For example, in many countries conscientious objectors can substitute military service with social service. The civil disobedience movement organized by Gandhi in India was a fundamental factor in winning independence from England. The civil rights movement in the United States led to the end of legalized segregation, and mass movements for social justice forced the end of apartheid in South Africa. With the emergence of alternative political actions, new political players have come on board: neighborhood organizations, communities, and even international organizations such as Greenpeace.

Politics, Ideology, and Consciousness Raising

The recognition of ideology's role in political phenomena has led to intense research in this area. The origins, causes, and ways of overcoming the effects of dominant ideologies have been the subject of study in many South American countries since the late fifties. Research on deideologization (fighting the effects of ideology) and consciousness raising in Brazil (Lane and Sawaia, 1991), Colombia (Fals Borda, 1985), Salvador (Martín-Baró, 1985a; 1986; 1990), and Venezuela (Montero, 1993) shows convergence between two fields: community psychology and political psychology. Both have proved that the process of community development is itself a mode of political action. Furthermore, the research shows that in order to become a full political actor it is necessary to break the vicious cycle of self-diminishing attributions and political alienation. People need to resist political alienation. That is, ordinary people have to fight the belief that politics is a world that is foreign to them, belonging exclusively to professional politicians and holders of power whose decisions cannot be questioned.

Ideology is constructed in language and expressed in discourse. It is a dynamic process of legitimation of certain ideas which need to be imposed as "truth" or as valid. Thus, ideology projects images designed to keep certain people in power. Acting through "common sense," ideology fosters certain beliefs about the social world as natural: those in power deserve their privileges, those subjected to power cannot do any better. But common sense, like science, is not devoid of contradictions. Common sense is made of presences and absences. To accept only the presences, what is explicit, can be misleading and biasing. As the French philosopher Derrida (1967) has put it, there is the text and there is nothing outside of it. But even the countertext can be found within it, by noticing what is missing. That is why political psychology has to deal with ideology and with forms to counteract it, what has been called *deideologization*.

Deideologization presupposes a political commitment: to promote the interests of the oppressed, and to put their interests above any other. An example of this work is the proposal made by Martín-Baró (1985b) to use public opinion polls as deideologizing tools. To achieve this objective, survey results need to be discussed with the people and used as a means of popular education. Questions such as whose interests are being served by these results can act as catalysts for change. By probing the nature of the results and examining their connection to the prevalent ideology, public opinion polls can challenge the dominant ideology.

Deideologization is closely linked to *consciousness raising.* To raise consciousness does not mean to fill a vacuum. Everyone has consciousness. The purpose of this work is to create awareness about life conditions, about causes and effects, and to promote change and empowerment. The process of change begins with placing people, through their own actions and efforts, in control of their immediate environment. Action and reflection are carried out in order to transform passivity into activity, and apathy into commitment, decision making, and the transformation of everyday life. This process helps people exert their own rights, fulfill their duties, and demand what is due. It both strengthens and changes democracy, building the democratic character and bridging the gap between the people and the government elected to serve them. Consciousness raising increases action well beyond the cyclical act of voting.

Politics and Democracy

The foregoing discussion points to the bond between political action and democracy (Sabucedo, 1990). But although political psychologists study diverse forms of political expression within democracies, attempts to undermine democracy are rarely explored. In many South American countries, this is a dangerous, if not lethal, topic of study, as many Chilean, Argentinian, Brazilian, and Uruguayan psychologists and social scientists have personally experienced.

If democracy is the best political system known, why do alternative modes of political action arise? Doesn't this indicate a failure in the system? Obviously, in a truly democratic democracy (and this is not a redundancy), multiple forms of action should coexist. Why, then, is it not so? If political psychology wishes to give a response to this question it must study democratic processes from a *deconstructionist* perspective. It needs to look for the concealed meaning of texts and practices, analyzing the manner in which they are presented and explained. Political psychology needs to reveal the contradictions, assumptions, gaps and strategies embedded in political texts. Presences and absences in these texts should be accounted for.

A deconstructionist analysis will reveal some interesting things, teaching us that a critical perspective must not assume certain concepts as natural or given. It is said that democracy is a system in which the government representatives and the legislators are elected by the people, where people is read as *everyone.* Consequently, it is assumed that any government in a democratic country has gained power by a decision of all the people. It follows that the government is legitimate and that it represents the people's will.

Nevertheless, in countries where a certain percentage of the vote is not necessary in order to win, it is often a minority of citizens who elect the representatives for all the people. For example, assume three political parties are competing, A, B and C, and that 45% of the electorate abstains from voting, 15% vote for A, 10% for B and 30% for C. So C wins the elections. However, this means that only 30% of the electorate has elected the winning party or person, that 25% was really not in favor of that person, and that 45% were not even interested in voting for any of the candidates. The will of 70% of the electorate was then discarded in favor of the will of the 30%. In some countries the number of abstainers is very high. In others there are strong suspicions that the electoral system is fraudulent. Moreover, as pointed out by Ibáñez (1992: 41), even within each political party only a minority elects representatives to government positions. These are decisions that very often, for good or bad, go against the tendencies of the majority of the people (for instance, invading or economically helping another nation, raising taxes, etc.). For this reason, Ibáñez expresses the need to have an alternative to democracy "that respects the right of the people not to be governed against their will" (1992: 43).

Chomsky (1989) pointed out how political authorities who see alternative legal actions as a threat, as an "excess of democracy," may strive for a "moderation in democracy." They introduce measures to dissuade citizens from participating in politics, promoting political apathy and unquestioned obedience and restricting the political arena to political psychology's main actors, the "professionals of politics." What this means is that democracy cannot be accepted at face value. If we dig a little we will find that in democracy's name, as in the name of liberty, many injustices are committed. (I will not say crimes, although sometimes they occur.) But despite that, it is still the best system of government we know.

Final Remarks

Based on the "absences" present in political psychology, I believe we need to regenerate the discipline. The political psychology we need should meet a few requirements. First, it should go beyond appearances, studying not only what is explicitly present in texts, but also what is absent. Second, it should explore the behavior of main as well as supporting actors in the political drama. Third, it should challenge the common sense through which we interpret the social world. And fourth, it should recognize the political character of private and public acts. Relegating certain actions to the private world, as well as making public what has been previously kept secret, constitute political acts. By making public the roots and mechanisms of ideological systems we can expose the power base of our social arrangements. If political psychology accomplishes that, it will contribute to the cause of critical psychology (Becker and Lira, 1990; Lira and Castillo, 1991).

Note

The author is grateful to the editors for their help with the English in this chapter.

PART III
CRITICAL THEORIES

16

Feminist Psychology

Sue Wilkinson

Editors' note *Feminist psychology's enormous influence on critical psychology is apparent throughout this book. Feminist psychologists have instigated and maintained much of the critical effort to redirect psychology's theoretical assumptions, research methods, professional practices, and ethical guidelines. But despite feminism's partial success in forcing mainstream psychology to make room for women's perspectives, Sue Wilkinson makes it clear in this chapter that the struggle is far from over.*

Wilkinson identifies a process we have seen earlier: psychologists seeking fundamental social change establish a new area or perspective within psychology only to see their political goals recede from the new field's concerns (see Chapters 10, 11, and 14). In this case, "although 'psychology of women' was established with clear feminist intentions, a large part of the field is rigidly conventional in its support for the status quo." This dynamic has parallels in the larger society, where movements for social change are often coopted as they become institutionalized in less confrontational form. Because feminism radically challenges psychology as well as society, it is not surprising that its success has been limited. Nor is it surprising that psychologists seeking liberal reform rather than more significant transformation now dominate the depoliticized field called "psychology of women."

Adding to feminist psychology's difficulties is that its proponents lack consensus on many issues, a situation many readers may find surprising and confusing. Wilkinson evaluates the strengths and weaknesses of competing feminist perspectives, making it clear there is no single correct approach. As we noted in Chapter 1, differing perspectives are common throughout critical psychology. These differences lead to many of the dilemmas critical psychologists confront as we try to determine how best to bring about emancipation and equality.

Feminist psychology is psychological theory and practice which is explicitly informed by the political goals of the feminist movement. Feminism embraces a plurality of definitions and viewpoints, but these different versions of feminism share two common themes (Unger and Crawford, 1992: 8–9). First, feminism places a high value on women, considering us as worthy of study in our own right, not just in comparison with men.

Second, feminism recognizes the need for social change on behalf of women: feminist psychology is avowedly political.

The terms "feminist psychology" and "psychology of women" are sometimes used interchangeably, particularly in mainstream North American psychology (e.g., Worrell, 1990). It is true that much of the research conducted under the banner of "psychology of women" is explicitly or implicitly feminist in intent, although it does not use that label. This has arisen because of mainstream psychology's opposition to any kind of overt politics. Mainstream psychology has polarized "science" (pure, objective scholarship) against "politics" (ideologically biased advocacy), and has actively resisted feminist psychology's clear *political* basis (Unger, 1982; Wilkinson, 1989).

Historically, this clash between mainstream psychology (purportedly "value-free") and feminist psychology (explicitly politically engaged) has had important consequences for the development of feminist psychology. This history illustrates some key problems confronted by critical psychology in general. It shows how psychological perspectives which are outside, or in opposition to, the mainstream are fundamentally shaped and controlled by that mainstream. Critical psychologies do not develop in a vacuum simply on the basis of the theories, methods and politics of their advocates. If critical psychologists want to make effective interventions in mainstream psychology, to have an impact through their journals, books and conferences, then they have to engage (to varying degrees) with the mainstream. Not surprisingly, the mainstream uses this opportunity to constrain what critical psychologists can say.

In the case of feminist psychology, the mainstream has defined a context within which the field has been allowed to develop, and has used its institutional power to shape and control the field as a whole. Across at least five English-speaking countries (the United Kingdom, the United States, Canada, Australia and New Zealand), the national organizations for academic and professional psychologists – for example, the British Psychological Society (BPS), the American Psychological Association (APA) – have strenuously opposed the formation of internal groupings (Sections, Divisions, Interest Groups) clearly identified as feminist (Wilkinson, 1990a). The cost of entry into mainstream institutions has been loss of the label "feminist."

So, for example, in the US in the 1960s, a number of feminist psychologists worked together *outside* the APA in a forum which was "a model of feminist practice and a site for practising feminism" (Tiefer, quoted in Parlee, 1991: 42). Their activities eventually led (in 1973) to the formation of the "Psychology of Women" Division (Division 35) *inside* the APA. Division 35's first president stated clearly that while the earlier grouping of feminist psychologists was "political-activist," "the new ["Psychology of Women"] Division would NOT be a political organisation" (cf. Mednick, 1978). Similarly, feminist psychologists in the UK in the 1980s were cautioned against allowing themselves to be construed as "a quasi-political pressure group concerned with feminist causes" (cf. Wilkinson, 1990b: 145), and their proposal for a formal grouping within the BPS (paralleling APA Division 35) was deliberately submitted under the title "Psychology of Women." In both countries, then, psychologists with explicitly feminist commitments were instrumental in forming groupings within their national professional bodies which avoided the term "feminist" in favor of "psychology of women." Psychologists doing feminist work have sometimes made strategic use of the label "psychology of women" as a less politically contentious euphemism.

Inevitably, however, the formation of these new groupings *within* the national psychological organizations meant that "psychology of women" (and *not* "feminist psychology") emerged as a newly reputable area of mainstream psychology. Any psychologists researching "women" or "women's issues" can now identify themselves as appropriately located within "psychology of women" as a field – without the necessity of expressing any interest in or commitment to feminist principles. Indeed, the institutional constraints of mainstream psychology mean that there is considerable pressure on people working within "psychology of women" to disavow any political dimension to their work. A recent survey of members of the BPS "Psychology of Women" Section reported concerns about the "stigma of feminism" (Walker, 1994: 8), and in its ten-year history the Section has held at least two formal discussions on "Should Psychology of Women be Political?" – implying that the answer "no" is a distinct possibility. Critical psychologists are unlikely to find the radical political analysis they might expect of feminist approaches in *Psychology of Women Quarterly*, the official journal of APA Division 35. Indeed, as was pointed out in a recent editorial, "the title of the Journal says nothing about feminism" (Worrell, 1990: 2).

In sum, although "psychology of women" was established with clear feminist intentions, a large part of the field is rigidly conventional in its support for the status quo. Much of "psychology of women" challenges neither the institutions and practices of psychology, nor the dominant conceptions of women which the discipline constructs and promotes. It does not engage with the damage psychology has done to many women's lives, nor does it struggle to end psychology's continuing oppressions. Incorporation into national psychological organizations necessarily involves feminists in attending to the business of those organizations, rather than in setting our own agenda as feminists (Wilkinson, 1991a; 1996). Critical psychologies in general are constrained not simply by the political limitations of their adherents, but by the institutional power of mainstream psychology.

Those who call themselves "feminist psychologists" often set out explicitly to differentiate themselves from the harmless and acceptable face of "psychology of women." They use the term "feminist" to highlight the political and critical aspects of their work. Feminist psychology challenges the discipline of psychology for its inadequate and damaging theories about women, and for its failure to see power relations as central to social life. The international journal *Feminism & Psychology* was founded in 1991, and, unlike *Psychology of Women Quarterly*, is deliberately not affiliated with any national psychological association. As its inaugural editorial makes clear: "Our title is a statement of intent: the journal is about the conjunction between feminism (not women, or gender, or sex roles) and psychology; and feminism comes first in our order of priority" (Wilkinson, 1991b: 9–10).

Feminist psychology has its origins in the work of feminists in psychology at the turn of the century. For example, Helen Thompson Wooley described mainstream psychological research on sex differences as characterized by "flagrant personal bias, logic martyred in the cause of supporting a prejudice . . . [and] sentimental rot and drivel" (1910: 340). More than half a century later, as second-wave feminism gathered momentum in the 1970s, feminists launched clear and direct challenges to psychology as a discipline. In one of the most commonly cited early critiques, Naomi Weisstein asserted that: "Psychology has nothing to say about what women are really like, what they need and what they want . . . because psychology does not know" (1968/1993: 197). In 1970 Phyllis Chesler took the platform at the annual APA conference not to deliver the expected academic paper, but to demand that the APA provide:

> one million dollars "in reparations" for those women who had never been helped by the mental health professions but who had, instead, been further abused by them: punitively labeled, overly tranquilized, sexually seduced while in treatment, hospitalized against their will, given shock therapy, lobotomized, and, above all, disliked as too "aggressive," "promiscuous," "depressed," "ugly," "old," "disgusting" or "incurable." (Chesler, 1989b: xvii)

Other feminist psychologists have characterized the discipline as "a psychology against women" (Nancy Henley, 1974: 20), which has "distorted facts, omitted problems, and perpetuated pseudoscientific data relevant to women" (Mary Parlee, 1975: 124).

Feminist psychology is distinguished by its insistence upon exposing and challenging the operation of male power in psychology:

> psychology's theories often exclude women, or distort our experience – by assimilating it to male norms or man-made stereotypes, or by regarding "women" as a unitary category, to be understood only in comparison with the unitary category "men" . . . Similarly, psychology [screens out] . . . the existence and operation of social and structural inequalities between and within social groups (power differentials are written out). (Wilkinson, 1991b: 7–8)

Feminist psychology also looks beyond the confines of psychology as an academic discipline, addressing the power it has in shaping everyday understandings and in producing real, material effects in the world. It emphasizes how psychology obscures the social and structural operation of male power by concentrating its analysis on people as individuals – and it points to the dangers of this individualism:

Feminist psychologists have also been critical of the harm that psychology (and the popularization of psychological ideas) has wrought in women's lives: primarily (but not exclusively) through the location of responsibility – and also pathology – within the individual, to the total neglect of social and political oppression. (Wilkinson, 1991b: 8)

Perhaps most important, according to feminist psychologist Michelle Fine, is that feminist psychology is a "a social change strategy" (1992a: viii). It aims to end the social and political oppression of women.

In the remainder of this chapter, I will present feminist psychology as a key form of critical psychology. First, I will illustrate the ways in which mainstream psychology has oppressed and controlled women. Second, I will describe feminist psychologists' challenges to the mainstream of their discipline, highlighting five distinctive theoretical traditions. Finally, I will consider the long-term goals of feminist psychology.

Psychology's Oppressions: the Social Control of Women

Psychology's central assertion has been that women are inferior to men. According to pioneering feminist psychologist Naomi Weisstein, whose much-reprinted article "*Kinder, Küche, Kirche* as Scientific Law. Psychology Constructs the Female" has become a "classic" of feminist psychology, women are characterized by psychology as:

> inconsistent, emotionally unstable, lacking in a strong conscience or superego, weaker, "nurturant" rather than productive, "intuitive" rather than intelligent, and, if they are at all "normal," suited to the home and the family. In short, the list adds up to a typical minority group stereotype of inferiority. (Weisstein, 1968/1993: 207)

All apparent "differences" between women and men are characterized by psychology as "inferiorities," except where women's differences equip us so naturally to excel in our roles as wives and mothers. The most blatant examples of psychology's characterization of "women-as-inferior" come from the early days of psychology; more recent formulations are rather more sophisticated. But over the last century or so, from the beginnings of psychology onwards, this characterization of women as inferior has been used to confine women to the kitchen, the bedroom and the nursery. It has also been used (historically) to deny women access to education and to professional careers; and (more recently) to "explain" and justify our limited successes within these spheres.

Women's traditional role as wives and mothers has been particuarly well enforced by clinical psychology and therapy. When the writer Charlotte Perkins Gilman collapsed with a "nervous disorder" in 1885, she was referred to S. Weir Mitchell, "the greatest nerve specialist in the country," and inventor of "the rest cure." Mitchell's prescription for Gilman included injunctions to "Live as domestic a life as possible," "Have your child with you all the time," "Have but two hours intellectual life a day" and "Never touch pen, brush or pencil as long as you live" (Gilman, quoted in

Ehrenreich and English, 1979: 102). Eventually, Gilman came to understand the source of her "illness:" she did not want to be a wife, but wanted to be a writer and an activist. She divorced her husband, and took baby, pen, brush and pencil off to California.

A century later than Charlotte Perkins Gilman, "Jane" experienced a "nervous breakdown." Initially diagnosed as suffering from "post-natal depression," and following three months' hospitalization (including a course of electroconvulsive therapy), and six further years of "unhappiness and violence," "Jane" came to realize that:

> like many women, I went from being someone's daughter to someone's wife and mother without developing any real identity of my own . . . I was trying to do what was expected of me as a woman, and when I "failed" I blamed myself. I somehow felt it was my fault when my husband stayed out all night. I even had the feeling he was justified whenever he hit me . . . I couldn't seem to keep the baby from crying, cook and clean perfectly, and keep myself attractive and desirable: I felt so "inadequate." We lived in two rooms, and there was very little money. I went mad. ("Jane," 1986: 10)

The feminist analysis offered in a women's studies course enabled "Jane" to attribute her "breakdown" to her life circumstances and the constraints of her expected social role, rather than to her own personal "inadequacy." Feminists have rigorously critiqued mainstream therapeutic practices for reinforcing stereotypical notions of women as wives and mothers. Today, hospital "occupational therapy" programs typically involve women in the activities of putting on makeup, sewing, and cooking for their families (Johnstone, 1992).

Psychological arguments have been used – again, since the very beginnings of psychology – not only to justify keeping (white middle-class) women in the home as wives and mothers, but also to explain their "unsuitability" for education and professional work. Sigmund Freud, for example, argued vehemently against educational reforms for women:

> It is really a stillborn thought to send women into the struggle for existence exactly as men . . . I believe that all reforming action in law and education would break down in front of the fact that, long before the age at which a man can earn a position in society, Nature has determined woman's destiny through beauty, charm and sweetness. Law and custom have much to give women that has been withheld from them, but the position of women will surely be what it is: in youth an adored darling and in mature years a loved wife. (Freud, quoted in Reeves, 1971: 163–164)

The "founding fathers" of psychology around the turn of the century (for example, James M. Cattell, G. Stanley Hall, Edward Thorndike, E. B. Titchener) all drew on the new science of evolution – including the view that women are less highly evolved and possess only primitive mental abilities – to support their arguments that women should be excluded from high academic rank and from professional organizations (Bohan, 1992a: 34). According to these psychologists (particularly Hall), education could threaten women's fertility, because the brain would compete with the uterus for blood and energy, leading – in "the mental woman" – to uterine atrophy and shrivelled, nonlactating breasts (Ehrenreich and English, 1979: 125–131).

Few psychologists would advance such arguments today, but discrimination against women in the professions is still justified in some contemporary writing with reference to psychological "findings." Take, for example, the work of Dr. Glenn Wilson, a Fellow of the British Psychological Society, who says that the reason 95% of bank managers, company directors, judges and university professors in Britain are men is because men are "more competitive" and because "dominance is a personality characteristic determined by male hormones" (1994: 62, 63). He also advances arguments to demonstrate that women in academic jobs are less productive than men, stating that "objectively speaking, women may already be over-promoted." Women who *do* achieve promotion to top management positions "may have brains that are masculinized" (1994: 65). The psychological research which enables Wilson to make these claims is derived in part from the psychometric testing industries which are particularly implicated in providing "scientific" evidence of women's inadequacies: for example, women lack mathematical ability (Benbow and Stanley, 1980), are less good at spatial tasks than men (Masters and Sanders, 1993) and suffer from impaired performance on visual spatial tasks during parts of the menstrual cycle (Hampson, 1990). Even if women are considered to have the ability to perform well in professional jobs, we have personality defects – in particular "low self-esteem" (Lenney, 1977) or "lack of assertiveness" (Alberti, 1977) – which impede our performance.

To summarize, then, psychology is deeply implicated in the patriarchal control of women. Psychologists have asserted that women are inferior to men, and they have used this assertion to justify women's exclusion from, or limited achievements within, education and the professions. Psychology is used to enforce normative sex roles for women and to justify and to perpetuate oppressive practices.

Central to psychology's success in perpetuating oppression is its individualism. By locating "causes" and "cures" within individuals, and by ignoring or minimizing the social context, psychology obscures the mechanisms of oppression. So, for example, women's unhappiness after childbirth is treated as a problem in individual functioning (with possible hormonal causes), thus distracting attention away from the difficult material situation in which many new mothers find themselves (e.g., Nicolson, 1986). Women's (allegedly) limited achievements in the workplace are treated either as the consequences of biological differences between the sexes, or as individual problems of social skills. The "solution" is either to accept those "differences" as given (and so not to expect women to perform as well as men in many domains) or to change women, through, for example, assertiveness training. This preoccupation with what is wrong with women in the workplace locates *women* as the problem and has nothing to say about organizational structure, policies or procedures. It ignores the *social context* within which women (and men) work (cf. Hollway, 1991). The whole field of sex differences exhibits a relentless focus on the individual and the internal at the expense of external circumstances and social systems. In giving precedence to individual and interpersonal explanations, mainstream psychology "explains" and justifies the structural oppression of women.

Feminist Challenges to Mainstream Psychology: Five Traditions

Since the 1970s, feminists have developed a wide range of different approaches, both within and against psychology. Feminist psychology is not a unified field with a single "politically correct" line. In the early days of feminist psychology, its adherents wrote for *nonfeminist* readers – attacking the theories and implicit political commitments of mainstream psychology. Now, feminist psychologists are equally likely to write for *feminist* readers with whose theories and politics they disagree. Contemporary feminist psychology is characterized by debate as much *within* the field as between feminist psychology and mainstream psychology. The field embraces a rich variety of incompatible – and at times conflicting – theoretical traditions, methodological approaches, and types of activism.

Feminist challenges to mainstream psychology's central assertion of women's inferiority are lodged within five distinctive (and contested) theoretical traditions. These five traditions argue against psychology's presentation of women as inferior in the following ways:

1 Psychology is poor science: it has *mismeasured women.*
2 The problem is not women, but women's *internalization of oppression.*
3 We can gain a different perspective by *listening to women's voices.*
4 We should *displace* the question of sex differences.
5 We should *reconstruct* the question of sex differences.

Feminists disagree with each other as to which of these (sometimes logically incompatible) approaches offers the most effective challenge to mainstream psychology, and there are *feminist* (as well as more conventional) criticisms of each. I will present each approach in turn, ending with brief summaries of both the benefits and the problems of each approach considered from a feminist perspective.

The Mismeasure of Women

This tradition of feminist research refutes mainstream psychology's statement that women are inferior by arguing that psychology as presently conducted is poor science. In particular, this tradition points to the fact that many of psychology's classic theories (for example, Kohlberg's theory of moral reasoning, Erikson's theory of lifespan development) were derived from all-male samples and the findings then generalized to all humankind. Women are judged according to how well they "measure up" to a male norm, and any findings of sex differences are interpreted as female deficits. As Carol Tavris (1992) points out, much of sex differences research is designed to find out why women are not "as something" as men: for example, as moral, as creative, as rational, as funny. Compared with *men*, women supposedly:

- have lower self-esteem
- undervalue their own efforts
- are less self-confident
- have more difficulty developing a separate sense of self
- are more likely to say they are "hurt" than to admit they are "angry."

An alternative reading of these "findings" is to say that, compared with *women*, men may be seen as:

- more conceited
- overvaluing the work they do
- less realistic in assessing their abilities
- having more difficulty in forming and maintaining attachments
- more likely to accuse and attack others when unhappy, rather than stating that they feel hurt and inviting sympathy.

For example, there is a fairly consistent sex difference in self-confidence: on tasks such as estimating how many points they think they earned on an exam before the actual grades are known, women estimate fewer points (on average) than men do. This finding has often been interpreted as indicating that women lack self-confidence. In fact, when estimated scores are compared with actual scores, it turns out that men *over*estimate their performance by about as much as women *under*estimate theirs (Hyde, 1994).

Another example of feminists exposing mainstream psychology as "poor science" is the successful institutional challenge to the USA mental health system via the *Diagnostic and Statistical Manual* (*DSM*) of the American Psychiatric Association. (This is its official diagnostic handbook, on the basis of which many mental health practitioners make their clinical judgments.) Feminist psychologists challenged two particular categories in the *DSM*, both predominantly applied to women: "Self-defeating Personality Disorder" ("masochistic personality"), and "Late Luteal Phase Dysphoric Disorder" ("premenstrual syndrome").

The *DSM* diagnostic criteria for "Self-defeating Personality Disorder" include: "chooses people and situations that lead to disappointment, failure or mistreatment," "incites anger or rejection responses from others," "engages in excessive self-sacrifice" and "fails to accomplish tasks crucial to his or her personal objectives" (American Psychiatric Association, 1987). Feminist psychologists argued that this category was "a way to call psychopathological the woman who had conformed to societal norms for a feminine woman" (Caplan, 1991: 171). A review of the evidence for "Self-defeating Personality Disorder" shows that the existence of the category is not supported by empirical data, that research in the field is seriously flawed methodologically, and that the category has poor diagnostic power. The idea that "suffering people – and especially women – consciously or unconsciously bring their suffering on themselves" (Caplan and Gans, 1991: 263) is not the result of objective scientific investigation but the ideological bias of white male psychiatrists. There is no parallel diagnostic category of "Delusional Dominating Personality Disorder" ("macho personality"), predominantly applied to men, and calling psychopathological the man who has conformed to social norms for a "masculine man." (See Caplan, 1991, for some suggested diagnostic criteria for "Delusional Dominating Personality Disorder.")

Feminists have used similar arguments about "bad science" and "ideological bias" to challenge the *DSM* category of "Late Luteal Phase Dysphoric Disorder" – a notion incorporating the idea that menstruation is a debilitating condition that makes women unfit for work. Such notions were common in the early part of this century and were used to exclude women from the workforce. However, as Emily Martin (1987) points out, at the start of World War II (when women were needed for war work), studies suddenly found that menstruation and "premenstrual tension" were not problems for working women; while immediately after World War II (when men wanted women back in the home), menstruation became a "problem" again. Further, research on "premenstrual syndrome" erupted in the 1970s when "women had made greater incursions into the paid work force for the first time without the aim of a major war" (Martin, 1987: 120). Many feminists have pointed to the scientific inadequacies of "premenstrual syndrome" research (e.g. Parlee, 1973), describing it as "plagued with methodological errors" and as "deeply flawed" (Caplan et al., 1992: 27).

In conclusion, feminists in this tradition point to the scientific errors rampant throughout the sex differences literature. They expose empirical studies as riddled with technical flaws, such as experimental biases, inadequate sampling techniques, lack of control groups, insufficiently sensitive measurement techniques, unreplicated "findings" and unspecified effect sizes (e.g., Hyde, 1994; Eagly, 1994; Tavris, 1992). In sum, weak data are used to support sexist prejudices. Naomi Weisstein, castigating sex differences research as "theory without evidence," indicts the practice of sexist researchers: "[They] simply refuse to look at the evidence against their theory and practice. And they support their theory and practice with stuff so transparently biased as to have no standing as empirical evidence" (1968/1993: 197).

Feminist psychologists' allegation of "bad science" challenges the mainstream on its own terms and raises the possibility – by doing "better science" – of beating the boys at their own game. On the other hand, this tradition does not challenge the game itself. Celia Kitzinger (1990b) advances an important critique of this kind of feminist research. She argues that, in challenging the scientific objectivity of mainstream psychology, feminist psychologists reinforce the notion that objectivity is potentially attainable. Such challenges also obscure the extent to which the practice of science is deeply enmeshed in the social and political practices of which it is a part.

Internalized Oppression

This feminist tradition *accepts* (to some extent) psychology's assertion of women's inferiority – but contends that such "inferiority" is not intrinsic to women. Rather, it is the result of our oppression. According to this argument, women are socialized differently from men in ways which encourage the development of personal characteristics detrimental to our happiness and achievement. This means that even when, with the recent successes of feminism, external constraints on women's progress are removed, we still oppress ourselves.

The classic work cited by many writers in this tradition is Matina Horner's (1972) research on "fear of success" in women. Matina Horner gave women undergraduates the opening sentence of a story to complete: "After first term finals, Anne finds herself at the top of her medical school class." (For undergraduate men the sentence was the same except that the character's name was "John.") On the basis of the resulting stories, Horner argued that women exhibit a "motive to avoid success." While for men, professional success was greeted with joy and a sense of achievement, the same success led women to feel "disconcerted, troubled or confused" and was associated with "the loss of femininity, social rejection, personal or social destruction." Stories written by young women included one in which Anne drops out of medical school to get married, another in which she is terrified of becoming a lesbian, and a third in which she is physically beaten and maimed for life by her jealous classmates. Women's alleged "fear of success" has subsequently provided a very popular explanation for women's failure to advance in professional life. Other explanations following in this same tradition include lack of assertiveness, low self-esteem, poor self-confidence, underestimation and undervaluation of achievement, and failure to develop an autonomous self (Tavris, 1993).

Innovative in its focus on women *as women* (rather than in relation to, or comparison with, men), this framework remains a dominant one in much contemporary feminist psychology. In particular, it underpins the large (and growing) feminist therapy industry which is seen as offering "compensatory socialization" (Crawford and Marecek, 1989) for women. It seems to be popular because it offers clear prescriptions for creating change in the world – at both a social and an individual level. Social change is conceptualized as something which comes about as a natural result of the cumulative change of a sufficient number of individuals; and individual change can be wrought by counseling and therapy so as to improve women's lives. Feminist therapies and counseling programs aim to help women to overcome internalized oppression by becoming more assertive, getting in touch with our "real" desires, and understanding the ways in which unhelpful messages from our childhoods control and limit us in our everyday lives.

This same idea – that women have internalized negative messages about ourselves which prevent us from succeeding as well as we might in the world – is also at the root of the (so-called "feminist") pop-psych, self-help manuals which have flooded the market since the 1980s (e.g., *The Cinderella Complex*, Dowling, 1981; *The Doormat Syndrome*, Namka, 1989). According to these popular books, women are oppressed less by "men" or "society" than by our own lack of self-esteem, our own passivity. This argument rests on the assumption that feminism has achieved most of its goals: women have power, equality, liberation from without. The problem now is to deal with the legacy of past oppression on our psyches: we need "revolution from within" (Steinem, 1992). External, structural changes take second place to internal transformation:

> In society in general, women have enough opportunity, experience, and dare I say it, power to demand great changes. But they have not done so . . . The reasons for this passivity lie . . . in aspects of the male and female psyche. (Coward, 1992: 13)

Although this approach is enormously popular in contemporary feminist psychology, many feminists (e.g., Sethna, 1992; Schilling and Fuehrer, 1993) have drawn attention to its victim-blaming implications, and to its perpetuation of mainstream psychology's relentless focus on the internal and individual at the expense of the social and political. Others have extended this critique by asking whether individual change must always precede social change (e.g., Kitzinger and Perkins, 1993).

Listening to Women's Voices

The third main approach of feminist psychologists is to agree that women *are* different from men, and to maximize and celebrate sex differences. Feminists working within this tradition (particularly those associated with, or influenced by, the Harvard Project on Women's Psychology and Girls' Development) identify the discipline of psychology as speaking with a male voice. As Carol Gilligan (initiator of the Harvard Project) has said in interview:

> I picked up what you're not supposed to pick up in psychology – that there was a voice, and I asked "Who's speaking?"; "Whose voice is this?," "Whose body and where's it coming from?" If you listen to the imagery of sexuality and separation . . . you realize this is a man's body. This is a man's voice speaking as if from nowhere. (Gilligan, in Kitzinger and Gilligan, 1994: 413)

These feminists argue that psychology, with its "male voice," has described the world from its own male perspective, which it has confused with absolute truth. The task of feminist psychology is to listen to the voices of women and girls who speak in a "different voice" (Gilligan, 1982; Brown and Gilligan, 1992) and have distinctive "ways of knowing" (Belenky et al., 1986). Lyn Mikel Brown and Carol Gilligan (1992) have developed a "voice-centered relational method" to enable them to listen responsively to the voices of women and girls. They emphasize the radical potential of starting from these voices:

> What we have learned most of all about women's psychology and girls' development . . . is the power of beginning with girls' voices. From listening to girls at the edge of adolescence and observing our own and other women's responses, we begin to see the outlines of new pathways in women's development and also to see new possibilities for women's involvement in the process of political change. (Brown and Gilligan, 1993: 32)

The work of Carol Gilligan and her associates has been enormously influential. The feminist magazine *Ms.* named Gilligan "Woman of the Year," and the *New York Times Magazine* put Gilligan on the front cover. Their approach has been enthusiastically embraced in a range of applied areas, particularly youth work and secondary education. It has been institutionalized in, for example, research on young women's experiences in schools commissioned by the American Association of University Women (1991); the development of feminist pedagogy and curriculum materials; and the launch of a glossy magazine called *New Moon*, which celebrates young women's growth, development and "self-affirmation" throughout their teenage years.

The importance of this tradition lies in reversing the frame of reference within which women have been conceptualized by mainstream psychology. Feminist psychologists have asserted, for example, that "Gilligan's work touched a nerve . . . women were being denied a voice; and philosophically, it meant there *was* an alternative voice in the culture – that there is more than one way of looking at the world" (Haste, 1994: 399–400). Equally, however, it has been criticized by feminists for unproblematically reproducing the notion of the "pure" voices of the oppressed – as though women, simply by virtue of being women, can utter truths about the world and thereby reveal our authentic selves. A key "discovery" which has arisen from listening to women's voices is that women inhabit a more "relational" world than do men: women are more "connected" with and "caring" about other people. Many feminists have pointed out how this feeds back into traditional ideas about women, and reinforces the social structures which impose on us the jobs of caring for small children and elderly relatives (e.g., Faludi, 1991). Feminists have also emphasized that women are not, as some work within this tradition seems to suggest, a cohesive group who speak in a single voice. These critics have argued that the Harvard Project imposes a false homogeneity upon the diversity of women's voices across differences of age, ethnicity, (dis)ability, class and other social divisions (e.g., Davis, 1994).

Displacing the Question of Sex Differences

The fourth theoretical tradition of feminist psychology argues that women are neither inferior nor superior to men. In fact, these researchers refuse to compare the sexes. They minimize, indeed undermine, the importance of sex differences, arguing that being male or female is not a central determinant of psychological functioning. Rather, there are elements of masculinity and femininity in everyone, and a key aspect of mental health and well-being is the ability to deploy these flexibly according to the situation (so we are able to be relatively confident and assertive in a job interview, say, while being relatively self-effacing and sympathetic to a friend in distress – regardless of whether we are male or female). Back in 1974, Sandra Bem first proposed such "psychological androgyny" as "a new standard of mental health, one that removes the burden of stereotype and allows people to feel free to express the best traits of men and women" (1974: 125).

Perhaps because it removes the critical spotlight *both* from psychology *and* from women, and also offers a reframing of the familiar concept of "sex roles" in the positive context of improving mental health, this work has had surprising success within mainstream psychological theory. Detached from its feminist intent, it sits comfortably with the discipline's liberal rhetorics – and also offers the bonus of an associated measuring scale: the Bem Sex Role Inventory (BSRI). This was widely used in the 1970s and 1980s to correlate androgyny with many different indices of mental functioning, and it is still one of the most popular scales in use in social psychology today.

The BSRI consists of a list of personality descriptions, some of which are classified as "feminine" and others as "masculine." In completing the BSRI, people are asked to indicate to what extent each of these personality descriptions is "like me." People score high on "masculinity" if they describe themselves as independent, aggressive and competitive; high on "femininity" if they describe themselves as caring, emotional and yielding. "Androgynous" people describe themselves as characterized by *both* sets of traits. Sandra Bem's early research suggested that "androgynous" people are able to be flexible and adaptive in response to different situations. People who are "masculine" only cope well in stereotypically masculine situations, and people who are "feminine" cope well only in stereotypically feminine situations, but "androgynous" people are competent in both. When under pressure to conform, they behave in a "masculine" way and stick to their own opinions; when listening to the problems of a lonely fellow student, they behave in a "feminine" way and are empathetic and caring (Bem et al., 1976).

At the time it was developed, the notion of androgyny and the minimizing of sex differences offered a powerful corrective to the "women-as-inferior" position common in mainstream psychology. It also disrupted traditional ideas about the essential qualities of being "male" and "female" – about what should count as "normal" gender identity. Although the scale and its associated concepts are still widely used, many feminists, including Sandra Bem herself, no longer consider it to be a particularly helpful approach (cf. Kitzinger, 1992b). It focuses (like traditional psychology) on individuals at the expense of social structure (Mednick, 1989) and it ignores the power differentials which shape "appropriate" male and female behavior. Moreover, in classifying items like "caring" as "feminine" and items like "competitive" as "masculine," the BSRI actually reinforces the very stereotypes it aims to undermine.

Reconstructing the Question of Sex Differences

Finally – and most recently – feminist psychologists working within the frameworks of *social constructionism* and *postmodernism* (e.g., Hare-Mustin and Marecek, 1994; Hollway, 1994; see also Chapter 17 in this volume) have argued that sex/gender should no longer be theorized as *difference between individuals*, but reconceptualized as a *principle of social organization*, structuring power relations between the sexes. This tradition of work is highly controversial and difficult to understand. Because it challenges some of our most taken-for-granted ways of thinking, it can even seem bizarre. Perhaps not surprisingly, social constructionism/postmodernism has gained very little recognition in psychology. Indeed, to most mainstream psychologists – and even many critical psychologists – it is unrecognizable as psychology.

In the previous section we saw how androgyny theory served to displace sex differences by refocusing attention on "masculinity" and "femininity" as personality attributes that cut across the "male"/"female" divide. Instead of questions about differences *between* the sexes, this approach enabled psychologists to think more clearly about differences *within* the sexes – and their implications for mental health and well-being. However, in the androgyny approach, sex (the state of being "male" or "female") is seen as the biological bedrock upon which gender differences (psychological attributes of "masculinity" or "femininity") are constructed. According to androgyny theory, there are two types of human being ("men" and "women") – and "masculinity" has been imposed on men and "femininity" on women in a way which serves to limit and constrain both sexes. The androgyny approach advocates cutting "masculinity" and "femininity" free from biological sex, so that *both* sexes have access to a wider range of human capacities.

The social constructionist perspective takes this a step further. It suggests that it is not just the psychological attributes of "masculinity" and "femininity" which are constructed by a sexist society – but the biologically based categories of "men" and "women." It questions the notion of biological sex and refuses the taken-for-granted "knowledge" that people are either men or women. This assumption that people come in two sexes is, feminist social constructionists argue, a political necessity for sexist oppression. Only by dismantling the assumption of biological "maleness" and "femaleness" as fundamental categories can we end that oppression.

The argument that people do not "naturally" come in two sexes is, of course, counter-intuitive. Feminist social constructionists suggest that this is because our "intuitions" are formed under male supremacy. They have asked why it seems so obvious to us that people are either male or female, and whether it is possible to imagine that we do not "naturally" exist as women and men – that these are fundamentally ideological, not biological, categories. This means that instead of asking questions about what the "real" differences are between men and women, feminist psychologists in this tradition ask questions about how people (including psychologists) *construct* men and women as different sexes. Sometimes these differences are constructed physically – for example, through surgery upon the genitals of intersexed infants (to bring them into conformity with the biological categories of male or female: Kessler, 1990) or upon transsexuals (to change the biological markers of their sex to those of the other sex: Blanchard et al., 1985). More often, the construction of gender differences is accomplished socially (and psychologically) – by repeated assertions about what "men" and "women" are "really" like. Historically, it is male psychologists who have made these pronouncements. Today, it is as likely to be feminists who do so – by saying, for example, that women are more caring than men, or that women have less self-esteem than men, or that women are just as mathematically competent as men. The effect is the same, whoever is making the pronouncements, and whatever the content of these pronouncements (whether they proclaim that women are inferior, women are superior, or that there is no difference between the sexes). It *reinforces* the *categories* of "men" and "women." According to feminist social constructionists:

> the psychological literature on male–female differences is not a record of cumulative knowledge about the "truth" of what men and women are "really" like. Rather it is a repository of accounts of gender organized within particular assumptive frameworks, and reflecting various interests. (Hare-Mustin and Marecek, 1994: 535)

Feminists argue, of course, that it is men's interests which are primarily reflected in these "accounts of gender."

Social constructionists suggest that feminists who try to show that women are "the same as," or "different from," men actually underwrite women's oppression, by reproducing in their research the category "woman" upon which that oppression is predicated. Some writers (e.g., the French feminist Monique Wittig, 1992) propose jettisoning the concept of "woman" altogether. They argue that, just as the concept of "race" was constructed only within the socioeconomic reality of black slavery (Guillaumin, 1995), so the concept of "woman" functions only as a marker of otherness and subordination within a social system based on male dominance. To describe woman as a "natural" category is to give an "essential," biological under-pinning to a historical situation of male dominance and female subordi-nation. This perspective in feminist psychology is a very radical one. It goes well beyond notions about the "sex role stereotypes" and "socialization processes" supposed to produce "masculine" men and "feminine" women. It challenges the very categories "men" and "women" themselves.

A social constructionist/postmodernist approach offers feminist psychologists opportunities for alliances outside psychology. Feminists and critical theorists are using such approaches in other disciplines and in a multi-disciplinary women's studies context. Although social constructionism/postmodernism offers a fundamental challenge to mainstream ways of thinking, the full implications of this challenge have rarely been appreciated. The approach has often been dismissed as too radical, or simply too outrageous. It has also been criticized for its unintelligibility – partly due to the difficulty of the concepts, but partly due, too, to the willful obscurity of much of its writing – and for the difficulty of translating its theoretical challenge into a clear political program (e.g., Weisstein, 1968/1993).

Feminist Psychology: Towards Reform or Revolution?

Despite the (sometimes virulent) disagreements between these different traditions of feminist research, all of them have enabled feminists to make important interventions in psychology – and some of them have also provided a basis for social change. All five traditions have been used to challenge psychology's oppressive practices. Equally, as we have seen, these different traditions incorporate within them aspects which are rather less "radical" or "critical" in their implications. The "mismeasure of women" approach reinforces psychology's attempt to be an objective "science" at the cost of the other "ways of knowing" emphasized by other feminists. Approaches which rely on notions of "internalized oppression" run the risk of reinforcing the individualism and victim-blaming biases of mainstream psychology. "Listening to women's voices" reinforces the whole idea that "women" naturally exist as a homogeneous and distinctive group – an assumption challenged by other feminists. In "displacing sex differences," theories of "androgyny" perpetuate the focus on individuals, reinforce "science," and underwrite the very notions of "masculinity" and "femininity" which they purport to challenge. Finally, social constructionist feminists who aim to "reconstruct the question" are often simply unintelligible in their refusal of our "intuitive" knowledge and "common-sense" understandings of the world. In any event, their theoretically sophisticated treatises rarely translate into any practical political action, either within psychology or beyond it in the wider social world.

Feminist psychologists are likely to agree that "transformation" of psychology, at least, is needed to create a better world for women (Burman, 1996; Crawford and Marecek, 1989; Wilkinson, 1996; Worrell and Etaugh 1994). There is also broad agreement that we are "still seeking" this transformation (Wilkinson, 1996) and that the process "has far to go" (Worrell and Etaugh, 1994: 448). Feminist psychologists disagree, however, on whether our project is primarily one of "reform," or one of "revolution" (Ferree and Hess, 1985): on whether we aim to *change* psychology, or whether we aim to *overthrow* it. Some argue that although feminism and psychology are "uneasy partners" (Ussher, 1990: 54), feminists should still be working to "reconstruct" psychology (Bohan, 1992b; Morawski, 1994) in line with feminist principles. Others argue that the whole notion of a "feminist psychology" is a contradiction in terms (Fine and Gordon, 1991); or that feminism is "antipsychology" (Squire, 1990). This is because psychology is, almost by definition, the study of the "individual" (albeit, in the case of social psychology, "the individual in society"), whereas feminism is fundamentally about social structures and institutionalized oppression. Furthermore, psychology claims to be an objective science, whereas feminism is an overtly political movement.

Celia Kitzinger argues that the "hybrid" feminist psychology "can be made conceptually coherent *either* through the politicization of psychology *or* through the depoliticization of feminism" (1990c: 134). The history of feminist psychology and its institutions provides more evidence of mainstream psychology incorporating feminism (and assimilating it as "psychology of women") than of a feminist revolution in psychology. It may well be that feminists are "forced to choose to give priority either to feminism or to psychology" and that there is "a point at which we may choose to separate from the mainstream rather than continue to engage with it" (Wilkinson, 1991b: 14). However, as Erica Burman warns, "the cost of separatism for feminist psychology is marginalization" (1996: 4). It seems that whether our goal as feminist psychologists is to change or to overthrow mainstream psychology, we have to continue some kind of critical engagement with it. More importantly, however, we must not lose sight of social activism as "the project within which we conduct our work" (Fine, 1992a: viii). Feminist psychology embraces the political goals of the feminist movement. Above all, it aims to end the social and political oppression of women.

17

Critical Theory, Postmodernism, and Hermeneutics: Insights for Critical Psychology

Frank C. Richardson and Blaine J. Fowers

Editors' note *As critical psychologists we seek social change not only because of our individual moral preferences, political inclinations, or frustrations with institutional norms. Central to critical psychology are theoretical critiques of how mainstream psychology pursues knowledge (see Chapter 5). In this chapter, Frank C. Richardson and Blaine J. Fowers explore the strengths and weaknesses of three interrelated perspectives in philosophy and social theory that have implications for a theoretically sound critical psychology. Paralleling what we have seen in earlier chapters, there are contending perspectives rather than a single "correct" approach.*

Critical theory shows us how the natural and social sciences have been obsessed with instrumental values of control and domination at the expense of emancipatory values such as justice, mutuality, and autonomy. To promote a just and caring society where conflicting interests can be reconciled peacefully, the critical theorist Habermas proposed a method called the "ideal speech situation." This situation is a model for promoting collaboration and democratic participation, but Richardson and Fowers point to potential drawbacks as well.

Postmodernism arose in reaction to the failings of modern philosophies. Naturalistic approaches, using methods from the natural sciences, fail to capture the essence of human experience. Descriptivist approaches describe people's experiences without acknowledging that describing is inherently subjective. But, the authors maintain, although postmodernism offers suggestions for understanding the human condition, its relativism in terms of values prevents it from improving that condition. Critical psychologists must learn how to value diversity, but not be immobilized by thinking that all moral arguments are equally worthy – that "everything is relative."

The authors conclude by outlining the hermeneutic or interpretive approach. This method of inquiry is sensitive to cultural context, an important ingredient missing from most modern approaches. According to Richardson and Fowers, hermeneutics is not only a better method of inquiry, but an improved tool for the pursuit of the Good Life and the Good Society.

One of the main thrusts of critical psychology is to expose the ways modern psychology and psychologists – even if they mean well – help to maintain a social and cultural status quo that is unjust, shallow, or in some way harmful to human welfare. A number of critics inside and outside psychology express sharp reservations about psychology's approach to studying human action and its contribution to social well-being. In this chapter, we review briefly three alternative approaches that are in some ways highly critical of mainstream social science. The first is the so-called *critical theory* of the Frankfurt school and the great contemporary German thinker Jürgen Habermas. The second approach usually goes by the name of *postmodernism* or *social constructionism*. The third approach is called philosophical or ontological *hermeneutics* (hermeneutics, by the way, simply means "interpretation"). Critical theory, postmodernism, and hermeneutics are often classified as types of "social theory." This refers to a kind of theorizing that falls somewhere between ordinary social science and pure philosophy. These three schools of thought are all significant resources for critical psychology because they examine mainstream psychology from a deep historical and critical perspective.

In this chapter, we first briefly review the main tenets of mainstream social science and some of the principal objections that have been leveled against it. Second, we discuss several key notions of Habermas's critical theory, which offers a major alternative to the mainstream outlook. Generally speaking, critical psychologists draw heavily on Habermas's ideas. Third, we suggest that contemporary postmodernism and hermeneutic thought help us see certain problems with Habermas's critical theory. These problems may be important for critical psychology to take into account. Finally, we argue that postmodern thought has several dangerous shortcomings. However, certain hermeneutic insights may be especially helpful in working toward a truly critical and ethical social science and applied psychology.

The reader should remember that the theoretical and philosophical viewpoints described in this chapter do not directly imply any stand on specific issues concerning justice or the Good Life that critical psychologists might want to take up. Rather, these ideas concern the basic assumptions in terms of which we frame these issues in the first place. However, as Paul Wachtel suggests, "We need to examine more closely the assumptions that underlie our questions. For our questions are our destiny" (1977: xvii). We try to point out some examples of this indirect but significant influence in what follows.

Mainstream Social Science

Naturalism and Empiricism

Philosophers commonly use the term "naturalistic" to describe the general outlook of mainstream social science in the twentieth century. By this they mean that social science treats the social realm as simply a part of nature to be analyzed by natural science's methods. Critics often label this approach "positivistic" or "scientistic." It rests upon a particular ideal of knowledge often termed "empirical theory." In this traditional view, knowledge or explanation consists of much more than just finding correlations among different behavioral and situational variables. By themselves, such correlations only provide interesting descriptions, not real explanations.

For example, it may seem interesting that subjects with an "internal locus of control" (i.e., they generally believe they can influence the course of events by their actions) persist longer than those with an "external locus of control" in trying to solve difficult problems in a laboratory setting. But who knows whether this belief system really causes such persistence? Perhaps both the belief system and the persistence are the coeffects of other unknown factors, psychological or physiological. According to positivism, this matter can only be sorted out in the long run by a more rigorous experimental science that finally reaches the goal of genuine empirical theory. Ideally, such theory consists of universal psychological or sociological laws that are logically derived from a few assumptions and definitions concerning the basic nature of the realm being investigated (for example, atomic and subatomic particles and forces in physics, or elementary behaviors linked to stimuli or reinforcing conditions in behavioristic psychology). Moreover, these laws must have been empirically confirmed by means of carefully controlled experimentation. The resulting theory and laws permit precise prediction about events that are remote in space and time. Such knowledge, of course, represents the power to manipulate events in the social realm.

Another feature of this mainstream approach is its claim that scientific knowledge is about "facts," not about "values." Values reflect only "subjective" attitudes or feelings about "objective" states of affairs. This reminds us how committed this approach is to the modern scientific outlook on the world which arose with the Enlightenment in Europe a few centuries ago. In older or traditional world views, like those of the Bible, the Greek philosophers, and almost all times and places outside the modern West, moral values or spiritual insights were considered anything but "subjective." People typically viewed themselves as playing a role in some meaningful cosmic order or larger spiritual drama. As a result, morality or ethics mainly concerned cultivating the virtues and maturity needed to carry out one's roles and responsibilities in this larger scheme of things.

A radically new kind of modern, scientific materialistic outlook arose in sixteenth and seventeenth century Europe. In Max Weber's famous phrase, this new outlook "disenchants" the world. The objective world is viewed as a giant collection of material objects to be mapped by empirical observation. Sometimes this new modern outlook is termed a "subject–object" ontology (*ontology* simply means a general view of what exists; see Chapter 5). In this view, individual minds are sharply distinguished from the world, each other, and the ordinary social realm's unthinking customs or traditions. Traditional "higher values" and mythical elements are relegated to the sphere of the merely subjective. We must look inward, not outward, for meaning and purpose in our lives. If that deprives us of the protection and comfort of traditional authorities and belief systems, it is simply the price we must pay for full autonomy and self-responsibility. Unless we fall prey to ignorance and superstition, we realize that we confront a world of objects to be known or represented with clear, explicit ideas and scientific explanations. These explanations alone provide objective and useful knowledge.

Problems and Discontents

From the very beginning of the modern age, critics have objected to this view of knowledge and its role in life. They consider this view excessively detached and rationalistic, too individualistic, too emotionally isolating, and overly preoccupied with instrumental control over events to the neglect of other important concerns and purposes in living. Critics have also pointed out a great paradox in this view: humans stand completely apart from the world as free thinkers and scientific investigators at the same time that their activities are part of the natural world governed by deterministic laws. Perhaps the most powerful and influential critique of this modern rationalistic outlook has come from writers associated with the Romantic movement. Romanticism began in the late eighteenth and early nineteenth century and has reverberated throughout our culture down to the present day It celebrates closeness to nature, instinct, mythical consciousness, and beauty and art. Romantic notions have had a great influence in psychology and psychotherapy. They are the main source of such key modern therapeutic ideas as "getting in touch" with one's basic or authentic feelings, "self-actualization," and "meaningful interpersonal relationships."

There is another major objection to mainstream social science: despite tremendous effort, enormous methodological sophistication, and years of trying, it seems to have failed completely to achieve the kind of explanatory theory needed for precise prediction and instrumental control (Bernstein, 1976; Taylor, 1985). Not everyone agrees with this conclusion. But many critics believe that just describing interesting patterns – which always have many exceptions – does not yield the technical control over events we associate with modern physics, biology, or engineering. Suppose, for example, we find that high self-esteem is roughly correlated with better grades in school. This finding does not tell us how to directly boost self-esteem in order to improve students' grades. Nor does it tell us to what extent that is really a worthwhile goal to pursue. By itself, it really tells us very little.

This failure and other considerations have led many to conclude that the epistemological ideal of empirical theory may not be appropriate for social science. Kenneth Gergen concludes that a "fundamental difference exists between the bulk of the phenomena of concern to the natural as opposed to the sociobehavioral scientist." Thus, "there appears to be little justification for the immense effort devoted to the empirical substantiation of fundamental laws of human conduct. There would seem to be few patterns of human action, regardless of their durability to date, that are not subject to significant alteration" (1982: 12).

In Gergen's view, human agents are not detached knowers. They are active participants in a historical and social realm, often called an inter-subjective "life-world." Human action is purposive and goal-oriented rather than determined by outside causes. It is deeply social and consists more in cooperative activities guided by common meanings and shared values than in radically self-interested behavior. After all, even in a competitive, individualistic modern society where most people view themselves as quite distinct individuals capable of doing their own thing, they do so in a very similar manner! They must follow largely the same detailed rules and customs to participate successfully in that society. From this perspective, human activities are governed by changing, periodically renegotiated social rules or conventions rather than by natural law. These ever evolving meanings and conventions shape both their outward practices and institutions and their most inward beliefs and feelings.

There may be a great deal of validity to these criticisms of the modern scientific outlook. But there are reasons it has persisted for so many years. First, it gives central importance to natural science and the technological achievements this science makes possible, upon which modern people understandably place great value.

Second, scientific rationalism seems to support our modern celebration of individual autonomy, a skeptical, critical attitude, and hatred of dogmatism, absolutism, and authoritarianism. It helps undermine the kind of superstitious belief, fanciful mythology, and arbitrary privilege to which dogmatisms usually appeal for support. Modern anti-authoritarianism has been accused, perhaps justly, of throwing out the baby with the bathwater. It may go to the extreme of leveling *all* authority (by making it merely subjective or relative) in order to banish arbitrary *false* authority. But it has helped support our battles against dogmatism and tyranny.

Third, no clear alternative to scientific rationalism has emerged. Some view Romanticism, its many virtues notwithstanding, as more of a protest than a genuine alternative. Many critical psychologists regard its one-sided emphasis on pure feeling and individual self-realization as somewhat escapist. Romanticism tends to be highly suspicious of modern society's hypocrisy, superficiality, fascination with power, and crass competitiveness. But it tends to retreat into the private realm rather than find a sense of purpose in seeking greater justice or a better society.

Descriptivisms

A minority viewpoint within mainstream social science vehemently rejects naturalism. It includes such approaches to human science as phenomenology, ethnomethodology, in some respects humanistic and existential psychology, and many traditional views of qualitative research (see Chapter 3). These approaches contend that human science mainly describes purposive human activities as part of a meaningful, holistic life-world. They reflect Romanticism's emphasis on spontaneity and appreciating cultural richness in contrast to our culture's Enlightenment rationalism.

Richard Bernstein (1976) labels these approaches to human science *descriptivisms*. Less scientistic and individualistic than mainstream positivistic psychology, they help put us back in touch with the varied practices and concerns of everyday life. According to the proponents of these approaches, people do something quite similar in both everyday life and more formal theorizing. First we explain human actions by discerning and describing their motives, reasons, or goals. Then we explain these reasons and purposes by describing the intersubjective rules, standards, or stories that constitute the wider "form of life" or "form of rationality" (Winch, 1977) of which they are an expression or part. However, Bernstein points out that descriptivist approaches ironically retain a key element of the positivistic outlook they mostly reject. They still adhere to a version of positivism's ideal of the disinterested theorist who seeks to give an account of social reality "over there" in a neutral manner. Their goal is not objective, value-neutral *explanations* of events but objective, value-neutral *descriptions* of social practices or psychological dynamics!

There is good reason to believe that this recommended objectivity or neutrality is not really objective or neutral at all. It only appeals to most of us because it expresses positive cognitive and ethical values of openness to, and respect for, the great variety of forms of life. The philosopher Peter Winch probably speaks for most human scientists who adopt this orientation. Winch says that by studying our own or other cultures we seek to gain wisdom from exposure to "new possibilities of good and evil, in relation to which people may come to terms with life" (1958: 103). But Bernstein observes that "such a 'wisdom' is empty unless it also provides some critical basis for evaluating these 'new possibilities of good and evil.' Certainly we can recognize that there are forms of life which are dehumanizing and alienating, and to remain uncommitted undermines any rational basis for . . . a critique of society" (1976: 74).

In the end, it is very hard to make sense out of the idea of a purely objective description. Of course, honest persons or social scientists will want to be objective or unbiased in certain particular ways. They will want to get their facts straight to the greatest extent possible. And they will try not to distort their accounts for secretive, manipulative, or otherwise unworthy purposes. However, it seems that every description is necessarily highly *selective*. It is also very much an *interpretation* of the events studied. Moreover, this interpretation inevitably reflects some *evaluation* of these happenings, an evaluation in line with the concerns and *commitments* of the investigator and his or her community or way of life. Investigators (one hopes!) will often change or develop their views and values as a result of their theorizing or research. But commitments and values of some kind influence not just the topics they choose to investigate, but the conclusions they reach.

The Critical Turn

To make what is sometimes called the "critical turn" means to acknowledge that all social theory and research findings are inescapably interpretive and evaluative. Critical psychologists find both positivistic and descriptivist approaches distinctly limited because of their difficulty in dealing with interesting contradictions or inconsistencies in human behavior.

Consider a few examples. Someone says he or she never gets angry but has crippling headaches for weeks after a confrontation. A leader of the religious right turns out to have a sexual relationship with his stepdaughter. An educational bureaucrat claims to support academic excellence but routinely discourages innovative teaching. Ordinary citizens claim to be dedicated to democracy but usually fail to vote. A demagogue touches on people's real frustrations but offers no real solutions, only enemies to blame for their troubles. Or an environmental activist advocating living in harmony with nature turns to violent politics to advance his or her aims. Very often it is just such inconsistencies that spur us to deeper thought and illuminating research. However, mainstream psychology has difficulty making sense of them. Its commitment to value neutrality tends to blind it to troubling contradictions and possible serious defects in our way of life. Since it thinks it only "tells it like it is," the mainstream has difficulty doing anything more than just describing these inconsistencies. To do more would involve interpreting their sources in social forces and human motivations in ways that inescapably make some evaluation about the human goods or moral evils involved.

Critical psychologists often discuss this issue as the problem of *ideology*. They suggest that a particular way of life may contain apparent contradictions because the self-understanding or beliefs of the social actors involved contain systematic distortions. These distortions may reflect the kind of repressions and rationalizations Freudians and Marxists analyze. In other words, they may represent inauthentic accommodations to force or threat. Perhaps unconsciously, one ignores problems or denies injustices for fear of losing one's income, one's status, or one's very life. That is why the abused child so often clings to and professes great love for the abusing adult. But this distortion means that our attempt to describe things in a "neutral" and "objective" manner will likely lead to error. Our accounts may portray oppressed workers as happy campers and grim workaholics as proud citizens, thus rationalizing the status quo and evading questions of justice and human welfare.

The critical theory of the Frankfurt school (Held, 1980) and Jürgen Habermas (Habermas, 1973, 1991; McCarthy, 1978) is concerned both with familiar evils and injustices and with new forms of domination and corruption that are unique to a modern technological society. The cornerstone of critical theory is its "critique of instrumental reason." According to Habermas, modern society to a great extent is built upon a damaging confusion of *praxis* with *techne*, Greek words meaning roughly culture and technology. This kind of society tends to collapse the cultural and moral dimensions of life into merely technical and instrumental considerations. It harmfully reverses their priority, putting *techne* on top. As a result, Habermas says, "the relationship of theory to *praxis* can now only assert itself as the purposive-rational application of techniques assured by empirical science." Unfortunately, such applications "produce technical recommendations, but they furnish no answer to practical [or moral] questions" (1973: 254). Too many spheres of life have become dominated by a calculating and instrumental viewpoint which discerns means–ends relationships, performs cost–benefit analyses, and seeks to maximize our control or mastery over events. This may increase our *instrumental prowess* in some areas. But its dominance undermines our ability to evaluate the *worth of ends* on any basis other than the sheer fact that they are preferred or desired.

Habermas points out that far from being value-neutral, positivism actually contains a tacit values system and even a tacit "critique of ideology" of its own (McCarthy, 1978: 5). In the tradition of the Enlightenment, positivism thinks of itself as doing battle with ignorance, superstition, dogmatism, and arbitrary authority. It seems to do this in order to promote some form of human rights, freedom, and dignity, values most of us share. The difficulty is, it does this by treating all values as merely subjective and by limiting knowledge to the findings of objective science. But this rather simplistic faith in individualism, science, and progress hides its own commitments behind a façade of value neutrality. In a similar vein, Sullivan (1986) argues that the typical moral outlook of modern times, first articulated clearly by the philosopher Kant, is a version of this individualistic faith often termed "liberal individualism." Unfortunately, Sullivan suggests, liberal individualism is a somewhat paradoxical and self-undermining viewpoint. It advocates a thoroughgoing neutrality toward all values as a way of promoting basic values of liberty and tolerance. But there is nothing to keep that neutrality and skepticism from eventually eroding those basic values as well. Thus, liberal individualism tends to undermine even its own best values of respect for human dignity and rights.

The critical theorist Horkheimer (1974) noted similar paradoxes. He argued that the modern outlook which glorifies instrumental reason actually turns into its opposite, or an "eclipse of reason." Scientific neutrality and regarding all values as merely subjective undermine our ability to reason together about the inherent quality of our way of life and about what ends we might best seek. As the means of control and influence grow, life gets more organized and complicated but we lose the ability to set priorities and impose needed limits. In this way, critical theory sheds light on our tendency to despoil the environment, our fascination with power and control to the neglect of other important values, and our stressful, over-extended lifestyles.

Erich Fromm, who had ties to the Frankfurt school, explored the consequences for personal or emotional life of instrumental reason's dominance. Fromm argues astutely that we suffer today from a "lag between 'freedom from' and 'freedom to.'" We suffer a "disproportion between the freedom *from* any tie and the lack of possibilities for the *positive* realization of freedom and individuality" (1969: 48–53). In other words, although we may have fewer restrictions than in the past, we also lack resources and options for self-determination. In assessing the socioeconomic system, Fromm notes that the "modern market is no longer a meeting place but a mechanism characterized by abstract and impersonal demand" (1975: 75ff). Commodities no longer have *use value* defined by the shared community standards. They only have an *exchange value* determined by impersonal market demand and often quite shallow or transient desires. Eventually, a widespread "personality market" develops: both professionals and laborers greatly depend for their material survival and success on a capricious kind of personal acceptance rather than on traditional use value or ethical qualities. Increasingly, one experiences oneself both as a commodity to be sold and as the seller of it. One's "self-esteem depends on conditions beyond [one's] control." The result is "shaky self-esteem," a "constant need of confirmation by others," and feelings of "depersonalization, emptiness, and meaninglessness." With these words, Fromm anticipates in the 1940s most of today's discussion about our "culture of narcissism."

Habermas contends that to restore our *praxis* we first need to appreciate that human action or social life is not fundamentally instrumental or "purposive-rational," even if the bulk of twentieth century social science assumes it is. Instead, "communicative action" or "interaction" is more basic (Habermas, 1991: 294ff). Communicative action is not instrumental activity governed by technical rules but "symbolic interaction" that is "governed by consensual norms, which define reciprocal obligations about behavior" (Habermas, 1970: 92). Most often, we cooperate with one another in terms of shared cultural, ethical, aesthetic, or religious meanings. Even when we disagree, it is usually within the framework of deeper common meanings. Also, the goals of instrumental activities are laid down by these shared values.

Habermas's Ideal Speech Situation

But how are we going to evaluate social norms and adjudicate social conflicts in a modern pluralistic context where disagreement and conflict are more common? We have the identical problem in choosing between different social or psychological theories with their different value commitments, and in deciding how to interpret research findings. The mainstream's majority stance pretends to maintain value neutrality and focuses on instrumental means–ends relationships. The mainstream's alternative approach – seeking purely objective descriptions of social life – likewise seems to collapse. Finally, it seems, we might have to admit that "anything goes." The question in both everyday life and social science is this: how can we restore a moral focus without reverting to dogmatism and arbitrary authority?

In Habermas's earlier work, he contended that humans have an inherent "interest" in or deep tendency toward "emancipation." Later he developed this view by suggesting that when current values or practices are questioned, it is possible to turn to an explicit kind of *discourse* to test the norms or the claims to rightness that are always an essential part of our *praxis*. We cannot, of course, appeal to standards of mere technical effectiveness. Nor should we ever rely dogmatically on an established authority or viewpoint. Thus, it seems we will have to do entirely without fixed decision procedures or explicit criteria. Instead, we must engage in the process of argument and discussion itself, and continue it until we reach as much of a consensus as possible.

Habermas argues that this kind of discussion and argumentation should follow the pattern of a certain "ideal speech situation." It is not possible to present the details of his argument in this brief chapter. Essentially, however, he contends that the pattern of such an ideal speech situation is built into our very nature as social, communicative beings. It defines how we should deliberate about such matters. Inherently, humans seek a consensus about issues of rightness or justice. We do this through discourse involving such things as full accountability to one another for the quality of our reasoning, arguing as many different points of view as possible in the search for a valid consensus, and excluding "all motives except that of the cooperative search for truth." Habermas feels that this kind of argumentation, although never perfectly achieved, can lead to consensus that is relatively more free of deception and ideology, and therefore more valid.

Discourse without fixed standards or established authorities might appear to be empty or circular. But Habermas's view does seem to capture something profound about the ethical search. Imagine a professor and a student carrying on a friendly argument about the need to protect the environment versus the desirability of more commercial development. Suppose the teacher picked up that the student was qualifying or backing down from her environmentalist views, perhaps fearing for her grade in a course. If the professor were to follow the principles of the ideal speech situation, she might switch to another role in the dialogue and suggest: "Perhaps I am overlooking something important in your position. After all, environmental considerations are very important. I feel their importance, too. Would you run over your main point again for me?" Thus, balance or equality might be restored and the joint search for understanding put back on track. In addition, in this kind of discourse individuals can directly challenge one another's arguments and even motives. Habermas feels that restored dialogue of this sort – concerned as it is with "needs that can be communicatively shared" (1975: 107–108) and with issues of rightness or justice – has the power to bring justice to light. It can counteract the distortion of our life-world by a one-sided instrumental reason.

A major difficulty with Habermas's critical theory concerns its claim that the kind of moral reasoning defined by the ideal speech situation is both universally valid and sufficient for moral purposes. In the end, his approach seems to be a rich, dialogical version of modern liberal individualism. Thus, it encounters some of liberal individualism's difficulties. Taylor (1985) calls this kind of ethical outlook *formalist*. He suggests the formalist outlook arose in part to avoid struggling with traditional moral views, including claims about virtue, the common good, or natural law. Partly this was because traditional approaches seem prone to dogmatism, even fanaticism. But liberal individualist or formalist thinkers also wish to escape the opposite, a complete moral relativism which, among other things, would undermine their own sense of justice and human dignity. So they try to legislate the *how* but not the *what* of ethical reasoning or debate. Examples are Kant's famous "categorical imperative" to treat others as ends and not as means to one's own ends, Lawrence Kohlberg's theory of moral development, and Habermas's definition of the ideal speech situation. Formalist thinking also undergirds our notion of the rule of law in modern liberal democracies, sometimes described as providing their citizens with a highly abstract or "procedural" kind of justice (see Chapter 14). It is hoped such principles will preserve a genuine moral sense while avoiding controversies about ultimate truth or the nature of the Good Life.

However, Taylor (1985: 231ff) argues that such ethical principles, while quite abstract, really reflect moral beliefs as substantive as any other. They reflect our civilization's commitment to the fundamental equality and dignity of *all* individuals. However, Taylor doubts it is possible to step out of history and demonstrate conclusively that our moral beliefs are anchored in any sort of moral or metaphysical absolute. We have only our historically contingent, never certain insights into what is decent or good. Also, Taylor argues that no society or tradition, even our own, ever strictly limits itself to formalist principles concerning moral matters or the Good Life. In fact, all societies are built around a "diversity of goods" (1985: 234ff). They incorporate diverse and sometimes conflicting ideals of maturity, success, integrity, honor, the social good, beauty, knowledge, existential meaning, or spiritual fulfillment. This situation always makes moral and political discussion both more interesting and a lot messier than the ideal speech situation.

Thus, Habermas's procedural universalism contains what Warnke calls an element of "Enlightenment dogmatism" (1987: 174). It *builds into* the ideal speech situation a specifically modern bias in favor of limiting moral discussion to broad, formal issues of justice and fairness. The ideal speech situation *presupposes* a distinctively modern moral outlook which cannot itself become the subject of critical inquiry! Many postmodern thinkers (e.g., Foucault, 1980a) feel that this modern outlook is self-absolutizing and tyrannical in its own way. Even hermeneutic writers more sympathetic to Habermas's ethics of dialogue (e.g., MacIntyre, 1981; Sullivan, 1986; Taylor, 1985) still feel that modernity involves losses or deficiencies that can be understood only from the standpoint of older traditions of thought.

This limitation could have practical or social consequences. For example, Moon points out that in his widely read book *Small Is Beautiful*, E. F. Schumacher argues that a certain "reverential conception of nature and of man's relationship to nature" (1983: 186) is part of the Good Life and may be essential to accepting needed limits and finding some greater sense of meaningfulness. Our "predatory" attitude toward nature, Moon suggests, might require stiffer medicine than mere Habermasian "generalizable interests." That may or may not be the case. Moon's point is only that the ideal speech situation rather arbitrarily rules out even discussing such issues.

It may be important for critical psychologists to reflect on these issues. Critical psychology tends to focus on questions of domination and injustice and their ideological concealment. Thus, it may implicitly embrace a version of the modern formalist ethical outlook which gives primacy to principles of justice and downplays the importance of other sorts of moral, cultural, and spiritual values. This outlook may inadvertently reinforce our society's one-sided individualism, which Fromm felt failed to provide a sufficient sense of healthy limits and common purpose. Even our best modern ideals of justice may be unachievable unless motivated and buttressed by other serious commitments or values.

Postmodern/Social Constructionist Viewpoints

A number of thinkers loosely grouped together as "postmodern" theorists offer, in part, a different kind of critique of the one-sided individualism and technicism of modern times. They complain in varied ways that twentieth century mainstream social science has uncritically and rather arrogantly assumed a "self-contained individualism." The mainstream pictures a decontextualized, "bounded, masterful self" (Cushman, 1990: 599) confronting an objectified world which it seeks to represent and manipulate. This "modern" picture of things, the postmodernists assert, is at the root of many dilemmas in living, including our confusions about the nature of social science and how it should relate to practical life.

Like Habermas, postmodern thinkers want to restore us to a sense of being embedded or contextualized in a historical culture or *praxis*. But they vehemently reject Habermas's attempt to define a universal standard or procedure for critically evaluating our values and practices. They see that sort of critical theory as just another example of modern Western society absolutizing its own way of life and arbitrarily insisting that all cultures and peoples be judged by its own ethnocentric point of view. They reject any sort of *foundationalism* that tries to reach beyond the shifting sands of

history and identify a metaphysical basis or moral standard as a "foundation" for judging our beliefs. They feel that any claim to have found such a
basis or standard is simply another historically influenced interpretation, a
mere projection of our particular community's viewpoint onto the universe.
It is time to bite the bullet, they say, and acknowledge the fundamental
truth (any irony intended) that all our beliefs and values are strictly
relative.

Postmodern thinkers generally concur with the philosopher Dreyfus's
view that "humanity is a self-interpreting way of being whose practices
have enabled it to act as if it had a whole series of different natures in the
course of history" (1987: 65). In other words, humans do not have a
transhistorical or transcultural nature. Rather, culture "completes" humans
by explaining and interpreting the world. Culture does not differently
clothe the universal human. Rather, it infuses individuals, fundamentally
shaping their natures and identities. In Cushman's words, "cultural conceptualizations and configurations of self are formed by the economies and
politics of their respective eras . . . There is no universal, transhistorical
self, only local selves; no universal theory about the self, only local
theories" (1990: 599). This view leads to a strong relativism, the view that
there are no moral absolutes because all values must be evaluated
"relative" to their surrounding culture.

Social Constructionism

One prominent branch of postmodern thought is represented by the
American philosopher Richard Rorty (1982; 1985; 1987) and the leading
social constructionist theorist in contemporary psychology, Kenneth
Gergen (1982; 1985b). In a clear and vivid way, Gergen (1985b: 267ff)
argues that the "terms in which the world is understood are social artifacts,
products of historically situated interchanges between people." As a result,
conceptions of "psychological process differ markedly from one culture to
another." Many of the findings and theories of empirical social science,
from this perspective, are quite distortive. They pretend that the world, the
self, and psychological processes are just *one* way, which is not the case,
and that they are *our* way, which is ethnocentric and erroneous. The
prevalence of a given form of understanding depends not "on the empirical
validity of the perspective in question, but on the vicissitudes of social
process (e.g., communication, negotiation, conflict, rhetoric)."

According to Gergen (1985b: 270ff), social constructionism helps us get
past the "traditional subject–object dualism." This means that psychological inquiry is deprived of any notion of "experience" as a "touchstone
of objectivity." So-called reports or descriptions of one's experiences are
really just "linguistic constructions guided and shaped by historically
contingent conventions of discourse." Therefore, there is "no 'truth through
method,'" no correct procedure that ensures our findings or theories are
objective. Moreover, social constructionism "offers no alternative truth

criteria." Instead, "the success of [our] accounts depends primarily on the analyst's capacity to invite, compel, stimulate, or delight the audience, and not on criteria of veracity."

Gergen and Rorty defend their postmodern approach against charges of irrationalism or destructive relativism. First, since there is an "inherent dependency of knowledge systems on communities of shared intelligibility," there can be "stability of understanding without the stultification of foundationalism" (Gergen, 1985b: 272ff). Second, since the "practitioner can no longer justify any socially reprehensible conclusion on the grounds of being a 'victim of the facts,' he or she must confront the pragmatic implications of such conclusions within society more generally." Not being able to hide behind a pretense of objectivity or façade of value neutrality actually "reasserts the relevance of moral criteria for scientific practice." Since our psychology theory and practice "enter into the life of the culture, sustaining certain patterns of conduct and destroying others, such work must be evaluated in terms of good and evil." Finally, Rorty (1985) even goes so far as to claim that this sort of relativism or contextualism will lead not to social fragmentation or personal directionlessness, but to a deepened sense of "solidarity." A sense of the enormous contingency of life will actually tend to undermine dogmatism and yield a positive sense of connectedness and shared purpose with fellow practitioners of our particular way of life.

Michel Foucault

Many contemporary thinkers in philosophy and the human sciences also have been influenced by the penetrating analyses of Michel Foucault (1979; 1980a; 1980b). Foucault presents a perhaps more realistic but much less cheery view of our embeddedness in culture than do Gergen and Rorty.

Initially, Foucault termed his primary unit of analysis *discourse*. In his later writings he discusses the same realities in terms of *relations of power*. Foucault tries to reveal sets of discursive rules which allow us to produce a field of knowledge, including all of its possible statements about what is true or false or good or evil. As a result, there can be no overall truth or falsity of a discourse. Rather, "truth" is simply an "effect" of the rules of discourse or the power relations that create and constitute a particular form of life. Typically, power relations are a matter of neither explicit consent nor violent coercion. Instead, they are the myriad ways people are constrained together to act within a particular, ultimately arbitrary, system of "power/knowledge." Foucault typically characterizes these power relations in terms of haphazard, incessant struggle and conflict. What we might call "domination" or "justice" are simply truth effects within our cultural order. They are in no way less dominating or morally superior to past or future "regimes of truth." They are only different.

Foucault suggests that the human sciences (he calls them the "dubious sciences") aim at "truth" but, in fact, deceptively classify and manage people in line with the current regime. They augment "biopower," Foucault's term for the kind of detailed surveillance and control that he feels power mainly takes in our era. This control is reflected in our peculiar modern obsession with creating a normal and healthy population. Foucault has illuminating things to say about how modern penology, psychiatry, and other human sciences contribute to this process. He not only analyzes how modes of domination form the modern subject. He also shows how certain practices, usually mediated by an external authority figure like a confessor or psychoanalyst, bring individuals' active self-formative processes in line with the current system (Foucault, 1980b). In other words, therapy clients are induced to scrutinize themselves interminably until they find (or even fabricate) certain problems or tendencies. Then they are persuaded to assume individual responsibility for suppressing or managing these desires in order to conform to current norms of health and productivity. Critical psychologists might find an analysis like this illuminating. They might think it shed light on how emotionally isolated modern individuals are trained to adapt to being cogs in the social and economic machinery, to do without lasting social ties, and to criticize only themselves and not the social order for problems in living (Hare-Mustin, 1991. 65).

However, Foucault does not moralize in this way. Instead of social science or ethical discussion, he recommends the practice of *genealogy*. Genealogy limits itself to uncovering the likely origins of "totalizing discourses"; it shows how their deceptive claims to unity and truth arose from historical accidents and the arbitrary influences exerted by those who had some advantage at the moment. In some ways, this approach resembles a highly austere "descriptivism." One might view it as a natural consequence of feeling the need strictly to abandon *all* traditional and modern value commitments, resulting in an extreme, existentialist-like sense of absurdity and meaninglessness. It is attractive to a number of thinkers today who perhaps despair at how, in a modern context, new "solutions" to human problems only seem to generate new confining entanglements and social evils to replace old ones. But for reasons discussed below, critical psychologists could easily argue that this approach is a somewhat defensive and escapist response to life's difficulties and disappointments. It undermines critical psychology's commitment to clarifying how personal and social dynamics relate to justice and oppression.

Critical psychologists might agree with the hermeneutic view, described in the next section, that it is neither desirable nor possible to remain as detached as Foucault recommends from the struggle for justice. Some support for this view might be found in the fact that Foucault himself often expressed support for those who "resist" or "refuse" what he took to be totalizing discourses. He seemed to place a positive value on resistance, which opened a space for the rediscovery of particular, fragmented, local sorts of knowledge or understanding that had been marginalized or suppressed. And, indeed, Foucault's theory and genealogical method may offer valuable additional tools for detecting the sort of rationalizations about historical inevitability or unquestionable validity that those in power sometimes use to dress up their views and values. Foucault never would have made such a statement, however. For him, "power" was simply the arbitrary, accidental way that social processes work and change, not something that could be limited or used in the service of any sort of better way of life.

Toward the end of his life Foucault took one additional step. He felt pressure from both friends and critics to go beyond merely engaging in the detached genealogy of endless and supposedly equally dominating regimes of truth. He was pressured, in other words, to articulate some sort of positive ethic. He finally relented to an extent: he suggested that we could infer from the lack of any fixed or universal human nature a practical program of ceaselessly creating and recreating ourselves "as a work of art" (Foucault, 1982a).

Concerns about Postmodernism/Social Constructionism

Both these versions of postmodern thought unmask our damaging modern pretensions to exaggerated autonomy, certainty, and control. Social constructionism helps restore a sense of belonging to a historical culture that has formed us. And it provides new helpful tools for recovering diverse and possibly valuable experiences and understandings that indeed have sometimes been "subjugated" by scientistic, rationalistic, or masculinist ways of thinking. Nevertheless, postmodern/social constructionist theory encounters serious difficulties.

The postmodern outlook sets forth a paradoxical and ultimately implausible view of the human self. On the one hand, it is radically determined by historical influences. Yet on the other hand, it is radically free to reinterpret both itself and social reality, for its own self-invented purposes. But where would such historically embedded beings get the leverage to reinvent themselves in this way? Moreover, why does this view not reproduce in another guise a *modern* view of the distance between self and world and *modern* pretensions to absolute freedom and indefinite control?

Also, postmodernists sometime suggest that just denying all metaphysical and moral universals will free us from tendencies toward dogmatism and domination. But where in this brave new world would we find the conviction or character needed to keep from discarding our society's ideals of freedom and universal respect for shallow diversions or some comforting new tyranny? Remember, postmodern theory asks us to believe that such ideals, when taken seriously, are dangerous illusions. Unfortunately, however, the social constructionist recommendation that we evaluate our values in terms of their "pragmatic implications" is a very weak interpretation of what it means to take responsibility in everyday life. One wonders if constructionist thinkers have really thought through what it would mean to collapse the distinction between feeling guilty merely from the fear of disapproval versus remorse from violating one's authentic personal standards.

Foucault, as we mentioned, clearly sides at times with those who resist or refuse totalizing discourses. But Philip (1985) argues that without a conception of the human good, Foucault cannot explain either *why* people should struggle at all or what they should struggle *for*. Similarly, Taylor (1985) suggests that Foucault's analyses of power/dominion and disguise/illusion really only make sense if some critical dimension or genuine goods are implicit in his own analysis. In fact, the denial of any such commitments by postmodern thinkers seems belied by their writings. Most convey a strong sense of opposition to arbitrary authority and domination. And they clearly suggest that it is more enlightened, mature, or wise *not* to be taken in by false absolutes and ethnocentric moral beliefs. Thus, in the end, it seems they advocate their own brand of wisdom and character ideal just like the rest of us. But they deny any such commitments. As a result, many critics worry, postmodernism encourages passivity or cynicism, thereby accelerating social atomization and personal malaise.

Philosophical Hermeneutics

Contemporary philosophical or ontological hermeneutics (e.g., Gadamer, 1975; 1981; Guignon, 1991; Ricoeur, 1992; Taylor, 1989; Warnke, 1987) offers a framework for thinking about social science, including critical psychology, that tries to go "beyond scientism and constructionism" (Richardson and Fowers, 1994) or beyond individualism and postmodernism. Agreeing partly with postmodernism, hermeneutics criticizes the residue of "Enlightenment dogmatism" and the one-sided emphasis on procedural justice in Habermas's critical theory. But it also endorses Habermas's general critical intent and rejects postmodernism/social constructionism's moral relativism as harmful and unnecessary.

Hermeneutic thinkers agree with critics of naturalistic philosophy that we have no direct or immediate access to a "real" world independent of our interpretation of things. (Again, "hermeneutics" means "interpretation.") The naturalistic view that "knowing" is simply forming accurate inner pictures of an outer reality seems absurd in light of our understanding of how social processes shape claims to knowledge. However, according to hermeneutics, the typical postmodern attempt to get past modern *representationalism* (the idea that our theories truly reflect or represent the external world) is overly hasty and incomplete. Hermeneutic philosophy views representationalism as more than just a philosophical mistake. It is one facet of the whole enterprise of modern emancipatory individualism, with its problematic central ethical ideal of "freedom as self-autonomy . . . to be self-responsible, to rely on one's judgment, to find one's purpose in oneself" (Taylor, 1995: 7). Sorting out the wheat from the chaff in this modern value outlook may be a task for centuries.

Rethinking Ontology

Hermeneutic thought begins by rethinking ontology, or the nature of what exists. To begin with, humans are "self-interpreting beings" (Taylor, 1985). It is the *meanings* they work out in the business of living that makes them to a great extent what they are. This view differs from the natural science focus on brute influences. Moreover, individual lives are "always 'thrown' into a familiar life-world from which they draw their possibilities of self-interpretation. Our own life-stories only make sense against the backdrop of possible story-lines opened by our historical culture" (Guignon, 1989: 109). In other words, our culture provides us with descriptions of possible meanings we can give to our lives. Instead of thinking of the self as an object of any sort, hermeneutic thought follows Heidegger in conceiving of human existence as a "happening" or a "becoming" (1962: 426). Individual lives have a temporal and narrative structure. They are a kind of unfolding "movement" that is "stretched along between birth and death." In Guignon's words, just as "events in a novel gain their meaning from what they seem to be pointing to in the long run . . . so our past lives and our present activities gain their meaning from a (perhaps tacit) sense of where our lives are going as a totality" (1993: 14).

In the hermeneutic view, a basic fact about humans is that they *care* about whether their lives make sense and what their lives are amounting to. Therefore, they have always taken some stand on their lives by seizing on certain roles, traits, and values. Humans do *not* simply desire particular outcomes or satisfactions in living. Rather, they always make "strong evaluations" (Taylor, 1985: 3). Even if only tacitly or unconsciously, they evaluate the quality of their desires and motivations and the worth of the ends they seek in terms of how they fit in with their overall sense of a worthwhile or decent life. According to Taylor (1989: 25ff) frameworks mapped by strong evaluations are "inescapably" part of human agency or social life.

This means we are always "insiders" with respect to some deep, defining set of commitments and identifications, even though their content varies greatly across cultures. Positivists and even postmodernists seem to feel it is appropriate to try to step outside or distance ourselves as much as possible from historical entanglements. Hermeneutic thinkers think this is not only impossible, but probably somewhat inauthentic. The only sort of human agency we can imagine takes place according to a "logic of question and answer" (Gadamer, 1975: 333) within a "space of questions" (Taylor, 1989: 26). These questions and answers are taken for granted by our culture or elaborated by us in some way. Outside that dialectic or disengaged from it, we would not gain a better grip on who we are. We would simply not know what meanings things have for us on basic matters and we would incur a frightening kind of dissociation.

We can and often should profoundly criticize various norms and practices. But we always critique them on the basis of other commitments or moral insights from our traditions that, for the moment, we take for granted. Our various cultural and moral traditions are rich resources for such critique. The common view of them as stable, monolithic authorities is actually a narrow, prejudiced outgrowth of the Enlightenment. In fact, "traditions" seem essentially to be multivocal, interminably noisy debates rather than static sets of rules (Fowers and Richardson, 1996).

The positivist and postmodern desire to disengage from all tradition and authority seems misguided and self-defeating, in the hermeneutic view. For example, many postmodernists stress detached irony and play as the most appropriate stance toward life, as in Foucault's view of life as purely aesthetic self-creation. This seems like a not terribly original blend of Enlightenment *anti*-authoritarianism and the Romantic reaction *against* the Enlightenment's excessive rationalism. But hermeneutic thinkers and critical psychologists, following Fromm, believe we should ask what freedom is "to" or "for" as well as "from." They worry that both positivism and postmodernism may represent, in part, a flight from life's inevitable risks and responsibilities, as if by extreme detachment we could defend or protect ourselves from uncertainty, mistakes, disappointments, and tragedy. Some deeper wisdom about life may be called for, but not mind-numbing detachment or the pretense that we really do not care.

According to hermeneutic thinkers, our moral and political judgments are always tied to specific cultural contexts and issues. They can never be final or certain. But there seems to be no good reason to think that all moral values are ultimately relative or invalid. Only a god could know that, in any case. In place of the modern "quest for certainty" and liberal individualist ethics, hermeneutics puts the process of hermeneutic dialogue (Taylor, 1989; Warnke, 1987: 100ff). Such dialogue is a kind of wide-open and multifarious version of Habermas's ideal speech situation. It also parallels what social constructionists refer to as the ongoing negotiation of cultural meanings. In this view, serious moral and political commitments actually encourage us to be as open as possible to challenges and possible insights from others or the past. They motivate us to be open because we want to get things right. And they give us the sense of self needed to withstand uncertainty and doubt. In turn, openness and the constant testing of our beliefs and values against new circumstances and unforeseen challenges deepen our understanding and refine our commitments.

We can always defensively or dishonestly distort this process. No sure-fire method or social arrangement of checks and balances can prevent this from happening. But this kind of hermeneutic ontology or general sketch of dialogue and interpretation might help us avoid familiar extremes of utopian ambition and resigned defeat, in critical endeavors and the moral life in general. In the hermeneutic view, social science and theory are a "form of practice" (Taylor, 1985; Richardson and Christopher, 1993). They are ethics and politics by other means, an extension of our search for justice, love, and wisdom in practical life.

18

Discursive Psychology

Ian Parker

Editors' note *It was not too long ago that psychologists used the generic "he" when talking about both men and women. Publication norms still encourage authors to describe research in neat, objective, detached, and sterile fashion, ignoring inevitably messy or subjective aspects. We're not supposed to talk about informal interactions with research participants (usually called "subjects"), or about the social context of the research process. These language norms and restrictions support psychology's image of a value-free science. It is not surprising, thus, that other chapters have emphasized how important it is for critical psychologists to examine terminology, ideology, and other aspects of communication and language use.*

In this chapter, Ian Parker's central focus is language and meaning. He describes how "discursive psychology" seeks to discover how language "works" by analyzing "discourses" or patterns of meaning. In studying how "forms of language serve social, ideological, and political interests," critical discourse analysts examine how written and verbal texts reveal the subjectivity of their authors – how the content of what authors write is related to their feelings, thoughts, and place in society. Discourse analysis, then, is the opposite of taking at face value printed or spoken material. In a sense, it tries to perfect the art of suspicion in getting at hidden meanings. Thus, when discourse analysts examine a text, they study the specific ways that the material predisposes readers to a particular interpretation. In this type of research, we can ask questions such as: what are the hidden ideological and political meanings of this text? How do particular discourses clarify or obscure oppressive relationships in society?

Parker distinguishes between a critical approach to discursive psychology and one that is more cautious. The first, relying heavily on work by Foucault, links psychological discourse with power and ideology. We learn from this tradition the intimate relation between language and politics. The second, relying on Potter and Wetherell, looks at the various and potentially contradictory discourses people use to explain facts and behaviors. This approach is more concerned with how people talk about phenomena, and less concerned about changing society or psychology.

We have seen contending positions within other areas of critical psychology such as feminist psychology (Chapter 16). Parker describes similar tensions within discursive psychology relevant to issues examined earlier in the book, such as psychology's individualistic bias and the use of qualitative methods. Agreeing with the critique of moral relativism expressed by Frank C. Richardson and Blaine J. Fowers in Chapter 17, Parker reminds us that "the fact that we can relativize phenomena does not mean that all explanations or moral positions are equally valid or equally useless."

Parker concludes by making explicit a point that is implicit in several other chapters: "A critical psychology has to be constructed from theoretical resources, life experiences and political identities outside the discipline. Only then does it make sense to deconstruct what the discipline does to us and to its other subjects." Using mainstream psychology's own norms and assumptions cannot lead to an adequate critique of the field – thus the importance of influences such as feminist theory, Marxism, liberation theology, and even utopianism. As psychology becomes more and more specialized, critical psychologists must become generalists, incorporating perspectives ranging from political philosophy to the everyday experience of those who suffer from the status quo and those who seek to change it.

The terms *discourse* and *discourse analysis* often present problems for researchers from a psychology background coming across them for the first time. This is because the terms do not have an easily understood everyday meaning as do *personality* or *development*. There are, in addition, strong disagreements amongst discourse analysts as to what it is they are actually studying and how they should study it.

In the following sections I provide definitions of key terms and a brief introduction to discourse analysis. Then I review the recent historical background to two different strands in discursive research. Later I discuss five axes of debate that have implications for a critical perspective, and conclude with some remaining questions for those who would like to do work in this area.

Defining Discourse

Discourse analysts study the way in which various forms of language work, and critical discourse analysts are concerned with the ways in which these forms of language serve social, ideological, and political interests. The different patterns of meaning that we use to talk about things like "mental illness" or "homosexuality," as if these things were fixed qualities of human psychology, are *discourses*. Discourses describe the aspects of the world in certain ways. A "medical discourse," for example, will lead us to speak about distressing experience as if it was a reflection of an underlying disease, and a "familial" discourse will define social relationships as if heterosexual couples raising their children were the only normal and natural way of living together.

The term "discourse" comprises the many ways that meaning is conveyed through culture, and so it includes speech and writing, nonverbal and pictorial communication, and artistic and poetic imagery. People develop and "express" their identity through the use of verbal, nonverbal, and other symbolic means of communication, such as art. Then, when they feel as if they are genuinely "expressing" something inside themselves, they pick up and reproduce certain discourses about the nature of the self, and they find it difficult to step back and question where those ways of describing the world may have come from, and what interests they may serve.

Discourse analysts treat the variety of things that psychologists tell us they have "discovered" inside us and among us as *forms of discourse*. We study accounts of action and experience as discourses, and as part of powerful discursive practices in Western culture that define certain kinds of activity and thinking as normal and other kinds as abnormal (Parker et al., 1995). There are two aspects to our critical activity here. First, traditional psychology is treated with suspicion, for it presents its stories about the mind and behavior as if they were factual accounts. Our analysis can unravel the ways in which those stories work, why they seem so plausible, and which institutions and forms of power they reproduce. Second, traditional psychology is seen as consistently misleading us about the place of mental phenomena, which it invariably locates inside individual heads rather than between people, in language.

Historical Resources: Two Traditions

Discursive approaches in psychology draw on debates outside the discipline. We can identify two approaches that have emerged from quite different theoretical traditions. This is not to say that there is no overlap, and we often find writers borrowing ideas and moving between theoretical frameworks.

Foucauldian Approaches to Discourse

The first strand is still the most radical. It develops the work of the French historian and philosopher Michel Foucault (Parker, 1995). This work was introduced into Anglo-American psychology in the late 1970s in the UK-based journal *Ideology and Consciousness* (Adlam et al., 1977), and then in the book *Changing the Subject* (Henriques et al., 1984). Foucault's detailed description and reflection on modern notions of madness (1971), punishment (1977a), confession (1981), and the self (1986) focused on the "rules of discourse" that allow our present-day talk about these things to make sense. He engaged in an "archaeology" of culture and a "genealogy" of knowledge which uncover the ways the phenomena psychology takes for granted came into being.

Many psychological and social phenomena can seem trivial if they are studied on their own, separated from culture. One of the main problems with traditional laboratory-experimental psychology is that it focuses on one issue at a time, such as memory or prejudice, and it then carries out thousands of studies exploring its different permutations in different contexts. There is an illusion in this type of research that the psychologist will be able to reveal the "essence" of the phenomenon, to discover what "memory" or "prejudice" really is. A discourse researcher asks instead, "How has this phenomenon come to be like this?" The most innocent bits of consumer culture can help us understand the workings of power, ideology and forms of subjectivity in a society if we ask what discursive conditions made them possible (Parker, 1994). Foucauldians would then look at how discourses constitute particular phenomena, elaborating them, making them natural and encouraging us to take them for granted.

Some of the original editors and authors of *Ideology and Consciousness* and *Changing the Subject* have extended this research into psychology (Rose, 1985; 1990), or have combined an analysis of discourse with psychoanalysis to look at gender, sexuality and class (Hollway, 1989; Walkerdine, 1991). Psychoanalysis has to be handled very carefully and skeptically in this work, and Foucault (1981) provides a powerful argument against treating psychoanalytic notions as underlying truths about the human mind.

The next generation of researchers were influenced by these ideas, and have worked on subjectivity and race (Mama, 1995) and on links between psychology, culture and political practice (Burman et al., 1996; Parker, 1992). A particularly useful idea that runs through this work is the notion of the *psy-complex*. The psy-complex is the network of theories and practices that comprise academic, professional and popular psychology, and it covers the different ways in which people in modern Western culture are categorized, observed and regulated by psychology, as well as the ways in which they live out psychological models in their own talk and experience.

The psy-complex is part of a particular "regime of truth" which makes our talk and experience about "the self," "personality" and "attitudes" make sense. While academic psychologists tell stories about people and so participate in certain discourses about the individual, professional psychologists make those stories come true and help police discursive practices. At the same time there is always room for resistance. Our study of the ways in which certain discourses reproduce power relations can also promote "counter-discourses" or alternative arguments for what is usually taken for granted (Foucault, 1977b).

Interpretative Repertoires

A second strand of discourse analysis emerged in the 1980s in social psychology. This was first presented as an alternative to traditional attitude research (Potter and Wetherell, 1987). The main theoretical resource for this strand was work on the sociology of scientific knowledge. This approach treated scientists' activities as procedures to be explained rather than as discoveries to be celebrated.

For example, scientists talk about what they do in contradictory ways. A close analysis of their discourse identified contrasting ways of explaining phenomena. The researchers in this tradition call these contrasting explanations *interpretative repertoires*. For example, one interpretative repertoire makes reference to observation and testing and objectivity, while another acknowledges the role of intuition and personal rivalries (Gilbert and Mulkay, 1984). The term "discursive psychology" was first coined in an extension of this work which looked at the way memory, attribution and "facts" were constructed in people's and scientists' talk (Edwards and Potter, 1993). The concept "interpretative repertoire" is still used in this tradition, even in research which moves closer to a critical approach to ideology and to some Foucauldian concepts (Edley and Wetherell, 1995; Wetherell and Potter, 1992).

This second strand of discursive work has proved more acceptable to social psychology and, to an extent, to psychology in general. This model is more accepted in psychology because it contains the work of discourse analysis within traditional psychological categories and because it evades reference to politics or power. Although the model relativizes categories that psychology likes to see as essential and unchanging, it restricts its analysis to a particular text rather than locating it in wider discursive practices. As a consequence, much of the research in this tradition is rather descriptive, and a range of techniques from micro-sociology make the description look more objective. This approach is less critical of the ideological and political discourses of psychology.

Discourse Analysis in Psychology

The second strand of discourse analysis, using interpretative repertoires, is more comfortable with the term "discursive psychology" than are critical Foucauldian writers. There are certainly advantages in this strand, for it makes some key aspects of discourse analysis accessible to a psychology audience. Potter and Wetherell (1987) helpfully draw attention to three characteristics of discourse. In the process, they lead researchers away from their dependence on traditional psychological notions.

Three Characteristics of Discourse, Power and Practice

Some ideas from philosophy and sociology have been useful to look at language. I will briefly describe how these have found their way into discursive psychology, and then connect each to some more critical perspectives on discourse. Attention to *variability, construction* and *function* takes the researcher several steps away from mainstream psychology, but we still need something more to help them leap over to a critical standpoint. Each of these three characteristics of discourse had already been described in Foucault's (1972) writings.

From Variability to Contradiction The first characteristic is *variability*. Psychologists tend to search for an underlying consistency of response, or for a set of items on a questionnaire or test that cohere, or for parsimony of explanation. Psychological explanation looks for tools that will predict consistently. Interpretation in traditional psychological work looks for a single meaning, whether in observational statements or in reports of experience. In contrast, discourse analysts will always attend to inconsistency, and to variations in accounts. This is not to catch people out, but to lead us to the diverse and sometimes contradictory fragments of meaning that come together in any particular discourse.

For example, Wetherell and Potter (1992) studied racial and cultural discourses of Pakeha (white) New Zealanders, and their views of the Maori people. Within these accounts there were competing descriptions of culture. On the one hand, culture was talked about as "heritage" with the Maori positioned as if they were a protected species. At other points in the conversation, people adopted a therapeutic tone, with worries that young Maori might behave badly because they were disconnected from their cultural group. These different interpretations or discourses could be found within the interview transcript of the same person

Foucault's historical research focused on *contradictions* between discourses and the ways in which the self is torn in different directions by discourse. The unified image of the "self" in contemporary psychology and society is no more than that, an image, and so discursive psychology has to take care not to assume something undivided in the person underneath discourse. The term *deconstruction* is sometimes used in this context to describe the way in which a text can be unravelled and the contradictions in it displayed so that it becomes clear what ideas are being privileged and what are the costs of that. A critical discursive reading is always, in some sense, a deconstruction of dominant forms of knowledge (Derrida, 1981; Eagleton, 1983). While the notion of variability tends to celebrate diversity of meaning in pluralist spirit, the notion of contradiction links more directly with struggle, power and the deconstruction of discourse in practice.

From Construction to Constitution The second characteristic of discourse is *construction*. This refers to the way in which every symbolic activity must make use of cultural resources to make sense to others. Traditional psychology treats individuals as if they could, in principle, be separated from culture, and it treats each individual mental process as if it were disconnected from the rest of the life-world of the "subject." Discourse analysis sees the meanings of terms, words, turns of phrase, arguments or other seemingly discrete aspects of language as intimately connected to other meanings and activities. An important resource here has been *ethnomethodology* (Garfinkel, 1967), which sees meaning as always defined by context. Another useful tool is *conversation analysis*, which looks at the mechanics of turn-taking and the way order is maintained in speech

(Atkinson and Heritage, 1984). People cannot make up the meaning of symbols as they go along, but participate in already existing meanings. Meanings are not transmitted from one head to another, but are produced in discourse as people participate in new texts. Discourses then construct ways in which people are able to relate to one another.

For example, Hollway (1989) analyzed the accounts of heterosexual couples, examining the ways in which notions of intimacy and sexuality were described. She highlighted three contradictory discourses which had powerful consequences for how the partners could experience themselves as men or women in a relationship. The "male sexual drive" discourse positions the man as impelled by forces out of his control and the woman only as object and recipient of his needs. The "have/hold" discourse positions the man and woman as bound together for life, with moral responsibilities to maintain the relationship having priority. The "permissive" discourse celebrates the possibility of other relationships and the freedom of each partner to find fulfillment as he or she wishes. These discourses not only prescribe certain behaviors, but produce "masculinity" and "femininity" as objects to be understood and positions to be lived out in ways that might be liberating or oppressive for those subject to them.

Foucault's (1970) study of different *epistemes* or forms of knowledge in Western culture, and of the emergence of the modern episteme in the nineteenth century, was a "structuralist" enterprise. That is, Foucault described structures of knowledge and how they penetrate our understanding of the world. His "archaeology" of the human sciences showed how the concepts we take for granted in psychology and in our daily lives have a long history which is marked by rapid changes in knowledge. The modern episteme governs the way we talk and think about science, progress and personal meaning. Our ideas are *constituted* within patterns of discourse that we cannot control. Foucault's later work emphasized the instability and struggles over meaning that mark human activity, and he came to prefer the term "genealogy" to refer to the messy and sometimes bloody way in which meanings emerge. Structures were now seen as always contested, and the power they hold always met by resistance. A Foucauldian account of the psy-complex, for example, focuses on the way that individuals are made to tell one coherent story about themselves to the authorities, to each other, and to themselves. In sum, the turn from construction to constitution helps us see that meanings are historically and politically constituted, and not just cognitively constructed in a social void.

From Function to Power   The third characteristic is *function*. Discourse does not provide a transparent window into the mind of the individual or into the world outside, as many psychologists seem to believe. Rather, language organized through discourse always does things. When we seem to be merely describing a state of affairs, our commentary always has other effects; it plays its part in legitimizing or challenging, supporting or ironizing, endorsing or subverting what it describes. In both everyday language and in psychological description, our utterances are "speech acts" (Austin, 1962). Discourse analysts will focus on what these acts do. Speech act theory saw everyday talk as an alternative to mentalistic explanations of individual activities, and Wittgenstein and other writers in this tradition see psychological phenomena as effects or products of ordinary language (Parker, 1996; Wittgenstein, 1958).

The attention to functions of discourse is also radicalized through Foucault's (1982b) account of *power*. A Foucauldian view sees power as bound up with knowledge. This view differs from many standard social scientific accounts, which reduce power to a kind of potential that an individual possesses and wields when he or she wishes (Ng, 1980). For example, Walkerdine (1991) analyzed the interaction between a female teacher and a little boy in class. In the brief piece of transcript, the teacher was able to control the boy until he responded with a stream of sexist abuse. She withdrew, and was then unable to reassert her authority. Walkerdine explored the way that competing discourses of devalued female sexuality and liberal education theory framed the way the participants could relate to one another. The boy was able to position the teacher as a woman, and so silence her, and the woman who had been trained to value the free expression of children positioned herself as a good teacher, and was unable to silence the boy. These discourses could only take place because of the wider systems of power in male–female relationships and systems of ideology in education. Power was played out in this classroom in such a way that the woman participated in, and reproduced, her own oppression.

Discourse locates people in "subject positions," places in the discourse which carry certain rights to speak and specifications for what may be spoken. People must assume these places for the discourse to work (Davies and Harré, 1990). The notion of "subject position" is a valuable tool for understanding abuses of power in psychology and its wider culture. Some will speak and some will remain silent. In this perspective, it is as much a problem when people speak in certain ways as when they are silent.

Axes of Difference in Discursive Research

As with any other approach in psychology, there is much disagreement about what discursive psychology is, and some doubt as to whether it could be seen as an off-the-shelf alternative to the mainstream discipline. It is certainly not consistently reliable as a critical tool for examining psychology when we get it home and try to use it. There are some important fault-lines in discursive approaches which bear serious attention. In this second half of the chapter I draw attention to some of the key debates and divisions in discursive research and their consequences for critical psychologists by laying out five axes around which conceptual differences revolve at the moment.

Micro–Macro

Reduction in explanation to the individual has long been a problem for critical approaches in psychology (Billig, 1976). Psychology is founded on the study of the person abstracted from social context. *Micro*-reduction, which sees the individual as the source of all psychological processes, is usually a conservative mode of explanation. In contrast, critical psychologists insist that it is necessary to focus on patterns of social relationships and structures of the wider culture to explain how psychological phenomena come about. Only then is it possible to connect psychology with questions of ideology and power.

In discourse analysis there is a good deal of work on the interpersonal level, and upon texts of conversations and interviews. There is a progressive movement away from the individual to the contexts in which they make and remake relationships with others. Micro-sociological perspectives such as *conversation analysis* and *ethnomethodology* have been imported here to describe, for example, how a person attributes and gains identity as part of a group through use of "membership categorization devices" (Sacks, 1974), or how a deviant career is constructed for others through what is made to seem unusual behavior (Smith, 1978). Some important issues around gender and power in language can also be picked up using conversation-analytic accounts of language (Crawford, 1995).

However, while conversation-analytic and ethnomethodological work is useful, this micro-sociological view is often quite stubborn in resisting a shift further up to higher-level social and cultural analysis. Critical psychologists will need at some point to refer to the character of a particular society, economic structures, classes and systems of oppression based, for example, on gender or race. The micro-sociological perspective prevents them from doing this. There is, then, little place in this micro-sociology for an analysis of the weight of history, for people are seen as freely creating a version of the world in their talk and in their own interpretations of other texts (Garfinkel, 1967). There is a danger, then, that discursive psychology could be restricted in its focus and refuse to take into account the role of ideology and power.

At the other side of the micro–macro axis lie various approaches that explore the historical and cultural background to this small-scale activity of sense-making. It is certainly necessary for critical discourse researchers to pay due attention to the micro level, rather than simply insisting that an analysis of historical forces and social structures is sufficient. The feminist argument that the "personal is political" (Rowbotham et al., 1979) is one that critical psychologists need to take to heart. An account of discourse should be able to identify the ways in which processes of ideology and power find their way into the little stories of everyday life (Smith, 1974).

A discursive psychology which is to reflect critically on the accomplishments of actors must explore the rules they have followed and the material they have worked upon. But to do that it must take seriously the way wider structures of power set the scene for the way we make sense of things and the way those structures limit our understanding of ourselves and the social world. As some realist writers have pointed out, we need to attend to unintended consequences, unacknowledged conditions, unconscious motivations and tacit skills that prevent the world from being a fully open and transparent place (Bhaskar, 1989; Parker, 1992).

Inside–Outside

As well as reducing explanation to the level of the individual, the conservative goal of most psychologists is to produce an account of what is happening *inside* the head. Psychology here reproduces the deeply felt experience of most people in Western culture, that their thinking first takes place in an interior private realm and is only then expressed and communicated to others. The danger with explanations which try to look inside the subject is that all too often they smuggle essentialism back into our picture of social action. *Essentialism* is a mode of explanation that looks to underlying fixed qualities that operate independently of social relations. Essentialism can be found in contemporary discursive accounts where there is a temptation to bring in some notion of the self to explain identity in discourse (e.g., Burr, 1995); where certain characteristics of thought are assumed to underpin what people are doing in discourse (e.g., Billig, 1991); or where there is an attempt to justify a discourse perspective by appealing directly to neurophysiology (e.g., Harré and Gillett, 1994).

However, there is also a danger with an alternative critical account which simply insists that everything is in language, and that all of our cognitive skills, decisions, experiences of selfhood and intentionality can be dissolved in discourse as it washes through us. The discursive argument against the existence of cognitive machinery inside the head can appear uncomfortably similar to traditional behaviorist accounts, and to their refusal to speculate about what is going on inside the mind as if it were a kind of closed box. It is true that a thoroughly discursive psychology is anti-humanist in that there is suspicion of the notion of a unified self that lies underneath discourse. The problem here is with the individualist essentialism that underpins much humanist rhetoric, not with its moral claims.

A critical discursive account reframes questions about the inside and the outside of the individual, turning the activity of speakers and listeners into places in discourse. The inside and the outside are dialectical aspects of people's subjectivity, where subjectivity refers to the sense of selfhood and to the production of that sense of self in relation to others. Humanist psychotherapy, for example, tries to uncover the self, as if it were always there under the surface. The integrity of the self is maintained independent of social relations. In contrast, discursive psychotherapy traces distress to networks of social relations and to patterns of language. Thus, a turn to discourse in therapy has helped therapists who want to link their work to wider issues of social justice. Discourse therapists deconstruct the client's problem by locating it in discourse, by "externalizing" it (White and Epston, 1990). This innovative therapeutic work leads to a more challenging and empowering social humanist practice.

Quantitative–Qualitative

The third axis runs from the quantification of discourse-analytic accounts to the more *hermeneutic qualitative* (interpretive) styles of explanation. Most traditional psychology operates on the conservative premise that the only things worth studying are those that can be measured. Quantification of psychological and interpersonal processes is seen as one of the guarantees that research is scientific. Critical psychology challenges this scientific status in a number of ways. One strategy has been to refuse to adopt the term "science" altogether and to argue, in ethnomethodological style, that scientific explanation is merely a particular way of making sense of the world (Woolgar, 1988). Another strategy has been to demonstrate that scientific inquiry need not resort to quantification, and that it is often a sign of bad science that practitioners want to quantify phenomena before carefully describing singular cases (Harré and Secord, 1972).

The difference between qualitative and quantitative tendencies in discourse analysis is seen in the debate between those who look for a theoretically informed critical "reading" and those who would take short-cuts with computer software to code the material. The problem is that this sort of coding must always operate as a form of content analysis. It saves time in skimming a large body of textual material. But all too often it leads to a view of language as a set of neatly labelled discrete packages of meaning that always carry the same value regardless of context.

Barthes (1977) talked about the "death of the author," assuming that we could not understand the meaning of a text by tracing it back to the person who "wrote" it. The other side of this argument, however, and just as important, is that the kinds of reading he was proposing required the "birth of the reader" as an active participant in the text. The critical discourse analyst is an active reader who encourages people to read the texts they live within and so to assume a position of understanding and greater control over their lives.

Quantitative approaches do not take us any further than description, than reading. Computers help us in doing this, but they also restrict us to this. Qualitative approaches, on the other hand, help us engage with the text for the purpose of action research. Qualitative discourse analysis looks for the intricate ways in which power suffuses texts.

The first three axes of difference sometimes find the more conservative varieties of discursive psychology in broad agreement with some of the key assumptions made by traditional psychology. They like reductionism, essentialism and quantification. The fourth and fifth axes are a little more complicated, and find critical psychologists having to make some difficult choices, and having to risk some strange alliances.

Relativism–Realism

There is a powerful tendency in discourse-analytic work toward a *relativist* position, and an understandable refusal to accept the "findings" that psychology claims to have made so far about what goes on inside human beings. There are, however, also serious risks in this social constructionist view of psychological concepts. The theoretical resources that critical and discursive researchers have drawn upon are part of a wider discursive turn in the human sciences that carry conservative as well as progressive prescriptions for social activity.

Deconstruction and discourse theory cut away the positivist ground from beneath traditional psychology and relativize their claims about the nature of human nature. That is to say, they challenge psychology's explanations of behavior because the discipline pretends to make universal claims about human nature. Psychology fails to see the importance of the time and location where behavior occurs. Psychology neglects also the social, historical, and political context of events. Discourse and deconstruction interpret behavior *relative* to the time and place in which it occurs, and *relative* to the person who describes the phenomenon. We *relativize* psychological phenomena when we ask questions such as: is this behavior likely to occur in another time or in another place? Is the explanation given determined by the cultural lenses of the researcher? Would a researcher with another set of basic assumptions give a different interpretation? Are class, gender, and power issues involved in the definition of the event? These questions relativize the nature of psychological experiences and explanations.

At the same time, these theoretical currents also relativize the truth claims of the critics, potentially sabotaging moral and political critiques of the discipline. For who is to say that the critics have a more ethical view of psychology? Deconstruction was mentioned earlier as a useful source of work for discourse analysts, but there is also a conservative variant of deconstruction which reduces the reading of a text to a free play of meaning in which no critical position can be taken toward it. This is a potential risk that critical psychologists need to take seriously. The fact that we can relativize phenomena does not mean that all explanations or moral positions are equally valid or equally useless. The position of critical psychologists will also be relative to their time, place, culture, and subjectivity, but it can still be more morally defensible than the positions they criticize.

Now the stakes are higher as some defences of relativism in discourse research seem to throw into question any position from which a critique could be developed. In one particularly pernicious example, "discursive psychologists" have analyzed the way in which references to the Holocaust function as part of a bottom-line argument against relativism (Edwards et al., 1995). They wish to make the case for relativism in research, but they also, in the process, undermine the truth claims of those who refer to the

Holocaust as a real historical event. A relativist position in social constructionism or discourse analysis makes it difficult for us to sustain the project of a critical psychology, and it is not surprising that feminist psychologists have been alert to this danger (Burman, 1990; Gill, 1995).

Critical realism appears to provide an answer to this problem. This orientation pays attention to the material, physical, and social bases of behavior, without neglecting the social nature of our interpretations and theories. Although it acknowledges external realities outside of our perceptions of the world, it differs from the traditional positivist approach in important ways. Critical realism does not reduce the human experience by breaking it into small bits, the way positivists do. While critical realists study the effects of systems on people, they do not accept the premise that human systems can be studied as if they were closed and controllable, like a test tube in sterile conditions, or the way experimental social psychologists study humans in laboratories. Unlike empiricists who set out to prove the truth or falseness of theories, as if we can ignore the social context and limitations in which these theories are created, critical realists examine the external world with the knowledge that their lenses not just examine it but also help to create it. Critical realism opposes relativism in the sense that it accepts an external reality outside of us, and somewhat independent of our views of it. Mindful, however, of the limitations of the positivist approach, critical realism acknowledges the complexity and unpredictability of human systems, and our inability to capture the essence of human beings by breaking it into small bits and pieces of behaviors, cognitions, and emotions.

Critical realism, then, exposes positivist psychology's pretensions to model itself after the natural sciences, at the same time that it examines the discursive accounts of social practices (Bhaskar, 1989; Parker, 1992). Critical realism runs alongside the social constructionist attacks on the discipline while preventing a wholesale collapse into discourse idealism, the position that there is nothing but discourse. Realism of different varieties, however, can always be mobilized by those sympathetic to mainstream psychology to warrant it as a science and to rebut social constructionist critiques (Greenwood, 1994). It seems, in this light, that even critical realists could end up falling into the arms of traditional science as they look for certainties in this confusing landscape.

There is a way out of this problem. A critical engagement with relativism and realism needs to address (a) how psychological facts are socially constructed, (b) how subjectivity is discursively reproduced within present social arrangements, *and* (c) how the underlying historical conditions emerged that gave rise to the psy-complex. Only by understanding how the discipline of psychology reproduces notions of individuality and human nature – a realist endeavor – will it be possible to transform it, and to socially construct it as something different, something better.

Although critical psychologists welcome the relativizing of normative notions of human nature advanced by traditional psychology, they resist the tendency to relativize moral critiques. While suffering and oppression are variously experienced by different groups, critical psychologists do not question the existence of patterns of domination. Critical realism helps us view oppression for what it is. Social structures of oppression and exploitation cannot be wished away by the relativist impulse. The voices of the oppressed make the experience of oppression very real and tangible. Letting relativism undermine the cause of social justice is something critical psychologists resist.

Common Sense–Theory

Although traditional psychology does not usually value the common-sense understanding that people have of their activities and psychological states, it does still rest upon common-sense assumptions about the mind and behavior. There is a two-way traffic of ideas here. On the one hand, psychologists base their theories upon hunches and intuitions about people that they gather from common sense. On the other hand, psychological "facts" and theories find their way out from the discipline into the real world and become part of common sense. Common sense in general, of course, consists of cultural and historical discourses which reproduce the very oppressive social relations psychology ratifies. Both common sense and psychology, for example, are saturated by racist imagery and are rooted in colonial imagery (Howitt and Owusu-Bempah, 1994).

On the other hand, critical perspectives often develop through researchers using their own experience to challenge the lies that the discipline peddles about them. The development of feminist psychology, for example, would be inconceivable without a challenge based on women's experience, and that experience can draw upon forms of common sense that are usually devalued (Wilkinson and Kitzinger, 1995).

The tension between common sense and expertise draws attention to two vital prerequisites for critical research. The first is an awareness of context, and the second is the use of theoretical resources. With respect to the first, an awareness of context, it is not surprising that some of the most radical discourse-analytic studies have been carried out in contexts where it has been impossible to feel comfortable with common sense. The development of discourse analysis in South Africa is an example. It occurred in a setting where the society and the academic world were politicized, where there were continual questions and struggles over identity, and where conflicts over culture and "race" had a run-on effect on the ways in which researchers understood power and ideology (Levett et al., 1997). In the liberal democracies, on the other hand, especially where the student population is skewed to the more comfortable middle-class side of the general population, there is little impetus to question what may be wrong with social arrangements and ways of speaking. It is more difficult to politicize language, but discourse analysis does at least help us to keep those questions around in psychology.

With respect to the second prerequisite for critical research, theory, it is necessary to draw upon frameworks which separate us from the language which makes the world seem "just so." Deconstruction has been discussed in this chapter because it enables us to step back from language and to understand how it informs our common sense. What is at stake here is the space for a critical standpoint to develop from which to view the ideological functions of the discipline of psychology. That standpoint is not given to us by common sense. Rather, we have to construct it, and we need good theory to do that. Critical psychology requires a critical distance from its object of study. Our task is to maintain that critical distance without devaluing the understanding that people have of their own lives.

Remaining Questions

Discursive psychology has been presented here as a radical alternative to most research in the discipline. There are, nevertheless, problems that cannot be solved within this framework. Moreover, it creates problems for researchers. Some critical psychologists will find elements of a discursive approach difficult to agree with. There will be occasions, for example, when good quantitative research into the impact of exploitation, overcrowding and poverty on people's lives will be better than reams of textual analysis. Aspects of a discursive approach, such as its relativism and celebration of common-sense categories of experience, have already made it something of a liability for critical researchers.

The different axes of debate in discourse theory in psychology constitute a field of theoretical and political struggle. One of the paradoxes in discourse research is that those who are critical will already, almost spontaneously, do "discourse analysis" on the texts they read and live, for they read and live at a distance from language, experiencing its ideological character and the effects of power. On the other hand, those who accept language and culture unquestioningly will dismiss critical discourse analysis on the basis that language does no more than represent the world as it is and as they think it should be. These arguments have been rehearsed before, along with a number of other problems in discourse analysis (Parker and Burman, 1993). What these issues come down to is that there is no place *in* psychology, or even in discursive psychology, for critical work to start. A critical psychology has to be constructed from theoretical resources, life experiences and political identities *outside* the discipline. Only then does it make sense to deconstruct what the discipline does to us and to its other subjects.

Note

I would like to thank Judith Arrowsmith, Erica Burman, Eugenie Georgaca, Sarah Grogan, Rhiannon Lloyd and Richard Mepham for their helpful comments on earlier versions of this chapter.

PART IV
CRITICAL REFLECTIONS

19

A Critical Look at Critical Psychology: Elaborating the Questions

Julian Rappaport and Eric Stewart

Editors' note *We asked Julian Rappaport and Eric Stewart to review the broad field of critical psychology as presented in this book. We asked them to do so critically, and they did. Going beyond the themes and dilemmas noted in Chapter 1 and elsewhere, they point to risks and limitations inherent in critical psychology's theory and practice. Their analysis pushes critical psychology further along by suggesting where we might go from here. No doubt the next edition of this book will benefit from their analysis.*

From their perspective as community psychologists, Rappaport and Stewart remind us how important it is to escape the trap of mere intellectualism and stay focused on the real-world consequences of our work. How can we transfer our insights from the academic setting to the community, changing not just the norms of psychologists but the lives of people less privileged than ourselves? At least equally important, how can we incorporate into our work the experiences and insights of those who live in the community, who often differ from us in many significant ways? Sensing that the gap between rhetoric and action is as present in critical psychology as it is in other critical fields, the authors invite us to join community members in social action and to try harder to solicit the participation of those with less privileged backgrounds.

In a field defined by a critical attitude, Rappaport and Stewart caution us not to become elitist and self-righteous. Expanding on this book's emphasis on acknowledging dilemmas, they caution us against too much certainty in our own positions. Comfort with our new conception of psychology can make us stop questioning our own assumptions. The lesson is clear: instead of rushing to confirm our presuppositions we should stop to appreciate the ironies, tensions, and contradictions inherent in our own ideas. We should be explicit about our values and our subjectivity.

Immersion in real-life "mid-level" settings is a good antidote to false conceptual dichotomies such as the "individual" and the "social system." Individuals are part of systems and systems are made up of individuals. It makes no sense to talk about people out of context. Conversely, it makes no sense to talk about systems without reference to real people. Critical psychologists wish to recapture the importance of larger social systems: many would not agree with an exclusive focus on the mid-level structures that Rappaport and Stewart find central. But we should not forget the individual, who remains both the subject of oppression and the hero of emancipation.

> But the problem is, precisely, to decide if it is actually suitable to place oneself within a "we" in order to assert the principles one recognizes and the values one accepts; or if it is not, rather, necessary to make the future formation of a "we" possible by elaborating the question. Because it seems to me that the "we" must not be previous to the question; it can only be the result.
>
> M. Foucault, "Polemics, Politics, and Problemizations"

In Eastern Europe there are new textbooks. Where these books used to say something like "Communism is the only way to a happy world" they now say something like "Capitalism is the only way to a happy world." These are not opposite statements. In fact, it is difficult to come up with a statement that might be opposite to either of these; it is hard because prescriptive statements tend to be answers without fully elaborated questions, and in fact foreclose on any such elaboration. We would argue that offering an end-state, a product, as an answer in advance produces the practices and postures we purport to challenge, and that we should rather offer a process, a means, an "elaboration of the question."

Of course, this is problematic for the writing of textbooks. It may even call into question the notion of textbooks. This is one of the ironies of *Critical Psychology: An Introduction*. As critical psychologists, we must ask our readers (and writers) to be critical (if not suspicious) of our criticism and prescriptions, to deconstruct even as we construct. We cannot rush to an answer or a product without risking becoming part of the received institution, becoming the status quo. We must articulate our own ideological commitments, but also understand their limitations. We need a vision of the future – empowerment and democracy for what? – and these stated goals should be made transparent: what does social justice mean? What is implied by self-determination? But we must also seek to enhance, rather than short circuit, the "social imagination" (Giroux, 1992). We have the rather difficult task of avoiding both perpetrating another ideology and of remaining simply another form of "cultural dissonance" (Giroux, 1992). And, we must be alert to, and elaborative of, the tensions and paradoxes that constitute our own enterprise.

But this book is offered at a time when psychology is only now emerging from a century of proudly proclaiming itself to be the discipline whose ambition is to "predict and control" human behavior. How odd such words sound to current sensibilities! Applying this self-description, organized psychology has mostly sought, in the interests of both compassion and guild, to assist individual adjustment to contemporary society – and less often to resist. The right to be the same (as whom?) is legitimate, the right to be different may even be championed. But the right to be different without loss of material, psychological or social resources poses problems that while surely "psychological" we have not well elaborated. Even less well elaborated are questions about how an enterprise that is supported by current social arrangements can question those very arrangements and retain its legitimacy.

Roles and role relationships among psychologists and subjects, clients or patients are defined by well established historical, economic and cultural expectations with respect to professionals and scientists. These expectations have not always encouraged or respected collegial, collaborative, diverse voices. When psychologists have attended to other than the individual it has most often been in search of efficient ways to exert social control in hospitals, schools or business organizations, consistent with the policies prevailing in our particular societies. It may be no accident that one of the leading architects of South African apartheid was a psychologist, trained to think in categories; nor is this more shocking than our complicity in the agreement that intelligence test scores, or other such measurements, are a reasonable standard for the allocation of educational or economic advantage.

Obviously, people who think about themselves as critical psychologists do not wish to accept such self-definitions and role relationships as desirable. Rather, critical psychologists want to think about how to make the discipline of psychology part of a much larger social movement, both in and outside academia. It is a movement that challenges institutional arrangements and looks toward the development of a more democratic, participatory, multi-voiced, "fairer" society in which psychology may have a role to play. As participants in this larger social movement psychologists take on the same responsibilities as other nonpsychologist participants. Every person lives and works in particular social arrangements. Each one of us can question our own.

The Project of Critical Psychology

If psychology is the discipline, critical psychology is a project of that discipline, though not necessarily confined to it. It is helpful for self-critique to make use of ideas, methods and practices developed in the context of world views different from one's own. Doing critical psychology includes elements of a sociology and anthropology of psychology and its practitioners. It encourages us to ask questions about the meaning and functions of our own work. This is a project that asks us to understand and change the ritual practices of our discipline. It is useful to keep in mind, however, that the very nature of a discipline that claims to be a science, as does psychology, means ideally that all of its members share in the ideal of a self-critical, ever changing understanding of its subject matter. In this sense the project of critical psychology is (theoretically) quite compatible with the goals and ambitions of the discipline of which it is a part. What may be different is that as critical psychology focuses inward as well as outward, using ideas that emerge from elsewhere, certain social values and voices other than our own become both salient and welcomed as a part of the "conversation" (Fowers and Richardson, 1996).

Since it is now well understood that all scientists work within particular historical value and paradigmatic perspectives, one might ask, "So, what is the news here; why decide to engage in the critical psychologist's project?" The only reason that makes sense to us is because all social arrangements are at best time-bound. Every generation must engage the central questions of its day in terms of its own time, place and context. Every generation will be faced with certain abstract questions of morality, fairness, justice and so on that will only find answers in concrete social arrangements. Past arrangements ("solutions") will always create burdens, injustice and new questions in the present. Being a part of how such questions are elaborated and addressed is a worthwhile vocation.

The editors of this volume provide a summary and the chapter authors provide definitions of critical psychology, each in accord with their own domain of interest. We do not offer yet another definition so much as our own sense of what those who would participate in the project of a critical psychology seem to be trying to do, and the sort of dilemmas inherent in such work. Our assigned task is to take a critical look at critical psychology, and this requires us, however unfairly, to be somewhat critical of the chapters that here precede our own. We do so quite selectively, with no intention of summarizing these chapters and with awareness of the advantage of having the last word. But we also offer our own vision. Central to that vision is (a) living with irony, tensions and contradictions; (b) a serious effort at boundary spanning in our conceptual work, our methodology and our collegiality; (c) a conscious search for mid-level constructs that avoid reification as individual, stable "traits" or as mystifying "social systems"; and (d) an effort to participate in small and documented ways in the real world of social action in the service of asking new questions as we pursue our values and goals.

Irony, Tensions and Contradictions

Critical psychologists want to be self-critical with respect to worldly realities such as psychology's functional relationships and "fairness" to the people studied and served. They call attention to political, economic, human rights and social justice issues in ways that seem to make certain demands on adherents. Indeed, the very nature of critical psychology calls into question roles and role relationships that doing psychology itself creates, an irony not to be lost if we are to grasp its essential elements. It is not the resolution of tensions that is the proper aim of a critical psychology, but rather exactly the opposite: a highlighting of tensions so as to illuminate the contradictions, choices and alternatives salient in our own time and place.

If doing critical psychology is, by its very nature, an ironic endeavor, full of tensions and contradictions, it is also necessarily about relationships and social regularities (Seidman, 1988) at multiple levels of analysis. It is about the meaning of justice, fairness and mutual respect, and cannot escape the dilemmas and tensions that mark all contexts where individuals live in collectivities. In social problem solving costs and benefits can at best be balanced momentarily; the definition and assignment of weights to such terms will remain contentious. Critical psychology cannot settle such matters, but it can question the ways in which they are being settled. Critical psychology, if it is to matter, cannot be limited to understanding without action, or to obtaining specific outcomes or providing specific services. It needs to ask how outcomes are reached, what counts as data, and how and by whom the data will be interpreted. Such concerns make aspects of this endeavor both action-oriented and a "meta-discipline," one that looks at the accepted ideas as a continuing part of its subject matter.

Critical psychology is ironic because its way of thinking cannot in itself become the dominant way of thinking. The moment any idea wins (becomes *the* way things are thought about or practiced by most members of a discipline or profession) that idea becomes the enemy of a critical psychology – that is, it becomes the status quo to which one is expected to adjust and the role relationship that becomes institutionalized. Ironically, the practitioner of this way of thinking wants to create change in roles and role relationships, ideas, methods and practices; but the changes themselves (the content) could never satisfy critical psychology's own criteria for justice, democratic participation and social change other than in a very momentary way.

Examples abound, however much one may wish to avoid simple versions of revisionist history (Harris, Chapter 2). It is not necessary to impugn the motives of reformers to know that history teaches us that reforms are transitory. Reform of the criminal justice system early in this century led to the development of the juvenile court as a means to divert children from the harsh cruelties and lack of wise discretion in an adult legal system. But well before the last quarter of this century it became obvious to those concerned with child welfare that children now need to be diverted from the arbitrariness that passes for wisdom in the juvenile justice system itself. The irony of "diversion from diversion" is paradigmatic and not a unique experience in the history of child welfare reforms. A cursory look at the ways in which state efforts to prevent child abuse create state-sponsored abuse of children will reinforce the point. And the same kind of history can be traced in the mental health system. State hospitals, intended to provide humane care for the destitute mentally ill, became "snake pits" in need of humanitarian reform in a community mental health movement that itself ultimately breeds increased homelessness and neglect as we cycle back to the original problem – a failure to respect those most in need and an inability to provide resources with respect. Having said this, we would do well to comprehend that each of these reforms was a momentary change for the better for those who immediately experienced them. The sad reality is that we quickly became more committed to the institutionalization of our reforms than to the kind of questions they were designed to elaborate: what does it mean to live in social arrangements that are just, fair and respectful?

When justice is the goal we must ask, "Who gets to decide what is just?" A critical psychology true to its own standard of fairness is a psychology of liberation in the context of mutually respectful relationships. Liberation in the context of respectful relationships is quite different than liberation in the context of individualism (where individual liberty, *per se*, is the prime value). Liberation in the context of relationships can never be perfectly known or obtained, but for an instant. It is only the moment of "change" itself, when a new comprehension, respect and pattern of behavior emerges, that liberates, albeit for an instant, before the dust of a new status quo settles on the product of reform or revolution, requiring yet another long battle against the forces of privilege. It is in the battle itself, when people cross boundaries to commune with one another in mutual respect, that one glimpses liberation.

Relationships are defined by more than content; fairness requires attention to the processes that underlie how specific decisions, behaviors, compromises and goals are arrived at. Nevertheless, procedural justice without substantive justice is like freedom without resources, the ultimate end of a heartless, albeit ordered, society (Fox, Chapter 14). Thus, although there are no final solutions to social problems, there are certain criteria by which all solutions may be judged. These criteria can be summarized in words as deceptively simple as "fairness," about which critical psychology seems to want to speak. But even as one grasps for what the critical psychologist says about fairness, there is an uneasy feeling that comfort will be found more in a process of representation that balances concern about equity with concern for freedom, than in some foreknowledge of what constitutes the quality of fairness itself in any particular context. As a practical matter, fairness may be a function more of the inefficient and messy democratic representation of more voices in the conversation, than of how a self-appointed elite group of critical psychologists go about getting our message right.

Beyond abstract ideas such as fairness and respect, a universal, context-free understanding will not be found in any statement of principles so much as in the elaboration of questions. Perfect solutions to problems in living will not be obtained, and social arrangements will only be relatively better or worse for more or fewer people for longer or shorter periods of time. While not unique to critical psychology, one element of irony its practice can illuminate is the value of questioning who (including the critical psychologist) gets to speak for whom, who gets to decide what is better or worse for whom, and how such decisions are arrived at and legitimated. These issues are never resolved, only more or less opened to question. They can be managed, if only for a time, in specific contexts. The application of mid-level theoretical constructs (Weick, 1974) and the practice of "boundary spanning" (Kelly, 1992) help create, understand and support the practices of mediating structures, i.e., settings that mediate between large social systems and individual lives. We elaborate on this point of view below.

Boundary Spanning Disciplines, Methods and Constituencies

Doing critical work can lead us, more than is typical for most disciplinary scholarly activity, to the work of people outside our own academic community. Boundary spanning (Kelly, 1992) is therefore an important part of the critical psychology project. It involves looking across disciplines, methods and communities. It means collaborating both with members of other disciplines and with the people we study and serve.

This work requires social action and political engagement with ordinary citizens if it is to be alive (i.e., crossing more than conceptual boundaries). But when we speak of it among ourselves in academia it is largely a conceptual-intellectual enterprise; it is associated with certain intellectual and social values that may be described (perhaps with a touch of self-righteousness) at the end of the twentieth century as "progressive." Progressive social values are those that emphasize inclusion, social justice, empowerment of diverse groups, equitable distribution of resources and other such notions of "fairness." There is an explicit critique of methods, construals and practices that emerge from a psychology that seems sadly destined only to perpetuate and reproduce long-standing institutionalized power relations among social groups based on categories of diagnosis, race or ethnicity, gender, sexual orientation, income and social class. Yet by the very analysis there is an implicit danger of reification lurking in the shadows of our work, making the abstract seem concrete. How can we analyze without being categorical, and be categorical without reification?

At its best, critical work is genuinely open to new (for psychology) methods of inquiry, such as various forms of qualitative and discourse analysis, without discarding mainstream quantitative methods on principle, as if they are irrevocably and inherently too sullied by association with the status quo to ever yield information of interest to a true "progressive." But new methodologies do provide fresh avenues and alternative ways to define the issues of the field. They open up the field to more voices, perspectives and means to legitimacy. They help us to span boundaries in new ways. They may even confuse rather than clarify standards and thus force new arguments on old problems. In critical psychology, as in any academic/ intellectual project, the power to frame the issues, define the terms of the debate, and set the agenda for discourse is to win the game before it begins. Thus, the critical psychologist engages in a reframing of the issues that are to be addressed by every area of psychology, in the "before the beginning" (Sarason, 1972) phase of engagement, before the actions of intervention or the data from research and scholarly analysis are presented. In a sense, critical psychology is a project that seeks to name the questions rather than to provide the answers.

*Mediating Structures, Mid-Level Constructs and Bottom-Up
Collaboration*

Above we have suggested that our own vision includes a search for constructs that avoid reification as individual, stable "traits" or as mystifying
"social systems," and an effort to participate in small (and documented)
ways in the real world of social action in the service of asking new
questions as we pursue our values and goals. If the critical psychologist is
to engage the status quo in more than theory, that is, in social action as a
participant rather than as a bystander who observes from a safe distance,
the question arises as to where such activity is to be engaged. Undoubtedly
we can address issues from the top down, as policy analysts to government,
or in mental health or social welfare departments or agencies, or in the
safety of our own offices where only certain people are able, or forced, to
seek us out. But more fruitful we think is a bottom-up participation, an
actual engagement, in local settings where we can both assist and learn
from collegial relationships with people who are themselves engaged in the
struggle for liberation. Such a stance provides several advantages for the
critical psychologist, not the least of which is learning about the uses of our
expertise in the context of not being in charge. This sort of role relationship
requires us both to listen better and to explain ourselves and our intentions
more fully.

Our own experience has sometimes led us to local settings and organizations under the control of local citizens (Rappaport, 1994; 1995; Rappaport
et al., 1975). The people who have allowed us to collaborate in such settings
have often taught us new ways to speak. They have sometimes enabled us to
observe their own acquisition of new narratives about their own lives and
communities, and to learn how they use such narratives to tell their own
stories and explore new power relations in their own community. We have
seen how participation in consumer-run mental health (Rappaport, 1993)
and other mutual help organizations (Humphreys and Rappaport, 1994),
neighborhood community arts groups, and those that express alternative
views of masculinity can create local, but nevertheless real, social changes
(Mankowski and Rappaport, 1995; Thomas and Rappaport, 1996).

In working with community-owned AIDS service and action organizations (Stewart and Weinstein, 1996), we have found that their definitions
and strategies have far outpaced professional understandings and solutions.
We have also had the experience of trying to maintain the precarious
balance between being useful and not playing expert and diagnostician in
our collaborations with an under-resourced neighborhood elementary
school (Good et al., 1996; Kloos et al., 1996). In these relationships we
have also come to appreciate the importance of social and personal
pleasure (performance, celebration, an experience of "being excellent for
others") in effective and sustained change efforts.

Karl Weick (1984; 1974), an organizational psychologist, has suggested
that those of us interested in understanding and facilitating social change

would do well to pay attention to what he called "small wins," or concrete implemented outcomes in particular times, places and settings. He has also suggested that we would do well to posit theoretical constructs that describe processes operating somewhere between large social structures and individual characteristics, what he called "mid-level constructs," and that these processes may be usefully implicated as we think about creating change in local settings (see also Geertz, 1984, on local knowledge).

Interestingly, although they emerge from a conservative political tradition, Berger and Neuhaus (1977) have discussed a similar notion in what they call "mediating structures," those settings that exist as real entities somewhere between isolated individuals and large-scale government or other social institutions. These are the places where real people live out their lives, and where both participation is accessible and its impact is visible to the participants. They cite four kinds of mediating structures – families, churches, voluntary associations and neighborhoods – as particularly appealing settings in terms of their own "empowerment" agenda. For the critical psychologist there will be much to be critical about in Berger and Neuhaus's particular description of such settings. But there is every reason to believe that these are good places to invoke such critique and to provide alternatives.

It would be no news to this audience that the idea of family is one that is steeped in traditions of heterosexist patriarchy. But in actually engaging and collaborating with the wide diversity of people who consider themselves to be families (see for example the work of the Cornell University Empowerment Group, 1989) one encounters concrete, accessible opportunities for progressive values and goals to take hold. Making known new ideas about what a family is, and providing concrete and visible documentation of alternative family settings, is one way the critical psychologist can contribute to the creation of new realities.

Similarly, if the status quo leaves spiritual and community life to be defined exclusively by traditional European and North American religious practice, then critical psychologists would do well to engage local people who are offering alternative contexts, narratives and understandings for the expression of these human values and interests. And if by voluntary organizations and neighborhoods we mean only those that inculcate the values of business or civic organizations we give up many opportunities to engage people where they actually live. One hopes that critical psychologists will be found engaging progressive community organizations that work for real social change, and that we would be documenting their work, spreading its message both in and outside of psychology, placing ourselves in role relationships that make us servants rather than masters, and using whatever expertise we think we have to help such organizations gain the resources they need to accomplish their work. These suggestions simply express, in the language of social science, ideas quite familiar to those who know the work of Saul Alinsky (1971) and a host of others who have engaged the real world of community organizing (see, e.g., Berkowitz,

1982; Hanna and Robinson, 1994; Kahn, 1994; Wineman, 1984; and many other activists). We suggest that direct, thoughtful participation by action-oriented critical psychologists, in collaborative work with local leaders, is important for learning about the circumstances we wish to change; and that the accumulation of small and documentable changes is one kind of activity that can enable the critical psychologist to test her ideas, and to modify them, in the real contexts in which our constituents live.

A Reading of the Text: Elaboration of Selected Questions

How then does this book fare when measured against the sort of critical stance we have taken here? Happily, throughout its pages many tensions and paradoxes, elaborations of taken-for-granted questions, and challenges to a social imagination are present. As might be expected from a critical approach, ironic contradictions abound. These contradictions are more likely to be useful to readers who use them for what they are – questions to be applied to one's own work – rather than for what they are not, or what they can never be: universal, timeless answers.

Some ironies and tensions are elaborated within a single chapter, others only emerge reading across chapters. Kitzinger (Chapter 13) and Wilkinson (Chapter 16) both make the elaboration of dilemmas and ironies a focus of their respective chapters. This may come from the fact that both of these authors bring experience with movements that have their own (often intersecting) histories of self-critique, contestation, and polyvalence. Harris (Chapter 2) points out the ironic benefits and losses of revisionist history. Kidder and Fine (Chapter 3) elaborate several pervasive tensions, between theory and experience for example, or between description and reinscription. Hare-Mustin and Marecek (Chapter 7) point to the not always clear difference between precision and mystification in the language and practices of psychology. Nightingale and Neilands (Chapter 5) help to find ways to make the distal and abstract proximal and lived. These are in addition to the value dilemmas and contradictions that emerge as soon as the lid of distanced objectivism is removed, some of which are highlighted in the introduction and by Prilleltensky and Nelson (Chapter 11). Still others emerge across chapters. As we have indicated above, to us this is cause for optimism rather than anxiety. Rather than glossing or deferring these ironies and paradoxes, we think a subjective and selective few deserve unpacking and elaboration, or maybe complication and mystification, as the case may be.

A good place to begin is where much of the criticism of mainstream psychology begins, with the notion of the individual. This is not a transparent notion, and is often no more transparent in the critical literature. Kitzinger (Chapter 13) elaborates a question of what we can/should do for the "suffering individual" while "waiting for the revolution." Hare-Mustin and Marecek (Chapter 7) frame their interrogation in terms of a lack of sociopolitical consciousness on the part of clinical psychologists (employing, in the process, many of the ideas and arguments that community psychologists have expounded for some time). Unfortunately, they stop short of questioning the enterprise of therapy and clinical/professional expertise as the major mode of fostering change. As recent analysis (Dawes, 1994) and recent reviews (Christiansen and Jacobson, 1994) of long-standing findings on the outcomes of expert as opposed to nonprofessional and ordinary citizen interventions have shown, there is every reason to question professional psychotherapy as the major means to individual, let alone social, change (see, e.g., Albee et al., 1988). It seems reasonable for the critical psychologist to ask if the implicit sanctification of psycho-therapy as the mode of intervention is not further reproduction of traditional and often oppressive relationships (see also Kitzinger and Perkins, 1993).

Aside from some apparent disagreement about the master's tools, and reform versus abolition of clinical practice, there is sometimes here a problematic reinscription, albeit in different ways, of the separation of "individual" and structure. The feminist and gay/lesbian/bisexual movements have had reason to interrogate this distinction. They have developed our understanding of the importance of creating small-group and community-level spaces for dialogue and personal and social interrogation, neither waiting for the revolution, accepting the professional/clinical understanding of "personal" suffering, nor writing off the personal suffering of individuals in the name of "larger" political struggle. That is, the conceptual polarization of the individual and the socio-politico-economic, the distal and the proximal, tends to be less than useful for practice, and may have little resonance to "the people" engaged in struggle for change.

Similarly, as we note above, many members of mental health consumer organizations have found both therapeutic value and social change embodied in the control of their own settings. So have many others, ranging from participants in African American churches and civil rights organizations to members of a wide variety of social action organizations where psychologists might work in collaboration without control, as partners who learn "the rules of the game" from those who actually live the battles rather than expecting others to play by our rules on our turf (Lykes et al., 1996).

On the other hand, do we really wish to dispose of consideration of the individual altogether, and what would be the price of such a decision? Parker (Chapter 18), Wilkinson (Chapter 16), Richardson and Fowers (Chapter 17), Kidder and Fine (Chapter 3), and Burman (Chapter 9) all offer compelling reasons to consider the specific, the localized, the lived, and the ideographic. There are dangers in positing "the individual" as an abstract, self-contained, universal entity opposed to the totalizing state (or economy or discourse). Such conceptualizations leave little room for understanding the variety of strategies of resistance, subversion, or oppression. What is needed is some theorizing about the individual as social actor, theorizing that takes account of post-structuralist, feminist, discursive, and hermeneutic insights, if not adopting entirely any of these paradigms. If our goals include democracy, empowerment, and "self-determination," then we have to reckon with the fact that many people not only participate in, but take pleasure in, various forms of their own oppression (e.g., Foucault, 1978; Gramsci, 1971), for example, and yet also that some people and groups have managed to appropriate and subvert forms of oppression to create spaces for liberation (e.g., Davis and Kennedy, 1989; Champagne, 1995). In other words, in the post-industrial, post/colonial world, it is very difficult to identify locations of oppression and liberation (e.g., Champagne, 1995; Duggan, 1992; Foucault, 1978; hooks, 1990; Spivak, 1990).

Another apparent tension, one that Celia Kitzinger again elaborates to an extent, is our relationship to empiricism. Another not too transparent term, empiricism is usually linked, as it is in some of the chapters here, to positivism. The empirical imperative has been rightly interrogated, on political and epistemological grounds, as a particularly powerful and insidious form of oppression and the constitution of marginal identities. Yet, there are some inconsistencies here. First, here we are, all in the business of psychology, many of us doing research, and generally assuming that we should use psychology's authority and legitimacy as leverage to bring about social change. We all also have the privilege of writing, thinking, and critiquing for a living because of the money, resources, and status that the empiricist project has gained psychology (even if the gravy train days are over). We are sitting squarely in the master's house. This may not pose a particular problem for many of us, there is, after all, something to be said for subversion from within, or for attempting to appropriate structures and resources for our presumably more transformative ends. But there is more to it. As Kitzinger points out, when we look back at psychology's more successful efforts for social change (if only reform or tolerance), we find, often, that they are creditable to empiricists. Furthermore, many of the authors in this text were willing to employ an objectivist standpoint for critique of past and present assumptions and research.

Part of the problem here comes from the critical position, and part from a lack of clarity of terms. Kidder and Fine (Chapter 3) and Parker (Chapter 18) offer more positive (as opposed to positivistic) ways out of this apparent dilemma, as do in certain ways Moghaddam and Studer (Chapter 12), Burman (Chapter 9), and others. Certainly we wish to be as honest and accurate as possible in our discussions and research. Certainly we would rather make an attempt to see if our ideas have any relevance "in the world." Some accounts are less careful, reflexive, or trustworthy than others, aren't they? Is grand theorizing sufficient? Is it less oppressive and reifying? Marx made mistakes that had to do with not checking his facts.

It is not our aim here to preserve the positivist-empiricist project. Rather, we wish to point out that we apparently have different relationships to, and different understandings of the meaning of, "empiricism." In fact, our argument is perhaps that the issue is not about whether or not we want to concern ourselves over the quality and trustworthiness of our and others' research, but rather about questions of whose knowledge gets to count, what are the terms of discourse and validity that circumscribe legitimacy, what we do with contradictory accounts and "facts." We should ask if we have made the positioning behind our questions and approaches as clear as possible, if we have sufficiently situated our interpretations, and if we are willing to subject ourselves and our own little culture to the same "objective" scrutiny we give our "subjects" in order to understand better how we construct our "findings" (e.g., Bourdieu, 1990). These are some questions that are as applicable to critical psychologists as to "mainstream positivist empiricists."

Finally, something that becomes a tension for many of us is the matter of to whom we are speaking. Throughout this book, critical psychology is framed as a dialogue between us (critical psychologists) and "mainstream psychology." At other times, the audience appears to be ourselves. Noticeably, none of these chapters seems to be addressed to "the people" or the "oppressed communities" that many profess to be their primary concern. The matter of our audience – to whom we are speaking – is not a small one, as it tends to dictate the language we use, the agenda, and the terms of discussion. Do we, for instance, want the terms of debate and the domains of our theorizing to be limited by the useful but by no means complete criticism of mainstream psychology? In this chapter, we have advocated a self-reflexive dialogue among ourselves (or even about whether there is an "ourselves" at all), which Harris (Chapter 2), Kitzinger (Chapter 13), Richardson and Fowers (Chapter 17), and Wilkinson (Chapter 16), among others, offer and usefully exploit. However, although we cannot without hypocrisy disavow academic exercises, purely critical engagements carry the danger of hovering over, rather than actively and positively engaging, the status quo that we putatively seek to transform. In other words, we should be more than critics.

As Prilleltensky and Nelson point out about community psychology, there has been considerably more research (and we would add, rhetoric) than action. That is certainly true, but we are suggesting more than a call to action. Consider how differently we would speak, what different priorities we might have, and how differently we might relate to our own (and mainstream psychology's) rhetoric if we spoke with "the people" and "oppressed communities" rather than to ourselves or other psychologists. For starters, they might cease to be the abstract placeholders of "the people" and "oppressed communities." We might also begin to see that our own practices and promises are sometimes naive, elitist, romantic, reifying, and/or obfuscating. We may also discover our own prescriptive imperialism. Our struggle for legitimacy and impact would be different if instead of being aimed at journal editors, department heads, and colleagues it were directed at those people and communities we profess to champion.

There is a more radical meaning to Miller's (1969) call to "give psychology away" than merely colloquially phrased debriefings and research summaries. Miller meant to share the process and not simply the results of our inquiry and interventions. This aligns well with Freire's (1970; 1990) goal of *conscientization*, a process that invites learners (which would include the putative educator) to critically engage the world, questions and knowledge about it, and the creators of that knowledge. That is, there is something potentially liberating to be gained from making our work available to the interrogation of "those people" whose circumstances we are trying to change, something for "us" and something for "them." As Giroux and McClaren (1991) succinctly point out, knowledge must be made meaningful to be made critical.

This is not to imply some romantic notion about the wisdom of the people, nor is it meant to devalue theoretical, critical and empirical work. But we do believe that choices of language and audience simultaneously provide and take away possibilities, different intelligibilities arise, different interests are structuring questions, different social relations are articulated and affirmed, and different systems of representation are produced and legitimated. Beyond those considerations, however, is our belief that critical psychologists need to create a "public language" (Giroux, 1992) that is deacademicized, compelling, and useful. Such a language would invite questions about how knowledges are (de)valued and hierarchically strati- fied, and undermine the relationship of psychologists to their "subjects" as subordinates or even consumers. And, because we *do* value theory and critical work, it is our belief that psychologists and other critical theorists should, as Barbara Kruger (1993) puts it, "cross the moats of academia" and speak a pleasurable, powerful, and evocative language of change; this might have the effect of simultaneously decentering ourselves as experts and preventing us from becoming peripheral, elitist, and superfluous to the struggle. It may also relieve the sense of impotence that Harris (Chapter 2) suggests haunts us as psychologists cum social activists.

After that lengthy improvisation on themes suggested by chapter authors, we have noted a few contentions and exceptions that in the interests of elaboration we want to briefly mention. We appreciated Laura Brown's (Chapter 4) injection of polemics into the heretofore constrained and overly cautious discussion of APA ethics. Still, we wish she had more fully theorized the implications of her vision. We wonder if there is not more potential for reproduction than for reformation in such an expanded domain of inquiry for the APA. The idea of a reformed or even trans- formed APA entering our personal lives and thoughts makes us as uncomfortable now as it would have in the 1950s. As might already be apparent, we are both more hopeful about postmodernism and Foucault and less hopeful about hermeneutics as a defining paradigm than are Richardson and Fowers (Chapter 17). It is worth noting the contrasting readings of Foucault presented by Parker (Chapter 18) and Richardson and Fowers (Chapter 17). (But we will resist providing our own reading here.) Parker (Chapter 18) has done a great service by his clear introduction of discourse theories, but in working with and representing people and communities, we find it worth remembering (paraphrasing Jameson, 1989) that all is not text. Although these comments reflect our values and theoretical positions, they are offered in the interest more of keeping questions on the table than of settling them in some kind of finality.

But, finally, as we warned, we are taking advantage of our own (literal or literary) positioning in taking the last word here. And as one of the editors of this volume has himself said elsewhere, "These are high standards for the discourse on oppression. Our own work only begins to answer some of its requirements. Nevertheless, we think it necessary to articulate a vision and principles to guide our efforts" (Prilleltensky and Gonick, 1994: 169).

Conclusions

Critical psychology is an ambitious attempt to speak about how we understand psychology in relationship to ourselves (the community of psychologists), our methods and ways of conducting our business (philosophy, methodology and interventions), and our social arrangements with other disciplines and with the larger society (our role relationships, sources of knowledge and legitimacy). Any attempt to speak about such things tends to be meta-analytic; that is, the critical psychological attitude tends to distance us from colleagues engaged in the activity of doing psychology so as to "comment on" those activities. Yet that same attitude may help us to think more directly about our relationship to the people who participate in our research and practice. Are they our subjects, our clients, or our collaborators? If collaborators, are they co-workers in defining the terms of our collaboration? While these matters should be important to doing critical psychology, they are not unique to it.

One challenge for those who would do critical work is to avoid the temptation of self-righteousness. By definition, critical psychology cannot be something most members of a particular disciplinary community do as their primary work at any moment in time, although it is theoretically possible for an entire profession or discipline to adopt the values and goals of progressive politics as the standard by which to make judgments about the worth of their field. It is also possible for people to engage in such work as a legitimate part of their disciplinary activities at least some of the time.

For those who do critical psychology as their primary work there is some danger that we may begin to see ourselves as an elite or "enlightened" minority, with some sort of special awareness lacking in others within the traditions of our own discipline. Critical work is of course not limited to psychology. It emerges in many human endeavors including most academic disciplines, and quite regularly in the social and behavioral sciences and the humanities, as well as in the professions of law, medicine and social work. It shows itself most often among a self-described politically motivated, and usually relatively small, minority within any particular intellectual community.

There is a long tradition of intellectual and social criticism in and of the social, behavioral and medical sciences. In a sense, critical psychology wishes to join in that tradition. Many of the ideas and concerns that have been raised by powerful observers and theorists (e.g., Goffman, Foucault, Szasz) who would not have described themselves as "critical psychologists" can be understood as placing the observer on the side of the outsider, the least powerful, the "inmate" (Jones and Fowles, 1984), in a way that changes our relationship to those we wish to understand or assist. Currently, many of the views of people who consider themselves to be feminists, or aligned with the interests of gay, lesbian and bisexual people, ethnic and racial minorities, or mental health consumer organizations (Chamberlin, 1978), can be embraced by those who do "critical work." These concerns are not easily confined to the boundaries of a single discipline, let alone a single subdiscipline of psychology. Nor are they confined to "academics."

Despite such an avowed interest, we must take note of the very real issue of representation. Perhaps it merely (?) reflects the demographics of academic psychology and the perseverant effects of racism in education, but we wonder at the absence of a chapter here on race and ethnicity issues inside and outside psychology (as if they were separate). We cannot say with certainty whether or not any of the chapter authors are people of color (as we can be sure that women and a gay/lesbian perspective were represented), but issues relating to race and ethnicity in the United States, to the extent they were mentioned, seem not to have been presented by anyone with embodied experience of it. This raises the issue of people being absent from the process of their own representation, or just being absent altogether, in critical psychology. Whatever the reasons for this absence here, it does communicate something in this age of scientistic complicity in institutional racism (Sternberg, 1995). Perhaps it is necessary to refer readers out of the critical psychology canon to thinkers like bell hooks (e.g., 1984; 1990; 1992), Cornel West (e.g., 1994) or Audre Lorde (1984), or perhaps at least to current books within psychology (e.g., Trickett et al., 1994; Wilson, 1995). It is an ironic absence given the extent to which psychology has participated in, and creatively perpetrated all on its own, the oppression and colonialist representation of people of color.

This raises another, perhaps paradoxical problem with representation. We understand that there are many good (primarily political) reasons to think, talk, and write about people – including ourselves – in terms of a sexual identity, a race, a gender, or a class position. Indeed, we do so ourselves. Our culture makes decisions and allotments based on these distinctions, and our systems of government often dictate that people organize themselves around one of these categories. But people are all simultaneously gendered, raced, classed, and sexually "oriented" (and aged, and healthed, and cultured, etc.). And the intersections of these distinctions rather unpredictably create lives and circumstances that are inadequately captured by "gay" or "woman" or "black" (e.g., Tessman, 1995). This is more than a question of identity politics versus a politics of difference, though it is related. It also has to do with the ways in which psychology uncritically adopts the category or checklist approach of government and society, and may therefore reinscribe ghettoization, marginalization, or reification of "identities." For critical psychology, it may also help to obscure a real understanding of the mechanisms of oppression by luring us into the "hierarchy of oppression" ideology (see hooks, 1984; Lorde, 1984). Perhaps this is itself a sufficiently ironic point on which to conclude our critical look at critical psychology.

Note

Order of authorship was determined in part by history (Rappaport was invited to write the chapter, and he asked Stewart to collaborate). Benefits to the authors turned out to be quite mutual – the product of lengthy discussions, shared drafts and emergent thoughts. We have both profited from sharing our individual and intellectual histories in the context of a critical look at critical psychology. Credit, or disdain, should be attributed more to the collaboration than to either individual author.

References

Abramovitch, R., Freedman, J. L., Thoden, K., and Nikolich, C. (1991). Children's Capacity to Consent to Participation in Psychological Research: Empirical Findings. *Child Development, 62,* 1100–1109.

Abrams, D., and Hogg, M. A. (1990). The Context of Discourse: Let's Not Throw Out the Baby with the Bathwater. *Philosophical Psychology, 3*(2), 219–225.

Adlam, D., Henriques, J., Rose, N., Salfield, A., Venn, C., and Walkerdine, V. (1977). Psychology, Ideology and the Human Subject. *Ideology and Consciousness, 1,* 5–56.

Adorno, T. W. (1973). *Negative Dialectics.* New York: Seabury.

Afshar, H., and Maynard, M. (Eds.). (1994). *The Dynamics of "Race" and Gender.* London: Taylor and Francis.

Ahrons, C. R. (1994). *The Good Divorce.* New York: HarperCollins.

Alatas, S. H. (1977). *The Myth of the Lazy Native.* London: Frank Cass.

Albee, G. W. (1986). Toward a Just Society: Lessons from Observations on the Primary Prevention of Psychopathology. *American Psychologist, 41,* 891–898.

Albee, G. W. (1988). Introduction. In P. A. Bronstein and K. Quina (Eds.), *Teaching a Psychology of People: Resources for Gender and Sociocultural Awareness* (pp. vii–x). Washington, DC: American Psychological Association.

Albee, G. W. (1990). The Futility of Psychotherapy. *Journal of Mind and Behavior, 11*(3,4), 369–384.

Albee, G. W. (Ed.). (1996). Social Darwinism and Political Models of Mental/Emotional Problems. Special issue of *Journal of Primary Prevention, 17*(1).

Albee, G. W., Joffe, J. M., and Dusenbury, L. A. (Eds.). (1988). *Prevention, Powerlessness, and Politics: Readings on Social Change.* Beverly Hills, CA: Sage.

Alberti, R. E. (Ed.). (1977). *Assertiveness: Innovations, Applications, Issues.* San Luis Obispo, CA: Impact.

Alinder, G. (1972). Gay Liberation Meets the Shrinks. In K. Jay and A. Young (Eds.), *Out of the Closets: Voices of Gay Liberation* (pp. 141–145). New York: Harcourt Brace Jovanovich.

Alinsky, S. D. (1971). *Rules for Radicals.* New York: Random House.

Alldred, P. (1996). "Fit to Parent"? Developmental Psychology and Non-Traditional Families. In E. Burman, P. Alldred, C. Bewley, B. Goldberg, C. Heenan, D. Marks, J. Marshall, K. Taylor, R. Ullah, and S. Warner (Eds.), *Challenging Women: Psychology's Exclusions, Feminist Possibilities* (pp. 141–159). Buckingham: Open University Press.

Allport, F. H. (1924). *Social Psychology.* Boston: Houghton Mifflin.

Allport, G. W. (1985). The Historical Background of Social Psychology. In G. Lindzey and E. Aronson (Eds.), *Handbook of Social Psychology* (3rd edn, Vol. 1, pp. 1–46). New York: Random House.

American Association of University Women (1991). *Shortchanging Girls, Shortchanging America.* Washington, DC: AAUW.

American Psychiatric Association (1987). *Diagnostic and Statistical Manual of Mental Disorders* (3rd edn, revised). Washington, DC: American Psychiatric Association.

American Psychiatric Association (1994). *Diagnostic and Statistical Manual of Mental Disorders* (4th edn). Washington, DC: American Psychiatric Association.

American Psychological Association (1953). *Ethical Standards for Psychologists: A Summary of Ethical Principles.* Washington, DC: American Psychological Association.

American Psychological Association (1977). Revised Ethical Standards of Psychologists. *APA Monitor*, March, 22–23.

American Psychological Association (1992). Ethical Principles of Psychologists and Code of Conduct. *American Psychologist, 47*, 1597–1611.

Anastasi, A. (1988). *Psychological Testing* (6th edn). New York: Macmillan.

Andeneas, A. (1995). . . . And What About the Sacred Cows? In B. Arve-Parás (Ed.), *Building Family Welfare: Contributions from a Seminar on Family, Gender and Welfare Policies in the Nordic Countries* (pp. 79–86). Stockholm: Nordsteds tryckeri.

Andeneas, A. (forthcoming). Theories of Development from the Perspective of the Children, Their Parents and the Scientists. *Researching Early Childhood, 3*, 1.

Anderson, C. A. (1989). Temperature and Aggression: Ubiquitous Effects of Heat on Occurrence of Human Violence. *Psychological Bulletin, 106*, 74–96.

Anderson, C. C., and Travis, L. D. (1983). *Psychology and the Liberal Consensus*. Waterloo, Ontario: Wilfrid Laurier University.

Anderson, C. M., Hogarty, G. E., and Reiss, D. J. (1986). *Schizophrenia and the Family: A Practitioner's Guide to Psycho Education and Management*. New York: Guilford.

Andreasen, N., Flaum, M., Swayze, V., O'Leary, D. S., Alliger, R., Cohen, G., Ehrhardt, J., and Yuh, W. T. C. (1993). Intelligence and Brain Structure in Normal Individuals. *American Journal of Psychiatry, 150*, 130–134.

Aries, P. (1962). *Centuries of Childhood: A Social History of Family Life*. New York: Vintage.

Aronson, E. (1990). Applying Social Psychology to Desegregation and Energy Conservation. *Personality and Social Psychology Bulletin, 16*, 118–132.

Aronson, E., and Gonzalez, M. H. (1988). Desegregation, Jigsaw, and the Mexican-American Experience. In P. A. Katz and D. A. Taylor (Eds.), *Eliminating Racism: Profiles in Controversy* (pp. 301–314). New York: Plenum.

Aronson, E., Stephan, C., Sikes, J., Blaney, N., and Snapp, M. (1978). *The Jigsaw Classroom*. Beverly Hills, CA: Sage.

Asch, S. E. (1951). Effects of Group Pressure upon the Modification and Distortion of Judgments. In H. S. Guetzkow (Ed.), *Groups, Leadership, and Man: Research in Human Relations* (pp. 177–190). Pittsburgh: Carnegie Press.

Ash, M. G., and Woodward, W. R. (1987). *Psychology in Twentieth-Century Thought and Society*. Cambridge, MA: Cambridge University Press.

Atkinson, J. M., and Heritage, J. C. (Eds.). (1984). *Structures of Social Action: Studies in Conversation Analysis*. Cambridge: Cambridge University Press.

Atkinson, R. L., Atkinson, R. C., and Hilgard, E. R. (1983). *Introduction to Psychology* (8th edn). New York: Harcourt Brace Jovanovich.

Augoustinos, M., and Walker, I. (1995). *Social Cognition: An Integrated Introduction*. London: Sage.

Austin, J. L. (1962). *How To Do Things with Words*. Oxford: Clarendon Press.

Avineri, S., and De-Shalit, A. (Eds.). (1992). *Communitarianism and Individualism*. New York: Oxford University Press.

Avis, J. M. (1991). Power Politics in Therapy with Women. In T. J. Goodrich (Ed.), *Women and Power: Perspectives for Family Therapy* (pp. 183–200). New York: Norton.

Baier, K. (1973). The Concept of Value. In E. Laszlo and J. B. Wilbur (Eds.), *Value Theory in Philosophy and Social Science* (pp. 1–11). New York: Oxford University Press.

Bakan, D. (1966). *The Duality of Human Existence: An Essay on Psychology and Religion*. Chicago: Rand McNally.

Balcazar, F., Mathews, R. M., Francisco, V. T., Fawcett, S. B., and Seekins, T. (1994). The Empowerment Process in Four Advocacy Organizations of People with Disabilities. *Rehabilitation Psychology, 39*(3), 189–203.

Barclay, H. (1982). *People without Government: An Anthropology of Anarchism*. London: Kahn and Averill.

Baritz, L. (1974). *The Servants of Power: A History of the Use of Social Science in American Industry*. Westport, CT: Greenwood.

Baron, R. A. (1972). Aggression as a Function of Ambient Temperature and Prior Anger Arousel. *Journal of Personality and Social Psychology, 21,* 183–189.

Baron, R. A., and Richardson, D. (1994). *Human Aggression.* New York: Plenum.

Barratt, B. B. (1993). *Psychoanalysis and the Postmodern Impulse: Knowing and Being since Freud's Psychology.* Baltimore: Johns Hopkins University Press.

Barthes, R. (1972). *Mythologies* (A. Lavers, Trans.). New York: Hill and Wang (original work published 1957).

Barthes, R. (1977). *Image-Music-Text.* London: Fontana.

Baumeister, R. F. (1995). The Personal Story of an Interpersonal Psychologist. In G. G. Brannigan and M. R. Merrens (Eds.), *The Social Psychologists: Research Adventures* (pp. 74–96). New York: McGraw-Hill.

Beals, K. L., Smith, C. L., and Dodd, S. M. (1984). Brain Size, Cranial Morphology, Climate, and Time Machines. *Current Anthropology, 25,* 301–330.

Becker, D., and Lira, E. (Eds.). (1990). *Derechos Humanos: Todo es Segun el Dolor con que se Mira* [Human Rights: The Pain Colors Everything]. Santiago: Instituto Latinoamericano de asistencia social y derechos humanos.

Bell, D. (1993). *Communitarianism and its Critics.* Oxford: Clarendon.

Bell, R., and Harper, L. (1977). *Child Effects on Adults.* Hillsdale, NJ: Lawrence Erlbaum.

Belle, D. (1994). Attempting to Comprehend the Lives of Low-Income Women. In C. Franz and A. Stewart (Eds.), *Women Creating Lives* (pp. 37–50). Boulder, CO: Westview Press.

Bem, S. L. (1974). The Measurement of Psychological Androgyny. *Journal of Consulting and Clinical Psychology, 42,* 155–162.

Bem, S. L., Martyna, W., and Watson, C. (1976). Sex Typing and Androgyny. Further Explorations of the Expressive Domain. *Journal of Personality and Social Psychology, 34,* 1016–1023.

Benbow, C. P., and Stanley, J. C. (1980). Sex Differences in Mathematical Ability: Fact or Artifact? *Science, 210,* 1262–1264.

Benjamin, J. (1988). *The Bonds of Love: Psychoanalytic Theory, Feminism, and the Problem of Domination.* New York: Pantheon.

Bennett, C. C., Anderson, L. S., Cooper, S., Hassol, L., Klein, D. C., and Rosenblum, G. (1966). *Community Psychology: A Report of the Boston Conference on the Education of Psychologists for Community Mental Health.* Boston: Boston University Press.

Bennett, E. M. (Ed.). (1987). *Social Intervention: Theory and Practice.* Lewiston, NY: Edwin Mellen Press.

Berg, I. K., and Jaya, A. (1993). Different and Same: Family Therapy with Asian-American Families. *Journal of Marital and Family Therapy, 19,* 31–38.

Berger, P. L., and Luckman, T. (1966). *The Social Construction of Reality: A Treatise in the Sociology of Knowledge.* Garden City, NY: Doubleday.

Berger, P. L., and Neuhaus, R. H. (1977). *To Empower People: The Role of Mediating Structures in Public Policy.* Washington, DC: American Enterprise Institute for Public Policy Research.

Berkowitz, L. (1962). *Aggression: A Social Psychological Analysis.* New York: McGraw-Hill.

Berkowitz, L. (1993). *Aggression: Its Causes, Consequences, and Control.* New York: McGraw-Hill.

Berkowitz, W. R. (1982). *Community Impact: Creating Grassroots Change in Hard Times.* Cambridge, MA: Schenkman.

Berlin, I. (1984). Two Concepts of Liberty. In M. J. Sandel (Ed.), *Liberalism and its Critics* (pp. 15–36). New York: New York University Press.

Berman, J. S., and Norton, N. C. (1985). Does Professional Training Make a Therapist More Effective? *Psychological Bulletin, 98,* 401–407.

Bernstein, R. (1976). *The Restructuring of Social and Political Theory.* Philadelphia: University of Pennsylvania Press.

Berrill, K. (1992). Anti-Gay Violence and Victimization in the United States: An Overview. In G. Herek and K. Berrill (Eds.), *Hate Crimes: Confronting Violence against Lesbians and Gay Men* (pp. 19–45). London: Sage.

Berry, J. W., Poortinga, Y. H., Segall, M., and Dasen, P. (1992). *Cross-Cultural Psychology: Theory, Method, and Application*. New York: Cambridge University Press.

Bersoff, D. N. (1994). Explicit Ambiguity: The 1992 Ethics Code as Oxymoron. *Professional Psychology: Research and Practice, 25*, 382–387.

Bettelheim, B., and Janowitz, M. (1950). *Dynamics of Prejudice*. New York: Harper.

Bhaskar, R. (1989). *Reclaiming Reality: A Critical Introduction to Contemporary Philosophy*. London: Verso.

Billig, M. (1976). *Social Psychology and Intergroup Relations*. London: Academic Press.

Billig, M. (1991). *Ideology and Opinions*. London: Sage.

Blanchard, R., Steiner, B. W., and Clemmensen, L. H. (1985). Gender Dysphoria, Gender Reorientation and the Management of Transsexualism. *Journal of Consulting and Clinical Psychology, 53*, 295–304.

Bloch, D. (1988). The Partnership of Dr. Biomedicine and Dr. Psychosocial. *Family Systems Medicine, 6*, 2–4.

Bloch, I. (1909). *The Sexual Life of Our Time*. London: Heinemann.

Bloom, C., Gitter, A., Gutwill, S., Kogel, L., and Vaphiropoulos, L. (1994). *Eating Disorders: A Feminist Psychoanalytic Model*. New York: Basic Books.

Bogardus, E. S. (1925). Measuring Social Distance. *Journal of Applied Sociology, 9*, 299–308.

Bohan, Janis S. (1992a). Prologue: Re-Viewing Psychology, Re-Placing Women – An End Searching for a Means. In Janis S. Bohan (Ed.), *Seldom Seen, Rarely Heard: Women's Place in Psychology* (pp. 9–53). Boulder, CO: Westview Press.

Bohan, Janis S. (Ed.). (1992b). *Seldom Seen, Rarely Heard: Women's Place in Psychology*. Boulder, CO: Westview Press.

Bollen, K. A. (1989). *Structural Equations with Latent Variables*. New York: Wiley.

Bond, M. (1995). Prevention and the Ecology of Sexual Harassment: Creating Empowering Climates. *Prevention in Human Services, 12*, 147–173.

Bonsignore, J. J. (1994). *Law and Multinationals: An Introduction to Political Economy*. Englewood Cliffs, NJ: Prentice-Hall.

Bonsignore, J. J., Katsh, E., D'errico, P., Pipkin, R. M., Arons, S., and Rifkin, J. (Eds.). (1994). *Before the Law: An Introduction to Legal Process* (5th edn). Boston: Houghton Mifflin.

Bordo, S. (1985). Anorexia Nervosa: Psychopathology as the Crystallization of Culture. *The Philosophical Forum, 17*, 73–103.

Boudon, R. (1977). *Effets Pervers et Ordre Social* [Perverse Effects and Social Order]. Paris: Presse Universitaire de France.

Bourdieu, P. (1990). *In Other Words: Essays towards a Reflexive Sociology*. Stanford, CA. Stanford University Press.

Boyd-Franklin, N. (1989). *Black Families in Therapy*. New York: Guilford.

Boyden, J. (1990). Childhood and the Policy Makers: A Comparative Perspective on the Globalization of Childhood. In A. James and A. Prout (Eds.), *Constructing and Reconstructing Childhood: Contemporary Issues in the Sociological Study of Childhood* (pp. 185–215). Basingstoke: Falmer Press.

Boyte, H. C., and Riessman, F. (Eds.). (1986). *The New Populism: The Politics of Empowerment*. Philadelphia: Temple University Press.

Bradley, B. (1989). *Visions of Infancy*. Oxford: Polity, Blackwell.

Braginsky, B. M., and Braginsky, D. D. (1974). *Mainstream Psychology: A Critique*. New York: Holt, Rinehart, and Winston.

Braginsky, D. D. (1985). Psychology: Handmaiden to Society. In S. Koch and D. E. Leary (Eds.), *A Century of Psychology as Science* (pp. 880–891). New York: McGraw-Hill.

Brainerd, C. (1973). Judgements and Explanations as Criteria for the Process of Cognitive Structures. *Psychological Bulletin, 79*(3), 172–179.

Brannigan, G. G., and Merrens, M. R. (1995). *The Social Psychologists: Research Adventures*. New York: McGraw-Hill.

Breggin, P., and Breggin, G. R. (1994). *Talking Back to Prozac*. New York: St. Martin's Press.

Brislin, R. W. (1990). *Applied Cross-Cultural Psychology*. Newbury Park, CA: Sage.

Bronstein, P. A., and Quina, K. (1988). *Teaching a Psychology of People: Resources for Gender and Sociocultural Awareness.* Washington, DC: American Psychological Association.

Broughton, J. (1986). The Psychology, History and Ideology of the Self. In K. Larsen (Ed.), *Dialectics and Ideology in Psychology* (pp. 128–164). Norwood, NJ: Ablex.

Broughton, J. (Ed.). (1987). *Critical Theories of Psychological Development.* New York: Plenum Press.

Broughton, J. (1988). The Masculine Authority of the Cognitive. In B. Inhelder (Ed.), *Piaget Today* (pp. 111–124). London: Erlbaum.

Brown, L. S. (1982). Ethical Issues in Feminist Therapy: What is a Feminist Ethic? Paper presented at the *First Advanced Feminist Therapy Institute*, Vail, CO, May.

Brown, L. S. (1984). Power and Responsibility: Developing Ethical Guidelines for Feminist Therapists. Paper presented at the *Third Advanced Feminist Therapy Institute*, Oakland, CA, March.

Brown, L. S. (1985). Power, Responsibility, Boundaries: Ethical Issues for the Lesbian-Feminist Therapist. *Lesbian Ethics, 1,* 30–45.

Brown, L. S. (1989). New Voices, New Visions: Toward a Lesbian/Gay Paradigm for Psychology. *Psychology of Women Quarterly, 13,* 445–458.

Brown, L. S. (1991). Anti-Racism as an Ethical Imperative: An Example from Feminist Therapy. *Ethics and Behavior, 1,* 113–127.

Brown, L. S. (1992). While Waiting for the Revolution: The Case for a Lesbian Feminist Psychotherapy, *Feminism & Psychology, 2*(2), 239–253.

Brown, L. S. (1993). Anti-Domination Training as a Central Component of Diversity in Clinical Psychology Education. *The Clinical Psychologist, 16,* 83–87.

Brown, L. S. (1994). *Subversive Dialogues: Theory in Feminist Therapy.* New York: Basic Books.

Brown, Lyn Mikel, and Gilligan, Carol (1992). *Meeting at the Crossroads: Women's Psychology and Girls' Development.* Cambridge, MA: Harvard University Press.

Brown, Lyn Mikel, and Gilligan, Carol (1993). Meeting at the Crossroads: Women's Psychology and Girls' Development. *Feminism & Psychology, 3*(1), 11–35.

Brown, P. M. (1973). *Radical Psychology.* New York: Harper and Row.

Bruner, J. (1986). *Actual Minds, Possible Worlds.* Cambridge, MA: Harvard University Press.

Bulhan, H. A. (1985). *Franz Fanon and the Psychology of Oppression.* New York: Plenum Press.

Bunch, C. (1987). *Passionate Politics.* New York: St. Martin's Press.

Burke, M. (1995). *Boys in Blue.* London: Cassell.

Burman, E. (1990). Differing with Deconstruction: A Feminist Critique. In I. Parker and J. Shotter (Eds.), *Deconstructing Social Psychology* (pp. 208–220). London: Routledge.

Burman, E. (1991). Power, Gender and Developmental Psychology. *Feminism & Psychology, 1*(1), 141–154.

Burman, E. (1992). Feminism and Discourse in Developmental Psychology: Power, Subjectivity and Interpretation. *Feminism & Psychology, 2*(1), 45–60.

Burman, E. (1993). Beyond Discursive Relativism: Power and Subjectivity in Developmental Psychology. In H. Stam, L. Mos, W. Thorngate, and B. Caplan (Eds.), *Recent Trends in Theoretical Psychology* (Vol. III, pp. 433–440). New York: Springer.

Burman, E. (1994). *Deconstructing Developmental Psychology.* London: Routledge.

Burman, E. (1995a). What is It? Masculinity and Femininity in the Cultural Representation of Childhood. In S. Wilkinson and C. Kitzinger (Eds.), *Feminism and Discourse* (pp. 49–67). London: Routledge.

Burman, E. (1995b). The Abnormal Distribution of Development: Policies for Southern Women and Children. *Gender, Place and Culture, 2*(1), 21–36.

Burman, E. (1996). Introduction: Contexts, Contests and Interventions. In Erica Burman, Pam Alldred, Catherine Bewley, Brenda Goldberg, Colleen Heenan, Deborah Marks, Jane Marshall, Karen Taylor, Robina Ullah, and Sam Warner (Eds.), *Challenging Women: Psychology's Exclusions, Feminist Possibilities* (pp. 1–16). Buckingham and Bristol, PA: Open University Press.

Burman, E. (forthcoming). Dis/Continuities in Interpretive and Textual Approaches in Developmental Psychology. *Human Development.*

Burman, E., Aitken, G., Alldred, P., Allwood, R., Billington, T., Goldberg, B., Gordo-López, A. J., Heenan, C., Marks, D., and Warner, S. (1996). *Psychology Discourse Practice: From Regulation to Resistance.* London: Taylor and Francis.

Burns, D. D. (1989). *The Feeling Good Handbook.* New York: William Morrow.

Burr, V. (1995). *An Introduction to Social Constructionism.* London: Routledge.

Burstow, B., and Weitz, D. (Eds.). (1988). *Shrink Resistant: The Struggle against Psychiatry in Canada.* Vancouver, BC: New Star Books.

Cain, D. P., and Vanderwolf, C. H. (1990). A Critique of Rushton on Race, Brain Size, and Intelligence. *Personality and Individual Differences, 11,* 777–784.

Camhi, L. (1993). Stealing Femininity: Department Store Kleptomania as Sexual Disorder. *Differences, 5*(1), 26–50.

Cantril, H. (1940). *The Invasion from Mars.* Princeton, NJ: Princeton University Press.

Caplan, N., and Nelson, S. D. (1973). On Being Useful: The Nature and Consequences of Psychological Research on Social Problems. *American Psychologist, 28,* 199–211.

Caplan, Paula J. (1991). Delusional Dominating Personality Disorder (DDPD). *Feminism & Psychology, 1*(1), 171–174.

Caplan, Paula J., and Hall-McCorquodale, I. (1985). Mother-Blaming in Major Clinical Journals. *American Journal of Orthopsychiatry, 55,* 345–353.

Caplan, Paula J., McCurdy-Myers, Joan, and Gans, Maureen (1992). Should "Premenstrual Syndrome" be Called a Psychiatric Abnormality? *Feminism & Psychology, 2*(1), 27–44.

Cartwright, D. (1979). Contemporary Social Psychology in Historical Perspective. *Social Psychology Quarterly, 1,* 82–93.

Cavaliere, F. (1995). Psychology-and-Law Field Well-Positioned for Growth. *APA Monitor,* August, 43.

Cernovsky, Z. Z. (1991). Intelligence and Race: Further Comments on J.P. Rushton's Work. *Psychological Reports, 68,* 481–482.

Cernovsky, Z. Z. (1992). J.P. Rushton's Aggregational Errors in Racial Psychology. Paper presented at the *25th International Congress of Psychology,* Brussels, Belgium, July.

Cernovsky, Z. Z. (1994). Rushton's Defenders and their Hasty Rejection of the Null Hypothesis. *Journal of Black Psychology, 20,* 325–333.

Chamberlin, J. (1977). *On Our Own.* London: MIND Publications.

Chamberlin, J. (1978). *On Our Own: Patient Controlled Alternatives to the Mental Health System.* New York: McGraw-Hill.

Chamberlin, J. (1990). The Ex-Patients' Movement: Where We've Been and Where We're Going. *Journal of Mind and Behaviour, 11,* 323–336.

Champagne, J. (1995). *The Ethics of Marginality: A New Approach to Gay Studies.* Minneapolis: University of Minnesota Press.

Chavis, D. M., and Wolff, T. (1993). *Public Hearing: Community Psychology's Failed Commitment to Social Change: Ten Demandments for Action.* Public meeting held at the *Biennial Conference of the Society for Community Research and Action,* Division 27 of APA, Williamsburg, VA, June.

Chesler, P. (1972). *Women and Madness.* Garden City, NY: Doubleday.

Chesler, P. (1989a). *Women and Madness* (2nd edn). New York: Harcourt Brace Jovanovich.

Chesler, P. (1989b). Preface. In *Women and Madness* (2nd edn). San Diego, CA: Harcourt Brace Jovanovich.

Chesler, P. (1992). Mothers on Trial: The Custodial Vulnerability of Women. *Feminism & Psychology, 1*(3), 409–426.

Chodorow, N. (1994). *Femininities, Masculinities, Sexualities: Freud and Beyond.* Lexington, KY: University of Kentucky Press.

Chodorow, N. (1995). Gender as a Personal and Cultural Construct. *Signs, 20,* 516–544.

Chomsky, N. (1989). *Necessary Illusions.* Boston: South End Press.

Christiansen, A., and Jacobson, N. S. (1994). Who (or What) Can Do Psychotherapy: The Status and Challenge of Nonprofessional Therapies. *Psychological Science, 5,* 8–14.

Coch, L., and French, J. R., Jr. (1948). Overcoming Resistance to Change. *Human Relations, 11*, 512–532.

Cohen, D. (Ed.). (1990). Challenging the Therapeutic State: Critical Perspectives on Psychiatry and the Mental Health System. Special issue of *Journal of Mind and Behavior, 11*(3/4).

Cohen, D. (Ed.). (1994). Challenging the Therapeutic State, Part Two: Further Disquisitions on the Mental Health System. Special issue of *Journal of Mind and Behavior, 15*(1/2).

Cohen, R. J., Swerdlik, M. E., and Smith, D. K. (1992). *Psychological Testing and Assessment.* Mountain View, CA: Mayfield.

Collins, P. H. (1991). *Black Feminist Thought: Knowledge, Consciousness, and the Politics of Empowerment.* London: Routledge.

Comas-Diaz, L., and Jansen, M. A. (1995). Global Conflict and Violence Against Women. *Peace and Conflict: Journal of Peace Psychology, 1*, 315–331.

Comely, L., Kitzinger, C., Perkins, R., and Wilkinson, S. (1992). Lesbian Psychology in Britain: Back into the Closet? *Feminism & Psychology, 2*(2), 265–268.

Committee on Ethical Guidelines for Forensic Psychologists (1991). Specialty Guidelines for Forensic Psychologists. *Law and Human Behavior, 15*, 655–665.

Constantino, V., and Nelson, G. (1995). Changing Relationships between Self-help Groups and Mental Health Professionals: Shifting Ideology and Power. *Canadian Journal of Community Mental Health, 14*(2), 55–70.

Cooper, J., and Mackie, D. (1986). Video Games and Aggression in Children. *Journal of Applied Social Psychology, 16*, 726–744.

Cooter, R. (Ed.). (1992). *In the Name of the Child.* London: Routledge.

Cornell University Empowerment Group (1989). *Networking Bulletin, 1*(3, October).

Costanzo, M., and White, L. T. (Eds.). (1994). The Death Penalty in the United States. Special issue of *Journal of Social Issues, 50*(2).

Coward, Ros (1992). *Our Treacherous Hearts: Why Women Let Men Get Their Way.* London: Faber and Faber.

Cowen, E. L. (1980). The Wooing of Primary Prevention. *American Journal of Community Psychology, 8*, 258–284.

Cowen, E. L. (1985). Person Centered Approaches to Primary Prevention in Mental Health: Situation-Focused and Competence Enhancement. *American Journal of Community Psychology, 13*, 31–48.

Cowen, E. L. (1991). In Pursuit of Wellness. *American Psychologist, 46*, 404–408.

Cowen, E. L. (1994). The Enhancement of Psychological Wellness: Challenges and Opportunities. *American Journal of Community Psychology, 22*, 149–180.

Cowen, E. L., Trost, M. A., Lorion, R. P., Dorr, D., Izzo, L. D., and Isaacson, R.V. (1975). *New Ways of School Mental Health: Early Detection and Prevention of School Maladaptation.* New York: Human Sciences Press.

Coyle, A., Kitzinger, C., Flynn, R., Wilkinson, S., Rivers, I., and Perkins, R. (1995). Lesbian and Gay Psychology Section (Letter). *The Psychologist, 8*(4), 151.

Cramer, D. (Ed.). (1995). Personal Relationships. Special issue of *The Psychologist, 8*(2).

Crawford, Mary (1995). *Talking Difference: On Gender and Language.* London: Sage.

Crawford, Mary, and Marecek, Jeanne (1989). Psychology Reconstructs the Female 1968–1988. *Psychology of Women Quarterly, 13*, 147–165.

Cross, W. E., Jr. (1991). *Shades of Black: Diversity in African-American Identity.* Philadelphia: Temple University Press.

Crusio, W. E. (1990). Intelligent Quantitative Genetics: Asking the Right Questions. *Cahiers de Psychologie Cognitive, 10*, 619–25.

Curti, M. W. (1926). The New Lombrosianism. *Journal of Criminal Law and Criminology, 17*, 246–253.

Cushman, P. (1990). Why the Self Is Empty. *American Psychologist, 45*, 599–611.

Cushman, P. (1995). *Constructing the Self, Constructing America: Studies in the Cultural History of Psychotherapy.* New York: Addison-Wesley.

D'Adamo, O., and García-Beaudoux, V. (1995). *El Argentino Feo* [The Ugly Argentinian]. Buenos Aires, Argentina: Losada.

D'Augelli, A. R. (1994). Identity Development and Sexual Orientation: Toward a Model of Lesbian, Gay, and Bisexual Development. In E. J. Trickett, R. J. Watts, and D. Birman (Eds.), *Human Diversity: Perspectives on People in Context* (pp. 312–333). San Francisco: Jossey-Bass.

D'Augelli, A. R., and Patterson, C. J. (Eds.). (1995). *Lesbian, Gay, and Bisexual Identities over the Lifespan: Psychological Perspectives.* New York: Oxford University Press.

Danziger, K. (1990). *Constructing the Subject: Historical Origins of Psychological Research.* New York: Cambridge University Press.

Davidson, W. S., and Redner, R. (1988). The Prevention of Juvenile Delinquency: Diversion from the Juvenile Justice System. In R. H. Price, E. L. Cowen, R. P. Lorion, and J. Ramos-Mckay (Eds.), *Fourteen Ounces of Prevention* (pp. 123–137). Washington, DC: American Psychological Association.

Davies, B., and Harré, R. (1990). Positioning: The Discursive Production of Selves. *Journal for the Theory of Social Behaviour, 19*(4), 43–63.

Davis, Kathy (1994). What's in a Voice? Methods and Metaphors. *Feminism & Psychology, 4*(3), 353–361.

Davis, M., and Kennedy, E. L. (1989). Oral History and the Study of Sexuality in the Lesbian Community: Buffalo, New York, 1940–1960. In M. Duberman, M. Vicinus, and G. Chauncey (Eds.), *Hidden from History: Reclaiming the Gay and Lesbian Past* (pp. 426–440). New York: Meridian.

Dawes, A., and Donald, D. (Eds.). (1994). *Children and Adversity: Psychological Perspectives from South African Research.* Cape Town: David Philip.

Dawes, R. M. (1994). *House of Cards: Psychology and Psychotherapy Built on Myth.* New York: Free Press.

Decker, B. (1984). Counseling Gay and Lesbian Couples. *Journal of Social Work and Human Sexuality, 2*(2/3), 39–52.

Denmark, F., Russo, N. F., Frieze, I. H., and Sechzer, J. (1988). Guidelines for Non-Sexist Research. *American Psychologist, 43,* 582–585.

Dent, H. E. (1995). Everything You Thought Was True about Testing, But Isn't. *Focus: Notes from the Society for the Psychological Study of Ethnic Minority Issues, 9,* 4–6.

Derrida, J. (1967). *De la Grammatologie* [Of Grammatology]. Paris: Editions de Minuit.

Derrida, J. (1981). *Positions.* London: Athlone Press.

Deutsch, M. (1975). Introduction. In M. Deutsch and H. A. Hornstein (Eds.), *Applying Social Psychology: Implications for Research, Practice, and Training* (pp. 1–12). Hillsdale, NJ: Lawrence Erlbaum.

Deutsch, M., and Collins, M. E. (1951). *Interracial Housing: A Psychological Evaluation of a Social Experiment.* Minneapolis: University of Minnesota Press.

Deutsch, M., and Steil, J. M. (1988). Awakening the Sense of Injustice. *Social Justice Research, 2,* 3–23.

Doherty, W. (1995). *Soul Searching: Why Psychotherapy Must Promote Moral Responsibility.* New York: Basic Books.

Dollard, J. (1937). *Caste and Class in a Southern Town.* Garden City, NY: Doubleday.

Dollard, J., Doob, L., Miller, N., Mowrer, O., and Sears, R. (1939). *Frustration and Aggression.* New Haven: Yale University Press.

Donaldson, M. (1978). *Children's Minds.* London: Fontana.

Dowling, Colette (1981). *The Cinderella Complex: Women's Hidden Fear of Independence.* London: Fontana.

Dreyfus, H. (1987) Foucault's Therapy. *PsychCritique, 2*(1), 65–83.

Dryden, W., and Feltham, C. (Eds.). (1992). *Psychotherapy and its Discontents.* Bristol, PA: Open University Press.

Duggan, L. (1992). Making It Perfectly Queer. *Socialist Review, 22*(1), 11–31.

Dumont, M. P. (1987). A Diagnostic Parable (Review of DSM-III-R). *Readings: A Journal of Reviews and Commentary in Mental Health,* December, 9–12.

Eagleton, T. (1983). *Literary Theory: An Introduction.* Oxford: Blackwell.

Eagly, Alice H. (1994). On Comparing Women and Men. *Feminism & Psychology, 4*(4), 513–522.

Earnest, W. R. (1992). Ideology Criticism and Interview Research. In G. C. Rosenwald and R. L. Ochberg (Eds.), *Storied Lives* (pp. 250–264). New Haven, CT: Yale University Press.

Eckensberger, L. H. (1972). The Necessity of a Theory for Applied Cross-Cultural Research. In L. H. Cronbach and P. J. D. Drenth (Eds.), *Mental Tests and Cultural Adaptation* (pp. 99–107). The Hague: Mouton.

Edley, N., and Wetherell, M. (1995). *Men in Perspective: Practice, Power and Identity.* London: Prentice-Hall.

Edwards, D., Ashmore, M., and Potter, J. (1995). Death and Furniture: The Rhetoric, Politics and Theology of Bottom Line Arguments against Relativism. *History of the Human Sciences, 8*(2), 25–49.

Edwards, D., and Potter, J. (1993). Language and Causation: A Discursive Action Model of Description and Attribution. *Psychological Review, 100*(1), 23–41.

Ehrenreich, Barbara, and English, Deidre (1979). *For Her Own Good: 150 Years of the Experts' Advice to Women.* London: Pluto.

Elliott, A. (1992). *Social Theory and Psychoanalysis in Transition.* Oxford: Basil Blackwell.

Ellis, M. L. (1994). Lesbians, Gay Men and Psychoanalytic Training. *Free Associations, 4*(4), 501–517.

Epstein, E. (Ed.). (1994). *Challenging Lesbian and Gay Inequalities in Education.* Buckingham: Open University Press.

Espin, O. M. (forthcoming). *Latina Realities: Essays on Healing, Migration, and Sexuality.* Boulder, CO: Westview Press.

Etzioni, A. (1993). *The Spirit of Community.* New York: Touchstone.

Evans, B., and Waites, B. (1981). *IQ and Mental Testing.* London: Macmillan.

Everingham, C. (1994). *Motherhood and Modernity.* Buckingham: Open University Press.

Fairchild, H. (1995). *The Bell Curve:* Pseudoscience Claptrap. *Focus: Notes from the Society for the Psychological Study of Ethnic Minority Issues, 9,* 7.

Falco, K. L. (1991). *Psychotherapy with Lesbian Clients: Theory into Practice.* New York: Brunner/Mazel.

Fals Borda, O. (1985). *Conocimiento y Poder Popular* [Knowledge and Popular Power]. Bogotá, Colombia: Siglo XXI.

Faludi, Susan (1991). *Backlash: The Undeclared War against Women.* London: Chatto and Windus.

Fancher, R. E. (1985). *The Intelligence Men: Makers of the IQ Controversy.* New York and London: Norton.

Fancher, R. E. (1988). Henry Goddard and the Kallikak Family Photographs: "Conscious Skulduggery" or "Whig History"? *American Psychologist, 42,* 585–590.

Fanon, F. (1968). *The Wretched of the Earth.* London: Macgibbon and Kee.

Fawcett, S. B., White, G. W., Balcazar, F. E., Suarez-Balcazar, Y., Mathews, R. M., Paine-Andrews, A., Seekins, T., and Smith, J. F. (1994). A Contextual-Behavioral Model of Empowerment: Case Studies Involving People with Physical Disabilities. *American Journal of Community Psychology, 22,* 471–496.

Fay, B. (1987). *Critical Social Science.* Ithaca, NY: Cornell University Press.

Febbraro, A. R. (1994). Single Mothers "At Risk" for Child Maltreatment: An Appraisal of Person-Centred Interventions and a Call for Emancipatory Action. *Canadian Journal of Community Mental Health, 13*(2), 47–60.

Feminist Therapy Institute (1990). Feminist Therapy Institute Code of Ethics. In H. Lerman and N. Porter (Eds.), *Feminist Ethics in Psychotherapy* (pp. 37–40). New York: Springer.

Ferree, M. M., and Hess, B. B. (1985). *Controversy and Coalition: The New Feminist Movement.* Boston, MA: Twayne.

Festinger, L. (1957). *A Theory of Cognitive Dissonance.* Evanston, IL: Row, Peterson.

Festinger, L., Riecken, H., and Schachter, S. (1956). *When Prophecy Fails.* Minneapolis: University of Minnesota Press.

Festinger, L., Schachter, S., and Back, K. (1950). *Social Pressures in Informal Groups: A Study of a Housing Project.* New York: Harper.

Fine, M. (1984). Coping with Rape: Critical Perspectives on Consciousness. *Imagination, Cognition and Personality: The Scientific Study of Consciousness, 3,* 249–267.

Fine, M. (1992a). *Disruptive Voices: The Possibilities of Feminist Research.* Ann Arbor, MI: University of Michigan Press.

Fine, M. (1992b). Coping with Rape: Critical Perspectives on Consciousness. In M. Fine (Ed.), *Disruptive Voices* (pp. 61–76). Ann Arbor, MI: University of Michigan Press.

Fine, M. (1995). Participatory Evaluation Research. Unpublished manuscript.

Fine, M., and Gordon, S. M. (1991). Effacing the Center and the Margins: Life at the Intersection of Psychology and Feminism. *Feminism & Psychology, 1*(1), 19–28.

Fine, M., Powell, L., Weis, L., and Wong, M. (Eds.). (1996). *Off-White: Theorizing Whiteness.* New York: Routledge.

Finison, L. J. (1976). Unemployment, Politics, and the History of Organized Psychology. *American Psychologist, 31,* 741–755.

Fiske, S. T., and Taylor, S. E. (1991). *Social Cognition* (2nd edn). New York: Random House.

Fitzgerald, L. F., and Nutt, R. (1986). The Division 17 Principles Concerning the Counseling/ Psychotherapy of Women: Rationale and Implementation. *The Counseling Psychologist, 14,* 180–216.

Flynn, J. R. (1987a). Race and IQ: Jensen's Case Refuted. In S. Modgil and C. Modgil (Eds.), *Arthur Jensen: Consensus and Controversy* (pp. 221–232). New York: Falmer Press.

Flynn, J. R. (1987b). Massive IQ Gains in 14 Nations: What IQ Tests Really Measure. *Psychological Bulletin, 101,* 171–191.

Flynn, J. R. (1989). Rushton, Evolution, and Race: An Essay on Intelligence and Virtue. *The Psychologist: Bulletin of the British Psychological Society, 9,* 363–366.

Flynn, J. R. (1990). Explanation, Evaluation, and a Rejoinder to Rushton. *The Psychologist: Bulletin of the British Psychological Society, 5,* 199–200.

Forel, A. (1908). *The Sexual Question: A Scientific, Psychological, Hygienic and Sociological Study* (C. F. Marshall, Trans.). New York: Physicians and Surgeons Book Co.

Foucault, M. (1970). *The Order of Things.* London: Tavistock.

Foucault, M. (1971). *Madness and Civilization: A History of Insanity in the Age of Reason.* London: Tavistock.

Foucault, M. (1972). *The Archaeology of Knowledge.* London: Tavistock.

Foucault, M. (1977a). *Discipline and Punish: The Birth of the Prison.* London: Allen Lane.

Foucault, M. (1977b). *Language, Counter-Memory, Practice: Selected Essays and Interviews.* Oxford: Blackwell.

Foucault, M. (1978). *The History of Sexuality: An Introduction.* New York: Vintage.

Foucault, M. (1979). *Discipline and Punish: The Birth of the Prison* (Alan Sheridan, Trans.). New York: Vintage.

Foucault, M. (1980a). *Power/Knowledge: Selected Interviews and Other Writings* (Colin Gordon, Ed.). New York: Pantheon.

Foucault, M. (1980b). *The History of Sexuality. Vol. I: An Introduction* (Robert Hurley, Trans.). New York: Vintage/Random House.

Foucault, M. (1981). *The History of Sexuality. Vol. I: An Introduction.* Harmondsworth: Penguin.

Foucault, M. (1982a). On the Genealogy of Ethics: An Overview of Work in Progress. Afterword in H. Dreyfus and P. Rabinow (Eds.), *Michel Foucault: Beyond Structuralism and Hermeneutics* (pp. 229–252). Chicago: University of Chicago Press.

Foucault, M. (1982b). The Subject and Power. *Critical Inquiry, 8,* 777–795.

Foucault, M. (1984). Polemics, Politics, and Problemizations. In P. Rabinow (Ed.), *The Foucault Reader* (pp. 381–390). New York: Pantheon.

Foucault, M. (1986). *The Care of the Self: The History of Sexuality. Vol. III.* Harmondsworth: Penguin.

Fowers, B. J., and Richardson, F. C. (1996). Why is Multiculturalism Good? *American Psychologist, 51,* 609–621.

Fox, D. R. (1985). Psychology, Ideology, Utopia, and the Commons. *American Psychologist, 40,* 48–58.

Fox, D. R. (1991). Social Science's Limited Role in Resolving Psycholegal Social Problems. *Journal of Offender Rehabilitation, 17,* 117–124.

Fox, D. R. (1993a). The Autonomy–Community Balance and the Equity–Law Distinction: Anarchy's Task for Psychological Jurisprudence. *Behavioral Sciences and the Law, 11,* 97–109.

Fox, D. R. (1993b). Psychological Jurisprudence and Radical Social Change. *American Psychologist, 48,* 234–241.

Fox, D. R. (1993c). Where's the Proof that Law is a Good Thing? *Law and Human Behavior, 17,* 257–258.

Fox, D. R. (1994). Observations on Disability Evaluation in the Social Security Administration. *Journal of Social Behavior and Personality, 9,* 237–246.

Fox, D. R. (1996). The Law Says Corporations Are Persons, but Psychology Knows Better. *Behavioral Sciences and the Law, 14,* 339–357.

Fox, D. R., and Prilleltensky, I. (1996). The Inescapable Nature of Politics in Psychology: A Response to Dyslin and O'Donohue. *New Ideas in Psychology, 14,* 21–26.

Frazer, E., and Lacey, N. (1993). *The Politics of Community: A Feminist Critique of the Liberal-Communitarian Debate.* Toronto: University of Toronto Press.

Freeman, A., Pretzer, J., Fleming, B., and Simon, K. M. (1990). *Clinical Applications of Cognitive Therapy.* New York: Plenum Press.

Freire, P. (1970). *Pedagogy of the Oppressed.* New York: Seabury.

Freire, P. (1981). *Education for Critical Consciousness.* New York: Seabury.

Freire, P. (1990). *Education for Critical Consciousness.* New York: Continuum.

Freire, P. (1993). *Pedagogy of the Oppressed.* New York: Continuum.

Freud, S. (1905/1963). *Dora: An Analysis of a Case of Hysteria.* New York: Collier.

Fromm, E. (1955). *The Sane Society.* New York: Holt, Rinehart, and Winston.

Fromm, E. (1941/1969). *Escape from Freedom.* New York: Avon.

Fromm, E. (1975). *Man for Himself.* New York: Fawcett Premier (original work published in 1947).

Furumoto, L. (1989). The New History of Psychology. In I. S. Cohen (Ed.), *The G. Stanley Hall Lecture Series, Vol. 9* (pp. 5–34). Washington, DC: American Psychological Association.

Gadamer, H.-G. (1975). *Truth and Method.* New York: Continuum.

Gadamer, H.-G. (1981). *Reason in the Age of Science.* Cambridge, MA: MIT Press.

Galbraith, J. K. (1996). *The Good Society: The Humane Agenda.* New York: Houghton Mifflin.

García, I., Giuliani, F., and Wiesenfeld, E. (1994). El Lugar de la Teoría en la Psicología Social Comunitaria: Comunidad y Sentido de Comunidad [The Place of Theory in Social-Community Psychology: Community and Sense of Community]. In M. Montero (Ed.), *Psicología Social Comunitaria [Social-Community Psychology]* (pp. 75–102). Guadalajara, Mexico: Universidad de Guadalajara.

Gardner, H. (1983). *Frames of Mind: The Theory of Multiple Intelligences.* New York: Basic Books.

Garfinkel, H. (1967). *Studies in Ethnomethodology.* New York: Prentice-Hall.

Garnets, L. D., Herek, G. M., and Levy, B. (1993). Violence and Victimization of Lesbians and Gay Men: Mental Health Consequences. In L. D. Garnets and D. C. Kimmel (Eds.), *Psychological Perspectives on Lesbian and Gay Experiences* (pp. 579–598). New York: Columbia University Press.

Garnets, L. D., and Kimmel, D. C. (Eds.). (1993a). *Psychological Perspectives on Lesbian and Gay Experiences.* New York: Columbia University Press.

Garnets, L. D., and Kimmel, D. C. (1993b). Conclusion: Implications for Practice, Research and Public Policy. In L. D. Garnets and D. C. Kimmel (Eds.), *Psychological Perspectives on Lesbian and Gay Experiences* (pp. 599–604). New York: Columbia University Press.

Garrison, D. (1981). Karen Horney and Feminism. *Signs, 6,* 672–691.

Gartrell, N. K. (Ed.). (1994). *Bringing Ethics Alive: Feminist Ethics in Psychotherapy Practice.* New York: Haworth.

Geen, R. G. (1990). *Human Aggression.* Pacific Grove, CA: Brooks Cole.

Geen, R. G. (1995). Human Aggression. In A. Tesser (Ed.), *Advanced Social Psychology* (pp. 383–417). New York: McGraw-Hill.

Geertz, C. (1979). From the Native's Point of View: On the Nature of Anthropological Understanding. In P. Rabinow and W. Sullivan (Eds.), *Interpretative Social Science* (pp. 225–241). Berkeley, CA: University of California Press.

Geertz, C. (1984). *Local Knowledge.* New York: Basic Books.

Gergen, K. J. (1973). Social Psychology, Science and History. *Personality and Social Psychology Bulletin, 2,* 373–383.

Gergen, K. J. (1976). Social Psychology as History. *Journal of Personality and Social Psychology, 26,* 309–320.

Gergen, K. J. (1982). *Toward Transformation in Social Knowledge.* New York: Springer.

Gergen, K. J. (1985a). Social Psychology and the Phoenix of Unreality. In S. Koch, and D. E. Leary (Eds.), *A Century of Psychology as Science* (pp. 529–557). New York: McGraw-Hill.

Gergen, K. J. (1985b). The Social Constructionist Movement in Modern Psychology. *American Psychologist, 40,* 266–275.

Gergen, K. J. (1992). Toward a Postmodern Psychology. In S. Kvale (Ed.), *Psychology and Postmodernism* (pp. 17–30). London: Sage.

Gilbert, L. A. (1993). *Two Careers/One Family.* Beverly Hills, CA: Sage.

Gilbert, N., and Mulkay, M (1984). *Opening Pandora's Box: A Sociological Analysis of Scientists' Discourse.* Cambridge: Cambridge University Press.

Gill, R. (1995). Relativism, Reflexivity and Politics: Interrogating Discourse Analysis from a Feminist Perspective. In S. Wilkinson and C. Kitzinger (Eds.), *Feminism and Discourse* (pp. 165–186). London: Sage.

Gilligan, Carol (1982). *In a Different Voice: Psychological Theory and Women's Development.* Cambridge, MA: Harvard University Press.

Gilman, C. P. (1892/1995). *The Yellow Wallpaper.* Manakato, MN: Creative Education.

Giroux, H. A. (1992). *Border Crossings: Cultural Workers and the Politics of Education.* New York: Routledge.

Giroux, H. A., and McClaren, P. L. (1991). Radical Pedagogy as Cultural Politics: Beyond the Discourse of Critique and Anti-Utopianism. In D. Morton and M. Zavarzadeh (Eds.), *Theory/Pedagogy/Politics: Texts for Change* (pp. 152–186). Urbana, IL: University of Illinois Press.

Glaser, B., and Strauss, A. (1967). *The Discovery of Grounded Theory.* Chicago: Aldine.

Gleitman, H. (1992). *Basic Psychology* (3rd edn). New York: Norton.

Goddard, H. H. (1912). *The Kallikak Family: A Study in the Heredity of Feeble-Mindedness.* New York: Macmillan.

Goddard, H. H. (1917). Mental Tests and the Immigrant. *Journal of Delinquency, 2,* 243–277.

Goffman, E. (1977). The Arrangement between the Sexes. *Theory and Society, 4,* 301–331.

Goldberger, N. R., and Veroff, J. B. (Eds.). (1995). *The Culture and Personality Reader.* New York: New York University Press.

Goldner, V. (1991). Toward a Critical Relational Therapy of Gender. *Psychoanalytic Dialogues, 1,* 249–272.

Goldner, V., Penn, P., Sheinberg, M., and Walker, G. (1990). Love and Violence: Gender Paradoxes in Volatile Attachments. *Family Process, 29,* 343–364.

Goldstein, M. J., Rodnick, E. H., Evans, J. R., May, P. R. A., and Steinberg, M. R. (1978). Drug and Family Therapy in the Aftercare Treatment of Acute Schizophrenics. *Archives of General Psychiatry, 35,* 1169–1177.

Gonsiorek, J. C. (1994). Foreword. In B. Greene and G. M. Herek (Eds.), *Psychological Perspectives on Lesbian and Gay Issues. Vol. 1: Lesbian and Gay Psychology: Theory, Research and Clinical Applications* (pp. vii–ix). Thousand Oaks, CA: Sage.

Gonsiorek, J. C. (1995). Gay Male Identities: Concepts and Issues. In A. R. D'Augelli and C.

J. Patterson (Eds.), *Lesbian, Gay, and Bisexual Identities over the Lifespan: Psychological Perspectives* (pp. 24–47). New York: Oxford University Press.

Gonsiorek, J. C., and Weinrich, J. D. (Eds.). (1991). *Homosexuality: Research Implications for Public Policy*. London: Sage.

Good, T., Wiley, A., Thomas, R. E., Stewart, E., McCoy, J., Kloos, B., Hunt, G., Moore, T., and Rappaport, J. (forthcoming). Community Organizing for Parent and Citizen Involvement. *Journal of Educational and Psychological Consultation*.

Goodrich, T. J. (Ed.). (1991). *Women and Power: Perspectives for Family Therapy*. New York: Norton.

Gorey, K. M., and Cryns, A. G. (1995). Lack of Racial Differences in Behavior: A Quantitative Replication of Rushton's (1988) Review and an Independent Meta-Analysis. *Personality and Individual Differences, 19*, 345–353.

Gottlieb, B. H. (Ed.). (1981). *Social Networks and Social Support*. Beverly Hills, CA: Sage.

Gottlieb, B. H. (1983). *Social Support Strategies: Guidelines for Mental Health Practice*. Beverly Hills, CA: Sage.

Gould, S. J. (1981). *The Mismeasure of Man*. New York: Norton.

Gramsci, A. (1971). The Study of Philosophy. In Q. Hoare and G. N. Smith (Eds.), *Selections from the Prison Notebooks* (pp. 321–377). New York: International Press.

Green, C. D. (1995). The Power Hour: Maybe Psychotherapy is Social Control after All. Unpublished manuscript, York University, Ontario, Canada.

Greene, B. (1994). Lesbian and Gay Sexual Orientations: Implications for Clinical Training, Practice, and Research. In B. Greene and G.M. Herek (Eds.), *Psychological Perspectives on Lesbian and Gay Issues. Vol. 1: Lesbian and Gay Psychology: Theory, Research and Clinical Applications* (pp. 1–24). Thousand Oaks, CA: Sage.

Greene, B., and Herek, G. M. (Eds.). (1994). *Psychological Perspectives on Lesbian and Gay Issues. Vol. 1: Lesbian and Gay Psychology: Theory, Research and Clinical Applications*. Thousand Oaks, CA: Sage.

Greenstein, F. I. (1973). Political Psychology: A Pluralistic Universe. In J. N. Knutson (Ed.), *Handbook of Political Psychology* (pp. 438–469). San Francisco: Jossey-Bass.

Greenwood, J. D. (1994). *Realism, Identity and Emotion: Reclaiming Social Psychology*. London: Sage.

Gregg, G. (1991). *Self-Representation: Life Narrative Studies in Identity and Ideology*. New York: Greenwood.

Griffin, C., and Phoenix, A. (1994). The Relationship between Qualitative Methods and Quantitative Research: Lessons from Feminist Psychology. *Journal of Community and Applied Social Psychology, 4*, 287–298.

Grisso, T. (1987). The Economic and Scientific Future of Forensic Psychological Assessment. *American Psychologist, 42*, 831–839.

Grisso, T. (1991). A Developmental History of the American Psychology-Law Society. *Law and Human Behavior, 15*, 213–232.

Grob, G. N. (1991). *From Asylum to Community: Mental Health Policy in Modern America*. Princeton, NJ: Princeton University Press.

Grob, G. N. (1994). The History of the Asylum Revisited: Personal Reflections. In M. S. Micale and R. Porter (Eds.), *Discovering the History of Psychiatry* (pp. 260–281). New York: Oxford University Press.

Grossman, D. (1995). *On Killing: The Psychological Cost of Learning to Kill in War and Society*. Boston: Little, Brown.

Groves, P. A. (1985). Coming Out: Issues for the Therapist Working with Women in the Process of Identity Formation. *Women and Therapy, 4*(2), 17–22.

Guba, E., and Lincoln, Y. S. (1989). *Fourth Generation Evaluation*. Newbury Park, CA: Sage.

Guignon, C. (1989). Truth as Disclosure: Art, Language, History. *The Southern Journal of Philosophy, 28*, 105–121.

Guignon, C. (1991). Pragmatism or Hermeneutics? Epistemology after Foundationalism. In J. Bohman, D. Hiley, and R. Schusterman (Eds.), *The Interpretive Turn*. Ithaca, NY: Cornell University Press.

Guignon, C. (1993). Overcoming Dualism: A Hermeneutic Approach to Understanding Humans. Unpublished manuscript, University of Vermont.

Guillaumin, Colette (1995). *Racism, Sexism, Power and Ideology*. London: Routledge.

Gulbrandsen, M. (1994). Boys and Girls in Cross-Gender Relations: A Social Psychological Approach to Gendered Development. In *The Social Construction of Gender in Children's Worlds* (pp. 5–12). Centre for Women's Research: Oslo.

Habermas, J. (1970). *Toward a Rational Society*. Boston: Beacon.

Habermas, J. (1971). *Knowledge and Human Interests*. Boston: Beacon.

Habermas, J. (1973). *Theory and Practice*. Boston: Beacon.

Habermas, J. (1975). *Legitimation Crisis*. Boston: Beacon.

Habermas, J. (1984). *The Theory of Communicative Action* (Vol. I). Boston: Beacon.

Habermas, J. (1987). *The Theory of Communicative Action* (Vol. II). Boston: Beacon.

Habermas, J. (1990). Justice and Solidarity: On the Discussion Concerning "Stage 6". In M. Kelly (Ed.), *Hermeneutics and Critical Theory in Ethics and Politics* (pp. 21–42). Cambridge, MA: MIT Press.

Habermas, J. (1991). *The Philosophical Discourse of Modernity*. Cambridge, MA: MIT Press.

Hall, M. (1984). Counselor–Client Sex and Feminist Therapy: A New Look at an Old Taboo. Paper presented at the *Third Advanced Feminist Therapy Institute*, Oakland, CA, March.

Hall, M. (1987). *The Lavender Couch: A Consumer's Guide to Psychotherapy for Lesbians and Gay Men*. Boston: Alyson.

Hall, P. M. (1983). Individualism and Social Problems: A Critique and an Alternative. *The Journal of Applied Behavioral Science, 19*(1), 85–94.

Hampson, E. (1990). Variations in Sex-Related Cognitive Abilities across the Menstrual Cycle. *Brain and Cognition, 14*, 26–43.

Haney, C. (1980). Psychological and Legal Change: On the Limits of a Factual Jurisprudence. *Law and Human Behavior, 4*, 147–200.

Haney, C. (1991). The Fourteenth Amendment and Symbolic Legality: Let Them Eat Due Process. *Law and Human Behavior, 15*, 183–204.

Haney, C. (1993). Psychology and Legal Change: The Impact of a Decade. *Law and Human Behavior, 17*, 371–398.

Haney, C., and Hurtado, A. (1994). The Jurisprudence of Race and Meritocracy: Standardized Testing and "Race-Neutral" Racism in the Workplace. *Law and Human Behavior, 18*, 223–248.

Hanna, M. G., and Robinson, B. (1994). *Strategies for Community Empowerment: Direct-Action and Transformative Approaches to Social Change Practice*. Lewiston, NY: Edwin Mellen Press.

Hansen, G. L. (1982). Measuring Prejudice against Homosexuality (Homosexism) among College Students: A New Scale. *Journal of Social Psychology, 117*, 233–236.

Haraway, D. (1988). Situated Knowledges: The Science Question in Feminism and the Privilege of Partial Perspective. *Feminist Studies, 14*(3), 575–597.

Haraway, D. (1989). Metaphors into Hardware: Harry Harlow and the Technology of Love. In D. Haraway (Ed.), *Primate Visions: Gender, Race and Nature in the World of Modern Science* (pp. 231–243). London: Verso.

Harding, S. (1991). *Whose Science? Whose Knowledge? Thinking From Women's Lives*. Milton Keynes: Open University Press.

Hare-Mustin, R. T. (1991). Sex, Lies, and Headaches: The Problem is Power. In T. J. Goodrich (Ed.), *Women and Power: Perspectives for Therapy* (pp. 63–85). New York: Norton.

Hare-Mustin, R. T. (1992). Cries and Whispers: The Psychotherapy of Anne Sexton. *Psychotherapy, 29*, 406–409.

Hare-Mustin, R. T. (1994). Discourses in the Mirrored Room: A Postmodern Analysis of Therapy. *Family Process, 33*, 19–35.

Hare-Mustin, R. T., and Marecek, J. (1986). Autonomy and Gender: Some Questions for Therapists. *Psychotherapy, 23*, 205–212.

Hare-Mustin, R. T., and Marecek, J. (1990). *Making a Difference: Psychology and the Construction of Gender*. New Haven, CT: Yale University Press.

Hare-Mustin, R. T., and Marecek, J. (1994). Asking the Right Questions: Feminist Psychology and Sex Differences. *Feminism & Psychology*, 4(4), 531–537.

Hare-Mustin, R. T., Marecek, J., Kaplan, A. G., and Liss-Levinson, N. (1979). Rights of Clients, Responsibilities of Therapists. *American Psychologist*, 34, 3–16.

Harré, R. (1986). Steps towards Social Construction. In M. Richards and P. Light (Eds.), *Children of Social Worlds* (pp. 287–296). Oxford: Polity.

Harré, R., and Gillett, G. (1994). *The Discursive Mind*. London: Sage.

Harré, R., and Secord, P. F. (1972). *The Explanation of Social Behaviour*. Oxford: Blackwell.

Harris, B. (1979). Whatever Happened to Little Albert? *American Psychologist*, 34, 151–160.

Harris, B. (1990). Psychology. In M. J. Buhle, P. Buhle, and D. Georgakas (Eds.), *Encyclopedia of the American Left* (pp. 610–612). New York: Garland.

Harris, B. (1993). "Don't be Unconscious, Join Our Ranks": Psychology, Politics and Communist Education. *Rethinking Marxism*, 6(1), 44–76.

Harris, B. (1994). Century of Progress? *Contemporary Psychology*, 39, 465–468.

Harris, B. (1995). The Benjamin Rush Society and Marxist Psychiatry in the United States, 1944–1951. *History of Psychiatry*, 6, 309–331.

Harris, B. (forthcoming). John B. Watson. In J. A. Garraty (Ed.), *American National Biography*. New York: Oxford University Press.

Haste, Helen (1994). "You've Come a Long Way, Babe": A Catalyst of Feminist Conflicts. *Feminism & Psychology*, 4(3), 399–403.

Hattie, J. A., Sharpley, C. F., and Rogers, H. J. (1984). Comparative Effectiveness of Professional and Paraprofessional Helpers. *Psychological Bulletin*, 95, 534–541.

Hawkins, J.D., Catalano, R.F., and Miller, J.Y. (1992). Risk and Protective Factors for Alcohol and other Drug Problems in Adolescence and Early Adulthood: Implications for Substance Abuse Prevention. *Psychological Bulletin*, 112, 64–105.

Hayduk, L. A. (1987). *Structural Equation Modeling with LISREL: Essentials and Advances*. Baltimore, MD: Johns Hopkins University Press.

Hearnshaw, L. S. (1979). *Cyril Burt: Psychologist*. London: Hodder and Stoughton.

Heidegger, M. (1962). *Being and Time*. New York: Harper.

Heilbrun, K. (1995). Psychology and Law: Taking New Directions, Finding New Partners. *American Psychology-Law Society News*, Fall, pp. 1–2.

Heilbrun, K. (1996). Looking to Hilton Head, and Some Updates. *American Psychology-Law Society News*, Winter, pp. 1–2.

Held, D. (1980). *Introduction to Critical Theory*. Berkeley, CA: University of California Press.

Helmreich, R. L. (1975). Applied Social Psychology: The Unfulfilled Promise. *Personality and Social Psychology Bulletin*, 1, 548–560.

Helms, J. (1995). We Are Due Something New: A Reaction to *The Bell Curve*. *Focus: Notes from the Society for the Psychological Study of Ethnic Minority Issues*, 8–10.

Hendrick, C. (1977). Social Psychology as an Experimental Science. In C. Hendrick (Ed.), *Perspectives on Social Psychology* (pp. 1–74). Hillsdale, NJ: Erlbaum.

Henley, Nancy (1974). Resources for the Study of Psychology and Women. *R.T.: Journal of Radical Therapy*, 4, 20–21.

Henriques, J., Hollway, W., Urwin, C., Venn, C., and Walkerdine, V. (1984). *Changing the Subject: Psychology, Social Regulation and Subjectivity*. London: Methuen.

Henshall, C., and McGuire, J. (1986). Gender Development. In M. Richards and P. Light (Eds.), *Children of Social Worlds* (pp. 135–166). Oxford: Polity, Blackwell.

Henwood, K., and Parker, I. (1994). Introduction: Qualitative Social Psychology. *Journal of Community and Applied Social Psychology*, 4, 219–213.

Henwood, K., and Pidgeon, N. (1994). Beyond the Qualitative Paradigm: A Framework for Introducing Diversity within Qualitative Psychology. *Journal of Community and Applied Social Psychology*, 4, 225–238.

Herek, G. M. (1989). Hate Crimes against Lesbians and Gay Men. *American Psychologist*, 44, 948–955.

Herman, E. (1995). *The Romance of American Psychology: Political Culture in the Age of Experts*. Berkeley, CA: University of California Press.

Herrnstein, R. J., and Murray, C. (1994). *The Bell Curve: Intelligence and Class Structure in American Life*. New York: Free Press.

Herskovits, M. J. (1930). *The Anthropometry of the American Negro*. New York: Columbia University Press.

Higbee, E. R., Millard, R. J., and Folkman, J. R. (1982). Social Psychology Research during the 1970s: Predominance of Experimentation and College Students. *Personality and Social Psychology Bulletin, 8,* 180–183.

Higbee, K. L., Lott, W. J., and Graves, J. P. (1976). Experimentation and College Students in Social-Personality Research. *Personality and Social Psychology Bulletin, 2,* 239–241.

Higbee, K. L., and Wells, M. G. (1972). Some Research Trends in Social Psychology during the 1960s. *American Psychologist, 27,* 963–966.

Hilgard, E. R. (1987). *Psychology in America: A Historical Survey*. San Diego, CA: Harcourt Brace Jovanovich.

Hill Collins, P. (1990). *Black Feminist Thought: Knowledge, Consciousness, and the Politics of Empowerment*. New York: Routledge.

Hilliard, A. G. (1995). The Nonscience and Nonsense of *The Bell Curve. Focus: Notes from the Society for the Psychological Study of Ethnic Minority Issues,* 10–12.

Hochschild, A. (with A. Machung) (1989). *The Second Shift: Working Parents and the Revolution at Home*. New York: Viking.

Hollway, Wendy (1989). *Subjectivity and Method in Psychology: Gender, Meaning and Science*. London: Sage.

Hollway, Wendy (1991). The Psychologization of Feminism or the Feminization of Psychology? *Feminism & Psychology, 1*(1), 29–38.

Hollway, Wendy (1994). Beyond Sex Differences: A Project for Feminist Psychology. *Feminism & Psychology, 4*(4), 538–546.

Holmes, D. R. (1989). *Stalking the Academic Communist: Intellectual Freedom and the Firing of Alex Novikoff*. Hanover, NH: University Press of New England.

Holzkamp-Osterkamp, U. (1991). Personality: Self-Actualization in Social Vacuums. In C. Tolman and W. Maiers (Eds.), *Critical Psychology: Contributions to an Historical Science of the Subject* (pp. 160–179). Cambridge: Cambridge University Press.

hooks, b. (1984). *Feminist Theory from Margin to Center*. Boston: South End Press.

hooks, b. (1990). Marginality as a Site of Resistance. In R. Ferguson, M. Gever, T. T. Minh-ha, and C. West (Eds.), *Out There: Marginalization and Contemporary Cultures* (pp. 341–343). New York: New Museum of Contemporary Art, and Cambridge: MIT Press.

hooks, b. (1992). *Black Looks: Race and Representation*. Boston: South End Press.

Horgan, J. (1993). Eugenics Revisited. *Scientific American, 268*(6), 123–131.

Horkheimer, M. (1974). *Eclipse of Reason*. New York: Continuum.

Horner, Matina S. (1972). Toward an Understanding of Achievement-Related Conflicts in Women. *Journal of Social Issues, 28,* 157–176.

Horney, K. (1926/1967). The Flight from Womanhood. In *Feminine Psychology* (pp. 54–70). New York: Norton.

Hornstein, G. A. (1994). The Ethics of Ambiguity: Feminists Writing Women's Lives. In C. E. Franz and A. J. Stewart (Eds.), *Women Creating Lives: Identities, Resilience, and Resistance* (pp. 51–68). Boulder, CO: Westview Press.

Horowitz, I. A., and Willging, T. E. (1984). *The Psychology of Law: Integrations and Applications*. Boston: Little, Brown.

Horwitz, M. (1977). *The Transformation of American Law*. Cambridge, MA: Harvard University Press.

Hovland, C. I., Lumsdaine, A. A., and Sheffield, F. D. (1949). *Experiments on Mass Communication*. Princeton, NJ: Princeton University Press.

Howard, G. (1985). The Role of Values in the Science of Psychology. *American Psychologist, 40,* 255–265.

Howitt, D. (1991). *Concerning Psychology*. Philadelphia: Open University Press.

Howitt, D., and Owusu-Bempah, J. (1994). *The Racism of Psychology: Time for Change.* New York: Harvester Wheatsheaf.

Hudson, B. (1977). Review of *The Science and Politics of I.Q.* by Leon Kamin. *International Socialist Review*, February 4, 11–12.

Hudson, W. W., and Ricketts, W. A. (1980). A Strategy for the Measurement of Homophobia. *Journal of Homosexuality, 5,* 357–372.

Huesmann, L. R., and Eron, L. D. (1986). *Television and the Aggressive Child: A Cross-National Comparison.* Hillsdale, NJ: Erlbaum.

Humphreys, K., and Rappaport, J. (1994). Researching Self-Help/Mutual Aid Groups and Organizations: Many Roads, One Journey. *Applied and Preventive Psychology, 3,* 217–231.

Hyde, Janet S. (1994). Should Psychologists Study Sex Differences? Yes, with Some Guidelines. *Feminism & Psychology, 4*(4), 507–512.

Ibáñez, T. (1992). La Increíble Levedad del ser Democrático [The Unbearable Lightness of Being Democratic]. *Archipielago: La Ilusión Democrática, 9,* 37–43.

Ingleby, D. (1985). Professionals as Socializers: The "Psy Complex". *Research in Law, Deviance and Social Control, 7,* 79–109.

Irigaray, L. (1985). *This Sex Which Is Not One* (C. Porter, Trans.). Ithaca, NY: Cornell University Press (original work published 1977).

Iyengar, S., and McGuire, W. J. (Eds.). (1993). *Explorations in Political Psychology.* Durham, NC: Duke University Press.

Jacoby, R. (1975). *Social Amnesia: A Critique of Contemporary Psychology from Adler to Laing.* Boston: Beacon.

Jameson, F. (1989). Afterword: Marxism and Postmodernism. In D. Kellner (Ed.), *Postmodernism/Jameson/Critique* (p. 386). Washington, DC: Maisonneuve Press.

"Jane" (1986). Going Mad. In Women in MIND (Eds.), *Finding Our Own Solutions: Women's Experience of Mental Health Care* (pp. 10–11). London: MIND (National Association for Mental Health).

Jensen, A. R. (1969). How Much Can We Boost I.Q. and Scholastic Achievement? *Harvard Educational Review, 39,* 1–123.

Jensen, A. R. (1992). Scientific Fraud or False Accusations? The Case of Cyril Burt. In D.J. Miller and M. Hersen (Eds.), *Research Fraud in the Behavioral and Biomedical Sciences* (pp. 97–124). New York: Wiley.

Joffe, J. M., and Albee, G. W. (1988). Powerlessness and Psychopathology. In G. W. Albee, J. M. Joffe, and L. A. Dusenbury (Eds.), *Prevention, Powerlessness, and Politics: Readings on Social Change* (pp. 53–56). Beverly Hills, CA: Sage.

Johnstone, Lucy (1992). *Users and Abusers of Psychiatry: A Critical Look at Traditional Psychiatric Practice.* London: Routledge.

Jones, E. E. (1985). Major Developments in Social Psychology during the Past Five Decades. In G. Lindzey and E. Aronson (Eds.), *Handbook of Social Psychology* (3rd edn, Vol. 1, pp. 47–107). New York: Random House.

Jones, J. (1995). Minister to Rebuke "Anti-Gay" Disciples of Freud. *The Observer,* June 18.

Jones, K., and Fowles, A. J. (1984). *Ideas on Institutions.* London: Routledge and Kegan Paul.

Jost, J. T. (1995). Negative Illusions: Conceptual Clarification and Psychological Evidence Concerning False Consciousness. *Political Psychology, 16,* 397–424.

Kagehiro, D. K., and Laufer, W. S. (Eds.). (1992). *Handbook of Psychology and Law.* New York: Springer.

Kahn, S. (1994). *How People Get Power* (rev. edn). Washington, DC: National Association of Social Workers Press.

Kairys, D. (Ed.). (1990). *The Politics of Law: A Progressive Critique* (rev. edn). New York: Pantheon.

Kameny, F. E. (1971). Gay Liberation and Psychiatry. *Psychiatric Opinion, 8,* 18–27.

Kamin, L. (1974). *The Science and Politics of I.Q.* Potamac, MD: Erlbaum.

Kamin, L. (1981). Chapters 12 to 20, and 22, in H. J. Eysenck and L. Kamin (Eds.), *Intelligence: The Battle for the Mind. H. J. Eysenck versus Leon Kamin.* London: Macmillan.

Kamin, L. (1995). Behind the Curve. *Scientific American, 272,* 99–103.

Kamin, L., and Grant-Henry, S. (1987). Reaction Time, Race, and Racism. *Intelligence, 11,* 299–304.

Kane, R. (1994). *Through the Moral Maze: The Search for Absolute Values in a Pluralistic World.* New York: Paragon House.

Kanuha, V. (1990). The Need for an Integrated Analysis of Oppression in Feminist Therapy Ethics. In H. Lerman and N. Porter (Eds.), *Feminist Ethics in Psychotherapy* (pp. 24–35). New York: Springer.

Katz, D., and Braly, K. (1933). Racial Stereotypes of One Hundred College Students. *Journal of Abnormal and Social Psychology, 28,* 280–290.

Kelly, J. G. (1986). An Ecological Paradigm: Defining Mental Health Consultation as a Preventive Service. *Prevention in Human Services, 4*(3/4), 1–36.

Kelly, J. G. (1992). On Teaching the Practice of Prevention: Integrating the Concept of Interdependence. In M. Kessler, S. E. Goldston, and J. M. Joffe (Eds.), *The Present and Future of Prevention: In Honor of George W. Albee* (pp. 251–264). Beverly Hills, CA: Sage.

Kelman, H. C., and Hamilton, V. L. (1989). *Crimes of Obedience: Toward a Social Psychology of Authority and Obedience.* New Haven, CT: Yale University.

Kessler, S. J. (1990). The Medical Construction of Gender: Case Management of Intersexed Infants. *Signs, 16,* 3–26.

Kidder, L. H. (1994). All Pores Open. Paper presented as part of a *Symposium on Irresistible Methods and Meanings.* American Psychological Association, Los Angeles, August.

Kidder, L. H., and Fine, M. (1987). Qualitative and Quantitative Methods: When Stories Converge. In M. M. Mark and L. Shotland (Eds.), *New Directions in Program Evaluation* (pp. 57–75). San Francisco: Jossey-Bass.

Kidder, L. H., Lafleur, R. A., and Wells, C. V. (1995). Recalling Harassment, Reconstructing Experience. *Journal of Social Issues, 51,* 53–67.

Kimball, M. M. (1994). The Worlds We Live In: Gender Similarities and Differences. *Canadian Psychology, 35,* 388–404.

Kimble, G. (1984). Psychology's Two Cultures. *American Psychologist, 39,* 833–839.

King, M. (1986). *Psychology in and out of Court: A Critical Examination of Legal Psychology.* Oxford: Pergamon.

Kitzinger, C. (1987). *The Social Construction of Lesbianism.* London: Sage.

Kitzinger, C. (1990a). Heterosexism in Psychology. *The Psychologist, 3*(9), 391–392.

Kitzinger, C. (1990b). The Rhetoric of Pseudoscience. In I. Parker and J. Shotter (Eds.), *Deconstructing Social Psychology* (pp. 61–75). London: Routledge.

Kitzinger, C. (1990c). Resisting the Discipline. In Erica Burman (Ed.), *Feminists and Psychological Practice* (pp. 119–136). London: Sage.

Kitzinger, C. (1991). Lesbians and Gay Men in the Workplace: Psychosocial Issues. In M. J. Davidson and J. Earnshaw (Eds.), *Vulnerable Workers: Psychosocial and Legal Issues* (pp. 223–240). London: Wiley.

Kitzinger, C. (1992a). The Individuated Self Concept: A Critical Analysis of Social-Constructionist Writing on Individualism. In G. M. Breakwell (Ed.), *Social Psychology of Identity and the Self-Concept* (pp. 221–250). London: Surrey University Press in association with Academic Press, Harcourt Brace Jovanovich.

Kitzinger, C. (1992b). Sandra Bem: Feminist Psychologist. *The Psychologist, 5*(5), 222–224.

Kitzinger, C. (1996). The Token Lesbian Chapter. In S. Wilkinson (Ed.), *Feminist Social Psychologies: International Perspectives* (pp. 119–124). Buckingham: Open University Press.

Kitzinger, C., and Gilligan, C. (1994). Listening to a Different Voice: Celia Kitzinger Interviews Carol Gilligan. *Feminism & Psychology, 4*(3), 408–419.

Kitzinger, C., and Perkins, R. (1993). *Changing Our Minds: Lesbian Feminism and Psychology.* New York: New York University Press.

Kloos, B., McCoy, J., Stewart, E., Thomas, E., Wiley, A., Good, T., Hunt, G., Moore, T., and Rappaport, J. (1996). Parent Involvement and Organizational Structure: An Ecological, Open-Systems Model for School Consultation. Manuscript submitted for publication.

Kluger, R. (1975). *Simple Justice* (Vol. 1). New York: Knopf.

Kluger, R. (1976). *Simple Justice.* New York: Knopf.

Knutson, J. N. (Ed.). (1973). *Handbook of Political Psychology.* San Francisco: Jossey-Bass.

Kohl, H. (1967). *Thirty-Six Children.* New York: New American Library.

Koocher, G. P. (1994). The Commerce of Professional Psychology and the New Ethics Code. *Professional Psychology: Research and Practice, 25,* 355–361.

Korten, D. C. (1995). *When Corporations Rule the World.* San Francisco: Berrett-Koehler.

Krafft-Ebing, R. (1882). *Psychopathia Sexualis* (M.E. Wedneck, Trans.). New York: Putnams, 1965.

Krebs, D. L., and Miller, D. T. (1985). Altruism and Aggression. In G. Lindzey and E. Aronson (Eds.), *Handbook of Social Psychology* (3rd edn, Vol. 2, pp. 1–71). New York: Random House.

Krech, D., and Cartwright, D. (1956). On SPSSI's First 20 years. *American Psychologist, 11,* 470–473.

Krieger, S. (1982). Lesbian Identity and Community: Recent Social Science Literature. *Signs: Journal of Women in Culture and Society, 8*(1), 91–108.

Krogman, W. M. (1970). Growth of Head, Face, Trunk, and Limbs in Philadelphia White and Negro Children of Elementary and High School Age. *Monographs of the Society of Research on Child Development, 35,* no. 136.

Kronemeyer, R. (1980). *Overcoming Homosexuality.* New York: Macmillan.

Kruger, B. (1993). Repeat after Me. In *Remote Control: Power, Cultures, and the World of Appearances* (p. 223). Cambridge, MA: MIT Press.

Kurtz, S. (1992). *All the Mothers Are One.* New York: Columbia University Press.

Kvale, S. (Ed.). (1992). *Psychology and Postmodernism.* London: Sage.

Kymlicka, W. (1990). *Contemporary Political Philosophy.* New York: Oxford University Press.

Ladner, J. A. (1971/1987). Introduction to *Tomorrow's Tomorrow: The Black Woman.* In S. Harding (Ed.), *Feminism and Methodology* (pp. 74–83). Bloomington, IN: Indiana University Press.

Lamb, H. R., and Zusman, J. (1979). Primary Prevention in Perspective. *American Journal of Psychiatry, 136,* 12–17.

Lambert, W. E., Moghaddam, F. M., Sorin, J., and Sorin, S. (1990). Assimilation vs. Multiculturalism: Views from a Community in France. *Sociological Forum, 5,* 387–411.

Lambert, W. E., and Taylor, D. M. (1990). *Coping with Cultural and Racial Diversity in Urban America.* New York: Praeger.

Landes, W. M., and Posner, R. A. (1987). *The Economic Structure of Tort Law.* Cambridge, MA: Harvard University Press.

Landrine, H. (1989). The Politics of Personality. *Psychology of Women Quarterly, 13,* 325–340.

Lane, S., and Sawaia, B. B. (1991). Psicología ¿Ciencia o Política? [Psychology: Science or Politics?]. In M. Montero (Ed.), *Acción y Discurso: Problemas de Psicología Política en América Latina* [Action and Discourse: Political Psychology Problems in Latin America] (pp. 59–84). Caracas, Venezuela: Eduven.

Larsen, K., Reed, M., and Hoffman, S. (1980). Attitudes of Heterosexuals toward Homosexuality: A Likert-Type Scale and Construct Validity. *Journal of Sex Research, 16*(3), 245–257.

Lavoie, F., Borkman, T. J., and Gidron, B. (1994). Self-Help and Mutual Aid Groups: International and Multicultural Perspectives – Part 1. Special issue of *Prevention in Human Services, 11*(1).

Le Bon, G. (1895). *Psicología de las Multitudes* [Psychology of the Masses]. Buenos Aires, Argentina: Albatros, 1952.

Le Bon, G. (1910). *La Psychologie Politique* [Political Psychology]. Paris: Flammarion.

Lederer, G. (1986). Protest Movement as a Form of Political Action. In M. Hermann (Ed.), *Political Psychology* (pp. 355–378). San Francisco: Jossey-Bass.

Lehne, G. K. (1976). Homophobia among Men. In D. Davis and R. Brannon (Eds.), *The Forty-Nine Percent Majority: The Male Sex Role* (pp. 43–59). Reading, MA: Addison-Wesley.

Lenney, E. (1977). Women's Self-Confidence in Achievement-Related Settings. *Psychological Bulletin, 84,* 1-13.

Lerman, H., and Porter, N. (Eds.). (1990a). *Feminist Ethics in Psychotherapy.* New York: Springer.

Lerman, H., and Porter, N. (1990b). The Contribution of Feminism to Ethics in Psychotherapy. In H. Lerman and N. Porter (Eds.), *Feminist Ethics in Psychotherapy* (pp. 5-13). New York: Springer.

Lerner, M. J. (1982). The Justice Motive in Human Relations and the Economic Model of Man: A Radical Analysis of Facts and Fictions. In V. J. Derlega and J. Grzelak (Eds.), *Cooperation and Helping Behavior: Theories and Research* (pp. 249-278). New York: Academic Press.

Levett, A., Kottler, A., Burman, E., and Parker, I. (Eds.). (1997). *Power and Discourse: Culture and Change in South Africa.* London: Zed Books.

Levine, M. L. (Ed.). (1995). *The International Library of Essays in Law and Legal Theory: Law and Psychology* (T. D. Campbell, Series Ed.). Aldershot: Dartmouth.

Lewin, K. (1946). Action Research and Minority Problems. *Journal of Social Issues, 2,* 34-64.

Lewin, K., Lippitt, R., and White, R. (1939). Patterns of Aggressive Behavior in Experimentally Created "Social Climates". *Journal of Social Psychology, 10,* 271-299.

Lewin, R. (1980). Is Your Brain Really Necessary? *Science, 210,* 1232-1234.

Lichtman, R. (1987). The Illusion of Maturation in an Age of Decline. In J. Broughton (Ed.), *Critical Theories of Psychological Development* (pp. 127-148). New York: Plenum Press.

Liebow, E. (1993). *Tell Them Who I Am: The Lives of Homeless Women.* New York: Free Press.

Lieven, E. (1981). If It's Natural We Can't Change It. In *Cambridge Women's Studies, Women in Society* (pp. 203-223). London: Virago.

Lifton, R. J. (1986). *The Nazi Doctors: Medical Killing and the Psychology of Genocide.* New York: Basic Books.

Lincoln, Y. S., and Guba, E. (1985). *Naturalistic Inquiry.* Beverly Hills, CA: Sage.

Lindzey, G., and Aronson, E. (1985). *The Handbook of Social Psychology* (3rd edn). New York: Random House.

Lira, E., and Castillo, M. I. (1991). *Psicologia de la Amenaza Politica y del Miedo* [The Psychology of Political Threats and Fear]. Santiago: Instituto Latinoamericano de asistencia social y derechos humanos.

Liss, M. B. (1992). Psychology and Law Courses: Content and Materials. *Law and Human Behavior, 16,* 463-471.

Llewelyn, S., and Kelly, J. (1980). Individualism in Psychology: A Case for a New Paradigm. *Bulletin of the British Psychological Society, 33,* 407-411.

Lombroso, C. (1899/1911). *Crime: Its Causes and Remedies.* Boston: Little, Brown.

Lonner, W., and Malpass, R. S. (1994). *Psychology and Culture.* Needham Heights, MA: Allyn and Bacon.

Loo, D., Fong, K. T., and Iwamasa, G. (1988). Ethnicity and Cultural Diversity: An Analysis of Work Published in Community Psychology Journals, 1965-1985. *American Journal of Community Psychology, 16,* 332-349.

Lord, J., and Hutchison, P. (1993). The Process of Empowerment: Implications for Theory and Practice. *Canadian Journal of Community Mental Health, 12*(1), 5-22.

Lorde, A. (1984). *Sister Outsider.* Trumansburg, NY: Crossing Press.

Lykes, M. B. (1989). Dialogue with Guatemalan Indian Women: Critical Perspectives on Constructing Collaborative Research. In R. K. Unger (Ed.), *Representations: Social Constructions of Gender* (pp. 167-185). Amityville, NY: Baywood.

Lykes, M. B., Liem, R., Banuazizi, A., and Morris, M. (Eds.). (1996). *Myths about the Powerless: Contesting Social Inequalities.* Philadelphia: Temple University Press.

Lykes, M. B., and Mallona, A. (forthcoming). Surfacing Ourselves: Gringa, White – Mestiza, Brown? In M. Fine, L. Powell, L. Weis, and M. Wong (Eds.), *Off-White: Readings on Society, Culture and Race.* New York: Routledge.

Lynn, R. (1993). Further Evidence for the Existence of Race and Sex Differences in Cranial Capacity. *Social Behavior and Personality, 21*, 89–92.

MacDonald, A. P. (1976). Homophobia: Its Roots and Meanings. *Homosexual Counseling Journal, 3*, 23–33.

MacDonald, A. P., and Games, R. G. (1974). Some Characteristics of Those Who Hold Positive and Negative Attitudes toward Homosexuals. *Journal of Homosexuality, 1*, 9–27.

Macedo, D. (1994). *Literacies of Power: What Americans Are Not Allowed to Know.* Boulder, CO: Westview Press.

MacIntyre, A. (1981). *After Virtue.* Notre Dame, IN: University of Notre Dame Press.

Mack, J. E. (1994). Power, Powerlessness, and Empowerment in Psychotherapy. *Psychiatry, 57*, 178–198.

Mama, A. (1995). *Beyond the Masks: Race, Gender and the Subject.* London: Routledge.

Mankowski, E., and Rappaport, J. (1995). Stories, Identity and the Psychological Sense of Community. In R. S. Wyer, Jr. (Ed.), *Advances in Social Cognition* (Vol. 8, pp. 211–226). Hillsdale, NJ: Lawrence Erlbaum.

Marcuse, H. (1955). *Eros and Civilization: A Philosophical Inquiry into Freud.* Boston: Beacon.

Marecek, J. (1993). Disappearances, Silences, and Anxious Rhetoric: Gender in Abnormal Psychology Texts. *Journal of Theoretical and Philosophical Psychology, 13*, 114–123.

Marecek, J., and Hare-Mustin, R. T. (1991). A Short History of the Future: Feminism and Clinical Psychology. *Psychology of Women Quarterly, 15*, 521–536.

Margolies, L., Becker, M., and Jackson-Brewer, K. (1987). Internalized Homophobia: Identifying and Treating the Oppressor Within. In Boston Lesbian Psychologies Collective (Ed.), *Lesbian Psychologies: Explorations and Challenges* (pp. 229–241). Urbana, IL: University of Illinois Press.

Mark, M. M., Cook, T. D., and Diamond, S. S. (1976). Fourteen Years of Social Psychology: A Growing Commitment to Field Experimentation. *Personality and Social Psychology Bulletin, 2*, 154–157.

Marrow, A. (1969). *The Practical Theorist: The Life and Work of Kurt Lewin.* New York: Basic Books.

Marsh, A., and Kaase, M. (1979). Background of Political Action. In S. H. Barnes and M. Kaase (Eds.), *Political Action: Mass Participation in Five Western Democracies* (pp. 97–136). Beverly Hills, CA: Sage.

Marshall, H. (1991). The Social Construction of Motherhood: An Analysis of Child Care and Parenting Manuals. In A. Phoenix, A. Wollett, and E. Lloyd (Eds.), *Motherhood: Meanings, Practices and Ideologies* (pp. 66–85). London: Sage.

Martin, Emily (1987). *The Woman in the Body: A Cultural Analysis of Reproduction.* Boston, MA: Beacon Press.

Martín-Baró, I. (1985a). La Desideologización Como Aporte de la Psicología Social al Desarrollo de la Democracia en Latinoamerica [Deideologization as a Contribution of Social Psychology to the Development of Democracy in Latin America]. *Boletín de la AVEPSO, 8*(3), 3–9.

Martín-Baró, I. (1985b). La Encuesta de Opinión Pública Como Instrumento de Desideologización [Public Opinion Polls as Deideologizing Tool]. *Cuadernos de Psicología* (Universidad del Valle, Cali, Colombia), 7(1–2), 93–108.

Martín-Baró, I. (1986). Hacia una Psicología de la Liberación [Towards a Psychology of Liberation]. *Boletín de Psicología de El Salvador, 22*, 219–231.

Martín-Baró, I. (1990). Retos y Perspectivas de la Psicología en América Latina [Challenges and Perspectives of Psychology in Latin America]. In G. Pacheco and B. Jiménez (Eds.), *Ignacio Martín-Baró. Psicología de la liberación para América Latina* (pp. 51–79). Guadalajara, Mexico: Universidad de Guadalajara Press.

Martín-Baró, I. (1994). *Writings for a Liberation Psychology* (A. Aron and S. Corne, Trans.). Cambridge, MA: Harvard University Press.

Martín-Baró, I. (1995). Procesos Psíquicos y Poder [Power and Psychic Processes]. In O. D'Adamo, V. García-Beaudoux, and M. Montero (Eds.), *Psicología de la Acción Política* [The Psychology of Political Action] (pp. 205–233). Buenos Aires, Argentina: Paidós.

Masters, M. S., and Sanders, B. (1993). Is the Gender Difference in Mental Rotation Disappearing? *Behavior Genetics, 23*, 337–341.

Matsumoto, D. (1994). *People: Psychology from a Cultural Perspective.* Pacific Grove, CA: Brooks Cole.

McAdams, D. P., and Ochberg, R. L. (Eds.). (1988). Psychobiography and Life Narratives. Special issue of *Journal of Personality, 56*(1).

McCarthy, T. (1978). *The Critical Theory of Jürgen Habermas.* Cambridge, MA: MIT Press.

McDougall, W. (1908). *Introduction to Social Psychology.* London: Methuen.

McFall, R. M. (1996). Making Psychology Incorruptible. *Applied and Preventive Psychology, 5*, 9–16.

McFarlane, W. R. (Ed.). (1983). *Family Therapy in Schizophrenia.* New York: Guilford.

McGoldrick, M., Anderson, C. M., and Walsh, F. (Eds.). (1989). *Women in Families: A Framework for Family Therapy.* New York: Norton.

McGuire, W. J. (1973). The Yin and Yang of Progress in Social Psychology: Seven Koan. *Journal of Personality and Social Psychology, 26*, 446–456.

McGuire, W. J. (1993). The Poly–Psy Relationship: Three Phases of a Long Affair. In S. Iyengar and W. J. McGuire (Eds.), *Explorations in Political Psychology* (pp. 9–35). Durham, NC: Duke University Press.

McKnight, J. (1995). *The Careless Society: Community and its Counterfeits.* New York: Basic Books.

McLean, C., Carey, M., and White, C. (Eds.). (1996). *Men's Ways of Being.* Boulder, CO: Westview Press.

McMillan, D. W., and Chavis, D. M. (1986). Sense of Community: A Definition and Theory. *Journal of Community Psychology, 14*, 6 23.

McNamee, S., and Gergen, K. J. (Eds.). (1992). *Therapy as Social Construction.* London: Sage.

McNicoll, P., and Rousseau, C. (1993). Cultural Diversity: Voice, Access, and Involvement. Special issue of *Canadian Journal of Community Mental Health, 12*(2).

Mednick, Martha T. S. (1978). Now We Are Four: What Should We Be When We Grow Up? *Psychology of Women Quarterly, 3*, 123–138.

Mednick, Martha T. S. (1989). On the Politics of Psychological Constructs. *American Psychologist, 44*, 1118–1123.

Melton, G. B. (1987). Children, Politics, and Morality: The Ethics of Child Advocacy. *Journal of Clinical Child Psychology, 16*, 357–367.

Melton, G. B. (1988). The Significance of Law in the Everyday Lives of Children and Families. *Georgia Law Review, 22*, 851–895.

Melton, G. B. (1990). Law, Science, and Humanity: The Normative Foundation of Social Science in Law. *Law and Human Behavior, 14*, 315–332.

Melton, G. B. (1991). President's Column. *American Psychology-Law Society News,* Summer, 1–3.

Melton, G. B. (1992). The Law Is a Good Thing (Psychology Is, Too): Human Rights in Psychological Jurisprudence. *Law and Human Behavior, 16*, 381–398.

Melton, G. B. (1994). Therapy Through Law (Review of the Book *Essays in Therapeutic Jurisprudence*). *Contemporary Psychology, 39*, 215–216.

Melton, G. B., Petrila, J., Poythress, N., and Slobogin, C. (1987). *Psychological Evaluations for the Courts: A Handbook for Mental Health Professionals and Lawyers.* New York: Guilford.

Melton, G. B., and Saks, M. J. (1986). The Law as an Instrument of Socialization and Social Structure. In G. B. Melton (Ed.), *The Law as a Behavioral Instrument* (pp. 235–277). Lincoln, NB: University of Nebraska Press.

Memmi, A. (1968). *Dominated Man: Notes toward a Portrait.* New York: Orion Press.

Miles, M. B., and Huberman, A. M. (1994). *Qualitative Data Analysis: A Source Book of New Methods* (2nd edn). London: Sage.

Miller, D. (1978). *Social Justice.* Oxford: Clarendon.

Miller, G. A. (1969). Psychology as a Means of Promoting Human Welfare. *American Psychologist, 24*, 1063–1075.

Miller-Jones, D. (1989). Culture and Testing. *American Psychologist, 44*, 360–366.

Mirkin, M. P. (Ed.). (1994). *Women in Context: Toward a Feminist Reconstruction of Psychotherapy.* New York: Guilford.

Moberly, E. R. (1983). *Psychogenesis: The Early Development of Gender Identity.* London: Routledge and Kegan Paul.

Moghaddam, F. M. (1987). Psychology in the Three Worlds: As Reflected by the Crisis in Social Psychology and the Move toward Indigenous Third World Psychology. *American Psychologist, 42,* 912–920.

Moghaddam, F. M. (1990). Modulative and Generative Orientations in Psychology: Implications for Psychology in the Three Worlds. *Journal of Social Issues, 46,* 21–41.

Moghaddam, F. M., and Harré, R. (1995). But Is It Science? Traditional and Alternative Approaches to the Study of Social Behavior. *World Psychology, 1,* 47–78.

Moghaddam, F. M., and Solliday, E. A. (1991). "Balanced Multiculturalism" and the Challenge of Peaceful Coexistence in Pluralistic Societies. *Psychology and Developing Societies, 3,* 51–72.

Moghaddam, F. M., and Taylor, D. M. (1987). The Meaning of Multiculturalism for Visible Minority Immigrant Women. *Canadian Journal of Behavioural Science, 19,* 121–136.

Moghaddam, F. M., Taylor, D. M., and Lalonde, R. N. (1987). Individual and Collective Integration Strategies among Iranians in Canada. *International Journal of Psychology, 22,* 301–313.

Moghaddam, F. M., Taylor, D. M., and Lalonde, R. N. (1989). Integration Strategies and Attitudes toward the Built Environment: A Study of Haitian and Indian Immigrant Women in Montreal. *Canadian Journal of Behavioral Science, 21,* 160–173.

Moghaddam, F. M., Taylor, D. M., and Wright, S. C. (1993). *Social Psychology in Cross-Cultural Perspective.* New York: Freeman.

Moghaddam, F. M., Taylor, D. M., Lambert, W. E., and Schmidt, A. E. (1995). Attributions and Discrimination: A Study of Attributions to the Self, the Group, and External Factors Among Whites, Blacks, and Cubans in Miami. *Journal of Cross-Cultural Psychology, 26,* 209–220.

Monahan, J., and Walker, L. (1988). Social Science Research in Law: A New Paradigm. *American Psychologist, 43,* 465–472.

Monahan, J., and Walker, L. (1991). Judicial Use of Social Science Research. *Law and Human Behavior, 15,* 571–584.

Monahan, J., and Walker, L. (1994). Judicial Use of Social Science Research after *Daubert. Shepard's Expert and Scientific Evidence Quarterly, 2,* 327–342.

Monckeberg, F. B. (1973). Effects of Nutrition on Brain and Intellectual Development. In F. Richardson (Ed.), *Brain and Intelligence* (pp. 207–236). Hyattsville, MD: National Educational Press.

Montero, M. (1985). *Ideología, Alienación e Identidad Nacional* [Ideology, Alienation, and National Identity]. Caracas, Venezuela: EBUC.

Montero, M. (1990). Autoimagen de los Venezolanos: Lo Negativo y lo Positivo [Venezuelan Self-Image: What Is Negative and What Is Positive]. In H. Riquelme (Ed.), *Buscando América Latina* [Looking for Latin America] (pp. 45–56). Caracas, Venezuela: Nueva Visión.

Montero, M. (1991). Psicología de la Liberación: Propuesta Para una Teoría Psicosociológica [Psychology of Liberation: Proposal for a Psychosociological Theory]. In H. Riquelme (Ed.), *Otras Realidades, Otras Vías de Acceso* [Other Realities, Other Paths] (pp. 133–150). Caracas, Venezuela: Nueva Sociedad.

Montero, M. (1993). De-Ideologization, Conversion, and Consciousness-Raising. *Journal of Community Psychology, 22,* 3–11.

Montero, M. (Ed.). (1994). *Psicología Social Comunitaria* [Social-Community Psychology]. Guadalajara, Mexico: Universidad de Guadalajara.

Montero, M. (1995). Modos Alternativos de Acción Política [Alternative Modes of Political Action]. In O. D'Adamo, V. García-Beaudoux, and M. Montero (Eds.), *Psicología de la Acción Política* [Psychology of Political Action] (pp. 91–109). Buenos Aires, Argentina: Paidós.

Moon, D. (1983). Political Ethics and Critical Theory. In D. Sabia and J. Wallulis (Eds.), *Changing Social Science* (pp. 171–188). New York: State University of New York Press.

Morawski, Jill G. (1994). *Practicing Feminisms, Reconstructing Psychology: Notes on a Liminal Science.* Ann Arbor, MI: University of Michigan Press.

Morin, S. F. (1977). Heterosexual Bias in Psychological Research on Lesbianism and Male Homosexuality. *American Psychologist, 19,* 629–637.

Morin, S. F., and Rothblum, E. (1991). Removing the Stigma: Fifteen Years of Progress. *American Psychologist, 46,* 947–949.

Morris, A. D., and Mueller, C. M. (Eds.). (1992). *Frontiers in Social Movement Theory.* New Haven, CT: Yale University Press.

Morss, J. (1990). *The Biologizing of Childhood.* Hillsdale, NJ: Erlbaum.

Morss, J. (1995). *Growing Critical: Alternatives to Developmental Psychology.* London: Routledge.

Moscovici, S. (1976). *Psychologie des Minorités Actives* [Psychology of Active Minorities]. Paris: Presse Universitaire de France.

Moscovici, S. (1985). Social Influence and Conformity. In G. Lindzey and E. Aronson (Eds.), *The Handbook of Social Psychology* (3rd edn, Vol. 2, pp. 347–412). New York: Random House.

Moscovici, S., and Mugny, G. (Eds.). (1987). *Psychologie de la Conversion: Etudes sur l'Influence Inconsciente* [Psychology of Conversion: Studies on Unconscious Influence]. Fribourg, Switzerland: Del Val.

Mulkay, M., and Gilbert, G. N. (1982). Accounting for Error: How Scientists Construct their Social Worlds When They Account for Correct and Incorrect Belief. *Sociology, 16,* 165–183.

Mulvey, A. (1988). Community Psychology and Feminism: Tensions and Commonalities. *Journal of Community Psychology, 16,* 70–83.

Münch, R. (1988). *Understanding Modernity.* London: Routledge.

Munné, F. (1986). *La Construcción de la Psicología Social como Ciencia Teórica* [The Construction of Social Psychology as a Theoretical Science]. Barcelona, Spain: Alamex.

Murchison, C. (1933). Preface. In C. Murchison (Ed.), *A Handbook of Child Psychology* (pp. ix–x). Worcester, MA: Clark University Press.

Murphy, S. T., Mohahan, J. L., and Zajonc, R. B. (1995). Additivity of Nonconscious Affect: Combined Effects of Priming and Exposure. *Journal of Personality and Social Psychology, 69,* 589–602.

Nahem, J. (1981). *Psychology and Psychiatry Today.* New York: International Publishers.

Nakano, Glenn E., Chang, G., and Rennie Forcey, L. (Eds.). (1994). *Mothering: Ideology, Experience, Agency.* New York: Routledge.

Namka, Lynn (1989). *The Doormat Syndrome.* Deerfield Beach, FL: Health Communications Inc.

Napoli, D. S. (1981). *Architects of Adjustment: A History of the Psychological Profession in the United States.* Port Washington, NY: National University Publications.

Neff, W. S. (1938). Social Problems and Intelligence. *Psychologists League Journal, 2,* 29–33, 41.

Neilands, T. (1993). The Time Course of the Self-Concept Threat Reduction Process among Low and High Self-Esteem Individuals. World Wide Web document. Available URL: http://uts.cc.utexas.edu/~neilands/psych/research/bigd/.

Nelson, G. (1994). The Development of a Mental Health Coalition: A Case Study. *American Journal of Community Psychology, 22,* 229–255.

Nelson, G., and Hayday, B. (1995). Advancing Prevention in Ontario, Canada: Follow-Up to a Utilization-Focused Evaluation. *Prevention in Human Services, 12*(1), 43–68.

Nelson, G., and Walsh-Bowers, R. (1994). Psychology and Psychiatric Survivors. *American Psychologist, 49,* 895–896.

Nelson, K. (1990). Mothering Others' Children: The Experiences of Family Daycare Providers. *Signs: Journal of Women in Culture and Society, 15*(31), 586–605.

Newbrough, J. R. (1992). Community Psychology in the Postmodern World. *Journal of Community Psychology, 20,* 10–25.

Newbrough, J. R. (1995). Toward Community: A Third Position. *American Journal of Community Psychology, 23,* 9–38.

Newman, F. (1991). *The Myth of Psychology.* New York: Castillo.

Newton, E. (1993). *Cherry Grove, Fire Island: Sixty Years in America's First Gay and Lesbian Town.* Boston: Beacon Press.

Ng, S. H. (1980). *The Social Psychology of Power.* London: Academic Press.

Nichols, M. (1987). Lesbian Sexuality: Issues and Developing Theory. In Boston Lesbian Psychologies Collective (Ed.), *Lesbian Psychologies: Explorations and Challenges* (pp. 97–125). Urbana, IL: University of Illinois Press.

Nicolson, P. (1986). Developing a Feminist Approach to Depression Following Childbirth. In Sue Wilkinson (Ed.), *Feminist Social Psychology: Developing Theory and Practice* (pp. 135–149). Milton Keynes and Philadelphia, PA: Open University Press.

Nisbett, R. E. (1993). Violence and U.S. Regional Culture. *American Psychologist, 48,* 441–449.

Nisbett, R. E., and Cohen, D. (forthcoming). *Culture of Honor: Violence and the U.S. South.* Boulder, CO: Westview Press.

Nisbett, R. E., and Wilson, T. D. (1977). Telling More Than We Can Know: Verbal Reports on Mental Processes. *Psychological Review, 84,* 231–259.

Nottingham Community NHS Trust (n.d.) *Statement of Philosophy.* (Available from Steve Melleish, Nottingham Community Health NHS Trust, Psychology Service, Linden House, 261 Beechdale Road, Aspley, Nottingham NG8 3DY, UK.)

Novaco, R., and Monahan, J. (1980). Research in Community Psychology: An Analysis of Work Published in the First Ten Years of the *American Journal of Community Psychology. American Journal of Community Psychology, 8,* 131–146.

O'Hagan, K., and Dillenburger, K. (1995). *The Abuse of Women within Childcare Work.* Buckingham: Open University Press.

Ogloff, J. R. P. (Ed.). (1992). *Law and Psychology: The Broadening of the Discipline.* Durham, NC: Carolina Academic Press.

Ogloff, J. R. P. (Ed.). (1993). *Psychology and Law Syllabi* (3rd edn). American Psychology-Law Society (available from James Ogloff, Department of Psychology, Simon Fraser University, Burnaby, British Columbia, Canada V5A 1S6).

Ogloff, J. R. P., Tomkins, A. J., and Bersoff, D. N. (1996). Education and Training in Psychology and Law/Criminal Justice: Historical Foundations, Present Structures, and Future Developments. *Criminal Justice and Behavior, 23,* 200–235.

Osipow, S. H., and Fitzgerald, L. T. (1993). Unemployment and Mental Health: A Neglected Relationship. *Applied and Preventive Psychology, 2,* 59–63.

Otto, R. K., Heilbrun, K., and Grisso, T. (1990). Training and Credentialing in Forensic Psychology. *Behavioral Sciences and the Law, 8,* 217–231.

Pancer, S. M. (1996). Program Evaluation. In S. W. Sadava and D. R. McCreary (Eds.), *Applied Social Psychology* (pp. 47–67). Englewood Cliffs, NJ: Prentice-Hall.

Parker, I. (1992). *Discourse Dynamics: Critical Analysis for Social and Individual Psychology.* London, New York: Routledge.

Parker, I. (1994). Discourse Analysis. In P. Banister, E. Burman, I. Parker, M. Taylor, and C. Tindall (Eds.), *Qualitative Methods in Psychology: A Research Guide* (pp. 92–107). Buckingham: Open University Press.

Parker, I. (1995). Michel Foucault, Psychologist. *The Psychologist, 8*(11), 214–216.

Parker, I. (1996). Against Wittgenstein: Materialist Reflections on Language. *Theory and Psychology, 6,* 363–384.

Parker, I., and Burman, E. (1993). Against Discursive Imperialism, Empiricism and Constructionism: Thirty-Two Problems with Discourse Analysis. In E. Burman and I. Parker (Eds.), *Discourse Analytic Research: Repertoires and Readings of Texts in Action* (pp. 155–172). London: Routledge.

Parker, I., Georgaca, E., Harper, D., McLaughlin, T., and Stowell-Smith, M. (1995). *Deconstructing Psychopathology*. London: Sage.

Parker, I., and Shotter, J. (1990). Introduction. In I. Parker and J. Shotter (Eds.), *Deconstructing Social Psychology* (pp. 1–14). London: Routledge.

Parlee, Mary Brown (1973). The Premenstrual Syndrome. *Psychological Bulletin, 80*, 454–465.

Parlee, Mary Brown (1975). Review Essay: Psychology. *Signs, 1*, 119–138.

Parlee, Mary Brown (1989). The Science and Politics of PMS Research. Paper presented at the *Meeting of the Association for Women in Psychology*, Newport, RI, March.

Parlee, Mary Brown (1991). Happy Birth-Day to *Feminism & Psychology*. *Feminism & Psychology, 1*(1), 39–48.

Patterson, C. J. (1994). Children of the Lesbian Baby Boom: Behavioral Adjustment, Self-Concepts, and Sex Role Identity. In B. Greene and G. M. Herek (Eds.), *Psychological Perspectives on Lesbian and Gay Issues. Vol. 1: Lesbian and Gay Psychology: Theory, Research and Clinical Applications* (pp. 156–175). Thousand Oaks, CA: Sage.

Patterson, C. J. (1995). Sexual Identity Development. Special issue of *Developmental Psychology, 31*(1).

Payton, C. R. (1994). Implications of the 1992 Ethics Code for Diverse Groups. *Professional Psychology: Research and Practice, 25*, 317–320.

Pearson, G. (1975). *The Deviant Imagination: Psychiatry, Social Work and Social Change*. London: Macmillan.

Peirson, L., and Walsh-Bowers, R. (1993). The First Decade of the *Canadian Journal of Community Mental Health. Canadian Journal of Community Mental Health, 12*(1), 23–35.

Pepitone, A. (1981). Lessons from the History of Social Psychology. *American Psychologist, 36*, 827–836.

Perelberg, R. J., and Miller, A. C. (Eds.). (1990). *Gender and Power in Families*. London: Routledge.

Perlin, M. L. (1991). Power Imbalances in Therapeutic and Forensic Relationships. *Behavioral Sciences and the Law, 9*, 111–128.

Perlin, M. L. (Ed.). (1993). Therapeutic Jurisprudence: Restructuring Mental Disability Law. Special issue of *New York Law School Journal of Human Rights, 10*(3).

Perlin, M. L. (1994). Therapeutic Jurisprudence: Understanding the Sanist and Pretextual Bases of Disability Law. *New England Journal on Criminal and Civil Confinement, 20*, 369–383.

Perlin, M. L., and Dorfman, D. A. (1993). Sanism, Social Science, and the Development of Mental Disability Law Jurisprudence. *Behavioral Sciences and the Law, 11*, 47–66.

Petrila, J. (1993). Paternalism and the Unrealized Promise of *Essays in Therapeutic Jurisprudence* (Review of *Essays in Therapeutic Jurisprudence*). *New York Law School Journal of Human Rights, 10*, 877–905.

Pettifor, J. L. (1996). Ethics: Virtue and Politics in the Science and Practice of Psychology. *Canadian Psychology, 37*, 1–12.

Philip, M. (1985). Michel Foucault. In Q. Skinner (Ed.), *The Return of Grand Theory in the Human Sciences* (pp. 65–82). Cambridge: Cambridge University Press.

Phillips, D. C. (1987). *Philosophy, Science and Social Inquiry*. Oxford: Pergamon.

Phillips, L. (1995). *Flirting with Danger: A Study of Multiple Meanings of Male Aggression in Women's Hetero-Relations*. Unpublished doctoral dissertation, University of Pennsylvania, Philadelphia.

Phoenix, A. (1987). Theories of Gender and Black Families. In G. Weiner and M. Arnot (Eds.), *Gender Under Scrutiny* (pp. 50–63). London: Hutchinson.

Phoenix, A. (1991). *Young Mothers?* Oxford: Polity Press.

Piaget, J. (1957). The Child and Modern Physics. *Scientific American, 197*, 46–51.

Pilgrim, D. (1992). Psychotherapy and Political Evasions. In W. Dryden and C. Feltham (Eds.), *Psychotherapy and its Discontents* (pp. 225–242). Bristol, PA: Open University Press.

Politzer, G. (1928). *Critique des Fondements de la Psychologie* [A Critique of Psychology's Fundamentals]. Paris: Editions Rieder.

Pope, K. S., Keith-Spiegel, P., and Tabachnick, B. G. (1986). Sexual Attraction to Patients:

The Human Therapist and the (Sometimes) Inhuman Training System. *American Psychologist, 41*, 147–158.

Potter, J., and Wetherell, M. (1987). *Discourse and Social Psychology: Beyond Attitudes and Behaviour*. London: Sage.

Powell, L. (forthcoming). Race Cubed. In M. Fine, L. Powell, L.Weis, and M. Wong (Eds.), *Off-White: Readings on Society, Culture and Race*. New York: Routledge.

Price, R. H., and Cherniss, C. (1977). Training for a New Profession: Research as Social Action. *Professional Psychology, 8*, 222–230.

Price, R. H., Cowen, E. L., Lorion, R. P., and Ramos-Mckay, J. (Eds.). (1988). *Fourteen Ounces of Prevention*. Washington, DC: American Psychological Association.

Prilleltensky, I. (1994a). *The Morals and Politics of Psychology: Psychological Discourse and the Status Quo*. Albany, NY: State University of New York.

Prilleltensky, I. (1994b). The United Nations Convention on the Rights of the Child: Implications for Children's Mental Health. *Canadian Journal of Community Mental Health, 13*(2), 77–93.

Prilleltensky, I., and Gonick, L. (1994). The Discourse of Oppression in the Social Sciences: Past, Present, and Future. In E. J. Trickett, R. J. Watts, and D. Birman (Eds.), *Human Diversity: Perspectives on People in Context* (pp. 145–177). San Francisco: Jossey-Bass.

Prilleltensky, I., and Gonick, L. (1996). Polities Change, Oppression Remains: On the Psychology and Politics of Oppression. *Journal of Political Psychology, 17*, 127–148.

Prilleltensky, I. (forthcoming). Values, Assumptions, and Practices: Assessing the Moral Implications of Psychological Discourse and Action. *American Psychologist*.

Quintero, M. P. (1993). *Psicología del Colonizado* [Psychology of the Colonized]. Mérida, Venezuela: ULA.

Rabinow, P. (Ed.). (1984). *The Foucault Reader*. New York: Pantheon.

Rae-Grant, N. I. (1994). Preventive Interventions for Children and Adolescents: Where Are We Now and How Far Have We Come? *Canadian Journal of Community Mental Health, 13*(2), 17–36.

Ransom, D. C., and Fisher, L. (1995). An Empirically Derived Typology of Families. II: Relationships with Adolescent Health. *Family Process, 34*, 183–197.

Rappaport, J. (1977). *Community Psychology: Values, Research, and Action*. New York: Holt, Rinehart, and Winston.

Rappaport, J. (1981). In Praise of Paradox: A Social Policy of Empowerment over Prevention. *American Journal of Community Psychology, 9*, 1–25.

Rappaport, J. (1987). Terms of Empowerment/Exemplars of Prevention: Toward a Theory for Community Psychology. *American Journal of Community Psychology, 15*, 121–148.

Rappaport, J. (1993). Narrative Studies, Personal Stories, and Identity Transformation in the Mutual Help Context. *Journal of Applied Behavioral Science, 29*, 237–254.

Rappaport, J. (1994). Empowerment as a Guide to Doing Research: Diversity as a Positive Value. In E. J. Trickett, R. J. Watts, and D. Birman (Eds.), *Human Diversity: Perspectives on People in Context* (pp. 359–382). San Francisco: Jossey-Bass.

Rappaport, J. (1995). Empowerment Meets Narrative: Listening to Stories and Creating Settings. *American Journal of Community Psychology, 23*, 795–807.

Rappaport, J., Chinsky, J. M., and Cowen, E. L. (1971). *Innovations in Helping Chronic Patients: College Students in a Mental Institution*. New York: Academic Press.

Rappaport, J., Davidson, W. S., Wilson, M. N., and Mitchell, A. (1975). Alternatives to Blaming the Victim or the Environment: Our Places to Stand Have Not Moved the Earth. *American Psychologist, 40*, 525–528.

Rappaport, J., Swift, C., and Hess, R. (Eds.). (1984). Studies in Empowerment: Steps toward Understanding and Action. Special issue of *Prevention in Human Services, 3*(2/3).

Rave, E. J., and Larsen, C. C. (1990). Development of the Code: The Feminist Process. In H. Lerman and N. Porter (Eds.), *Feminist Ethics in Psychotherapy* (pp. 14–23). New York: Springer.

Rave, E. J., and Larsen, C. C. (Eds.). (1995). *Ethical Decision-Making in Therapy: Feminist Perspectives*. New York: Guilford.

Rawls, J. (1972). *A Theory of Justice*. New York: Oxford University Press.

Reeves, N. (1971). *Womankind*. Chicago: Aldine-Atherton.

Reich, J. W. (1981). An Historical Analysis of the Field. In L. Bickman (Ed.), *Applied Social Psychology Annual* (Vol. 2, pp. 45–70). Beverly Hills, CA: Sage.

Reich, W. (1933). *The Mass Psychology of Fascism*. Harmondsworth: Penguin, 1970.

Reicher, S. (1996). "The Battle of Westminster": Developing the Social Identity Model of Crowd Behaviour in Order to Explain the Initiation and Development of Collective Conflict. *European Journal of Social Psychology*, *26*, 115–134.

Reid, P. M. (1993). Poor Women in Psychological Research: Shut Up and Shut Out. *Psychology of Women Quarterly*, *17*, 133–150.

Reinharz, S. (1992). *Feminist Methods in Social Research*. Oxford: Oxford University Press.

Reinharz, S., and Davidman, L. (1992). *Feminist Methods in Social Research*. Oxford: Oxford University Press.

Ribbens, J. (1994). *Mothers and Their Children*. London: Sage.

Rich, A. (1980). *Of Woman Born*. London: Virago.

Richardson, F., and Christopher, J. (1993). Social Theory as Practice. *Journal of Theoretical and Philosophical Psychology*, *13*, 137–153.

Richardson, F., and Fowers, B. (1994). Beyond Scientism and Constructionism. Paper presented at the *Annual Meeting of the American Psychological Association*, Los Angeles, CA, August.

Ricoeur, P. (1992). *Oneself as Another*. Chicago: University of Chicago Press.

Riger, S. (1993). What's Wrong with Empowerment? *American Journal of Community Psychology*, *21*, 279–292.

Riley, D. (1983). *War in the Nursery: Theories of Child and Mother*. London: Virago.

Riley, D. (1987). "The Serious Burdens of Love"? Some Questions on Child Care, Feminism and Socialism. In A. Phillips (Ed.), *Feminism and Equality* (pp. 166–197). Oxford: Blackwell.

Ring, K. (1967). Experimental Social Psychology: Some Sober Questions about Some Frivolous Values. *Journal of Experimental Social Psychology*, *3*, 113–123.

Roback, A. A. (1961). *History of Psychology and Psychiatry*. New York: Philosophical Library.

Robertson, J., and Fitzgerald, L. F. (1990). The (Mis)Treatment of Men: Effects of Client Gender Role and Life-Style on Diagnosis and Attribution of Pathology. *Journal of Counseling Psychology*, *37*, 3–9.

Roden, R. G. (1983). Threatening Homosexuality: A Case Treated by Hypnosis. *Medical Hypnoanalysis*, *4*, 166–169.

Rodríguez, I. (1993). *El Discurso de la Democracia Venezolana* [The Discourse of Venezuelan Democracy]. Dissertation, Universidad Central de Venezuela, Escuela de Psicología, Caracas.

Rodríguez, A. and Seoane, J. (Eds.). (1988). *Psicología Política* [Political Psychology]. Madrid, Spain: Pirámide.

Roesch, R. (1990). From the Editor. *Law and Human Behavior*, *14*, 1–3.

Roesch, R. (1995). Creating Change in the Legal System: Contributions from Community Psychology. *Law and Human Behavior*, *19*, 325–343.

Roesch, R., Dutton, D. G., and Sacco, V. S. (Eds.). (1990). *Family Violence: Perspectives in Research and Practice*. Burnaby, BC: Simon Fraser University Press.

Roesch, R., Golding, S. L., Hans, V. P., and Reppucci, N. D. (1991). Social Science and the Courts: The Role of *Amicus Curiae* Briefs. *Law and Human Behavior*, *15*, 1–11.

Rorty, R. (1980). *Philosophy and the Mirror of Nature*. Oxford: Basil Blackwell.

Rorty, R. (1982). *Consequences of Pragmatism*. Minneapolis: University of Minnesota Press.

Rorty, R. (1985). Solidarity or Objectivity? In J. Rajchman and C. West (Eds.), *Post-Analytic Philosophy* (pp. 3–19). New York: Columbia University Press.

Rorty, R. (1987). Method, Social Science and Social Hope. In M. Gibbons (Ed.), *Interpreting Politics* (pp. 241–260). New York: New York University Press.

Rose, N. (1985). *The Psychological Complex: Psychology, Politics and Society in England 1869–1939*. London: Routledge and Kegan Paul.

Rose, N. (Ed.). (1990). *Governing the Soul: The Shaping of the Private Self*. London: Routledge.

Rosenblum, G. (Ed.). (1971). *Issues in Community Psychology and Preventive Mental Health*. New York: Behavioral Publications.

Rosenhan, D. L. (1973). Being Sane in Insane Places. *Science, 179*, 250–258.

Rosenthal, R. (1991). *Meta-Analytic Procedures for Social Sciences*. London: Sage.

Rosenthal, R., and Rubin, D. B. (1985). Statistical Analysis: Summarizing Evidence versus Establishing Facts. *Psychological Bulletin, 97*, 527–529.

Rosenwald, G. C. (1985). Hypocrisy, Self-Deception, and Perplexity: The Subject's Enhancement as Methodological Criterion. *Journal of Personality and Social Psychology, 49*, 682–703.

Rosenwald, G. C. (1988). Toward a Formative Psychology. *Journal for the Theory of Social Behavior, 18*, 1–32.

Rosenwald, G. C., and Ochberg, R. L. (Eds.). (1992). *Storied Lives: The Cultural Politics of Self-Understanding*. New Haven, CT: Yale University Press.

Ross, E. A. (1908). *Social Psychology*. New York: Macmillan.

Roubertoux, P. L., and Capron, C. (1990a). Are Intelligence Differences Hereditarily Transmitted? *Cahiers de Psychologie Cognitive, 10*, 555–594.

Roubertoux, P. L., and Capron, C. (1990b). Now to the Future: The Heritability of IQ versus the Cognitive-Genetic Analysis. *Cahiers de Psychologie Cognitive, 10*, 715–721.

Rowbotham, S., Segal, L., and Wainwright, H. (1979). *Beyond the Fragments: Feminism and the Making of Socialism*. Newcastle and London: NSC/ICP.

Ruse, M. (1984). Nature/Nurture: Reflections on Approaches to the Study of Homosexuality. *Journal of Homosexuality, 10*, 141–151.

Rushton, J. P. (1988). Race Differences in Behavior: A Review and Evolutionary Analysis. *Personality and Individual Differences, 9*, 1009–1024.

Rushton, J. P. (1990a). Race, Brain Size, and Intelligence: A Reply to Cernovsky. *Psychological Reports, 66*, 659–666.

Rushton, J. P. (1990b). Race, Brain Size, and Intelligence: A Rejoinder to Cain and Vanderwolf. *Personality and Individual Differences, 11*, 785–794.

Rushton, J. P. (1990c). Race and Crime: Reply to Roberts and Gabor. *Canadian Journal of Criminology, 32*, 315–334.

Rushton, J. P. (1991). Do r/K Strategies Underlie Human Race Differences? A Reply to Weizmann et al. *Canadian Psychology, 32*, 29–42.

Rushton, J. P. (1995). *Race, Evolution, and Behavior*. Brunswick, NJ: Transaction.

Ryan, C., and Bradford, J. (1993). The National Lesbian Health Care Survey: An Overview. In L. D. Garnets and D. C. Kimmel (Eds.), *Psychological Perspectives on Lesbian and Gay Experiences* (pp. 541–556). New York: Columbia University Press.

Ryan, W. (1971). *Blaming the Victim*. New York: Pantheon.

Sabucedo, J. M. (1990). Psicología y Participación Política [Psychology and Political Participation]. In J. Seoane (Ed.), *Psicología Política de la Sociedad Contemporánea* [Political Psychology in Contemporary Society] (pp. 23–36). Valencia, Spain: Promo-libro.

Sacks, H. (1974). On the Analyzability of Stories by Children. In R. Turner (Ed.), *Ethnomethodology* (pp. 216–232). Harmondsworth: Penguin.

Saks, M. J. (1986). The Law Does Not Live by Eyewitness Testimony Alone. *Law and Human Behavior, 110*, 279–280.

Salazar, J. M. (1983). *Bases Psicológicas del Nacionalismo* [Psychological Bases of Nationalism]. México: Trillas.

Sales, B. D. (Ed.). (1995). Therapeutic Jurisprudence. Special issue of *Psychology, Public Policy, and Law, 1*(1).

Samelson, F. (1974). History, Origin Myth, and Ideology: Comte's "Discovery" of Social Psychology. *Journal for the Theory of Social Behavior, 4*, 217–231.

Samelson, F. (1975). On the Science and Politics of the IQ. *Social Research, 42*, 467–488.

Samelson, F. (1979). Putting Psychology on the Map: Ideology and Intelligence Testing. In A. R. Buss (Ed.), *Psychology in Social Context* (pp. 103–168). New York: Irvington.

Samelson, F. (1992). Rescuing the Reputation of Sir Cyril [Burt]. *Journal of the History of the Behavioral Sciences, 28,* 221–233.

Sampson, E. E. (1977). Psychology and the American Ideal. *Journal of Personality and Social Psychology, 35,* 767–782.

Sampson, E. E. (1983). *Justice and the Critique of Pure Psychology.* New York: Plenum.

Sampson, E. E. (1989a). The Deconstruction of the Self. In J. Shotter and K. J. Gergen (Eds.), *Texts of Identity* (pp. 1–19). London: Sage.

Sampson, E. E. (1989b). The Challenge of Social Change for Psychology: Globalization and Psychology's Theory of the Person. *American Psychologist, 44,* 914–921.

Sampson, E. E. (1993). *Celebrating the Other: A Dialogic Account of Human Nature.* London: Harvester Wheatsheaf.

Sandel, M. J. (1996). *Democracy's Discontent: America in Search of a Public Philosophy.* Cambridge, MA: Harvard University Press.

Sanford, N. (1970). Whatever Happened to Action Research? *Journal of Social Issues, 26,* 3–23.

Sarason, S. B. (1972). *The Creation of Settings and the Future Societies.* San Francisco: Jossey-Bass.

Sarason, S. B. (1974). *The Psychological Sense of Community: Prospects for a Community Psychology.* San Francisco: Jossey-Bass.

Sarason, S. B. (1976). Community Psychology and the Anarchist Insight. *American Journal of Community Psychology, 4,* 243–261.

Sarason, S. B. (1981). *Psychology Misdirected.* New York: Free Press.

Sarason, S. B. (1988). *The Psychological Sense of Community: Prospects for a Community Psychology* (rev. edn). Cambridge, MA: Brookline.

Sarbin, T. R., and Kitsuse, J. I. (Eds.). (1994). *Constructing the Social.* London: Sage.

Saul, J. R. (1995). *The Unconscious Civilization.* Toronto: Anansi.

Scherer, K. R. (Ed.). (1992). *Justice: Interdisciplinary Perspectives.* New York: Cambridge University Press.

Schilling, Karen M., and Fuehrer, Ann (1993). The Politics of Women's Self-Help Books. *Feminism & Psychology, 3*(3), 418–422.

Schmidt, G., and Schorsch, E. (1981). Psychosurgery of Sexually Deviant Patients. *Archives of Sexual Behavior, 10,* 301–321.

Schonemann, P. (1989). Some New Results on the Spearman Hypothesis Artifact. *Bulletin of the Psychonomic Society, 27,* 462–464.

Schonemann, P. (1990). Environmental versus Genetic Variance Component Models for Identical Twins: A Critique of Jink and Fulker's Reanalysis of the Shields Data. *Cahiers de Psychologie Cognitive, 10,* 451–473.

Schonemann, P. (1992). Extension of Guttman's Result from g to PCI. *Multivariate Behavioral Research, 27*(2), 219–224.

Schonemann, P. (1995). Totems of the IQ Myth and its Heritabilities: g and h2. Paper presented at *Meeting of the American Association for the Advancement of Science,* Atlanta, Georgia, February.

Schopp, R. F. (1993). Therapeutic Jurisprudence and Conflicts among Values in Mental Health Law Scholarship. *Behavioral Sciences and the Law, 31,* 31–45.

Schopp, R. F. (1995). Sexual Predators and the Structure of the Mental Health System: Expanding the Normative Focus of Therapeutic Jurisprudence. *Psychology, Public Policy, and Law, 1,* 161–192.

Schrecker, E. W. (1986). *No Ivory Tower: McCarthyism and the Universities.* New York: Oxford University Press.

Schulman, J., Shaver, P., Colman, R., Emrich, B., and Christie, R. (1973). Recipe for a Jury. *Psychology Today,* May, 37–44, 77–84.

Schultz, D. P. (1969). *A History of Modern Psychology.* New York: Academic Press.

Scott-Jones, D. (1995). *The Bell Curve* Critique. *Focus: Notes from the Society for the Psychological Study of Ethnic Minority Issues*, 14–16.

Sears, D. O. (1986). College Sophomores in the Laboratory: Influences of a Narrow Data Base on Social Psychology's View of Human Nature. *Journal of Personality and Social Psychology, 51*, 515–530.

Segall, M. H., Dasen, P. R., Berry, J. W., and Poortinga, Y. H. (1990). *Human Behavior in Global Perspective: An Introduction to Cross-Cultural Psychology.* New York: Pergamon Press.

Seidman, E. (1988). Back to the Future, Community Psychology: Unfolding a Theory of Social Intervention. *American Journal of Community Psychology, 16*, 3–24.

Senn, D. J. (1989). Myopic Social Psychology: An Overemphasis on Individualistic Explanations of Social Behavior. In M. R. Leary (Ed.), *The State of Social Psychology: Issues, Themes and Controversies* (pp. 45–52). Newbury Park, CA: Sage.

Serrano-García, I. (1990). Implementing Research: Putting Our Values to Work. In P. Tolan, C. Keys, F. Chertok, and L. Jason (Eds.), *Researching Community Psychology: Issues of Theory and Methods* (pp. 171–182). Washington, DC: American Psychological Association.

Serrano-García, I., and Bond, M. A. (Eds.). (1994). Empowering the Silent Ranks. Special issue of *American Journal of Community Psychology, 22*(4).

Serrano-García, I., and Rosario, W. (Eds.). (1992). *Contribuciones Puertorriqueñas a la Psicología Social Comunitaria* [Puerto-Rican Contributions to Social-Community Psychology]. San Juan de Puerto Rico: EDUPR.

Sethna, Christabelle (1992). Accepting "Total and Complete Responsibility": New Age, Neo-Feminist Violence against Women. *Feminism & Psychology, 2*(1), 113–119.

Sève, L. (1978). *Man in Marxist Theory and the Psychology of Personality.* Atlantic Highlands, NJ: Humanities Press.

Shakur, S. (1993). *Monster: The Autobiography of an L.A. Gang Member.* New York: Penguin.

Sherif, M. (1936). *The Psychology of Social Norms.* New York: Harper.

Sherif, M. (1951). Experimental Study of Intergroup Relations. In J. H. Rohrer and M. Sherif (Eds.), *Social Psychology at the Crossroads* (pp. 388–426). New York: Harper and Row.

Sherif, M., Harvey, O. J., White, B. J., Hood, W. R., and Sherif, C. W. (1988). *The Robbers Cave Experiment: Intergroup Conflict and Cooperation.* Middletown, CT: Wesleyan University Press.

Sherif, M., and Sherif, C. W. (1953). *Groups in Harmony and Tension: An Integration of Studies on Intergroup Relations.* New York: Harper.

Sherif, M., White, B. J., and Harvey, O. J. (1955). Status in Experimentally Produced Groups. *American Journal of Sociology, 60*, 370–379.

Shidlo, A. (1994). Internalized Homophobia: Conceptual and Empirical Issues in Measurement. In B. Greene and G. M. Herek (Eds.), *Psychological Perspectives on Lesbian and Gay Issues. Vol. 1: Lesbian and Gay Psychology: Theory, Research and Clinical Applications* (pp. 176–205). Thousand Oaks, CA: Sage.

Shinn, M. (1978). Father Absence and Children's Cognitive Development. *Psychological Bulletin, 85*(3), 286–324.

Shinn, M. (1987). Expanding Community Psychology's Domain. *American Journal of Community Psychology, 15*, 555–574.

Shotter, J. (1984). *Social Accountability and Selfhood.* Oxford: Blackwell.

Shotter, J., and Gergen, K. J. (Eds.). (1989). *Texts of Identity.* London: Sage.

Shweder, R. A. (1990). Cultural Psychology: What is It? In R. A. Stigler, R. A. Shweder and G. Herdt (Eds.), *Cultural Psychology* (pp. 1–43). New York: Cambridge University Press.

Silverman, I. (1977). Why Social Psychology Fails. *Canadian Psychological Review, 18*, 353–358.

Sinha, D. (1986). *Psychology in a Third World Country: The Indian Experience.* New Delhi: Sage.

Skinner, B. F. (1971). *Beyond Freedom and Dignity.* New York: Knopf.

Skutnabb Kangas, T., and Cummins, J. (Eds.). (1988). *Minority Education: From Shame to Struggle.* Avon: Multilingual Matters.

Sloan, T. S. (1986). Breaking the Objectivist Hold on Personality Psychology. *Annals of Theoretical Psychology*, *4*, 226–231.

Sloan, T. S. (1987). Lucien Sève: Foundations for a Critical Psychology of Personality. In R. Hogan and W. Jones (Eds.), *Perspectives on Personality*, (Vol. 2, pp. 125–142). Greenwich, CT: JAI Press.

Sloan, T. S. (1994). La Personalidad como Construcción Ideológica [Personality as Ideological Construction]. In M. Montero (Ed.), *Construcción y Crítica de la Psicología Social* [Social Construction and Critique of Social Psychology] (pp. 177–188). Barcelona: Anthropos.

Sloan, T. S. (1996a). *Damaged Life: The Crisis of the Modern Psyche*. New York: Routledge.

Sloan, T. S. (1996b). *Life Choices: Understanding Dilemmas and Decisions*. Boulder, CO: Westview.

Slobogin, C. (1995). Therapeutic Jurisprudence: Five Dilemmas to Ponder. *Psychology, Public Policy, and Law*, *1*, 193–219.

Small, M. A. (1993). Advancing Psychological Jurisprudence. *Behavioral Sciences and the Law*, *11*, 3–16.

Small, M. A., and Wiener, R. L. (Eds.). (1993). Jurisprudence. Special issue of *Behavioral Sciences and the Law*, *11*(1).

Smith, D. (1974). Theorizing as Ideology. In R. Turner (Ed.), *Ethnomethodology* (pp. 41–44). Harmondsworth: Penguin.

Smith, D. (1978). K is Mentally Ill: The Anatomy of a Factual Account. *Sociology*, *12*, 23–53.

Smith, D. (1987). *The Everyday World as Problematic*. Boston: Northeastern University Press.

Smith, J. A., Harré, R., and Van Langenhove, L. (1995). *Rethinking Methods in Psychology*. London: Sage.

Smith, M. B. (1972). Is Experimental Social Psychology Advancing? *Journal of Experimental Social Psychology*, *8*, 86–96.

Smith, M. B. (1973). Is Psychology Relevant to New Priorities? *American Psychologist*, *28*, 463–471.

Smith, P., and Bond, M. (1994). *Social Psychology across Cultures*. Needham Heights, MA: Allyn and Bacon.

Snyder, M., and Ickes, W. (1985). Personality and Social Psychology. In G. Lindzey and E. Aronson (Eds.), *The Handbook of Social Psychology* (pp. 883–948). New York: Random House.

Sokal, M. M. (1987). *Psychological Testing and American Society*. New Brunswick, NJ: Rutgers University Press.

Solberg, A. (1990). Negotiating Childhood: Changing Constructions of Age for Norwegian Children. In A. James and A. Prout (Eds.), *Constructing and Reconstructing Childhood: Contemporary Issues in the Sociological Study of Childhood*, Basingstoke: Falmer Press.

Spivak, G. (1990). The Post-Modern Condition. In S. Harasym (Ed.), *The Post-Colonial Critic* (pp. 162–163). New York: Routledge.

Spring, B., Pingitore, R., Bourgeois, M., Kessler, K. H., and Bruckner, E. (1992). The Effects and Non-Effects of Skipping Breakfast: Results of Three Studies. Paper presented at the *100th Annual Meeting of the American Psychological Association*, Washington, DC, August.

Squire, Corinne (1990). Feminism as Antipsychology: Learning and Teaching in Feminist Psychology. In Erica Burman (Ed.), *Feminists and Psychological Practice* (pp. 76–88). London: Sage.

Squire, Corinne (forthcoming). Who's White? Daytime Talk Shows' Constructions of Whiteness. In M. Fine, L. Powell, L. Weis, and M. Wong (Eds.), *Off-White: Readings on Society, Culture and Race*. New York: Routledge.

Stack, C. (1974). *All Our Kin*. New York: Harper and Row.

Stainton Rogers, R., and Stainton Rogers, W. (1992). *Stories of Childhood: Shifting Agendas of Child Concern*. Hemel Hempstead: Harvester Wheatsheaf.

Stampp, K. M. (1956). *The Peculiar Institution: Slavery in the Antebellum South*. New York: Knopf.

Stanfield, J. H. (1994). Ethnic Modeling in Qualitative Research. In N. K. Denzin and Y. S.

Lincoln (Eds.), *Handbook of Qualitative Research* (pp. 175–188). Thousand Oaks, CA: Sage.

Stanton, W. (1965). *The Leopard's Spots*. Chicago: University of Chicago Press.

Steinem, Gloria (1992). *Revolution from Within: A Book of Self-Esteem*. New York: Little, Brown.

Steiner, I. D. (1974). Whatever Happened to the Group in Social Psychology? *Journal of Experimental Social Psychology, 10*, 94–108.

Sternberg, R. J. (1995). For Whom the Bell Curve Tolls: A Review of *The Bell Curve*. *Psychological Science, 6*, 257–261.

Stewart, E., and Weinstein, R. (1996). Volunteer Participation in Context: Motivations and Political Efficacy in three AIDS Organizations.

Stigler, R. A., Shweder, R. A., and Herdt, G. (Eds.). (1990). *Cultural Psychology*. New York: Cambridge University Press.

Stone, W. F. (1974). *The Psychology of Politics*. New York: Free Press.

Stone W. F. (1981). Political Psychology: A Whig History. In S. L. Long (Ed.), *The Handbook of Political Behavior* (Vol. 1, pp. 1–67). New York: Plenum Press.

Storfer, M. D. (1990). *Intelligence and Giftedness*. San Francisco: Jossey-Bass.

Strauss, A. L., and Corbin, J. (1990). *Basics of Qualitative Research: Grounded Theory Procedures and Techniques*. Newbury Park, CA: Sage.

Striegel-Moore, R., Silberstein, L., and Rodin, J. (1986). Toward an Understanding of Risk Factors for Bulimia. *American Psychologist, 41*, 246–263.

Stromberg, C. (1993). Privacy, Confidentiality and Privilege. *The Psychologist's Legal Update, Vol. 1*. Washington, DC: National Register of Health Service Providers in Psychology.

Strommen, E. F. (1993). "You're a What?": Family Member Reactions to the Disclosure of Homosexuality. In L. D. Garnets and D. C. Kimmel (Eds.), *Psychological Perspectives on Lesbian and Gay Male Experiences* (pp. 248–266). New York: Columbia University Press.

Suarez-Balcazar, Y., Durlak, J. A., and Smith, C. (1994). Multicultural Training Practices in Community Psychology Programs. *American Journal of Community Psychology, 22*, 785–798.

Sue, S. (1995). Implications of *The Bell Curve*: Whites are Genetically Inferior in Intelligence? *Focus: Notes from the Society for the Psychological Study of Ethnic Minority Issues*, 16–17.

Sullivan, E. V. (1984). *A Critical Psychology*. New York: Plenum.

Sullivan, W. (1986). *Reconstructing Public Philosophy*. Berkeley, CA: University of California Press.

Surrey, J. L. (1991). Relationship and Empowerment. In J. V. Jordan, A. G. Kaplan, J. B. Miller, I. P. Stiver, and J. L. Surrey (Eds.), *Women's Growth in Connection: Writings from the Stone Center* (pp. 162–180). New York: Guilford.

Swift, C., Bond, M. A., and Serrano-García, I. (forthcoming). Women's Lives in the Community. In J. Rappaport and E. Seidman (Eds.), *Handbook of Community Psychology*. New York: Plenum Press.

Szapocznik, J., and Kurtines, W. (1993). Family Psychology and Cultural Diversity: Opportunities for Theory, Research, and Application. *American Psychologist, 45*, 400–407.

Szasz, T. (1981). *The Manufacture of Madness*. London: Routledge and Kegan Paul.

Tamasese, K., and Waldegrave, C. (1996). Culture and Gender Accountability in the "Just Therapy" Approach. In C. McLean, M. Carey, and C. White (Eds.), *Men's Ways of Being* (pp. 51–62). Boulder, CO: Westview Press.

Tapp, J. L. (1974). The Psychological Limits of Legality. In J. R. Pennock and J. W. Chapman (Eds.), *The Limits of Law: Nomos xv* (pp. 46–75). New York: Lieber-Atherton.

Tapp, J. L., and Levine, F. J. (Eds.). (1977). *Law, Justice, and the Individual in Society: Psychological and Legal Issues*. New York: Holt, Rinehart.

Tavris, Carol (1992). *The Mismeasure of Woman*. New York: Touchstone/Simon and Schuster.

Tavris, Carol (1993). The Mismeasure of Woman. *Feminism & Psychology, 3*(2), 149–168.

Taylor, C. (1985). *Philosophy and the Human Sciences: Philosophical Papers* (Vol. 2). Cambridge: Cambridge University Press.

Taylor, C. (1989). *Sources of the Self*. Cambridge, MA: Harvard University Press.

Taylor, C. (1992). *Multiculturalism and the "Politics of Recognition"*. Princeton, NJ: Princeton University Press.

Taylor, C. (1995). *Philosophical Arguments*. Cambridge, MA: Harvard University Press.

Taylor, D. M., and Moghaddam, F. M. (1994). *Theories of Intergroup Relations: International Social Psychological Perspectives* (2nd edn). New York: Praeger.

Taylor, H. F. (1980). *The IQ Game: A Methodological Inquiry into the Heredity–Environment Controversy*. New Brunswick, NJ: Rutgers University Press.

Terman, L. (1919). *The Measurement of Intelligence*. London: Harrap.

Tessman, L. (1995). Beyond Communitarian Unity in the Politics of Identity. *Socialist Review, 24*, 55–83.

Thomas, R. E., and Rappaport, J. (1996). Art as Community Narrative: A Resource for Social Change. In M. B. Lykes, R. Liem, A. Banuazizi, and M. Morris (Eds.), *Myths about the Powerless: Contesting Social Inequalities* (pp. 317–336). Philadelphia: Temple University Press.

Thompson, B. W. (1995). *A Hunger So Wide and Deep*. Minneapolis, MN: University of Minnesota Press.

Thompson, J. (1984). *Studies in the Theory of Ideology*. Berkeley, CA: University of California Press.

Tiefer, L. (1994). *Sex is Not a Natural Act and Other Essays*. Boulder, CO: Westview Press.

Tizard, B., and Hughes, M. (1984). *Young Children Learning*. London: Fontana.

Tobias, P. V. (1970). Brain Size, Grey Matter, and Race: Fact or Fiction? *American Journal of Physical Anthropology, 32*, 3–25.

Tocqueville, A. de (1831/1973). *Democracy in America*. New York: Knopf.

Tolman, C. (1994). *Psychology, Society, and Subjectivity: An Introduction to German Critical Psychology*. London: Routledge.

Tolman, C., and Maiers, W. (Eds.). (1991). *Critical Psychology: Contributions to an Historical Science of the Subject*. Cambridge: Cambridge University Press.

Tomes, N. (1994). Feminist histories of psychiatry. In M. S. Micale and R. Porter (Eds.), *Discovering the History of Psychiatry* (pp. 348–383). New York: Oxford University Press.

Tomkins, A. J. (1990). Training and Career Options. Special issue of *Behavioral Sciences and the Law, 8*(3).

Tomkins, A. J., and Cecil, J. S. (1994). Treating Social Science like Law: An Assessment of Monahan and Walker's Social Authority Proposal. *Shepard's Expert and Scientific Evidence Quarterly, 2*, 343–387.

Tomkins, A. J., Victor, B., and Adler, R. (1992). Psycholegal Aspects of Organizational Behavior: Assessing and Controlling Risk. In D. K. Kagehiro and W. S. Laufer (Eds.), *Handbook of Psychology and Law* (pp. 523–541). New York: Springer.

Triandis, H. C. (1994). *Culture and Social Behavior*. St. Louis: McGraw-Hill.

Triandis, H. C., Lambert, W. W., Berry, J. W., Brislin, R. W., Draguns, J., Lonner, W., and Heron, A. (Eds.). (1980). *Handbook of Cross-Cultural Psychology* (6 vols.). Boston: Allyn and Bacon.

Trickett, E. J., Irving, J. B., and Perl, H. (1984). Curriculum Issues in Community Psychology: The Ecology of Program Development and the Socialization of Students. *American Journal of Community Psychology, 12*, 264–279.

Trickett, E. J., Watts, R. J., and Birman, D. (Eds). (1994) *Human Diversity: Perspectives on People in Context*. San Francisco: Jossey-Bass.

Triplett, N. (1898). The Dynamogenic Factors in Pacemaking and Competition. *American Journal of Psychology, 9*, 507–533.

Turkel, G. (1996). *Law and Society: Critical Approaches*. Boston: Allyn and Bacon.

Tyler, F. B., Pargament, K. I., and Gatz, M. (1983). The Resource Collaborator Role: A Model for Interactions Involving Psychologists. *American Psychologist, 38*, 388–398.

Tyler, T. R. (1990). *Why People Obey the Law*. New Haven, CT: Yale University Press.

Tyler, T. R., and Mitchell, G. (1994). Legitimacy and the Empowerment of Discretionary Legal Authority: The United States Supreme Court and Abortion Rights. *Duke Law Journal, 43*, 703–802.

Tyler, T. R., Rasinski, K. A., and Griffin, E. (1986). Alternative Images of the Citizen: Implications for Public Policy. *American Psychologist, 41*, 970–978.

Unger, D. (1983). The Critical Legal Studies Movement. *Harvard Law Review, 96*, 592–621.

Unger, R. M. (1984). *Passion: An Essay on Personality.* New York: Free Press.

Unger, Rhoda (1982). Advocacy versus Scholarship Revisited: Issues in the Psychology of Women. *Psychology of Women Quarterly, 7*(1), 5–17.

Unger, Rhoda, and Crawford, Mary (1992). *Women and Gender: A Feminist Psychology.* New York: McGraw-Hill.

Urwin, C. (1985). Constructing Motherhood: The Persuasion of Normal Development. In C. Steedman, C. Urwin, and V. Walkerdine (Eds.), *Language, Gender and Childhood* (pp. 164–202). London: Routledge and Kegan Paul.

US Congress. House (1954). *Hearings on Subversion and Espionage in Defense Establishments.* House Committee on Un-American Activities. 83rd Congress, 1st Session, January 15 (pp. 22–32). Washington, DC: GPO.

Ussher, Jane M. (1990). Choosing Psychology, *or* Not Throwing the Baby Out with the Bathwater. In Erica Burman (Ed.), *Feminists and Psychological Practice* (pp. 47–61). London: Sage.

Vasquez, M. J. T., and Eldridge, N. S. (1994). Bringing Ethics Alive: Training Practitioners About Gender, Ethnicity and Sexual Orientation Issues. In N. K. Gartrell (Ed.), *Bringing Ethics Alive: Feminist Ethics in Psychotherapy Practice* (pp. 1–16). New York: Haworth.

Venn, C. (1984). The Subject of Psychology. In J. Henriques, W. Hollway, C. Urwin, C. Venn, and V. Walkerdine (Eds.), *Changing the Subject: Psychology, Social Regulation, and Subjectivity* (pp. 119–152). London: Methuen.

Visweswaran, K. (1994). *Fictions of Feminist Ethnography.* Minneapolis: University of Minnesota Press.

Wachs, T. D., Moussa, W., Bishry, Z., Yunis, F., Sobhy, A., McCabe, G., Jerome, N., Galal, O., Harrison, G., and Kirksey, A. (1993). Relations between Nutrition and Cognitive Performance in Egyptian Toddlers. *Intelligence, 17*, 151–172.

Wachtel, P. L. (1977). *Psychoanalysis and Behavior Therapy.* New York: Basic Books.

Wachtel, P. L. (1983). *The Poverty of Affluence: A Psychological Portrait of the American Way of Life.* New York: Free Press.

Wahlsten, D. (1994). The Intelligence of Heritability. *Canadian Journal of Psychology, 35*, 244–260.

Walker, Anne (1994). Psychology of Women Publications Survey. *British Psychological Society Psychology of Women Section Newsletter, 13*(Spring), 4–12.

Walkerdine, V. (1988). *The Mastery of Reason: Cognitive Development and the Production of Rationality.* London: Routledge.

Walkerdine, V. (1991). *Schoolgirl Fictions.* London: Verso.

Walkerdine, V., and Lucey, H. (1989). *Democracy in the Kitchen: Regulating Mothers and Socialising Daughters.* London: Virago.

Walkerdine, V., and the Girls and Mathematics Unit (1989). *Counting Girls Out.* London: Virago.

Wallach, M. A., and Wallach, L. (1983). *Psychology's Sanction for Selfishness: The Error of Egoism in Theory and Therapy.* San Francisco: Freeman.

Walters, M., Carter, B., Papp, P., and Silverstein, O. (1988). *The Invisible Web: Gender Patterns in Family Relations.* New York: Guilford.

Warnke, G. (1987). *Gadamer: Hermeneutics, Tradition, and Reason.* Stanford: Stanford University Press.

Watson, J. B., and Rayner, R. (1920). Conditioned Emotional Reactions. *Journal of Experimental Psychology, 3*, 1–14.

Weick, K. (1974). Middle Range Theories of Social Systems. *Behavioral Science, 19*(6), 357–367.

Weick, K. (1984). Small Wins: Redefining the Scale of Social Issues. *American Psychologist, 39*, 40–49.

Weinberg, G. (1973). *Society and the Healthy Homosexual.* New York: Anchor.

Weiss, C. H. (1983). The Stakeholder Approach to Evaluation: Origins and Promise. In A. S. Bryk (Ed.), *Stakeholder-Based Evaluation* (pp. 3–14). San Francisco: Jossey-Bass.

Weiss, C. B., and Dain, R. N. (1979). Ego Development and Sex Attitudes in Heterosexual and Homosexual Men and Women. *Archives of Sexual Behavior, 8*, 341–356.

Weisstein, Naomi (1968/1993). Psychology Constructs the Female, *or* the Fantasy Life of the Male Psychologist (with some Attention to the Fantasies of his Friends, the Male Biologist and the Male Anthropologist). Reprinted 1993 in *Feminism & Psychology, 3*(2), 195–210.

Weizmann, F., Wiener, N. I., Wiesenthal, D. L., and Ziegler, M. (1990). Differential K Theory and Racial Hierarchies. *Canadian Psychology, 31*, 1–13.

Weizmann, F., Wiener, N. I., Wiesenthal, D. L., and Ziegler, M. (1991). Eggs, Eggplants, and Eggheads: A Rejoinder to Rushton. *Canadian Psychology, 32*, 43–50.

West, C. (1994). *Race Matters*. New York: Vintage.

Wetherell, M., and Potter, J. (1992). *Mapping the Language of Racism: Discourse and the Legitimation of Exploitation*. Hemel Hempstead: Harvester Wheatsheaf.

Wexler, D. B. (Ed.). (1990). *Therapeutic Jurisprudence: The Law as a Therapeutic Agent*. Durham, NC: Carolina Academic Press.

Wexler, D. B. (1992). Putting Mental Health into Mental Health Law. *Law and Human Behavior, 16*, 27–38.

Wexler, D. B. (1993). Therapeutic Jurisprudence and Changing Conceptions of Legal Scholarship. *Behavioral Sciences and the Law, 11*, 17–29.

Wexler, D. B. (1995). Reflections on the Scope of Therapeutic Jurisprudence. *Psychology, Public Policy, and Law, 1*, 220–236.

Wexler, D. B., and Schopp, R. F. (1992). Therapeutic Jurisprudence: A New Approach to Mental Health Law. In D. S. Kagehiro and W. S. Laufer (Eds.), *Handbook of Psychology and Law* (pp. 361–381). New York: Springer.

Wexler, D. B., and Winick, B. J. (Eds.). (1991). *Essays in Therapeutic Jurisprudence*. Durham, NC: Carolina Academic Press.

Wexler, D. B., and Winick, B. J. (1993). Patients, Professionals, and the Path of Therapeutic Jurisprudence: A Response to Petrila. *New York Law School Journal of Human Rights, 10*, 907–914.

White, A. (1989). *Poles Apart? The Experience of Gender*. London: Dent.

White, M., and Epston, D. (1990). *Narrative Means to Therapeutic Ends*. Adelaide: Dulwich Centre Press, and New York: Norton.

Wiener, R. L., and Small, M. A. (1992). Social Cognition and Tort Law: The Roles of Basic Science and Social Engineering. In D. K. Kagehiro and W. S. Laufer (Eds.), *Handbook of Psychology and Law* (pp. 435–454). New York: Springer.

Wiener, R. L., Watts, B. A., and Stolle, D. P. (1993). Psychological Jurisprudence and the Information Processing Paradigm. *Behavioral Sciences and the Law, 11*, 79–96.

Wilkinson, Sue (Ed.). (1986). *Feminist Social Psychology: Developing Theory and Practice*. Philadelphia: Open University Press.

Wilkinson, Sue (1989). The Impact of Feminist Research: Issues of Legitimacy. *Philosophical Psychology, 2*(3), 261–269.

Wilkinson, Sue (1990a). Women's Organisations in Psychology: Institutional Constraints on Disciplinary Change. *Australian Psychologist, 25*(3), 256–269.

Wilkinson, Sue (1990b). Women Organizing within Psychology. In Erica Burman (Ed.), *Feminists and Psychological Practice* (pp. 141–151). London: Sage.

Wilkinson, Sue (1991a). Why Psychology (Badly) Needs Feminism. In Jane Aaron and Sylvia Walby (Eds.), *Out of the Margins: Women's Studies in the Nineties* (pp. 191–203). London: Falmer Press.

Wilkinson, Sue (1991b). *Feminism & Psychology*: From Critique to Reconstruction. *Feminism & Psychology, 1*(1), 5–18.

Wilkinson, Sue (1996). Still Seeking Transformation: Feminist Challenges to Psychology. In Liz Stanley (Ed.), *Borderlands: Feminisms in the Academy*. London: Sage.

Wilkinson, Sue, and Kitzinger, Celia (1993). *Heterosexuality: A "Feminism and Psychology" Reader*. London: Sage.

Wilkinson, Sue, and Kitzinger, Celia (Eds.). (1995). *Feminism and Discourse*. London: Sage.

Wilkinson, Sue, and Kitzinger, Celia (1996). *Representing the Other: A "Feminism and Psychology" Reader*. London: Sage.

Wilson, Glenn (1994). Biology, Sex Roles and Work. In Caroline Quest (Ed.), *Liberating Women . . . From Modern Feminism* (pp. 59–71). London: Institute of Economic Affairs, Health and Welfare Unit.

Wilson, M. N. (Ed.). (1995) African American Family Life: Its Structural and Ecological Aspects. Special issue of *New Directions for Child Development*, 68, 1–109.

Winch, P. (1958). *The Idea of Social Science and its Relation to Philosophy*. London: Routledge and Kegan Paul.

Winch, P. (1977). Understanding a Primitive Society. In F. Dallmayr and T. McCarthy (Eds.), *Understanding and Social Inquiry* (pp. 159–188). Notre Dame, IN: University of Notre Dame Press.

Wineman, S. (1984). *The Politics of Human Services: Radical Alternatives to the Welfare State*. Boston: South End Press.

Wittgenstein, L. (1958) *Philosophical Investigations*. Oxford: Blackwell.

Wittig, M. A., and Bettencourt, B. A. (Eds.). (1996). Social Psychological Perspectives on Grassroots Organizing. Special issue of *Journal of Social Issues*, 52(1).

Wittig, Monique (1992). *The Straight Mind*. Boston: Beacon.

Wojciechowski, G. (1994). Data Group's Links Concern BCA Leaders. *Los Angeles Times*, March 16, C7.

Wolcott, H. F. (1995). *The Art of Fieldwork*. Walnut Creek, CA: AltaMira/Sage.

Wooley, Helen Thompson (1910). Psychological Literature: A Review of the Recent Literature on the Psychology of Sex. *Psychological Bulletin*, 7, 335–342.

Woolgar, S. (1988). *Science: The Very Idea*. London: Ellis Horwood/Tavistock.

World Health Organization (1978). *Mental Disorders: Glossary and Guide to their Classification in Accordance with the Ninth Revision of the International Classification of Diseases*. Geneva: World Health Organization.

Worrell, Judith (1990). Feminist Frameworks: Retrospect and Prospect *Psychology of Women Quarterly*, 14(1), 1–5.

Worrell, Judith, and Etaugh, Claire (1994). Transforming Theory and Research with Women. *Psychology of Women Quarterly*, 18(4), 443–450.

Worrell, Judith, and Riemer, P. (1992). *Feminist Perspectives in Therapy: An Empowerment Model for Women*. New York: Wiley.

Wylie, M.S. (1994). Endangered Species. *The Family Therapy Networker*, March/April, 20–33.

Wylie, M. S. (1995). Diagnosing for Dollars? *The Family Therapy Networker*, May/June, 23–34, 65–69.

Yllo, K., and Bograd, M. (Eds.). (1988). *Feminist Perspectives on Wife Abuse*. Beverly Hills, CA: Sage.

Yoshikawa, H. (1994). Prevention as Cumulative Protection: Effects of Early Family Support and Education on Chronic Delinquency and its Risks. *Psychological Bulletin*, 115, 28–54.

Zane, N. (forthcoming). Interrupting Historical Patterns: Bridging Race and Gender Gaps between Senior White Men and Other Organizational Groups. In M. Fine, L. Powell, L. Weis, and M. Wong (Eds.), *Off-White: Readings on Society, Culture and Race*. New York: Routledge.

Zenderland, L. (1987). The Debate over Diagnosis: Henry Herbert Goddard and the Medical Acceptance of Intelligence Testing. In M. M. Sokal (Ed.), *Psychological Testing and American Society* (pp. 46–74). New Brunswick, NJ: Rutgers University Press.

Zimbardo, P., Haney, C., Banks, W. C., and Jaffee, D. (1975). The Psychology of Imprisonment: Privation, Power and Pathology. In D. Rosenhan and P. London (Eds.), *Theory and Research in Abnormal Psychology* (pp. 271–287). New York: Holt, Rinehart, and Winston.

Zimmerman, J.L., and Dickerson, V. C. (1996). *If Problems Talked – Adventures in Narrative Therapy*. New York: Guilford.

Zimmerman, M. A., and Perkins, D. D. (Eds.). (1995). Empowerment Theory, Research, and Application. Special issue of *American Journal of Community Psychology, 23*(5).

Zimmerman, M. A., and Rappaport, J. (1988). Citizen Participation, Perceived Control, and Psychological Empowerment. *American Journal of Community Psychology, 16*, 725–750.

Zuckerman, M. (1987). Affect of the Game Player. *Personality and Social Psychology Bulletin, 12*, 390–402.

Zuckerman, M., and Brody, N. (1988). Oysters, Rabbits, and People: A Critique of "Race Differences in Behavior" by J. P. Rushton. *Personality and Individual Differences, 9*, 1025–1033.

Index

Printed in the United Kingdom
by Lightning Source UK Ltd.
112906UKS00001B/34-219